RELIGION

A CROSS-CULTURAL ENCYCLOPEDIA

ENCYCLOPEDIAS OF THE HUMAN EXPERIENCE

David Levinson, Series Editor

RELIGION

A CROSS-CULTURAL ENCYCLOPEDIA

David Levinson

ABC-CLIO

Santa Barbara, California
Denver, Colorado
Oxford, England

Library of Congress Cataloging-in-Publication Data

Levinson, David, 1947–
    Religion : a cross-cultural encyclopedia / David Levinson.
        p.   cm. — (Encyclopedia of the human experience)
    Incudes bibliographical references and index.
    1. Religions—Encyclopedias.   I. Title.   II. Series.
    BL80.2.L463   1996   200'.3—dc21   96-45172

ISBN 0-87436-865-0

03 02 01 00 99 98 97 96   10 9 8 7 6 5 4 3 2 1

ABC-CLIO, Inc.
130 Cremona Drive, P.O. Box 1911
Santa Barbara, California 93116-1911

This book is printed on acid-free paper ∞.
Manufactured in the United States of America

CONTENTS

Preface, vii

Chronology of World Religions, ix

Maps, xv

ANCESTOR WORSHIP, 3
ANIMISM, 7
ASCETICISM, 9
ASTROLOGY, 14

BAHA'I, 23
BUDDHISM, 25

CANNIBALISM, 33
CHRISTIANITY, 38
CHRISTIAN SCIENCE, 41
CONFUCIANISM, 43
COSMOLOGY, 46

DIVINATION, 53
DREAMS, 55

EASTERN ORTHODOXY, 59
EVIL EYE, 64

FESTIVALS, 69

GEOMANCY, 77

HINDUISM, 81

ISLAM, 91

JAINISM, 99
JUDAISM, 102

LIFE-CYCLE RITES, 109

MAGIC, 123
MANA, 127
MEDITATION, 128
MISSIONS, 133
MONOTHEISM AND POLYTHEISM, 138
MORMONISM, 141

NEW AGE, 145

ORDEALS, 147

PENTACOSTALISM, 149

Contents

Pilgrimage, 153
Possession and Trance, 159
Prayer, 170
Protestantism, 171
Purity and Pollution, 176

Reincarnation, 181
Religious Objects, 182
Religious Specialists, 184
Revitalization Movements, 189
Ritual, 194
Roman Catholicism, 194

Sacrifice and Offering, 201
Shamanism, 206
Shinto, 212
Sikhism, 217
Sorcery, 220
Soul, 222

Supernatural Beings, 226
Supernatural Explanations for Illness, 235
Syncretic Religions, 236

Taboo, 239
Taoism, 245
Totemism, 247

Vision Quest, 251

Witchcraft, 255

Zoroastrianism, 261

Bibliography, 265

Illustration Credits, 277

Index, 279

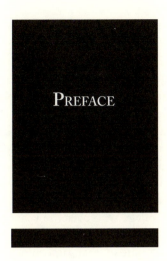

PREFACE

Religion is about the relationship between human beings and the supernatural world. Of the dozens of definitions of religion that have been suggested by theologians, historians, sociologists, anthropologists, and others, this one cuts to what is common to all religious systems. The term *religious system* is used here to mean all of the shared religious beliefs and practices that comprise the human-supernatural relationship of a particular indigenous culture or a particular world religion. A world religion is a religious system whose adherents are spread widely around the world and/or a religious system that has significantly influenced other religious systems. The term *indigenous religion* is used here to mean the religious system of a non-industrialized, non-Western society.

This volume focuses on both world religions and indigenous religions. Sixteen major world religions are described in separate entries, a chronology of world religions is provided, and topical entries cover various aspects of world religions such as missionary activity and monotheism. The purpose of these sixteen world religion articles is to provide a basic profile of each religion, with a focus on the official beliefs and practices of each religion. Although various denominations within some of these religions are also covered, little attention is given to the cross-cultural variation in the practice of these religions. For example, no comparison is offered of Roman Catholicism as practiced in Italy, Ireland, Poland, Germany, the Philippines, and Nigeria. Both the focus of this volume and the Human Experience series on indigenous cultures and space limitations make it impossible to include this type of information here.

The information on indigenous religions is not presented as profiles of specific religious systems, as we would need some 2,500 entries to cover them all (readers interested in this type of survey should consult the *Encyclopedia of World Cultures*) but instead is spread through the forty-three other articles in the volume, each of which focusses on some aspect of religion. As with the preceding six volumes in the Human Experience series, each of these articles describes cross-cultural similarity and variability for the topic and provides discussions of the various explanations social scientists and others have suggested for these patterns of similarity and variability. And, as with other volumes in the series, hundreds of examples are provided from accounts in the ethnographic record. Although the emphasis of this volume is on religion at the societal level—that is, customary beliefs and practices—it is also true that in all cultures religion is experienced at the individual level and emotions and meanings can vary widely from person to person even when they are adherents of the same religion. To make sure that this dimension of religion is covered, some examples have been included—such as passages of text and accounts of religious behavior—that highlight the personal, emotional nature of religious belief and practice around the world.

In discussing the various social science explanations for religious beliefs and practices, one difficulty was reaching some common ground in the perspectives brought by social scientists and the adherents themselves. A common thread through much cross-cultural research on religion is that the religious beliefs and practices of a culture are created by the adherents themselves and often reflect the world of the adherents. For example, in cultures with a strong political leader there is usually a single, all-powerful high god. Adherents in all religions tend to see the human-supernatural relationship as the opposite. Humans and the human and natural worlds were created by supernatural forces or beings in the image of the supernatural world. For example, the Book of Genesis tells us that God created the world in six days and man was made in his image. This notion is by no means peculiar to Judeo-Christianity. It is impossible to reconcile these two views and therefore throughout the volume when one viewpoint is mentioned, I have tried also to remind the reader of the opposing one. The purpose here is not to decide which approach is correct, but rather to make readers aware of different perspectives used to explain religion.

In closing, I want to thank Erik Bruun and Laura Gaccione for much of the research and writing on the world religions articles, Patricia Andreucci for answering numerous questions on Christianity in general and Roman Catholicism in particular, and my students at Albertus Magnus College who over the years raised and answered various questions about religion. I should also point out that some information provided here was acquired through my own research conducted in the Berkshire region of western Massachusetts, in northern New Mexico, and in France, Germany, Great Britain, and Japan.

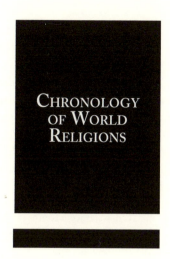

CHRONOLOGY
OF WORLD
RELIGIONS

Islam, Jainism, Judaism, Mormonism, Pentecostal Christianity, Protestantism, Roman Catholicism, Shinto, Sikhism, and Zoroastrianism. In addition, there is an overview article of Christianity. Some of these entries cover various denominations within world religions, and the articles on Festivals, Missions, Monotheism and Polytheism, Pilgrimage, and Syncretic Religions also deal with world religions.

The following table is a chronology of world religions with some additional information on indigenous religions and provides a comparative time frame for the information on the development of world religions spread through the volume.

A world religion is a religious system the adherents of which are spread around the world and/or a religious system that has significantly influenced other religious systems. The religious life of the world today is dominated by world religions. An overwhelming majority of the people on earth are adherents of world religions. Most, if not all, indigenous religions have been influenced by world religions. And some world religions are the official or unofficial national religions of various nations. Most world religions are characterized by a number of features that tend to separate them as a category from indigenous religions. These include a human founder of the religion, written religious texts, a belief in one high god, full-time religious practitioners, and a centralized administrative structure. The world religion that differs from this profile to the greatest extent is Hinduism, although Islam, Buddhism, Shinto, and others do not fit this model completely, either.

In this volume sixteen world religions are covered, with attention given to their histories, major beliefs and practices, texts, and current status: Baha'i, Buddhism, Christian Science, Confucianism, Eastern Orthodoxy, Hinduism,

Chronology of World Religions

BEFORE THE COMMON ERA (B.C.E.)

c. 50,000	Shamanism emerges
c. 5000	Evil eye beliefs emerge along with agriculture and cities in the Middle East
c. 2000	Abraham, one of the Hebrew forefathers, teaches of one supreme God
c. 1700–c. 500	Hinduism emerges and the basic texts are written
c. 1300	Ten Commandments announced to Hebrews by Moses
c. 1000	Torah, the basic laws of Judaism, written
c. 940	First Temple built by Hebrews in Jerusalem
c. 620	Judaism emerges as a monotheistic religion
c. 600	Ascetics rebel against Hindu doctrines in India
c. 587–538	Jewish Temple in Jerusalem destroyed and Jewish dispersal to Babylon, beginning of Jewish world diaspora

569	Jainism founded in India
550–250	Development of Confucianism and Taoism in China
c. 550	Hindu sects emerge in India
c. 538	Jews return to Jerusalem and Temple rebuilt
c. 528	Siddhartha, the Buddha, discovers enlightenment and announces the Four Truths and the Eightfold Path
c. 500–400	Zoroastrianism emerges and develops in Persia
c. 483	Buddha dies and his work is carried out by followers who convene the First Buddhist Council and write the first text
481–221	Emergence and development of Taoism in China
479	Confucius dies and followers compile basic text of Confucianism
c. 383	Second Buddhist Council
c. 340	Buddhism splits into what will become the Mahayana and Theravada branches
330	Zoroastrianism declines in Persia after Greek conquest
c. 300	Modern astrology develops in Greece
	Astrology develops in India, later influenced by Greek astrology
	Main texts of Jainism written
250	Third Buddhist Council and Buddhist law compiled
247–c.e. 227	Reemergence and growth of Zoroastrianism in Persia
221	Confucianism repressed in China
c. 206–c.e. 8	Geomancy (feng shui) develops in China
200	Buddhism has spread from India to Nepal, Sri Lanka, and Central Asia
175	Repression of Judaism by Greek rulers

141	Confucianism reemerges in China
c. 100	Modern form of Judaism begins to emerge
63	Romans conquer Jerusalem and Palestine
	Jewish sects begin to emerge in Palestine
c. 4	Jesus of Nazareth born

THE COMMON ERA (C.E.)

c. 24–26	Christianity emerges as Jesus begins ministry and gains a following
c. 30	Jesus crucified and followers report his resurrection
c. 33–49	Paul (Saul of Tarsus) converts to Christianity and spreads the teachings of Jesus
c. 55	Paul takes control of church in Rome, establishing the Papacy
c. 61	Buddhism spreads to China
66	Second Jewish Temple in Jerusalem destroyed by Romans
67	Roman Emperor, Hero, begins repression of Christianity
c. 100	Christian churches appear in Africa, Asia, and southern Europe
	Fourth Buddhist Council
c. 135–500	Jews defeated by Romans and disperse to Europe, Asia, and Africa
c. 200–400	Hindu Vaisnava cult emerges, worships Hindu God Vishnu
215	Taoism recognized as a religion in China
220	Confucianism declines in China
c. 249–305	Christians persecuted by Roman emperors
300	Taoism dominant religion in northern China
c. 300–800	Hindu devotion to gods Brahma, Vishnu, and Shiva deepens and

| | Hinduism spreads to Southeast Asia | 618 | Confucianism reemerges in China |
312 Roman Emperor Constantine converts to Christianity

622 Muhammad leaves Mecca and settles in Medina

313 Christians granted full rights by Constantine

624 Muhammad breaks with Judaism and makes Mecca rather than Jerusalem the focus of worship

325 First Catholic Ecumenical Council at Nicaea declares divinity of Jesus Christ

630 Muhammad and his followers capture Mecca

330 Constantine builds city of Constantinople as capital of the Roman Empire

632 Buddhism becomes official religion of Tibet

Muhammad dies and Islam begins split into two divisions of Sunni and Shiite Islam

372 Buddhism spreads to Korea

380 Roman Empire makes Christianity its official religion

650 Official version of the Koran written

381 Second Catholic Ecumenical Council at Constantinople

651 Muslims conquer Persia and Zoroastrianism begins to decline

395 Roman Empire splits between Eastern and Western Empires, with Roman Catholicism in Rome under the Pope and Eastern Orthodoxy in Constantinople under the Patriarch

680 Sixth Catholic Ecumenical Council at Constantinople

691 Islamic mosque, Dome of the Rock, built in Jerusalem

c. 700 Hindu caste system established as basis of rural social organization in India

Zoroastrians begin fleeing Persia and settle in India, forming the Parsi community

431 Third Catholic Ecumenical Council at Ephesus declares Mary as mother of God and Christ

451 Fourth Catholic Ecumenical Council of Chalcedon declares Jesus Christ to be man and god

705 Great Mosque in Damascas built

750 Islam has spread across North Africa and into Spain

c. 500 The Talmud, Jewish law, codified in Babylonia

Beginning of Islamic Abbasid period lasting until 1258, the most powerful Islamic empire in history

c. 529 Benedictine Order established in Italy

538 Buddhism spreads to Japan

787 Seventh Catholic Ecumenical Council at Nicaea is last one so recognized by both the Roman Catholic and Eastern Orthodox Churches

c. 550 Shinto first used as a name for related religious practices of ancient Japan

Shinto, Buddhism, and Confucianism begin to merge in Japan

794–1192 Period of merging of Buddhism and Shinto in Japan

553 Fifth Catholic Ecumenical Council at Constantinople

800 Charlemagne made Emperor by Pope Leo III, establishing secular authority of Roman Catholic Church

c. 570 Muhammad born in Mecca

c. 610 Muhammad has revelation of prophecy

800	Karaites emerge as rivals of Talmudic Judaism	1261	Eastern Orthodox rule reestablished in Constantinople
c. 800–900	Sufism emerges as distinct sect within Islam	c. 1290–1500	Major period of persecution of Jews in Europe
864	Bulgarian Orthodox Church emerges	1448	Russian Orthodox Church becomes independent
867	Split between Eastern and Western Orthodox Churches	1453	Ottoman Turks defeat Byzantine Empire and Islam achieves dominance in region
712–927	Shinto texts written	1478	Spanish Inquisition aimed at Jews and Muslims begins and lasts two centuries; Jews disperse throughout Europe and the Mediterranean region
950	Catholicism has spread to all of Europe		
960	Neo-Confucianism emerges in China		
988	Eastern Orthodoxy becomes state religion of Russia		
1021	Muslim rule begins in India leading to periods of repression of Hinduism and periods of relative freedom for several centuries	c. 1500	Sikhism emerges in northern India
		1517	Protestant Reformation begins when Martin Luther protests church corruption in Germany
	Jainism repressed by Muslims and declines	1518	Swiss Protestant Reformation begins
1054	Split between Roman Catholic Church and Eastern Orthodox Church	1520	Martin Luther excommunicated from Roman Catholic Church
			Anabaptism begins in Switzerland and Germany
1095	First of eight Christian Crusades with goal of displacing Muslims from Jerusalem.	1521	Martin Luther condemned by the Diet of Worms
c. 1200	Kabalah, Jewish mysticism, emerges in southern Europe	1529	Lutheranism becomes state religion of Denmark
	Muslim conquest of northern India eliminates Buddhism in India		Protestantism named and given official recognition at the Diet of Speyer
1204	Fourth Crusade conquers Constantinople and Roman Catholicism becomes dominant	1534	Church of England separates from Roman Catholic Church
			Society of Jesuits founded
1209	Franciscan Order founded	1536	Calvinism begins
1216	Dominican Order founded	1544	Lutheranism becomes state religion of Sweden
1220	Serbian Orthodox Church emerges	1545–1563	Ecumenical Council of Trent begins Catholic Reformation
1233	Inquisition established by Pope Gregory IX as means of identifying and converting or removing nonadherents of Roman Catholicism	1549	Church of England liturgy and practice codified
		1555	Pope authorizes placement of Jews in segregated neighborhoods (ghettos) in Italy

1560	Scottish Reformation begins	1868	Shinto designated the official religion of Japan and Buddhism repressed
1562–1598	Religious wars between Catholics and Protestants (Huguenots) in France	1869–1870	First Vatican Council leads to reforms in Roman Catholic Church and solidifies central role of the papacy
1587	Christian missionaries banned from Japan		
c. 1590	Effort to create single religion based on Islam and Hinduism in India begins and ultimately fails		End of papal secular authority in Europe
1608	Baptist church founded	1870	American Indian Ghost Dance Movement begins
1620	English Puritans settle in North America	1871	Romanian Orthodox Church becomes independent
1639	Baptist Church established in North America	1879	Christian Science founded by Mary Baker Eddy in the United States
1642–1649	English Civil War with Puritans and Presbyterians versus Anglicans and Catholics		Serbian Orthodox Church becomes independent
c. 1700–1900	Period of relative freedom for Jews in Europe	1880	Christianity and Buddhism allowed in Japan but as secondary religions to Shinto
1706	Presbyterian Church established in North America	c. 1880	Astrology reemerges in Europe
1720–1760	Development and spread of Christian Revival in North America	c. 1880–1917	Attacks on Jews in Russia
		1884	Baha'i emerges in Persia
1729	Methodism founded in England	1886	Term *Zionism* first used in reference to political movement seeking reestablishment of Jewish nation in Israel
1781	Spanish Inquisition ends		
1789	Protestant Episcopal Church founded in the United States		
1794	Eastern Orthodoxy brought to North America		American Indian Ghost Dance Movement reappears
1814	Baptist General Covention founded in the United States	1900	Pentecostal Christianity emerges in the United States
1830	Mormonism founded in western New York by Joseph Smith, Jr.	1905	Baptist World Alliance established
1833	Greek Orthodox Church becomes independent	1906	Pentecostal Christianity formally begins
1836	First Mormon Temple built in Kirtland, Ohio	1917	Code of Canon Law established by Roman Catholic Church
1844	Joseph Smith, Jr., killed	1918	Eastern Orthodoxy repressed in Russia
1845	Southern Baptist Convention founded in the United States	1926	First international Islamic organization founded
1847	Mormons migrate to Utah	1929	Vatican City established as independent republic
1850	Confucianism declines in China		

c. 1930	Rastafarian Movement begins in Jamaica	1978	Islamic fundamentalist revolution in Iran
1937	Albanian Orthodox Church becomes independent	1985	Conservative and Reform Judaism allow ordination of women as rabbis
1944–1945	Persecution and killing of Jews in Germany and German-occupied Europe	1990	Native American Grave Protection and Repatriation Act in the United States
1945	End of Shinto as the state religion of Japan		United States Supreme Court rules that use of peyote in Native American religious ceremonies is not protected by the U.S. Constitution
1948	World Council of Churches formed by Protestant denominations	c. 1990	Eastern Orthodoxy reemerges in Russia
	Establishment of the State of Israel	c. 1990–1996	Ethnic conflict in India involving Hindus and Muslims and Hindus and Sikhs
1949	Untouchable caste category outlawed in India		Ethnic conflict among Roman Catholic Croats, Orthodox Serbs, and Muslim Bosnians in Yugoslavia
	Religion repressed in China		
1950	World Council of Buddhists established		Islamic fundamentalists compete for power in a number of Middle East nations
1955–1956	New laws in India end Hindu practices regarding women, widows, marriage, and land ownership		Reemergence of anti-Semitism in Russia and Eastern Europe
c. 1960	Transcendental Meditation (TM) introduced		Pentecostalism spreads to all continents
	Revival of Pentecostalism		Hindu nationalist party does well in elections running on pro-Hindu, anti-Muslim platform
	New Pentecostalism emerges		
1962–1965	Second Vatican Council leads to major reforms in Roman Catholicism		
1965	Relations reestablished between Roman Catholic and Eastern Orthodox Churches		

Eliade, Mircea. (1977) *From Primitives to Zen.*

Eliade, Mircea, ed. (1987) *The Encyclopedia of Religion.*

Nigosian, S. A. (1994) *World Faiths.*

c. 1970	Islamic fundamentalism emerges in the Middle East
c. 1971	New Age movement emerges
1976	World of Islam festival in London

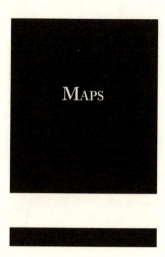

MAPS

The following maps show approximate locations of the cultures mentioned in the text.

Africa and the Middle East

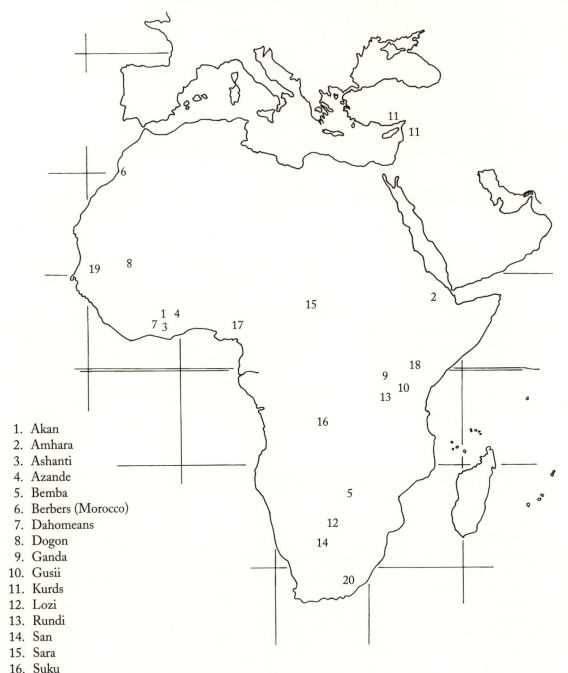

1. Akan
2. Amhara
3. Ashanti
4. Azande
5. Bemba
6. Berbers (Morocco)
7. Dahomeans
8. Dogon
9. Ganda
10. Gusii
11. Kurds
12. Lozi
13. Rundi
14. San
15. Sara
16. Suku
17. Tiv
18. Turkana
19. Wolof
20. Zulu

Central and South America

1. Amahuaca
2. Aymara
3. Aztec
4. Bahia Brazilians
5. Bahimians
6. Cuna
7. Goajiro
8. Guarani
9. Haitians
10. Huichol
11. Jivaro
12. Rastafarians
13. Tarahumara
14. Toba
15. Tucano
16. Tzeltal

Europe and Asia

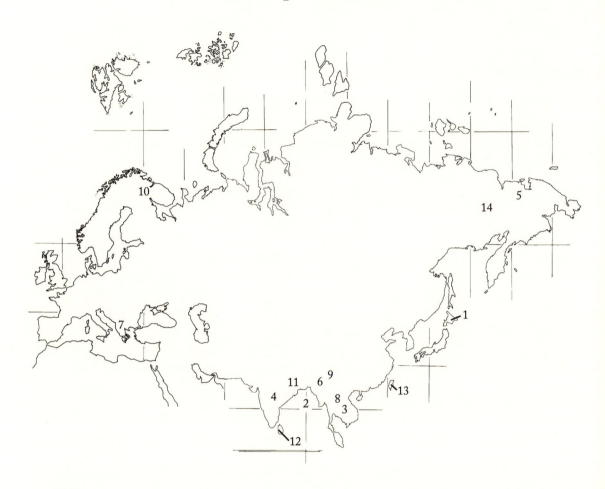

1. Ainu
2. Andaman Islanders
3. Central Thai
4. Chenchu
5. Chukchee
6. Garo
7. Greeks (Northern)
8. Kachin
9. Khasi
10. Saami
11. Santal
12. Sinhalese
13. Taiwanese
14. Yakut

North America

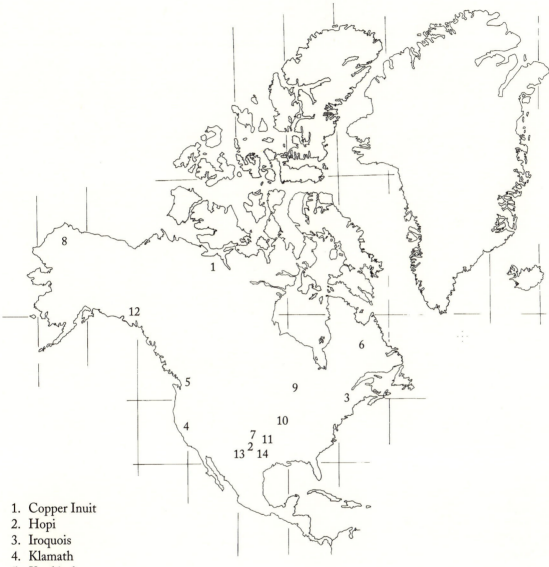

1. Copper Inuit
2. Hopi
3. Iroquois
4. Klamath
5. Kwakiutl
6. Naskapi
7. Navajo
8. North Alaskan Eskimo
9. Ojibwa
10. Pawnee
11. Taos
12. Tlingit
13. Western Apache
14. Zuni

Oceania

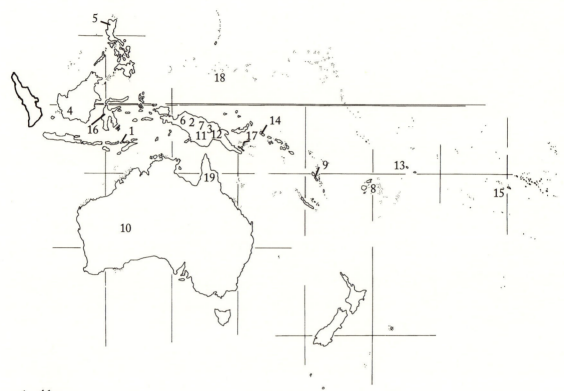

1. Alorese
2. Dani
3. Fore
4. Iban
5. Ifugao
6. Kapauku
7. Kimam
8. Lau Fijians
9. Malekula
10. Mardudjara
11. Melpa
12. Orokolo
13. Pukapuka
14. Siuai
15. Tahitians
16. Toradja
17. Trobriand Islanders
18. Turkese
19. Yir Yoront

RELIGION

A CROSS-CULTURAL ENCYCLOPEDIA

ANCESTOR WORSHIP

Ancestor worship refers to beliefs and customs centered on the worship of deceased kin. Ancestor worship across cultures has three major components. First, it is always deceased kin who are venerated and worshiped and it is the living kin of the ancestors who are required to perform the rituals associated with ancestor worship. This focus on kinship relationships distinguishes ancestor worship from what is called the "cult of the dead," although the two terms are sometimes used to mean the same set of religious beliefs and practices. The key difference is that in the cult of the dead it is spirits of the dead, whether they are kin or not, who are worshiped. The focus on specific kin also distinguishes ancestor worship as a specific form of religious practice from general ancestor worship in a culture, in which ancestors in other forms—ghosts, shadows, spirits, totems, and souls—are worshiped. This general form is found in all cultures, while ancestor worship is practiced in only some cultures—cross-cultural surveys indicate that ancestor worship is part of the religious system of about 60 percent of cultures. Second, the underlying belief in ancestor worship is that deceased ancestors take an interest in and can influence the lives of their living descendants. Third, the worship of ancestors is an obligatory activity that differs in intensity, degree, and duration from religious rites associated with death and afterlife. Although in nearly all cultures the death of kin is an important matter and attended to with religious ritual, ancestor worship is not practiced in all cultures. For example, the Garo of India acknowledge the death of kin through the erection of shrines and the carving of memorial posts, but they do not believe that ancestors can influence the lives of their living descendants and make no effort to influence them ritually. Similarly, the major Western religions do not include ancestor worship, although in major Eastern religions such as Hinduism, Buddhism, and Confucianism ancestors are worshiped in a limited way. In all world religions, the death and burial of kin is marked with much ritual activity and the anniversaries of their deaths are often noted. In no culture does ancestor worship constitute a religion in and of itself. Rather, as in Confucianism, ancestor worship is always one part of a broad religion system and, in some cultures, is often accompanied by other forms of religious activity, such as the use of mediums to communicate with ancestors or the use of geomancers to select suitable sites for burial that will make the ancestors happy and supportive of their living descendants. In addition, in no culture are ancestors the only type of recognized supernatural beings: gods, spirits, and other beings are always also recognized.

Ancestor worship has drawn much attention in East Asia as it is a major feature of religious systems in Korea, China, and Japan, although it varies in meaning and form across these societies and across communities and individuals in the communities. Ancestor worship is found in its most elaborated form in many rural villages in China and Taiwan. The

3

following summary of ancestor worship in rural Taiwan indicates the major beliefs and practices often involved in many communities. Taiwanese worship their ancestors for four primary reasons: (1) to repay debts they own them; (2) to express the fond feeling they have for them; (3) to reap benefits from benevolent ancestral influence such as wealth, a rich harvest, or many children; and (4) to avoid punishment in the form of poverty or illness that might result from angering an ancestor. The Taiwanese believe that the ancestors continue to live in three forms—in the ancestor tablets displayed in the village halls, in the bones in the grave, and in the underworld. Thus, Taiwanese ancestor worship is about keeping the ancestors in these three forms satisfied and pleased with the behavior of their living descendants.

Ancestor worship is both private and public. Private worship—which is perhaps less elaborated and less significant—centers on the worship of ancestor tablets in the home. The tablets contain the names of deceased ancestors three or four generations deep and usually the woman of the house conducts the rituals. After three or four generations, the tablets are removed and domestic worship of those ancestors ends. The tablet may be destroyed and the ancestor forgotten or it may be placed along with other tablets in the family's section of the village ancestor lineage hall, where much of the public worship takes place. The hall is a building built especially for and used almost exclusively for the worship of ancestors of people in the village and other people who are members of the same lineage.

A lineage is one's kinship line; in the case of the Taiwanese, the key lineage is one's patrilineage, or all relatives one is related to through one's father's line. In addition to the display of the ancestor tablets in the ancestor hall, the ancestors remembered in the hall are worshiped through offerings of food, feasts given

in their honor, rites on the anniversaries of their deaths, and special rites on general feast days. While the public function of the hall is religious, the size, placement, and condition of the hall, which groups worship their ancestors there, and the condition of the individual tablets all reflect political and social dynamics in the village and within and across the different lineages. In Taiwan, as elsewhere, one becomes an ancestor worthy of worship by dying. Thus, ancestor worship begins at or sometimes shortly before death. If death is near, the person is placed in the hall to die.

Following death, the family begins immediately to make preparations for the funeral and burial. Usually a geomancer is hired to determine the best day for the funeral, to select the site for the grave, and to orient the body in the grave. A geomancer may also be consulted in the future to make sure that the site is still an auspicious one and that changes in the landscape or the placement of new graves have not disturbed the harmony of the grave with the surrounding environment. The funeral involves internment and worship at the grave. The funeral rites are especially important because the correct performance will cancel out any wrongs the person committed during his life and thereby guarantee that he will be happy in the underworld. Subsequently, in addition to the domestic and public worship of the tablets, the survivors look after the ancestral bones by keeping the grave clean and making offerings of food at it.

As suggested by Taiwanese ancestor worship, ancestor worship in nearly all cultures has a political and social dimension as well as a religious one. In fact, the key characteristic that distinguishes cultures with ancestor worship from those without it is the presence of unilineal descent groups in the former. A unilineal descent group is a kinship group composed of all persons one is related to through either one's father's (patrilineage) or one's mother's line (matrilineage). In cultures with bilateral descent (where one reckons his or her kin through both parent's lines), ancestor worship is less common. The explanation for this patterned variation across cultures is that in cultures with unilineal descent systems, wealth and power are passed directly from one generation to the next only through one line and are of considerable importance to the living survivors. Thus, across cultures ancestor worship is found more often in cultures where political power and property are directly inherited by specific descendants, rather than shared among a group of kin. For example, among the Taiwanese, the greatest ritual obligations fall on individuals who inherit property directly from the deceased ancestor. They are required to worship the ancestor on feast days, worship him on the anniversary of his death, and make a tablet. On the other hand, a direct descendant who received no property is required to perform the first two forms of worship but is not expected to make a tablet. Additionally, some people in Taiwan who choose not to worship ancestors are often poor or in ill health and thus view themselves as having inherited little of benefit from their ancestors. In addition to social and political relations, in some cultures ancestor worship reflects a belief that the dead continue to be part of the kinship group. Perhaps the clearest example of this is found among the Suku of Africa, who have no word that means "ancestor." Rather, Suku lineages are made up of both the living and deceased, with relations based on level of seniority.

Benevolent and Punishing Ancestor Worship

One of the major concerns people have about their ancestors is whether the ancestors will be benevolent or punishing. In about 60 percent of cultures with ancestor worship, deceased ancestors are believed to be supportive and helpful to their living descendants. In the other 40 percent

of cultures with ancestor worship, ancestors range from being malicious to punishing to either benevolent or punishing, although in many cultures they are benevolent so long as their descendants worship them correctly. Among the Taiwanese, ancestors are thought to be mainly benevolent, although people believe that failure to worship in the appropriate way may anger the ancestor and that he will not be helpful in the future. In other cultures, ancestors are not seen as necessarily benevolent. Among the Alorese of Indonesia, ancestral spirits are malicious and are feared more than any other, and people try to avoid offending them. Among the Gusii of Kenya, ancestors are seen as capable of punishing their kin if the kin offend them by failing to make suitable sacrifices to them or by committing crimes such as murder or perjury. For the Ifugao of the Philippines, ancestors remain a part of the kin group and are believed to look favorably upon it unless they are forgotten and ignored; then they will cause illness or death.

Social scientists have devoted considerable effort to trying to explain why cultures vary in their beliefs about their ancestors. Most of these explanations rest on the assumption that the nature of ancestor-descendant relations is a reflection of the relationship between the individuals when both were living. Particularly since ancestors are older, the relations and people's beliefs about how their ancestors will treat them are an extension of parent-child relationships. Thus, in cultures where parents are rejecting toward their children, ancestors will more likely also be seen as rejecting—that is, as capricious and malicious. This is the case among the Alorese mentioned above, where parents are rejecting and hostile. In other cultures, people may fear their ancestors because of an ambivalent parent-child relationship in adulthood that made the children wish for their parent's death. This may especially be the case in cultures where adult children inherit much from their parents—such as family land for farming—but must wait until the parent dies to receive it. In these cases the psychological mechanism of projection might come into play, and people believe that since they wished harm to their parent, the parent will wish them harm. This fear is reflected in various ways—fear of ancestors, respect for them, or rituals such as sacrifices or offerings to keep them happy and pleased.

Superior Ancestor Worship

Superior ancestor worship is a form of religious practice in which a certain category or categories of ancestors are believed to be able to influence the lives of an entire community or society, not just their kin. A cross-cultural survey of ninety-four cultures indicates that superior ancestor worship is found in only 20 percent of cultures. In 1 percent of the surveyed cultures superior ancestors are believed to be aware of human affairs but do not interfere in them, in 2 percent they may or may not interfere, and in 17 percent they do involve themselves in human affairs. Past civilizations such as the Egyptians, Inca, and Imperial Romans worshiped superior ancestors while in the contemporary world the practice is most common in sub-Saharan Africa. For example, the Bemba worship two categories of ancestors. First, each family worships its own ancestors, with each hut serving as a shrine to ancestors, who are believed to influence the lives of their descendants, especially during times of crisis such as illness. Second, each village considers the headman's hut a shrine and people worship there the spirits of the headman's ancestors, who are believed to influence matters that effect the entire village. For the Bemba and other cultures with superior ancestor worship the practice evidently serves a political function as it consolidates power in the kin group of the village headman.

See also GEOMANCY; SOUL; SUPERNATURAL BEINGS.

Ahern, Emily M. (1973) *The Cult of the Dead in a Chinese Village.*

Freedman, Maurice. (1958) *Lineage Organization in Southeastern China.*

Hsu, Francis L. K. (1948) *Under the Ancestors' Shadow.*

Janelli, Dawnhee Yim, and Roger L. Janelli. (1982) *Ancestor Worship in Korean Society.*

Kopytoff, Igor (1971) "Ancestors as Elders in Africa." *Africa* 41: 129–142.

Lambrecht, Francis. (1954) "Ancestor's Knowledge among the Ifugaos and Its Importance in the Religious and Social Life of the Tribe." *Journal of East Asiatic Studies* 3: 359–365.

Playfair, A. (1909) *The Garos.*

Sheils, Dean. (1975) "Toward a Unified Theory of Ancestor Worship: A Cross-Cultural Study." *Social Forces* 54: 427–440.

———. Sheils, Dean. (1980) "The Great Ancestors are Watching: A Cross-Cultural Study of Superior Ancestral Religion." *Sociological Analysis* 41: 247–257.

Somersan, Semra. (1981) *Death Symbolism: A Cross-Cultural Study.*

Steadman, Lyle B., Craig T. Palmer, and Christopher F. Tilley. (1996) "The Universality of Ancestor Worship." *Ethnology* 35: 63–76.

Swanson, Guy E. (1968) *The Birth of the Gods: The Origin of Primitive Beliefs.*

Tatje, Terrence, and Francis L. K. Hsu (1969) "Variations in Ancestor Worship Beliefs and Their Relation to Kinship." *Southwestern Journal of Anthropology* 25: 153–172.

Whiteley, Wilfred (1950) "Bemba and Related People of Northern Rhodesia." *Ethnographic Survey of Africa: East Central Africa.* Part II, 1–32, 70–76.

Wolf, Arthur P. (1974) *Religion and Ritual in Chinese Society.*

ANIMISM

Animism and the related concepts of preanimism, animatism, and dynamism refer to stages in the evolutionary development of religion postulated by scholars of religion such as Edward B. Tylor and Robert R. Marett in the late nineteenth and early twentieth centuries. These stages were claimed to be the earliest stages in the evolution of religion or the original forms of religion and as such were thought to be characteristic of the religions of non-Western peoples, who were thought to be survivals from earlier stages of human evolution. At the opposite end of these evolutionary schemes were features of European culture such as Christianity and science, which were thought to be the highest form of religion or human understanding of the universe. Although these nineteenth-century evolutionary theories have been discarded, the concept of animism has survived and is sometimes used as a label for religious systems or a form of religious belief characterized by the belief that all or many nonhuman features of the environment have a supernatural dimension that can influence human life. Thus, the religious systems of some cultures are sometimes labeled as animistic if this is one of the features of the religious system. And, in some cases, the members of a culture may be described as Animists (as in Catholics, or Muslims) if the people are not adherents of a world religion. This is, of course, a misuse of the concept as lack of adherence to a world religion does not mean that the indigenous religious system is animistic or even that it contains animistic beliefs. Additionally, animism is rarely, if ever, the sole component of a religious system and cultures that are animistic in religious belief also have other features of religion such as creation myths and beliefs in the human soul, magic, witchcraft, shaman, or general spirits.

The key features of animism are the beliefs that animals others than humans, plants, and material objects and places are imbued with a sacred or supernatural quality and that inanimate objects are animate. The supernatural quality of an object is often labeled as the spirit or the soul of the animal, plant, or object. For people in cultures with animism the world around them is filled not just with other living things and inanimate objects but also with the spirits and souls of those things and objects, all of which influence human life.

A cross-cultural survey of sixty cultures indicates that a belief in animism occurs in about 50 percent of cultures. This belief is very common in cultures that subsist by hunting and gathering, fairly common in cultures that subsist through horticulture, and rare in cultures that subsist through agriculture. In addition, other than beliefs in general spirits not tied to any specific animal, plant, or object and in magic, animistic beliefs are the most common type of religious belief across hunter-gatherer societies. Such beliefs also constitute a central element of the worldview of hunter-gatherers. For example, the Ainu of northern Japan traditionally believed that animals, plants, and objects such as clothing, weapons, tools, and tents possessed a soul in addition to the objects' physical qualities. In addition to the soul, all living things and all features of nature such as lakes, mountains, the sun, the moon, and stars were also thought to possess a supernatural force that owned or possessed the object and resided within it. These possessors could be male or female and good or bad. When in contact with the animal, plant, or object, and especially when using it, the Ainu prayed, made offerings, or adhered to the appropriate ritual behavior in order to please the possessors so that the possessor and the souls of the animals and objects would continue to be benevolent toward humans. Ainu animism suggests a number of basic features of animism in general: the supernatural forces inhabiting animals, plants, and objects are usually conceptualized as spirits or souls; they are believed to be embodied in specific objects; they are not personified although they may be categorized as male or female; they are believed to influence human affairs; and they are believed to be responsive to human religious behavior meant to influence them. This behavior, in the form of prayer, offerings, and adherence to ritual is meant to keep benevolent souls and spirits satisfied and to placate potentially harmful ones.

The association of animism with a hunting-gathering subsistence economy is apparently a reflection of environmental uncertainty in hunter-gatherer societies. Hunter-gatherers in comparison to other peoples are far more directly dependent on their environments for survival and at the same time have less direct control of their environments. Thus, hunter-gatherers are more likely to view other features of the environment—and especially those they are most dependent on—as similar to themselves in some ways: like humans these animals, plants, and objects have physical and spiritual dimensions, both of which influence their behavior and their relations with other features of the environment, including their relations with humans. In addition, hunter-gatherers come to believe that one way to reduce environmental uncertainty is by trying to control this spiritual dimension of other objects in the environment through religious activity.

An example of this is provided by the Eskimos of northern Alaska, who believe that animal behavior is controlled by spirits resident in the animals. Hunting success depends on the inclinations of these spirits of the species (*inua*), the breath spirits (*ilitkusiq*), and the spirit doubles (*taktok*). To ensure that the species spirit will not warn the animals away from the hunters, rituals are performed before the hunt. For example, to prevent contamination of sea life with land life, all weapons used in hunting caribou are cleaned before hunting whales. Failure to clean the weapons would cause the whale spirit to direct the whales away from the hunters. After the hunt, the breath spirit and the spirit double need to be satisfied with ritual. The Eskimos believe that the animals allow themselves to be killed because they want something from humans. To ensure that the breath spirit tells other animals of its good treatment by humans, the head is cut from the body to free the breath spirit and special wishes of the spirit are granted. These special wishes often relate to the needs of the animal's spirit double, which is a spirit of another species living in the opposing environmental resource zone. For example, the spirit doubles of sea mammals are land mammals and vice versa. Giving the spirit of a whale fresh water or the spirit of a caribou whale blubber, or the performance of some other ritual activity satisfies the requirement to attend to the needs of the spirit double.

Davis, William D. (1974) *Societal Complexity and the Nature of Primitive Man's Conception of the Supernatural.*

Marett, Robert R. (1909) *The Threshold of Religion.*

Minc, L., and K. Smith. (1989) "The Spirit of Survival: Cultural Responses to Resource Variability in Alaska." In *Bad Year Economics: Cultural Responses to Risk and Uncertainty,* edited by Paul Halstead and John O'Shea, 8–39.

Murdock, George P. (1934) *Our Primitive Contemporaries.*

Tylor, Edward B. (1958) *Primitive Culture.* Originally published in 1871.

ASCETICISM

Asceticism refers to religious practices in which an individual voluntarily forgoes gratifying activities either permanently or for some set period of time in order to enhance his or her spirituality. Asceticism is a cultural universal and while the specific customs and the meanings associated with those customs vary widely, across cultures four forms of asceticism are most common: (1) fasting, (2) sexual continence or celibacy, (3) poverty, and (4) seclusion. Similarly, those who engage in ascetic behavior also vary widely across cultures. They may be the entire population of adherents of a particular religion who engage in ascetic behavior temporarily, such as Muslims who fast during daylight hours during the month of Ramadan, Jews who fast on the Day of Atonement, or Catholics who give up certain foods during Lent. Or they may be certain categories of people who do so only on certain occasions, such as Tlingit hunters who fast and avoid sexual relations before the hunt, or Tamil Brahman, men who when they become old may choose to live a life of poverty, isolation, and meditation. Or ascetics in a society may all be adherents of a particular religion or sect who choose a permanent ascetic lifestyle, such as the Old Order Amish, who wear plain clothing and obtain energy only from human or animal sources, or Mormons, who do not consume alcohol or tobacco products. Finally, ascetics may be religious specialists such as Catholic or Buddhist priests or Eastern Orthodox monks, to list just a few, whose rules require that they live an ascetic life.

Across cultures, individuals choose an ascetic lifestyle or engage in ascetic behavior for a variety of reasons. The most important are (1) to reach a deeper state of spirituality, including a closeness with supernatural beings or the sacred; (2) to escape the demands of everyday life so as to have more time to devote to spiritual activities such as prayer and meditation; (3) to achieve salvation; (4) to earn rewards or a better life in the afterlife or in a reincarnated form; and (5) to experience and share the suffering of a deity or of one's ancestors.

As a cultural universal, asceticism is found in all religious systems and in all major world religions. However, religions differ widely in the importance attached to asceticism and its role. Asceticism is most pronounced in Therevada and Tibetan Buddhism, Hinduism, and Roman Catholicism and is less important in contemporary Protestantism, Judaism, Confucianism, Shinto, Islam, and Zoroastrianism. However, asceticism has been an important element of various Jewish and Protestant sects in the past and remains a defining element of the Sufi school of Islam today.

Forms of Asceticism

As noted above, activities that are considered ascetic vary across cultures, with fasting, food restrictions, celibacy, seclusion, and poverty the most common. In religious systems where asceticism is important, such as Buddhism, many different forms of asceticism may be required. For example, Buddhist priests fast, avoid certain food, are sexually continent, reject possession of worldly goods, and live in temples apart from the general population.

Probably the most common form of asceticism across cultures is fasting and dietary restrictions. Fasting may be undertaken to prepare for an important event, to purify one's body, or to call the attention of supernatural beings. Virtually all major religions have a day or period during which adherents are required to fast or avoid certain foods. While fasting and food avoidances are seen as techniques of bringing adherents closer to the supernatural, they also serve other functions, such as conserving certain types of food and creating social solidarity among the adherents, who thus share a common ascetic experience that differentiates them from adherents of other religions. For Muslims, fasting during the ninth month—Ramadan—is one of the five pillars of Islam. Ramadan is the month when God sent the Quran to Gabriel who then revealed it to Muhammad. The fast period begins with the dawn of the day following the first full moon of the month and lasts 28 days. During this period, Muslims may not eat, drink, smoke, engage in sexual relations, or shed blood from dawn until sunset, although they may eat and drink during the night hours. Frequent prayer at the mosque, contemplation, meditation, and reading the Quran are preferred activities during Ramadan, although only the wealthy can engage routinely in such activities. Most Muslims must continue their daily work during Ramadan, which can create a considerable burden for people living in hot climates with long days. Jews fast on Yom Kippur—the Day of Atonement—and are also restricted from eating leavened bread during Passover. Catholics avoid certain foods during Lent and in the past avoided meat on Fridays. Mormons utilize fasting as a way of improving their physical health, stimulating intellectual activity, and enhancing their spirituality. Mormon fasting also has a practical benefit in that it is a mechanism for distributing wealth in the community and supporting poorer members. The first Sunday of each month is a fast day (people fast from the previous evening to Sunday evening), and each family is expected to make a donation to the church of money, clothing, food, etc., equivalent to the price of the food that would have been consumed, which is then used to support the poor or needy.

Sexual restrictions are a second common form of asceticism. In a sample of seventy cultures around the world, only 17.1 percent customarily allow men and women to engage in sex whenever they wish to do so. The remaining 82.9 percent impose constraints of some kind on sexual intercourse. Customs that regulate

sexual activity are connected to beliefs that too much sex is unhealthy or debilitating or that the effects of sexual activity interfere with other important human pursuits. Also commonly associated with celibacy and sexual continence, these cultures believe that the absence of sex will bring one closer to the supernatural world and perhaps will please the spirits and bring good fortune in earthly pursuits. For example, the Kimam of New Guinea avoid sexual intercourse when ceremonial crops are being planted or harvested and after a child has been born. Among the Tlingit, when a leading shaman died his entire kinship group was expected to fast for eight days and remain continent for a longer period of time, perhaps as long as one year. For the Guarani of South America continence is a prerequisite for achieving the role of religious leader or curer. Both men who become religious leaders and women who become curers are expected to have no interest in sexual relations and not to marry until they have completed their apprenticeship. Sex and marriage are avoided because they are believed to interfere with communication with the supernatural world, which is a key component of the apprenticeship process. The consequences of violating proscriptions for ascetic behavior are indicated by the Hopi of Arizona, who require all men to be continent at the time of ceremonies for fear "that the 'smell' of women is displeasing to the clouds, and hence no rain will fall if people have intercourse during the performance of sacred rituals" (Titiev 1971: 206). The condition of a Hopi man who was born with a disability was believed to be the result of his mother having sex with a man who was still wearing his ceremonial costume.

Poverty as a form of asceticism is most commonly associated with the asceticism of religious specialists, such as the vows of poverty taken by Roman Catholic priests and nuns and by Orthodox monks, and the rules restricting the ownership of material wealth by Buddhist priests. Poverty is also a major component of the asceticism of Hindu ascetics (*sadhu*) in South Asia, who subsist, as do Buddhist priests, by collecting alms from the population they serve. One interesting feature of poverty is that while it separates ascetics from the general community, it also ties them to it, as they are often totally dependent on contributions made by others for their survival. For example, Buddhist priests in Central Thailand collect alms daily as they move from house to house in rural communities, which indicates their continual dependence on the local community and also ensures continual contact with that community. And young men who become priests often enter novice status knowing much about the daily routine of priests from the contacts with priests they have had every day of their lives.

For ascetics seclusion is a method of separating oneself from the affairs of the secular world; of creating the opportunity for quiet meditation, contemplation, and prayer; and of moving closer to the supernatural world. In general, the greater the seclusion, the closer one is to achieving these goals. For example, Buddhist Sinhalese in Sri Lanka believe that true meditation can be achieved not by just removing oneself from the world but by also removing oneself from the temple and living instead in small hermitages where most of one's time can be given to meditation. Similarly, the most highly respected Sinhalese is the one who leaves his family and lives alone in the forest where he seeks salvation. Seclusion is an especially common feature of initiation rituals, with the adolescent boy or girl secluded in a separate building or room or in the forest so he or she may better communicate with the supernatural world. For example, an Ojibwa boy fasted and prayed in seclusion in order to communicate with the supernatural spirit that would protect him throughout his life. An Ojibwa girl also contacted her protective spirit while in seclusion for the ten days following her first menstruation.

Asceticism and Religious Specialists

Asceticism is most highly elaborated among religious specialists. These may be specialists whose identity and role as specialists are defined in part by asceticism or specialists who are defined as ascetics. Catholic and Buddhist priests and Eastern Orthodox monks are examples of the former, while the Hindu sadhu in South Asia are an example of the latter.

The essence of Buddhist asceticism is summarized in the following verse from the *Patimokkha*, the catalog of rules followed by Buddhist priests in Central Thailand (Bunnag 1973: 29):

> Shed thou householders' finery
> As coral tree its leaves in fall:
> And going forth in yellow clad,
> Fare lonely as rhinoceros.

The *Patimokkha* section of the *Vinaya-pitaka* contains 227 rules of conduct for Buddhist priests, many of which are ascetic in their requirements. The purpose of these rules is to remove the priest from the world and aid in his quest for salvation. Among the most important rules are those concerning poverty, celibacy, inoffensiveness (not killing living things), and dietary restrictions. The purpose of the restrictions is to aid the priest in reaching the highest spiritual goals by removing him from contact with the tasks of society. Adherence to these ascetic rules distinguishes the "way of the monk" from the "way of the world." The rules concerning food for Buddhist priests in central Thailand provide a good example of the importance of asceticism for Buddhist priests. Priests may not eat after noon and therefore eat two meals before noon (the second about 11 A.M.) and drink only liquids until the next morning. They may not drink milk (which is a food) nor pulp in juice (which is a meat). Priests may never take food, but must wait until it is offered and then eat it only because it is necessary to do so. Priests eat as a group and some twenty-five rules govern etiquette. These rules cover the mixing of different foods, hand and arm movements, and the size of portions. Priests also do not drink alcoholic beverages although they do smoke, as tobacco was introduced after the rules were written. All of these rules serve two purposes. First, they differentiate priests from laymen and remove priests from village life so that they may devote their energies to sacred activities. Second, by differentiating priests from laymen, they create solidarity among the priests and strengthen the temple community.

It is typical for ascetics such as Buddhist priests to live in communities separate from the general population they serve. One form of such a community is the monastery, which serves as the home of religious specialists. One such community is Mount Athos in northeast Greece, the home to dozens of monasteries and other dwellings that house several thousand Eastern Orthodox monks. Some monks live in the main monasteries, others in small monasteries, others live alone or in small groups in houses or on farms, and a few live as hermits in caves. Through a combination of meditation, asceticism, control of one's desires, admission of one's imperfection, and separation from the world the monks hope to experience the mystical divine light present at the transfiguration of Jesus Christ. Among ascetic behaviors are celibacy, wearing black robes, not eating meat, performing physical labor, controlling all forms of self-assertion and pride, living apart from the general population, and giving up all personal possessions. Monks live an ascetic lifestyle and engage in the other activities

so that they "have died to life" and after death be immediately resurrected.

Estimates suggest that in India and Nepal there are some five million or more individuals known as *sadhu* (men) or *sadhvin* (women). Each sadhu is associated with a Hindu religious order, with the largest number associated with orders affiliated with the Shaiva sect of Hinduism. Asceticism is institutionalized in Hinduism in the four-fold division of life—pupil, householder, forest hermit, and wandering beggar. Sadhus are socially defined as such by their mendicant and ascetic lifestyle, physical appearance, and the specific services they provide for other Hindus. As mendicants, sadhus are supported by voluntary contributions from others, by begging, or by collecting payment for services they provide, such as fortune telling, dream interpretation, selling herbs, tattooing, and casting spells. As these religious activities suggest, sadhus often serve as diviners for other Hindus. In addition, sadhus must worship regularly, study the Hindu literature, and make pilgrimages. Many sadhus live in monasteries (*ashrams*) while others live a peripatetic lifestyle, using pilgrimage shrines as occasional homes. As ascetics sadhus do not marry (although many had been previously married); mark their bodies and wear clothing associated with their sect or go naked; shave off all their body hair or leave hair only on their heads, armpits, upper jaw, chin, and pubic area; give up worldly possessions; survive on donations made by others; and engage in purifying and spiritual activities every day. There are three major ways a Hindu becomes a sadhu. First, he may choose to leave his marriage and family and adopt the role of a sadhu. Such a step is often taken in times of personal crisis. Second, he may serve an order as a child and then be trained as a sadhu. Or, third, an individual may progress through the four life stages, of which sadhu is the last.

Asceticism in Daily Life

In some cultures people engage in ascetic behavior on an ongoing basis. However, whether this constitutes asceticism as a cultural practice is open to interpretation. There are a number of arguments for not classifying such behavior as asceticism. First, since the individuals are more or less compelled by tradition or local custom to engage in these behaviors, such everyday asceticism often lacks the voluntary nature of asceticism in world religions. Second, the ascetic behavior is often linked in a cause-and-effect fashion to very specific desired outcomes such as a successful hunt rather than to more amorphous notions such as enhancing one's spirituality or closeness with the supernatural world. Third, such everyday asceticism is sometimes difficult to distinguish from taboos as both are subject to supernatural punishment.

Asceticism in daily life is found mainly in traditional cultures where no clear distinction is made between the secular and supernatural worlds and where the supernatural is seen as a constant influence on the affairs of humans. In these cultures asceticism is an important component of food-getting activities. For example, Tlingit hunters traditionally fasted, isolated themselves from the community, and abstained from sexual relations:

> It's like the rule in the Bible. We used to live like God created us. . . . Hunters stay away from their wives four months before hunting. They [the animals] know if you cheat. Some boys stay eight, nine months. Then a certain month they come together. From December the hunters are apart—just the hunters, because they supply the whole family. (de Laguna 1972: 362)

As this quote suggests, Tlingit hunters fasted, isolated themselves, and were sexually continent so as to favorably influence the spirits of the animals they were hunting. Similarly, the Tiv of Nigeria believe that if one wants the assistance of spirits in hunting, the hunter must remain sexually continent for six days before the hunt. The Trukese of the Pacific believe that the water spirit, Djsnuken, will cause them harm unless fisherman adopt an ascetic lifestyle before a fishing expedition. Thus, for two or three weeks before the expedition, the fisherman sleep without their families in the boathouse, drink only coconut milk, and avoid pandanus fruit and oranges.

See also JAINISM; LIFE-CYCLE RITES; RELIGIOUS SPECIALISTS; TABOO; VISION QUEST

Allison, Robert W. (1992) "Mount Athos." In *Encyclopedia of World Cultures. Vol. 4: Europe.* Edited by Linda Bennett, 174–177.

Ames, Michael M. (1964) "Magical-Animism and Buddhism: A Structural Analysis of the Sinhalese Religious System." *Journal of Asian Studies* 23: 21–52.

Bohannan, Paul, and Laura Bohannan. (1969) *A Source Notebook on Tiv Religion in Five Volumes.*

Bunnag, Jane. (1973) *Buddhist Monk, Buddhist Layman: A Study of Urban Monastic Organization in Central Thailand.*

de Laguna, Frederica. (1972) *Under Mount Saint Elias: The History and Culture of the Yakutat Tlingit.*

Eliade, Mircea. (1969) *Immortality and Freedom.*

Ford, Clellan S., and Frank A. Beach (1951) *Patterns of Sexual Behavior.*

Frayser, Suzanne G. (1985) *Varieties of Sexual Experience.*

Ingersoll, Jasper C. (1969) *The Priest and the Path: An Analysis of the Priest Role in a Central Thai Village.*

Jenness, Diamond. (1935) *The Ojibwa Indians of Parry Island: Their Social and Religious Life.*

Kraemer, Augustin. (1932) *Truk.*

Rogers, Erik N. (1976) *Fasting: The Phenomenon of Self-Denial.*

Schaden, Egon. (1962) *Fundamental Aspects of Guarani Culture.*

Serpenti, I. M. (1965) *Cultivators in the Swamps.*

Titiev, Mischa. (1971) *Old Oraibi: Study of the Hopis Indians of the Third Mesa.*

Tripathi, B. D. (1978) *Sadhus of India.*

ASTROLOGY

Astrology is a form of divination in which the positions of the planets and stars are used to explain and predict events or states of being on earth. Astrology rests on the holistic view that there are interrelationships among and parallels between all aspects of the natural and supernatural world. Consistent with this orientation is the belief in modern, Western astrology that the psychological makeup of every individual is a microcosm of the entire universe. It contains all qualities of experience, all talents, all predilections of behavior and feeling. The sun, moon, and planets represent specific qualities. What makes a personality—and what life experiences are played out within this personality—is defined by the particular alignment of planets present within the zodiacal circle of star constellations that encircles the earth. This information is then mapped over a circle of twelve "houses," or aspects of experience, at the time of a person's birth.

The belief that heavenly bodies—stars, planets, sun, moon, asteroids, etc.—can influence life on earth is found in all cultures. Astrology in the contemporary world is based on the astrology developed by the ancient Greeks about 2,300 years ago from the star-lore of the ancient Mesopotamian peoples they had conquered. Astrology developed independently in India at about the same time and was influenced by Greek astrology before diffusing to other regions of South and Southeast Asia. Astrology has been rejected by Christianity since the end of the Roman Empire, but it has been employed at times in Islam and Judaism and is a component of Hinduism, Jainism, and Buddhism. Because it was not accepted by Christianity, astrology waxed and waned in Europe over the centuries and has enjoyed widespread acceptance only since the late 1880s. Perhaps the two major factors that led to the revival of astrology were the changing social order in Europe, which enabled people to take greater control of their lives and move up the social ladder, and the spread of literacy, which meant that many people could now practice astrology and read the results (horoscopes and charts) of astrology.

Initially, astrology was a tool used by priests for predicting events for royalty—the ones who represented the divine on earth. Court astrologers would advise on the wisdom of taking particular courses of action and the most advantageous time to do so. Philosophical or humanistic astrology, which deals with aspects of personality for individuals and groups of people, came only in the twentieth century, as individual human rights grew and people began to see themselves as the center of the universe. Today some astrologers practice growth-oriented astrology, which uses astrological analysis as a tool for facilitating the spiritual growth of individuals, couples, families, and organizations. Some astrologers view astrology as being partly scientific and partly spiritual. The scientific part is the observation and measurement of the heavenly bodies and the mathematical calculations, with the underlying basis of astrology and its interpretations being more spiritual. Other astrologers claim that astrology is a science and that predictions made on the basis of astrological calculations can be verified as accurate by scientific research. Critics of astrology view it as unscientific and its results as unverifiable.

Modern astrology is divided between Western (tropical) and Asian (sidereal) astrology. While there are numerous differences between the two, and variations within each, two distinctions are most important. First, they differ in what is predicted. In Western astrology most attention is given to predicting individual personality traits and behavioral patterns on the basis of the individual's date of birth. This goal is in accord with the individuality, personal freedom, and emphasis on personal growth and achievement in Western cultures. In Asian astrology, and especially Hindu astrology, most attention is given to predicting the events and state of the individual's life. This goal is in accord with Indian society, in which a person's status in society and fate is established by the status of their family. The caste system severely limits opportunities for personal growth and achievement for many Indians. The second major difference is the starting point of the zodiacs used in the two systems. The zodiac is made up of the twelve signs that represent the movements of the planets in relation to the movement of the sun across the sky. In Western astrology the tropical zodiac is based on the seasons of the solar year. In Asian astrology the sidereal zodiac is based on the fixed stars. Thus the zodiacs begin in different places and the twelve segments do not align. Some astrologers who use both systems use a mathematical formula to control the variation and make predications from either system comparable to the other.

Basics of Western Astrology

To understand astrology, one needs to know some aspects of astronomy as it relates to the movement of heavenly bodies. The perspective is pre-Copernican: it is from the earth looking outward, rather than from the sun as center of the solar system.

People have long observed that the sun, moon, and planets move in our field of vision through the stars. Stars themselves move only incrementally. But as the earth rotates, twelve constellations, or star groups, appear to be circling overhead in a band around the earth. These constellations were discerned by ancient astrologers as the twelve signs of the zodiac, each having a different meaning, together representing all of human experience. This band is called the ecliptic or zodiacal circle.

At different times during the day, month, and year, and depending on where on the earth you are looking out from, the sun, moon, and planets are seen against a backdrop of a particular star group or constellation. The planet is said to be in a particular zodiacal sign, for example, Venus is in Cancer. Due to the movement of the stars, called the precession of the ages, the correspondence is not exact.

Using a reference work called an ephemeris, which contains the positions of the sun, moon, and planets as they move through the zodiac, and mathematical calculations, astrologers plot these planets on a paper chart that includes the zodiacal circle and the twelve houses (arranged like twelve unequal pie slices in 360 degrees of pie). When referencing the date and place of someone's birth, the resulting chart is called a birth chart, natal chart, or horoscope.

The qualities ascribed to the planets (it is an astrological convention to refer to the sun and moon as planets as well) are modified by those of the signs of the zodiac they appear in. They function within the realm of life experience presented by the house in which they appear, forming the basis for describing the life experience of an individual.

The completed chart then contains planets and signs in each of the twelve houses. The interpretation of the interrelationship of all of these qualities, energies, and life dramas will identify talents, potential character strengths and defects, hobbies, career choice, quality of relationships with family, friends, and mate, and a host of other possibilities. The goal of humanistic astrology is to obtain information about these life patterns and innate tendencies from birth to death so that we can be active in the events and turning points in our lives in pursuit of spiritual evolution.

Signs of the Zodiac

The placement of the sun at the time of one's birth determines one's astrological sign. The signs of the zodiac are as follows:

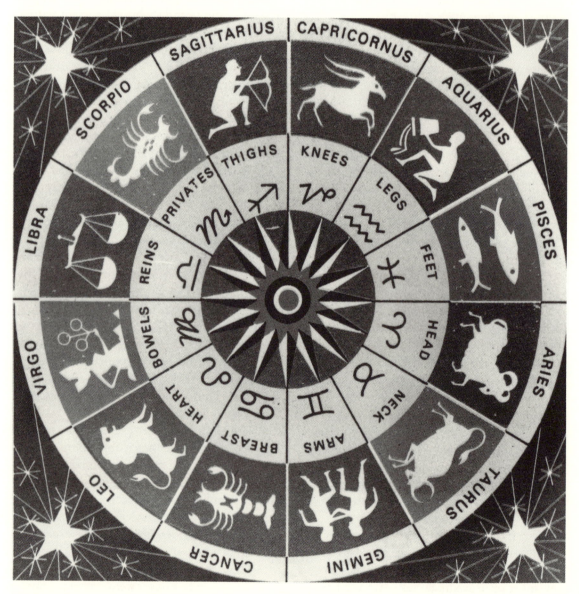

Astrology is a form of divination in which the spatial relationship between planets and stars is used to predict events and states of being on earth. This chart, for Western astrology, is based on the solar year's seasons and shows zodiacal signs and lists the parts of the body they are said to affect.

- Aries, the ram
  (March 21–April 20)
- Taurus, the bull
  (April 21–May 21)
- Gemini, the twins
  (May 22–June 21)
- Cancer, the crab
  (June 22–July 23)
- Leo, the lion
  (July 24–August 23)
- Virgo, the virgin
  (August 24–September 23)
- Libra, the scales of balance
  (September 24–October 23)
- Scorpio, the scorpion
  (October 24–November 22)
- Sagittarius, the archer
  (November 23–December 21)
- Capricorn, the goat
  (December 22–January 20)
- Aquarius, the water carrier
  (January 21–February 19)
- Pisces, the fish
  (February 20–March 20).

Aries starts the first day of spring and the signs always follow each other in the same order in thirty-degree increments around the circle. They are represented on the chart with a symbolic letter, or glyph. The signs will be of earth, water, fire, or air element and their mode can be cardinal, fixed, or mutable and expressed as masculine or feminine. Cardinal signs initiate, fixed signs stabilize, and mutable signs are receptive to change.

Aries is the ram, the life force, the will to exist. Its element is fire, and its mode is cardinal. It represents unyielding force in the face of life's challenges. Its lesson is courage, but its shadow side is a daredevil mentality and getting caught in the very crises that are meant to teach that lesson. Aries needs a force to push up against. Other Aries qualities are honesty, intensity, and directness.

Taurus the bull is the most physical sign, preferring the communication of music to that of words. Its element is earth and its mode is fixed. Taureans love silence, nature, simplicity, solidity. Its shadow side is the proverbial stubbornness of the bull, possessiveness, predictability, and a security bred from fear rather than choice.

Gemini represents the twins. Its element is air, its mode is mutable. Geminis are quick-thinking, intelligent collectors of information who strive to see clearly and who straddle unconventional and seemingly irreconcilable ideas regardless of how unorthodox their position may be. They revel in making sense of confusion. Their shadow side is the flip side of their quick minds—they never lose an argument and can reconstruct the elements of the truth to fit a less-than-true outcome. Geminis embody curiosity, vitality, and wonder in life.

Unlike Gemini, Cancer's exploration of the universe is an internal affair: Cancer leads with his or her feelings. Cancer's element is water, its mode is cardinal, and its archetype is the mother. Cancers develop an armor to protect their soft insides. The challenge for Cancer is to develop and evolve to the point where he or she outgrows his or her shell. Its shadow side is a tendency to hide from life, to hide beyond a nurturing persona instead of confronting the crises and challenges that are needed to grow.

Leo the lion's strength is brash self-aggrandizement. Leo's element is fire, its mode is fixed. Leo trusts in life and knows how to be happy. Leo is the sign of the actor, the politician, the creative personality. You always know that Leo is in the room. Leo's shadow side is when the people in the room are put off by his or her seemingly huge ego. Pride is another pitfall.

Virgo is the sign of wholeness, of the purity of mind embodied in Eastern philosophies like Buddhism and Taoism. Virgo's element is earth, his mode mutable. Perfection, unfettered freedom of the mind, is the goal of Virgo. Virgo loves order, and may tend to seriousness and self-absorption, but service is the key to happiness. Self-criticism and self-abnegation are pitfalls for Virgo.

Libra's symbol is the scales of harmony and balance, the reconciliation of opposites. Libra's element is air, its mode is cardinal. Libra both appreciates and creates beauty in the search for a harmonious mental and spiritual structure within which to live or a harmonious relationship where he or she can dare to be his or her most vulnerable self. Libras are always able to see both sides of an issue, but this ability often makes decision making agony. Indecisiveness and dalliance are the shadow side of Libra.

Scorpio is intensely focused on the present, using feelings rather than reason to move forward in life. Scorpio's element is water and its mode fixed. Actions based on feelings lead to satisfaction; Scorpio wants his. Emotional encounters must be lived at a fever pitch. Repression is not a part of Scorpio's makeup, but introspection is intense. Self-absorption and despair, a lack of balance in the consciousness, are the shadow sides of Scorpio.

Sagittarius is the wanderer, the student, the thinker. The search for meaning through travel and intellectual stimulation is paramount. Sagittarius' element is fire, its mode is mutable. Enthusiasm, free-spiritedness, and resilience mark the Sagittarian. There is not much from which Sagittarius cannot recover. In Sagittarius's search for wholeness, he or she seeks to discover his or her true place in life. Naiveté and placing too much faith in others may lead to tragedy.

Capricorn's vision is to have self and public personality become one. Capricorn's power, cunning, and ambition must be tempered with introspection and solitude to achieve balance. Capricorn's element is earth, his mode is cardinal. Patience, practicality, and self-discipline are hallmarks of his or her success. Its shadow side is difficulty in forming close interpersonal relationships; feelings are a challenge.

Aquarius is the sign of human freedom, the rebellion against social conformity. Aquarius's element is air and its mode is fixed. Single-mindedness may lead to loneliness as Aquarians search for truth. Alienation is the shadow for this sign.

Pisces, the fish, lives in the mother ocean of emotions. Its element is water and its mode is mutable. An easy awareness of higher consciousness is central to the Piscean personality—formless, structureless, and creative. Subjectivity and madness may be a shadow side of Pisces, as well as escaping into addiction.

Planets

Planets activate a particular energy in an area of life experience determined by the house and colored by the sign or signs in the house. Qualities of the "planets" are as follows:

1. the sun represents the essential self
2. the moon represents the expressed self or personality
3. the rising sign, which is the astrological sign and degree of the zodiac that was rising on the eastern horizon at the time and place of birth, represents the body through which this self and personality are anchored
4. Mercury is the trickster, the messenger, and represents mind, daily experience, and communication
5. Venus represents beauty and love, the emotional realm
6. Mars represents the ability to be aggressive and effective in the world
7. Jupiter represents hospitality, faith, and trust and expansion into the benefit in community
8. Saturn represents patience, limitation, and structure
9. Uranus represents the higher mind, the warrior

10. Neptune helps discern what is illusion and challenges us to go with what is real

11. Pluto rules transmutation and transformation, death, and birth at a cellular level.

Every planet rules a sign of the zodiac or has a natural affinity with one. Mercury rules Gemini, for example. Mercury is the planet of communication, and Gemini the sign of connections. Planets can rule more than one sign.

When a planet appears in the corresponding sign, its qualities are amplified and said to be "exalted." They may be said to be "in detriment" if the qualities of the planet are in conflict with those of the sign. In this case, the ruling planet of a sign appears in its opposite sign—180 degrees around the chart. Worse yet is if a planet is in its "fall."

The positions of the planets in relation to each other are significant and are called aspects. At 120 degrees, the aspect is called a trine, and represents major harmony aspects of the chart. At 60 degrees is the sextile, which is not as strong and exerts minor benefit. At 90 degrees, the planets are square, which represents a challenging opportunity for growth. At 180 degrees, they are in opposition and determining how to embrace both natures of the planets must be explored. When planets are said to be conjunct, they appear within a few degrees of each other.

Planets may be clustered in various ways, which are referred to as the bowl, the bucket, the seesaw, the scatter, the cluster, the splay, and the locomotive.

Houses of the Zodiac

The houses of the zodiac are a function of the angles created by the division of the horizon line into unequal pie-like pieces. There is more than one house system: the most commonly used house system in the United States

is called Placidus; the most commonly used house system in Europe is called Koch. There is also an equal-house system. The boundary line that separates one piece of "pie" from another is called a cusp.

The first house begins in the east and represents the way we put ourselves out in the world, the expression of our physical, genetic heritage and clothing styles. It includes the rising sign, and begins the east to west movement. The second house has to do with possessions, valuables, and income. The third house rules communication, humor, community, siblings, the elementary school years, and short-distance travel or commuting. The fourth house is the psychic ground we stand on: the unquestioned assumptions about the world and one's family of origin. It represents the home that we create.

The fifth house rules gambling, love affairs, and children, as well as all aspects of creativity. The sixth house represents health, community service, and more mundane life activities. Traditional relationships are the basis of the seventh house—major commitments like marriage and business partnerships.

In the eight house power issues come to the foreground. Death, taxes, other people's money, and legacies are also at issue, as are natural ways of accessing healing energy and connection with inner divinity. In the ninth house, higher education and consciousness are played out, as well as long-distance travel, expansion of the mind, and goals and planning. The tenth house is the place of career or vocation and how we are seen in the world. In the eleventh house, larger groups of people, organizations, friendship groups, and manifesting one's dreams are key. The twelfth house is the house of karma—meaning the inter- and intrapersonal issues that are part of our life's work to solve. The challenge it holds out is growth on a soul level.

Basics of Indian Astrology

Indian astrology is based on the stars, whose position is seen as fixed, with the most important being the constellations that the moon appears to move through each month. There are twenty-seven such constellations, which are called lunar mansions. While the other aspects of Indian astrology were influenced by peoples from Mesopotamia and the Greeks, the lunar mansions are of ancient Indian origin. Interpretation of the zodiac is quite similar to Western practice and astrologers have developed techniques for using both Western and Indian systems as equivalents.

The Signs of the Zodiac (Rasi)

1. Mesa, the ram: Aries
2. Vrsabha, the bull: Taurus
3. Mithuna, the couple, with the woman holding a *vina* (stringed instrument) and the man a mace: Gemini
4. Karkata, the crab: Cancer
5. Simha, the lion: Leo
6. Kanya, the maiden, often depicted in a boat and holding a lamp and grain: Virgo
7. Tula, the scales, often shown as a merchant weighing his goods in the marketplace: Libra
8. Vrscika, the scorpion: Scorpio
9. Dhanus, the bow, often, as in the West, a centaur archer: Sagittarius
10. Makara, the sea-monster, a mythical aquatic beast, typically resembling an ornate crocodile with an elephant's trunk, although the astrological version is often shown as a deer with a fish's tail: Capricorn
11. Kumbha, the water-pot, sometimes, as in the West, shown as a man emptying a water-pot carried on his shoulder: Aquarius
12. Mina, the fish: Pisces

Houses (Bhava)

1. Ascendant: body, appearance, personality
2. Wealth: property, family, speech
3. Brothers and sisters, courage, food
4. Kin: mother, early life, roots
5. Sons: offspring, intelligence, actions done in past lives
6. Enemies or Wounds: ill health, other obstacles
7. Wife: marriage partner, love, respect
8. Death: lifespan, death, future rebirth
9. Religion: spiritual teacher, father, the proper way of life
10. Work: career, status, knowledge
11. Gain: income, prosperity, success
12. Loss: expenditure, misfortune, travel.

Planets (Graha)

1. Surya or Ravi: the sun
2. Candra or Soma: the moon
3. Mangala (Auspicious) or Angaraka, (Burning Charcoal): Mars
4. Buddha (Knower): Mercury
5. Brhaspati (Lord of Sacred Speech) or Guru (Spiritual Teacher): Jupiter
6. Sukra (White or Sperm): Venus
7. Sani (Slow) or Sanaiscara (Slow-goer): Saturn

Lunar Mansions (Naksatra)

1. 0° Aries: *Asvini* (Possessing Horses, the Horsewoman): a horse's head
2. 13° 20' Aries: *Bharani* (Bearing): female sexual organ
3. 26° 40' Aries: *Krttika* (the Cutters): a weapon or flame
4. 10° Taurus: *Rohini* (the Growing [or Red] One): a temple, an ox-cart, or a cow's head
5. 23° 20' Taurus: *Mrgasiras* (the Deer's Head): a deer's head

6. 6°40' Gemini: *Ardra* (the Moist One): a tear drop

7. 20° Gemini: *Punarvasu* (the Two Good-Again): a quiver of arrows

8. 3°20' Cancer: *Pusya* (Nourishing): a cow's udder

9. 16°40' Cancer: *Aslesa* (the Clinging): a coiled snake

10. 0° Leo: *Magha* (the Great, the Bountiful): a royal throne-room

11. 13°20' Leo: *Purvaphalguni* (the Former Reddish [or Small] One): a swinging hammock

12. 26°40' Leo: *Uttaraphalguni* (the Latter Reddish [or Small] One): a bed or couch

13. 10° Virgo: *Hasta* (the Hand): a hand

14. 23°20' Virgo: *Citra* (Bright, Many-Colored, Wonderful): a bright jewel

15. 6°40' Libra: *Svati*, (Self-Going): a young shoot blown by the wind

16. 20° Libra: *Visakha* (the Forked or Two-Branched) or *Radha* (Delightful): a gateway decorated with leaves

17. 3°20' Scorpio: *Anuradha* (Additional Radha, After-Radha): a staff, or a row of offerings to the gods

18. 16°40' Scorpio: *Jyestha* (the Eldest): a circular talisman

19. 0° Sagittarius: *Mula* (the Root): a tied bunch of roots.

20. 13°20' Sagittarius: *Purvasadha* (the Former Unconquered): a winnowing basket or fan

21. 26°40' Sagittarius: *Uttarasadha* (the Latter Unconquered): an elephant's tusk; Intercalary Mansion. *Abhijit* (the Victorious): a triangle or three-cornered nut

22. 10° Capricorn: *Sravana* (Hearing or Limping): three footprints side by side

23. 23°20' Capricorn: *Sravistha* (the Most Famous) or *Dhanistha* (the Wealthiest): a musical drum

24. 6° 40' Aquarius: *Satabhisaj* (The Hundred Physicians): a circle enclosing a space

25. 20° Aquarius: *Purvabhadrapada* (the Former Lucky Feet): the first end of a bed

26. 3°20' Pisces: *Uttarabhadrapada* (the Latter Lucky Feet): the other end of the bed

27. 16°40' Pisces: *Revati* (Wealthy): a drum.

Applications of Astrology

The most popular use of astrology is the charting of natal or birth horoscopes, which tell individuals about their personalities or significant events in their life. Horoscopes printed in newspapers and magazines are of this type, although serious astrologers do not take them seriously. Horary astrology, in which charts are made to answer specific questions such as "where is a lost child?," is another common application. So too is event astrology, in which the astrologer predicts the date of occurrence of a specific event such as an earthquake. In recent years election astrology, in which the outcome of political elections are predicted, has become a popular application as well. In some Asian nations such as China, local space astrology is common as experts are consulted to help people pick an auspicious sight for a house or grave. Less common and somewhat more complicated are mundane astrology and astro-cartography. In mundane astrology, the focus is on an entire group or even a nation, with the group or national horoscope used to predict future significant events. Astro-cartography is a recent development made possible by computer mapping and computerized astrology and is based on the analysis of the location of heavenly bodies at one point in time relative to different locations on earth. Although most astrologers limit their practice to offering information and predictions, some have also added mitigation to their practices. Mitigation, often based on Burmese Mahabate astrology, involves providing clients with advice based on the horoscope.

A recent and rapidly growing form of astrology is growth-centered astrology. Rather than take the view that astrological calculations set our lives in stone, most growth-centered astrologers take the view that the birth chart represents a spectrum of possibilities, and the individual knows best which aspects can be best applied. What is not written is how the soul responds to the set-up; how these life patterns are played out depends on the person's own evolution. Particular energetic situations can warn of time of upheaval or trouble and can make the person mindful during that time. It need not portend disaster. Creative analysis of the chart can result in a picture of the best possible reality for the person being charted.

Astrologer Stephen Forrest (1984: 8–9) set forward seven principles of growth-oriented astrology:

1. Astrological symbols are neutral. There are no good ones, no bad ones.
2. Individuals are responsible for the way they embody their birth charts.
3. No astrologer can determine a person's level of response to his birth chart from that birth chart alone.
4. The birth chart is a blueprint for the happiest, most fulfilling, most spiritually creative path of growth available to the individual.
5. All deviations from the ideal growth pattern symbolized by the birth chart are unstable states, usually accompanied by a sense of aimlessness, emptiness, and anxiety.
6. Astrology recognizes only two absolutes: the irreducible mystery of life and the uniqueness of each individual viewpoint on that mystery.
7. Astrology suffers when wedded too closely to any philosophy or religion. Nothing in the system matters except the intensification of a person's self-awareness.

See also DIVINATION; GEOMANCY

Avery, Jeanne. (1982) *The Rising Sign: Your Astrological Mask.*

Braha, James T. (1986) *Ancient Hindu Astrology for the Modern Western Astrologer.*

Cameron, Barbara. (1981) *Mahabote: The Little Key.*

———. Cameron, Barbara. (1984) *Turning the Tables: A Mitigation Manual.*

Forrest, Steven. (1984) *The Inner Sky, The Dynamic New Astrology for Everyone.*

Jones, Marc Edmund. (1972) *Astrology: How and Why It Works.*

Jordan, Mary Kate. Personal communication.

Lofthus, Myrna. (1980) *A Spiritual Approach to Astrology.*

Matthews, John. (1992) *The World Atlas of Divination.*

Moore, Marcia, and Mark Douglas. (1948) *Astrology: The Divine Science.*

Tester, Jim. (1987) *A History of Western Astrology.*

followers throughout Persia. Alarmed by his success, the clergy and government cracked down on the religion, arrested the Bab, and in 1850 sentenced him to death by firing squad. On the day of execution, he was suspended in a public square by ropes, but when the squad of soldiers fired their volley at him, the Bab disappeared. He was soon discovered, however, in a nearby building talking calmly with a disciple. The next day, on July 9, he was brought before a firing squad again. This time the bullets found their mark. A brutal campaign against Baha'i ensued in which an estimated 20,000 followers were executed.

Just prior to the Bab's death he announced that there would be a new leader greater than himself to carry on his work of establishing a universal religion. One of the Bab's surviving followers was a man named Mizra Hussain Ali, who because of family connections escaped persecution. He had changed his family name, however, to Baha'u'llah. Two years after the Bab's execution, an attempted assassination attempt on the Iranian shah led to the banishment of Baha'u'llah and several other followers to Baghdad. Just outside of Baghdad the group encamped in the garden of Ridvan for twelve days (April 21–May 2). Baha'u'llah announced at this time that he was the one foretold by the Bab. Remarkably, almost all of those in attendance acknowledged him as the Chosen of God and became devoted followers.

Baha'u'llah and his followers spent the next several years moving from Baghdad to Istanbul to Adrianople and finally to Acre in Palestine, a Turkish community reserved for exiled criminals. During this time Baha'u'llah accomplished several things. He was able to build a community in exile of followers devoted to his teachings. He wrote a series of books, including The Book of Certitude, Seven Valleys, and Hidden Words, which became the foundation for Baha'i scriptures. And he aggressively pursued his

BAHA'I

Advocating a life of humanity and universal religion, Baha'i has a worldwide following. Baha'i is a relatively new religion, founded in 1844 in Iran. The term Baha'i comes from the founder's name, Baha'u'llah, literally meaning "Glory of God." "To be a Baha'i simply means to love all the world; to love humanity and try to serve it; to work for universal peace and universal brotherhood," explained Baha'u'llah's eldest son, Abdul Baha.

Historical Development

Baha'i traces its roots to Islam. Shiite Muslims believe that there were twelve legitimate descendants of the Prophet Muhammad, known as *imams*. The twelfth imam (or *bab*, meaning gate to the true faith) disappeared in the ninth century. Shiites have expected this lost imam to reappear as the Messiah. On May 22, 1844, 'Ali Mohammed, a young Persian descendent of Mohammed, declared himself to be the missing twelfth imam. He dubbed himself the Bab and succeeded in attracting a growing number of

mission of establishing a universal religion, preaching peace and harmony, including sending letters to the president of the United States, leaders of most European nations, the pope, and Christian and Muslim clergy. He and his followers were eventually allowed to leave Acre and settled in Mount Carmel. Baha'u'llah died on May 29, 1892. The Shrine of the Bab was built in 1909 in his memory and still stands in Haifa, Israel.

Baha'u'llah designated his eldest son, Abbas Effendi, as the sole interpreter of his teachings and as his successor. For thirty years the new leader, who changed his name to Abdul Baha (Servant of God), continued his father's work, spreading the message throughout the world and expanding on his writings, including the publication of his work *The Divine Plan.* Upon his death on November 28, 1921, his grandson Shoghi Effendi became the new leader. Shoghi Effendi (The Guardian), established an administration to oversee the religion and a supreme legislative body called the Universal House of Justice. He died on November 2, 1957, without leaving a successor.

Religious Beliefs

Baha'u'llah taught that God is unknowable. "No tie of direct intercourse can possibly bind Him to His creatures," he wrote. "No sign can indicate His presence or His absence." To make his presence known, however, God revealed himself through messengers, including Jesus, Moses, Mohammed, Zoroaster, Buddha, and the Bab. All of the messengers offered "manifestations" of God's will. Each of the religions the messengers espouse offer essentially the same beliefs aimed at peace and good will. The goal of Baha'i is to bring about a unity of mankind. The Baha'i, wrote Shoghi Effendi, "proclaims the necessity and inevitability of the unification of mankind, asserts that it is gradually approaching, and claims that nothing short of the transmuting

spirit of God, working through His chosen Mouthpiece in this day, can ultimately succeed in bringing it about."

The route to this goal for followers is to condemn prejudice and superstition, promote amity and compassion, advance science as the agent of orderly progress in society, adhere to the principle of equal rights between the sexes and among all races, and eliminate extreme poverty and wealth. Baha'is are urged to pursue education, live a monogamous lifestyle, and develop an international language to serve as a unifying force. The ultimate goal of Baha'i is to establish and the perpetuate peace of mankind.

Baha'is try to adhere to these principles every day. They view each day as a Judgment Day of their conduct. Upon death, a Baha'i's soul is called to account and evolves into different states and conditions. The more pure the soul or its spiritual qualities were during life, the closer it lies to God, which is considered heaven, the state of perfection. If the soul is placed far away from God, it is considered hell. Baha'is, however, do not believe that there is an evil force, but rather an absence of divine qualities. Thus, the joys of heaven are spiritual, and in hell the occupants suffer from the absence of those joys.

Texts and Practices

The sacred literature of Baha'i consists of the writings of the Bab, Baha'u'llah, Abdul Baha, and Shoghi Effendi. These include hundreds of texts, the most important of which are considered to be the Kitab-i-Aqda (Most Holy Book), describing Baha'i laws and institutions, and the Kitab-i-Iqan (Book of Certitude) consisting of Baha'u'llah's revelations. Both books were written by Baha'u'llah, who also wrote the Book of Covenant, in which he offers a clear interpretation of his own writings and authorizes future interpretations by his son. Since the death of Shoghi Effendi no one has been authorized to offer official interpretations of the writings.

Baha'i does not use professional priests, boast a monastic order, or prescribe complicated ceremonial rituals or initiation ceremonies. Membership to the Baha'i community is open to anyone who accepts the teachings of Baha'u'llah and professes faith in him. Every Baha'i, however, must pray daily (this can include service work), fast nineteen specified days a year going without food or drink from sunup to sundown, abstain from any use of alcohol or narcotics except for medicinal purposes, and gain permission from parents for marriage and, once married, be monogamous. Baha'i parents are obligated to educate their children.

Baha'i communities hold regular meetings for worship under the direction of a respected, unpaid person in the community. The meetings consist of reading from Baha'i and other religious scriptures, prayers, and on occasion discussions about religion. Every Baha'i community with nine or more members elects a nine-person administrative body annually on April 21 (the date that Baha'u'llah announced he was the chosen one) to govern the local community; the number nine represents the universal unity as it is the largest single-digit number. The next level of administration is the national spiritual assembly, which is also elected annually. The ultimate administrative body is the Universal House of Justice, which is elected every five years.

Although most Baha'i meetings take place in members' homes, there are some spectacular Baha'i houses of worship, built according to the designs of Baha'u'llah. The buildings have nine sides, and are surrounded by gardens adorned with fountains and trees as well as other buildings used for education, charity, and social purposes. Contributions are only accepted from Baha'i members and must be given voluntarily without any solicitation. Many Baha'is have sacrificed their homes and careers on behalf of spreading the faith, which now has a worldwide following.

Festivals

Baha'is hold several festivals a year to mark the anniversaries of important dates in their history, such as the birthdays of the Bab and Baha'u'llah, the death of the Bab, the ascension of Baha'u'llah and his son, and other events. The most important festival is the Feast of Ridvan, held from April 21 to May 2 to commemorate Baha'u'llah's announcement of his mission. The Nineteen-Day Fast is also very important and is celebrated on the first day of each of the nineteen months in the Baha'i calendar.

Esslemont, J. E. (1980) *Baha'u'llah and the New Era.* First published in 1923.

BUDDHISM

Founded in the sixth century B.C.E. as a reaction against Hinduism, Buddhism grew into the dominant religion in Asia for many centuries and now has a global following. Buddhism is based on the life and teachings of Siddhartha Gautama, later known as Buddha, or "the enlightened one." Many rulers and governments throughout the centuries have attempted to suppress Buddhism, most recently in communist China. There are more than 300 million followers of Buddhism, with the vast majority in Asia.

History

Buddhism grew out of a widespread disenchantment with Hinduism in India in the sixth century B.C.E. Many lay and religious leaders were dissatisfied with Hindu practices and principles. Siddhartha Gautama, who was born in 563 B.C.E. in what is now Nepal, counted himself among this group. He gave up his position of privilege as a member of the warrior class (*kshatriya*) to become a wandering ascetic. Even before his birth, Saddhartha's life seemed destined for greatness. Shortly before he was born his mother dreamed that a white elephant entered her womb. Dream interpreters declared this as a sign that the child would become a universal teacher or a universal leader. After his birth a Hindu priest identified markings on the child's body as indications that he would become a great teacher, or Buddha. Another Hindu predicted that if the child stayed in his home he would become a great ruler, but if he grew up somewhere else, he would become a Buddha. One week after Siddhartha was born his mother died, and the child was placed in the care of his mother's sister. After growing up in luxury, he was married in his teens and had a son.

Despite having a stable family and great wealth, Siddhartha was dissatisfied. When he was twenty-nine years old he witnessed four events that changed his life. First, he saw a frail old man leaning on his staff as he walked. Second, he witnessed a sick, suffering man who soiled himself because of his weakened condition. The third sight was the image of a human corpse being taken to a funeral pyre. The final sight was an ascetic monk in solitude. The combination of these images suddenly struck Siddhartha. Suffering is the condition of human life, he realized. He decided to leave his home, become a wandering ascetic, and search for the solution to human suffering. The search, which became known as the "great renunciation," lasted six years and became a critical foundation of Buddhist teachings.

Siddhartha placed himself under the tutelage of two different Hindu gurus who taught him to meditate to reach higher states of being as part of the Hindu philosophical path to enlightenment. Dissatisfied with these teachings, he then followed severe austerity practices in the search for truth. During this time he joined five other ascetics. Siddhartha subjected himself to extreme self-abuse in the company of his com-

panions. He refused to cleanse himself, ate disgusting types of food, and sat on a couch of thorns, eventually putting himself close to death. While recuperating, however, he rejected austerity as the path toward enlightenment, much to the disgust of his companions, who abandoned him. Frustrated by his inability to find the truth, Siddhartha found a tree off the road and sat cross-legged at its foot, determined to stay there in meditation until he discovered enlightenment.

During this meditation Siddhartha was approached by three temptations from Mara, the personification of evil. Mara first tried to convince Siddhartha that a former archenemy had led a revolt against his father, imprisoned him, and taken Siddhartha's wife. Unmoved by this first effort, Mara presented three sensuous goddesses surrounded by dancers who attempted to seduce Siddhartha. Finally, Mara called upon several demons to scare Siddhartha. Instead of being fearful, Siddhartha scattered Mara and the demons by placing his right-hand fingers on the ground, which produced a tremendous sound that scared his tormentors off. Siddhartha then spent the night lost in meditation, experiencing his former lives, discovering the cycles of birth and the reasons for them, and absorbing the cosmic truth, or *dharma*. This discovery was accompanied by a swelling of the earth and a great burst of light as the new day dawned. Armed with this new knowledge, Siddhartha became the Buddha.

Unsure of what to do with his newfound enlightenment, Buddha meditated for several weeks on whether to spread the word. He finally decided to do so. He first approached the five ascetics with whom he formerly associated. The five rejected Buddha several times as being unworthy of their companionship, much less as their leader. But they finally listened to his description of what he had learned (known as Setting in Motion the Wheel of Truth) and became

A second-century B.C.E. relief sculpture from a museum in India shows Buddha, "the enlightened one," surrounded by monks, princes, and bodhisattvas. *Buddhism, based on the life and teachings of Siddhartha Gautama, has expanded from its sixth-century B.C.E. Asian roots to become a global religion.*

the first members of Buddha's *sangha,* or monastic order. Buddha soon converted family members and many others, including people from all different Hindu castes; from brahman priests to the lower castes. Once a person became a disciple of Buddha as a member of the sangha, the distinctions of caste were no longer applied. Buddha spent the next forty-five years of his life teaching his followers. Sixty "perfected" disciples, *arhats,* who had reached enlightenment were sent all over India to spread Buddha's message of compassion, peace, and truth. A cousin

of Buddha, Ananda, convinced him to include women, and Buddha established an order of nuns. By the time of his death, Buddha had a large following of people he had taught and trained to continue his message through wisdom and compassion. His last words were, "And now, O monks, I take leave of you; transient are all conditioned things. Try to accomplish your aim with diligence."

According to tradition, a council was held immediately after Buddha's death to establish rules and an authorized canon to direct the early

Buddhist monasteries. A century later another council was convened. At this council, however, Buddhism split into two factions, the Mahasanghika, which interpreted Buddha's teachings liberally, and the Theravadins, which adhered to more conservative and orthodox principles. Although several other factions formed then and in subsequent centuries, they all fell under these two groups. At a third council held in the third century B.C.E., Buddhists wrote the Tripitaka, the Buddhist canon. Up until then most of Buddha's teachings were passed down through oral tradition.

Buddha held annual gatherings for his disciples, who continued the tradition after his death. The sites of these gatherings became permanent settlements or monasteries as centers for Buddhist learning. The monasteries eventually spread as Buddhist missionaries went forth to China, Tibet, Japan, and southeastern Asia. Buddhism is believed to be the first religion to create a monastic order, and many scholars believe that Christian practitioners adopted the idea of monasteries for their own purposes. Within Buddhism, many of the monasteries developed their own characteristics. Several Buddhist sects evolved in very different ways. In Japan, for example, Buddhist monasteries hired mercenaries and armed monks to wage wars against other religious orders during the tenth to thirteenth centuries, a practice that would have been condemned according to more traditional Buddhist teachings.

How Buddhism spread in its early years is unknown. But in the third century B.C.E., the king of India, Asoka, converted to Buddhism, renounced warfare, and spread the religion throughout India. He sponsored missionaries to the Middle East, China, Africa, Ceylon, and Southeast Asia. Buddhism established itself in China by the first century B.C.E. In the middle of the second century C.E., Buddha was worshiped in the imperial court. The influence of Buddhism continued to grow in China. In 399, the first Chinese Buddhist monk completed a pilgrimage to India and returned to China to teach Buddhism. Two years later Kumarajiva, a Buddhist monk, was captured by Chinese raiders and brought to the capital of China, where Kumarajiva oversaw the work of hundreds of scholars who translated Buddhist scriptures into Chinese. Chinese leaders increasingly embraced Buddhism and encouraged its development despite periodic efforts by the occasional emperor to retard its development. Buddhism reached its peak in China with the start of the Sui dynasty in 581 when the Emperor Wen declared himself a Buddhist and used the religion as a way to unify northern and southern China. This golden age of Chinese Buddhism lasted nearly three centuries. The era came to an end in 845 when a one-year purge of Buddhism was initiated by a Chinese emperor.

From China, Buddhism spread even further in Asia, including to Japan and Tibet. Buddhism was introduced to Japan in the sixth century and became a state religion in the eighth century. Not only did many Japanese adopt Buddhism as their own religion, but Buddhism also heavily influenced the development of Shintoism in the island nation. Tibet was first exposed to Buddhism in the seventh century, but their religion did not take hold until a century later when it eclipsed local beliefs. Buddhism evolved in a sporadic and factionalized fashion that was filled with rivalries. Now known as Lamaism, the localized religion fused a wide variety of local beliefs with Indian and Chinese forms of Buddhism.

Although Buddha taught tolerance of other religions, many leaders from other religions often did not reciprocate the belief. As a result Buddhists have continuously been subjected to persecution and opposition. In India, intolerant Hindu leaders periodically stomped down on Buddhist monasteries, resulting in a decline of Buddhism in northern India in the thirteenth century and in southern India in the fifteenth century. There are now virtually no Buddhists in India, where Buddhism first established itself. In the late nineteenth century, the Japanese government attempted to squash Buddhism. And in this century, communist China persecuted Buddhist monks and confiscated Buddhist temples. Nevertheless, Buddhism continues to flourish throughout most of east Asia. Increasingly, the teachings of Buddha are finding audiences throughout the rest of the world, including Europe, the United States, and Africa, as Asian Buddhists send missionaries to seek converts.

Religious Beliefs

Buddhism is based on the teachings of Buddha, who outlined his beliefs in opposition to Hinduism. Although there are some similarities, Buddha rejected the Hindu idea of liberation from the cycle of rebirths through philosophic, ascetic, or devotional paths. Liberation for Buddhists refers to the extinguishing of *tanha*, or selfish craving for physical or material pleasure. Buddha rejected the Hindu concept of an individual soul as part of the Atman. He said that people consist of five components, or *skandhas:* body, perceptions, feelings, dispositions, and consciousness. The cycle of rebirth, he said, is caused by the constantly changing condition of the world. There is a constant flow of becoming. The original condition is ignorance, which then expands to include predisposition, consciousness, individuality, the five senses and the mind, self-desire (tanha), attachment to existence, the process of becoming, different states of being, and human suffering. Rather than a constant cycle of rebirths, Buddha described a dharma, or cosmic truth, as a wheel in which a condition constantly moves and changes.

Buddha explained the dharma as the Four Noble Truths, which are the foundation for Buddhist teaching. The Four Truths are:

1. All things are in a state of dissatisfaction, called *dukkha,* that includes suffering, pain, and frustration. The condition of all these things is in a never-ending process of change. Nothing is permanent. Life and the conditions of life are all temporary. Indeed, the only thing that is permanent is the fact that there is an endless process of impermanence, change, and decay.
2. The dissatisfaction, or dukkha, is a result of tanha, a desire for physical things and intellectual stimulation. People convince themselves that possessions, relationships, and accomplishments will satisfy their restless desires. But Buddha said that the opposite is true: tanha is the cause of dukkha.
3. To break this process, a person must eliminate tanha. The only way to find inner peace is to eliminate all selfish desires.
4. The path to freedom is the Middle Way. This route shuns both extreme self-denial and unrestrained self-indulgence. The route to enlightenment involves a wide category of practical, day-to-day techniques described as the Noble Eightfold Path.

The Noble Eightfold Path consists of the following:

1. Right Understanding, in which a person believes in the Four Noble Truths.
2. Right Intention, whereby a person turns his or her back on worldly pursuits and accepts living in a "homeless" state.

3. Right Speech, in which one must always act in consideration of others and never lie, abuse someone else, or engage in idle talk.
4. Right Conduct, meaning a person must behave with respect to others and thus abstain from stealing, hurting other people, committing adultery, or using intoxicants.
5. Right Occupation, meaning a person must never hold a job that would violate the above prohibitions.
6. Right Endeavor, whereby a person must always attempt to do good and stay away from evil.
7. Right Contemplation, meaning that one must control his or her thoughts so that neither joy nor sorrow disturbs one's inner calm.
8. Right Concentration, which can only be achieved after having successfully accomplished the other principles, whereby one is able to control one's own mind to bring it to higher and higher states of being, even beyond reasoning.

The ultimate goal is to reach a state of *nirvana,* or extinguishment, in which a person rids himself or herself of tanha. This takes place when the enlightened person dies and thus breaks all connections to life. At that point the person is liberated from the cycle of rebirth. Nirvana is the end of transitory states for the individual, a final bliss that ends the constant process of change for the individual and is an absolute transcendent state.

Texts

Buddhism has hundreds of important texts and canons that have been written over the centuries describing a wide variety of philosophical beliefs, religious practices, and symbolic stories. However, the vast majority of these pertain to the many different sects that have developed.

The most important collection of writings for all Buddhists is the Tripitaka (the Three Baskets), written during the third great council after Buddha's death. The Tripitaka consists of the Vinayana Pitaka (the rules of the Buddhist order), the Sutta Pitaka (dialogues between Buddha's disciples and Buddha), and the Abhidhamma Pitaka (metaphysical teachings).

Sects

There are two main branches of Buddhism: Theravada (the conservative or orthodox interpretation of Buddha's teaching) and Mahayana (the liberal interpretation). Under these two broad categories fall many, many other forms of Buddhism that have formed because of the wide variety of ways that groups have prioritized, interpreted, or altered Buddha's original teachings.

Theravada Buddhism places the monk as the central figure and is generally limited to monastic orders because of the complete devotion required to comply with its tenets. Following rigorous daily schedules that include solitary meditation and monastic discipline, monks attempt to reach the ideal goal of nirvana through their personal conduct. Monks must faithfully abide by the daily schedule to gain merit in the quest for personal liberation. Theravada Buddhists regard Buddha as a flesh-and-blood man who discovered the path to nirvana and taught others how to follow him to that state.

Mahayana Buddhism interprets Buddha's life differently. Rather than looking upon him as a human being, Mahayana Buddhists regard Buddha as a living incarnation of the Buddha spirit. He appeared among humans out of compassion for people to instruct them in the way to nirvana. In addition, Mahayana Buddhists believe that a person can take steps toward a state of nirvana without entering the homeless position of a cloistered or wandering monk. These two beliefs stimulated a great diversity of ways to interact with Buddha. If Buddha is an eternal spirit, then in the eyes of many he becomes an object of worship, or a deity. In addition, others who reach the state of nirvana can become "saviors" worthy of worship. Known as *bodhisattvas,* they too became objects of worship and leaders of different sects. Two of the more important sects that have influenced the intellectual development of Buddhism are (1) Madhyamika, which emphasizes the importance of the middle position between opposites and (2) T'ien-t'ai (Tendai in Japan), which describes a threefold truth of emptiness, temporary existence, and the presence of a middle state in which everything is empty and temporary at the same time.

One of the most popular of the Mahayana Buddhist sects is the Pure Land, which describes a place overseen by the Buddha of Infinite Light that is called upon by followers for assistance and during meditation. The Pure Land offers a step for those who are not monks to reach the ultimate goal of nirvana. Followers believe that by constantly reciting the name of the sacred Buddha of Infinite Light, Amitabha, a person can reach the Pure Land. Another popular sect is Ch'an, or Zen in Japan. The Ch'an or Zen believe that a person can achieve enlightenment through strict self-discipline and intuitive meditation. Merit, good deeds, and the reading or reciting of scripture play no role in the quest for enlightenment in this sect. Rather, a person awakens the "Buddha" that exists in everyone through meditation that aims at taking a person's thought out of the realm of reason. Achieving this more personal enlightenment, or *satori,* is accomplished by contemplating different riddles or situations (known as *koans*) that cannot be solved through rational thought. How, for example, can a person make a sound by clapping one hand? The goal is to make a person think beyond known intellectual boundaries to take him or her into a different realm of thought.

Religious Practices

Buddhist temples are built around stupas or pagodas that contain relics of Buddha, including his body parts. Worshipers visit the temples to observe Buddha's significance as a way of gaining religious merit. Followers circle the stupa three times and then worship it. While images of Buddha were not used in the religion's early history, it is now commonplace for Buddhist temples and homes to have images of Buddha either seated, lying down, or standing that serve as symbolic objects for offerings. When worshiping Buddha, every follower must recite "Homage to Him, the Blessed One, the Exalted One, the fully Enlightened One." This is followed by a recitation of the Three Refuges: "I go to Buddha as my refuge. I go to the Dharma as my refuge. I go to the Sangha as my refuge." This is then followed by pledges to abstain from killing life, stealing, sexual misconduct, lying, and taking intoxicants. Followers often recite these invocations several times a day. Increasingly, followers meet once a week in temples for group worship. This is especially true in Western societies.

Festivals

All Buddhists observe three events in Buddha's life: his birth, enlightenment, and death, which was also his entry into nirvana. Theravada Buddhists commemorate all three events on a single day, Vesak, or Full Moon Day in the April–May time period. Mahayana Buddhists commemorate Buddha's birth at Hanamasturi (Flower Festival) on April 8, his day of enlightenment on Bodhi Day, December 8, and his entry into nirvana on February 15. In addition to these days, different Buddhist groups hold their own festivals and ceremonies according to their own beliefs.

March, Arthur C. (1986) *A Glossary of Buddhist Terms.*

Humphreys, Christmas. (1984) *A Popular Dictionary of Buddhism.*

Spiro, Melford. (1970) *Buddhism and Society: A Great Tradition and Its Burmese Vicissitudes.*

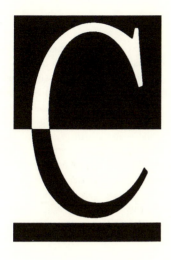

CANNIBALISM Cannibalism, or anthropophagy as it is technically known, is the consumption of human flesh, organs, or bones by other humans. Because it is both repulsive and fascinating (perhaps it is fascinating because it is repulsive), cannibalism has drawn considerable attention in the popular media and from nonscientific observers of other cultures, although it has been somewhat ignored by anthropologists until quite recently. Reports of early explorers, missionaries, and government officials in the New World, Oceania, and Africa often described cannibalism among the native peoples of those regions. This image persists, as evidenced by cartoons that depict native peoples boiling pith-helmeted Westerners in large pots. This image does not reflect reality, and, in fact, there is some question as to whether cannibalism as a regular practice has ever existed in any society and, therefore, whether it has ever been a major component of religious systems.

Anthropological interest in cannibalism among non-Western peoples grew following the publication of Arens's 1979 survey that led him to conclude that it is very unlikely that cannibalism ever existed in any culture. Other experts have subsequently taken a less firm view about its nonexistence, although the consensus now is that the past wisdom about its wide distribution and frequency was a gross exaggeration. The evidence supporting the view that cannibalism never existed as a regularly practiced custom in any society is considerable. It can be summarized as follows.

1. Most of the evidence for cannibalism comes from the reports of early European explorers, missionaries, and government agents. These individuals likely embarked on their voyages already believing that the people they would encounter were cannibals. This idea that the inhabitants of unexplored regions of the world were cannibals was an established part of classical writings and was also reported by Columbus, who claimed that the Carib people in the Caribbean were cannibals when they were not. The word *cannibal* is probably derived from the name of the Carib people, their name being misspelled as Canib by Columbus's party. Thus, early arrivals in the New World and Africa reported what they expected to find, whether or not the practice actually existed.

2. Westerners who established contact with indigenous peoples often had an interest in describing these cultures as uncivilized as they often coveted indigenous people's land, labor, natural resources, and souls. Defining people and cultures as less than human has been long used as a justification for killing them, enslaving them, or taking their land.

3. In addition to having a vested interest, these early reporters of cannibalism were not trained, objective observers and many did not speak the native language.
4. The early reports were often contradictory in their descriptions of how often cannibalism occurred, who was eaten, how the body was prepared, etc.
5. Most reports of cannibalism by trained ethnographers refer to the past and do not claim that cannibalism existed when the ethnographer was there. This is known as memory ethnography and is a less trustworthy method of collecting information than reporting what one actually observes.
6. People the world over are often quite willing to claim that others are cannibals. Just as Europeans believed that non-Europeans were cannibals, some native peoples claimed the reverse, while Koreans have accused the Chinese of cannibalism and the Chinese the Koreans. Often the people accused of being cannibals are enemies of the accuser or people who are already considered to be inferior, such as suspected witches, social misfits, religious minorities, and women in cultures where men consider them inferior.

The two following examples indicate how—and how easily—outside observers as well as members of the culture can claim that cannibalism is practiced when it is not. For the Andaman Islanders of South Asia, the information came from the first Europeans to settle the islands:

> There are no records of an attempt to land before 1825, when an English naval officer, T. E. Alexander, managed to do so, and was the first to report, in England, the existence of a fierce tribe of naked Onges. The encounter was bloody, as were many after-wards. Rumours (erroneous) were spread of cannibalism, as some English sailors who had managed to save themselves saw their companions being torn to pieces by the Onges: their hands, feet, legs and arms were cut off and the living remains were thrown into a great fire. This was, in fact, not cannibalism, but the satisfying of a superstition . . . that the spirit is immortal and stays by its bones. The spirit of an enemy could thus become a disturbing influence, which is to be avoided by totally destroying the living body with fire, so that the spirit flies with the smoke towards the sky, where it remains. (Cipriani 1966: 9)

For the Kapauku of New Guinea, cannibalism was alleged by Dutch colonists and claimed by the Kapauku themselves. An anthropologist, however, concluded otherwise:

> The Dutch authorities told the writer about cannibalistic practices of the Kapauku. Also the people themselves pointed out recent cases of cannibalism. All the instances reported to the writer which he has closely investigated brought out nothing more than the belief in ghouls. By a careful checking of the graves of several recent "victims," the writer discovered that the graves had never been disturbed. Moreover, the individuals claimed by the people to be the victims of the above described murderous assault, and later of endo-cannibalism, died of natural causes like dysentery, pneumonia, or heart attack. . . . It is the opinion of the present writer that all of the cannibalistic stories about the Kapauku, at least in the Kamu Valley, refer to a belief in ghouls rather than to true cannibalism. (Pospisil 1958: 32)

Despite misgivings about the trustworthiness of reports about cannibalism, there have been two worldwide surveys of the practice, based on available information of questionable reliability. In one, a survey of 240 cultures, cannibalism was present in 25 percent; in the other, cannibalism was present in 34 percent of 156

A drawing from the Florentine Codex, a compilation of Aztec practices made by Roman Catholic priests following the 1532 Spanish conquest, shows an instance of cannibalism. It is not known if cannibalism, humans eating humans, has ever been a major component of religious systems.

cultures. Both surveys counted only institutionalized cannibalism and ignored private cannibalism that was considered abnormal by people in the culture. Cannibalism comes in two primary forms—endocannibalism and exocannibalism. Endocannibalism is the eating of people from one's own culture and is reported as usually occurring as part of funeral rites and apparently often symbolizes the continuity of the culture from one generation to the next by physically passing the flesh or organs of one generation to the next. Exocannibalism is the eating of people from other cultures and reportedly often takes the form of trophy cannibalism where the heart, brain, or other body part of an enemy warrior is eaten to denigrate the defeated warrior, control his soul, or gain power from him. Survival cannibalism—the eating of human flesh to survive during environmental disasters or famine—is generally without religious import but is fairly common throughout human history and is the one type of cannibalism reliably documented. As regards the distribution of alleged cannibalism, it is most frequently reported for cultures in South America and Oceania, less frequently for Africa, and not at all for Europe, the Middle East, and Asia. However, if the medieval blood libel of Jews, where they were accused of killing Christian children to use their blood in religious rituals, is considered to be an actual case of cannibalism, Europe then belongs on the list.

Whether or not cannibalism is actually practiced, the belief and associated symbolic rituals are an important component of many religious systems around the world. For example, transubstantiation, the belief by Roman Catholics that during Communion the wafer and wine are transformed into the body and blood of Jesus Christ, can be seen in part as symbolic cannibalism.

In many cultures, cannibalism may not actually take place, but a belief in cannibalism and cannibalistic images and symbolism are prominent in conceptions of the universe and the mythology. In contemporary American culture, cannibalistic ideation continues to exist in popular culture in the Dracula story, where the vampire must drink fresh human blood to survive, and in popular movies such as *Night of the Living Dead*, where the dead return to eat the living. Among the Amhara of Ethiopia, cannibalism is evident in religious beliefs, religious art, and folktales. The Amhara conception of cannibalism is indicated in this child's tale:

> Once there was a cannibal. He lived among many people. He had no food in his house; he was poor. But even if he had not been poor, he just liked to eat the flesh of man. In his house was a big hole which he covered with carpet. He would invite somebody into his house and tell him to sit down on the chair over the hole. When the person sat down and fell into the hole, he would climb down by a ladder and eat him. In this way he ate all the people in his village one by one—about a hundred people. When he had eaten all the people in his village, he returned to live in the forest, because there was nobody left to eat. (Levine 1965: 229)

This belief that cannibals are dangerous supernatural beings is common across cultures. For the Ojibwa of North America, the cannibal spirit is "made out of the sorcerer's dreams" and is feared more than any other spirit. Only the work of a powerful sorcerer can divert him from destroying entire villages. For the Chukchee of Siberia, cannibals form a class of evil spirits who live far away but always fight against the Chukchee.

The linkage of cannibalism to evil is also found among the Tlingit of Alaska, who attribute the beginning of witchcraft to cannibalism:

> Therefore witchcraft came to Alaska through the sons of Aya'yi and through the Haida [a neighboring group]. Aya'yi, said to be a Haida name, was a cannibal at Yakutat who ate his brothers-in-law. Raven taught his sons how to avenge their dead uncles, by making a canoe of the dead men's skins, sewn with human hair, and a drum of human skin. When they came to their father's town in their canoe and beat on the drum, the entire town sank with all its inhabitants. Then Raven taught the sons how to restore their dead uncles to life. (de Laguna 1972: 733)

This linkage of cannibalism and danger is transmitted from one generation to another in many cultures through cannibal stories told to children, such as "Little Red Riding Hood," a tale told in variable form in other cultures as well. For example, the Tucano of Brazil tell their children tales of the *abuhuwa*, cannibalistic forest monsters. While the stories may be scary, they are not meant to create fear and thus the humans usually triumph:

> The story is told of an old woman alone in the maloca with two young children. Abuhuwa entered the house and the children were able to escape by climbing up to the house beams. But the old woman was caught. An abuhuwa rolled her between the palms until she became all soft and he sucked her out of the top of the head in the way a Cubeo child eats a banana. He hung her skin over the branch of a tree. When the others of the maloca returned they saw an abuhuwa family within. They set capsicum afire at the door of

the house and as the abuhuwa sought to escape its acrid smoke, that is noxious to all unwanted spirits, they struck them down with clubs and killed them all. (de Silva 1962: 256)

Ongoing interest in and discussion of cannibalism in many cultures seem to reflect the various elements of the human experience symbolized by cannibalism, including the meaning of one's own existence, social order, and cultural continuity over time.

Two cultures have drawn special attention as purveyors of cannibalism: the Aztec Empire of pre-Colombian Mexico and the Fore of New Guinea. Aztec cannibalism, as described by the Spanish conquistadors and writers who arrived shortly after the conquest, was closely tied to Aztec human sacrifice, which estimates place at anywhere from 20,000 to 250,000 persons per year. Scholars have suggested a variety of explanations for Aztec sacrifice and cannibalism, with sacrifice considered the socially and religiously more important of the two practices. Explanations focus on the possible need to obtain protein from human flesh due to a shortage of other foods, the central role played by the heart and blood in the Aztec conception of the universe, and sacrifice as an aspect of the social stratification system.

Alleged cannibalism by the Fore people came to the attention of outsiders because of its possible link to an infectious neurological disease called *kuru,* a slow infection of the central nervous system whose discovery and study won the Nobel Prize for Physiology/Medicine for Dr. D. Carleton Gajdusek in 1976. Kuru is a degenerative viral disease and reported cannibalism in which women and children ate the brains of deceased relatives was cited as one possible means of transmission. Reports of this Fore pattern of cannibalism all date to early contact times and mostly come from Fore men who themselves did not consume human flesh. More recent analysis of the information suggests that Fore cannibalism—if it actually existed—did not cause the trans-

mission of kuru. Rather, it was likely transmitted to women and children by women who handled the corpses and brains (which were extracted for ritual use) of persons who died from kuru.

See also SACRIFICE AND OFFERING; SUPERNATURAL BEINGS

Arens, W. (1979) *The Man-Eating Myth: Anthropology and Anthropophagy.*

Bogoras, Waldemar. (1904–1909) *The Chukchee.*

Brown, Paula, and Donald Tuzin, eds. (1983) *The Ethnography of Cannibalism.*

Cipriani, Lidio. (1966) *The Andaman Islanders.* Translated by D. Taylor Cox.

de Laguna, Frederica. (1972) *Under Mount Saint Elias: The History and Culture of the Yakutat Tlingit.*

de Silva, Alcionilio Bruzzi Alves. (1962) *The Indigenous Civilization of the Uaupes.*

Hallowell, A, Irving. (1942) *The Role of Conjuring in Salteaux Society.*

Harner, Michael. (1977) "The Ecological Basis for Aztec Sacrifice." *American Ethnologist* 4: 117–135.

Harris, Marvin. (1977) *Cannibals and Kings: The Origins of Cultures.*

Levine, Donald N. (1965) *Wax and Gold: Tradition and Innovation in Ethiopian Culture.*

Montellano, Bernard R. Ortiz de. (1978) "Aztec Cannibalism: An Ecological Necessity?" *Science* 200: 611–617.

Pospisil, Leopold. (1958) *Kapauku Papuans and Their Law.*

Price, Barbara. (1978) "Demystification, Enriddlement, and Aztec Cannibalism: A Materialistic Rejoinder to Harner." *American Ethnologist* 5: 98–115.

Sahlins, Marshall. (1979) "Cannibalism: An Exchange." *New York Review of Books* 26: 45–47.

Sanday, Peggy R. (1986) *Divine Hunger: Cannibalism as a Cultural System.*

Shankman, Paul (1969) "Le Rôti et le Bouilli: Lévi-Strauss' Theory of Cannibalism." *American Anthropologist* 71: 54–69.

Steadman, Lyle B., and Charles F. Merbs. (1982) "Kuru and Cannibalism." *American Anthropologist* 84: 611–627.

CHRISTIANITY

Christianity is the world's largest religion with close to two billion followers. It encompasses hundreds of denominations worldwide that fall under three broad categories: Roman Catholicism, Protestantism, and Eastern/Oriental Orthodoxy. All of the denominations focus on the relatively short life of Jesus Christ and his teachings. Christianity has been a cornerstone of Western Civilization for close to two thousand years, its influence so pervasive in philosophy, government, the arts, and society that in many cases its own history is indistinguishable from the unfolding of European history.

Jesus of Nazareth was born in Palestine two thousand years ago during the reign of the Roman Empire. Because Jesus did not record his teachings, we are forced to rely on secondhand accounts of his beliefs as described in the four Gospels (Matthew, Mark, Luke, and John), which serve as the core of the New Testament and were written in the centuries after his death. These texts are supplemented by the Acts of the Apostles, which describe the early history of Christian missionaries; a collection of letters written by Paul and other Christian disciples, called the Epistles; and a visionary book called Revelation describing the final triumph of God. The New Testament combined with the Old Testament, or Jewish Bible, constitute the Christian Bible, the source of inspiration and at times wildly different interpretations of God's will.

Christians of all denominations celebrate the important events in Jesus's life—his birth, crucifixion, and resurrection—as religious holidays.

Christians believe that Jesus was immaculately conceived by the Virgin Mary as the Son of God. Born in the town of Bethlehem, he was a direct descendent of the Jewish King David. He led an unremarkable life as a carpenter in Nazareth for thirty years until an ascetic Jew named John the Baptist announced to the world that the judgment from God would arrive soon with the coming of the Messiah, who would free the Jews from Roman rule. Jesus was among those baptized by John. Shortly afterward Jesus came to the conclusion that he was the foretold Messiah and revealed himself to his peers. Despite initial scorn from his fellow citizens in Nazareth, Jesus soon attracted twelve disciples who helped him spread God's message of love and redemption in the countryside.

Jesus outlined his message in the Sermon on the Mount and conveyed it with parables, such as that of the "Good Samaritan," about ordinary people who often broke the norms of society. This story is about a man who is beaten up by bandits and severely injured. Leading members of society, such as a priest and a lawyer, walked by the person and ignored his plight before he was finally helped by a Samaritan, a member of a minority race that was looked upon with scorn by most people. The message of this story, like many of Jesus' parables, was that status does not determine good conduct or humanity; these can only been determined by the individual. Jesus invited all people, but particularly the poor and oppressed, to become part of the "Kingdom of God" in which the peace of God would bring harmony. Jesus acted out the morals of the parables himself by dining, conversing, and embracing the disreputable and unacceptable, all of which became a threat to the establishment when Jesus brought his message to Jerusalem. Shortly after arriving in

*A third-century sculpture shows Jesus Christ as a good shepherd, a symbol found
frequently in Christianity, the religion based on the life and teachings of Jesus Christ.*

Jerusalem, Jesus was arrested and crucified. Christians believe his death was an atonement for the sins of humanity.

What happened next provided the meaning of Christianity. Three days after his death, Jesus rose from the dead and periodically reappeared to speak with some of his disciples and followers. When Adam in the Old Testament sinned by eating the forbidden fruit God punished him by making him mortal. With Jesus rising from the dead it proved to Christians that salvation was possible through the love and mercy that Jesus preached. Jesus' disciples and followers spread "the word" and converted many people to Christianity over the course of the next few centuries. Paul, who had a vision of Jesus while traveling to Damascus, was the most important person in popularizing Christianity. Unlike many other Christians, Paul believed that Jesus had widened God's covenant with the Jews to all people, meaning that Gentiles could become Christians without converting to Judaism first. Further, he resolved the dilemma of Judaism, as described in the Book of Job, of good deeds not necessarily resulting in happiness. Paul declared that the righteous will ultimately be vindicated, just as Jesus had been even though he had been tortured and put to death. Finally, he said that the power of Christianity is not so much knowing to do good rather than bad, which he said most people already knew, but actually having the strength to do good. The answer was in the power of grace as exemplified by Jesus, who could provide a person with the inner strength to do what is right.

Paul was not the only person to expound upon Jesus' teaching at this time, however, and several different sects were formed, including some involving mysticism. Christianity grew in spite of sporadic repression by the Romans that sometimes resulted in Christians being fed to lions as a form of public entertainment. But in the early fourth century the Roman Emperor Constantine I converted to Christianity after his troops won a battle in which he placed a Christian cross on their weapons. He soon called for an ecumenical council of the various leaders of the Christian church to settle internal disputes and develop a single unified vision for Christianity that would be applied to the entire Roman Empire. The council, which met in the city of Nicea, came up with the Nicene Creed (which members of many churches continue to repeat to this day), declaring that Jesus was "one in being with the father." Furthermore, Constantine issued an imperial edict that forbade Christians who disagreed with Nicea from meeting and confiscated their places of worship. The enforcement of doctrinal conformity resulted in the squashing of alternative forms of Christianity and led to the idea of heresy, whereby Christians believe that those who do not conform to their beliefs are mistaken or hold wrong ideas. Ironically, in a short time the tendency of Christians to define conformity with belief rather than behavior took hold. Before long, instead of being persecuted by Romans, Christians were enlisting Romans to persecute other religious groups, including nonconforming Christian sects.

Constantine also inadvertently played a major role in the future division of Christianity by building a "new Rome" five hundred miles to the east that he named after himself, Constantinople. Constantine moved to the new city, leaving Rome to be ruled by leaders from northern Europe. The two centers of Christianity grew further and further apart, with Catholic Rome representing the Latin branch and Orthodox Constantinople the Greek branch. The two did not officially split until 1054, but major differences had made their appearance centuries earlier.

The Catholic Church became institutionalized under Roman rule throughout the Mediterranean basin, and the pope became the spiritual head of a hierarchical church structure.

The rise of Islam in the seventh and eighth centuries led to an eclipse of Christianity in northern Africa and Asia, but at the same time Christianity had spread to much of northern Europe. The Catholic Church went through periodic eras of reform to cleanse itself of internal abuses and division, one of which was the calling for a Christian Crusade—which was launched off and on for close to three hundred years—to recapture Jerusalem from the Muslims.

In the sixteenth century the second major division in Christianity occurred with the advent of the Reformation, a widespread and diverse revolt against the Catholic Church, mainly in northern Europe, that resulted in the rise of a variety of Protestant sects. Bitter division between Catholicism and Protestantism resulted in wars, persecution, and massacres that did not abate for many years. At the same time, however, as European powers came to dominate the world through imperialist and military expansion, they spread Christianity to all corners of the globe, often with the mission of converting non-Christians into Christians, sometimes under the threat of death. The emergence of rationalism and scientific scrutiny during the Enlightenment in the eighteenth century, and nationalism and industrialism in the nineteenth, considerably diminished the role of Christianity in people's lives as many of the fundamental precepts of the Bible were called into question.

By the twentieth century hundreds of Christian denominations existed, placing different interpretations on the life of Jesus and the actions required to fulfill his message. But the level of rancor diminished to the point that an ecumenical movement arose in which some Christian groups are actually merging and most have adopted a new attitude of cooperation and united action. The most important manifestation of this is the World Council of Churches, formed in 1948.

See also EASTERN ORTHODOXY; JUDAISM; MISSIONS; PROTESTANTISM; ROMAN CATHOLICISM.

Barrett, David B., ed. (1982) *World Christian Encyclopedia: A Comparative Study of Churches and Religions in the Modern World, A.D. 1900–2000.*

Cross, F. L., ed. (1993) *The Oxford Dictionary of the Christian Church.*

CHRISTIAN SCIENCE

Christian Science is a religious system of metaphysics and therapy that was founded by Mary Baker Eddy in 1879 in Boston. Although Christian Science uses the Bible as the source of many of its fundamental beliefs, Eddy applied a radically different interpretation to the events of Jesus' life than do traditional Christian churches. The religion blends a quest for spiritual satisfaction with personal and societal healing. Christian Science, which does not have an ordained clergy or ritually observed sacraments, has a worldwide, if scattered, following in most countries with large Protestant populations, especially the United States. There are believed to be about 400,000 adherents. Despite its small size, Christian Science has played an influential role in the rise of spiritual healing movements and in public affairs through the publication of a daily newspaper, the *Christian Science Monitor.*

History
Mary Baker Eddy (1821–1920) developed the Christian Science system of thought in the 1860s and 1870s while she pursued a dual quest for divine spirituality and personal health. Eddy claimed to have a lifelong desire for the divine that was characteristic of New England Puritanism. "From my very

childhood, I was impelled, by a hunger and thirst after divine things—a desire for something higher and better than matter, and apart from it—to seek diligently for the knowledge of God as the one great and ever-present relief from human woe." At the same time, Eddy vigorously explored alternative healing methods. She became a pupil of the mental healer Phineas P. Quimby, who attempted to cure patients by correcting their thoughts.

In 1866 Eddy experienced a miraculous recovery from an accident while reading a description of Jesus healing the sick. This event triggered a revelation to Eddy that she developed into the religious system described in her book, Science and Health with Key to the Scriptures, published in 1875. When Protestant churches proved reluctant to incorporate Eddy's beliefs, she founded the Church of Christ, Scientist, or Christian Science Church, in Boston in 1879. Two years later she opened the Massachusetts Metaphysical College to train teachers of Christian Science. The church went through an early period of rapid growth as graduates spread the message of Christian Science. Some of the practitioners, however, strayed from Eddy's ideas and formed rival movements.

Eddy initiated a series of reforms to centralize control of the church. She closed the college, defined all local churches as branches of the Mother Church in Boston, and made membership to the Mother Church obligatory for all practitioners. A few years later, in 1895, she cemented her control by replacing all pastors at the branch churches with readers, who simply recited sermons from set readings of the Bible and *Science and Health*. Eddy started the *Christian Science Monitor* in 1908 as a way for the church to demonstrate the political and social expression of her practical idealism. The newspaper, which continues to have an international reputation for its standards, avoids sensational news and applies the Christian Science idea that

the very discussion of evil helps perpetuate and expand the power of evil. The newspaper focuses on the good in the world. When Eddy died in 1910, control of the church was given to a board of five directors, the corporate body that continues to exert control over the church. The growth of modern medicine and the secularization of Western society have held back the church's growth in this century. In addition, the church has gone through phases of internal turmoil over the way the directors have led the church. Nevertheless, the church has more than 3,000 congregations in 50 countries and continues to exert an influence that belies its relatively small numbers.

Scriptures

Science and Health with Key to the Scriptures is the only official text describing Christian Science. The book went through many revisions by Eddy after it was first published in 1876 before being finalized with a definitive version in 1891. Eddy also wrote in 1895 the Manual of the Mother Church, which outlines the duties of all branches to the Mother Church. The Bible is used by Christian Scientists as a source of inspiration.

Religious Beliefs

Christian Science applies a radically different interpretation to the life of Jesus Christ. Rather than viewing Jesus Christ as a supernatural entity from the spiritual world in the natural and material world as traditional Christianity does, Christian Scientists view Jesus Christ as a man who was able to transcend himself to the kingdom of heaven by breaking the bounds of ordinary sense perception in the material world. Jesus Christ, according to Christian Science, laid the path to salvation through his example as an ordinary human being. His life of sacrifice is viewed as the way for others to follow for their own salvation. This spiritual selfhood is identified as the eternal Christ, as opposed to the person Jesus. God did not create the world in the traditional Christian sense, but rather is divine Principle, Mind, Soul, Spirit, Life, Truth, and Love. Man is a reflection of those qualities but most people cannot see beyond their own bodies and minds, which are counterfeits. Christian Science attempts to overcome man's misconception that he suffers, sins, or even dies. Realization of this concept restores or keeps a person's health as a physical confirmation of the truth of spiritual thinking.

Salvation requires prayer, self-renunciation, and an unremitting fight against the evils of man's condition. This includes defending oneself and others against evil thought or malicious animal magnetism. Christian Scientists obey Jesus' command to heal the sick through the application of their belief in the "distinction between absolute and real beings and the human mortal concept of man," according to Eddy. Christian Scientists deny that medicine and drugs in and of themselves heal a person. Rather, Eddy says, they alter the patient's thoughts to make them think they are getting healthier.

Religious Practices

Church services, with the exception of hymns, are uniform at Sunday worship. Readers conduct the service by reciting lesson-sermons selected by a committee in Boston. Sermons cover twenty-six subjects, presented in succession twice each year. Devotees are expected to read the texts daily before they are read in public. Followers are also expected to read the church's religious periodicals, attend Christian Science lectures, attend Sunday schools, and participate in intensive two-week courses of class instruction. All churches maintain a reading room. Services are austere and emphasize silent prayer. Wednesday "testimony meetings" are held for members to share experiences of healing and spiritual guidance. Christmas and Easter are not

celebrated and there is no baptism or other sacrament. Twice a year the congregation kneels to commemorate the morning meal beside Lake Galilee attended by the risen Christ.

Cather, Willa, and Georgine Milmine. (1993) *The Life of Mary Baker Eddy and the History of Christian Science.*

Peel, Robert. (1989) *Health and Medicine in the Christian Science Tradition: Principle, Practice, and Challenge.*

CONFUCIANISM

Confucianism is a system of thought that developed in China beginning in about 500 B.C.E. and has been a major force in Chinese society ever since. Experts disagree about whether Confucianism is a religion or a humanistic philosophy. Confucianism does have some features common to religion, including a belief in heaven, ancestor worship, rituals, sacrifices, temples, and rules governing ethical and moral behavior. However, unlike other religions, it lacks clear beliefs about the supernatural world. Whether a religion or not, Confucianism has played a major role in Chinese social, political, and religious life for over 2,000 years. Not only have the principles of Confucianism been a major guiding force in Chinese life, but some experts view them as the essence of traditional Chinese culture. It has also been of influence in Vietnam, Korea, and Japan, and at times has competed with Buddhism and Taoism in China and these other countries.

Confucianism is named after Confucius, the founder of the belief system. Confucius was born in northern China in 551 B.C.E. and died in 479 B.C.E. What is known of his life comes from published accounts years after his death and is of questionable accuracy. He was evidently self-

Confucius (551 B.C.E.–479 B.C.E.), whose life and teachings form the basis of Confucianism.

taught and became a low-level government official who at the age of 51 became disenchanted with the inefficient and corrupt nature of government. He then traveled about China lecturing and teaching his ideas about social and political reform. Confucius lived during a period of considerable social and political turmoil in China and also a time of much intellectual creativity. Thus, his ideas were but one set of many discussed and taught by scholars during this time. Confucius argued for a return to the ways of the past to create a better society. These included (1) humaneness to create peace and justice; (2) the study of history to better understand heaven; (3) use of rituals and music from the earlier Chou period to symbolize and spread virtue; (4) the correct performance of social roles; and (5) learning in order to correct one's weaknesses.

Confucius died at age 72 believing that his work had little influence; in fact, his teaching did gain little attention from the political leaders of his time, who spent most of their effort on wars with each other. After his death, his work was carried on by a number of followers, most importantly Meng Tzu and then Hsün Tzu.

The development of Confucianism halted during the short Ch'in dynasty (221 to 206 B.C.E.), when state power was centralized and Confucian philosophers who differed with the state were killed and the Five Classic texts containing Confucius's teachings were burned. Confucianism reappeared at the state level during the Han dynasty (206 B.C.E. to 220 C.E.) when Confucius and his family received special honors and the learning of Confucianism became a requirement for government service. Although Confucianism remained important at the state level, from about 100 until 960 C.E., it was in competition with Buddhism, Taoism, and other philosophies and at times different emperors stressed Buddhism or Taoism over Confucianism.

During the Sung dynasty (960 to 1279 C.E.) Confucianism reemerged in a form now called Neo-Confucianism as the major philosophical force in Chinese life and remained so until the early twentieth century. Neo-Confucianism is characterized by an effort to remove elements such as meditation that had been borrowed from Buddhism and a return to traditional Confucian principles of purity, humaneness, virtue, peace, and learning. Early in the period two schools emerged, the school of principle and the school of mind, each with its own scholars, students, and varied interpretations of Confucian principles. Confucianism also became a guiding force for the organization of Chinese society, with property, individual, family, and state all seen as closely integrated with one another. Neo-Confucian practice emphasizes ancestor worship, the sacrifice of animals, and the offering of specially prepared foods to Confucius and other important persons at temples. At various times there have been attempts to deify Confucius but all have ultimately been rejected and he continues to be viewed as a great scholar and teacher.

The texts of Confucianism are an enormous collection of material. While adherents claim that Confucius wrote or edited the primary works, scholars believe that all were written after his death. In addition, the destruction of the Five Classics during the Ch'in dynasty meant that the versions used since then were reconstructed and rewritten by scholars some 600 years after Confucius's death. While the texts that form the core of the Confucian canonical texts have varied at times, for the past 1,000 years they have been the Five Classics (*Shu Ching, Shih Ching, I Ching, Chun Chiu,* and *Li Chi*) and Four Books (*Lun-Yü, Chung Yung, Ta Hsüeh,* and *Meng Tzu*). The study and mastery of these books was a requirement for status as a learned person in Chinese society, a status one had to achieve if one desired a position in the government. The requirement was ended in 1905.

In the twentieth century Confucianism has declined in China, at least at the official level.

In 1905 the Confucian examination requirement for government employment was ended, and sacrifice to Confucius by the state ended in 1928 as did its status as a state religion. Confucianism has been repressed in the People's Republic of China but is stressed in Taiwan.

Chan, W. T. (1963) *A Sourcebook on Chinese Philosophy*.

Nivison, D. S., and A. F. Wright, eds. (1959) *Confucianism in Action*.

Thompson, L. G. (1979) *Chinese Religion*. 3d ed.

COSMOLOGY

Cosmology refers to people's ideas about the origin and structure of the universe and the place of humans in it. In all cultures it is an attempt to come to terms with and make sense of the world. Across cultures and within cultures, people's beliefs about the origin of the universe (cosmogeny), the structure of the universe (cosmology), and their place in the universe (worldview) vary greatly. In some cultures, such as Western and Asian civilizations, ideas about the universe can be quite complex and encompass the supernatural and natural worlds, their origins and structures, the place of humans in these worlds, and ethics and morals that govern human action. In other cultures, notions of the universe are more restrictive. The Tlingit of the Northwest Coast of North America, for example, have no clear set of ideas that explain the universe, although they do have clear notions about its structure and humanity's place in it. Australian Aborigines are more concerned with the immediate features of nature and their functioning than with their origins, and the Copper Eskimo of northern Canada also concern themselves mainly with the physical features of their environment such as snow and ice and the sun and the moon. And agricultural peoples tend to see their universe in terms of the seasons as seasonal changes dictate their annual cycle of economic and ritual activities.

Although it is impossible to generalize completely across cultures, three beliefs about the nature of the universe are typical of people in many cultures: (1) that the universe consists of multiple layers or phenomena; (2) that a set of core elements comprise the universe; and (3) that some elements of the universe are polluting.

In nearly all societies people believe that the universe is composed of two or more layers or phenomena. The Copper Eskimo, for example view the universe as composed of (1) the earth, a vast expanse covered by snow and ice, and (2) the sky, inhabited by animals such as the caribou, which are also found on earth, as well as spirit beings such as the sun and the moon. The Amhara of Ethiopia also have a dualistic view of the structure of the universe, although they differentiate between the physical world and the world populated by all living things. The Western Apache of Arizona view the universe as composed of three categories: (1) *hindfa*—animals and objects capable of generating their own movement; (2) *desta*—immobile objects such as environmental features; and (3) *godiyo*—items and thoughts of religious significance.

The idea found in the Western world since the time of the classical Greek philosophers that the basic elements of the universe are earth, air, fire, and water is common across cultures, although in some, such as China, a fifth category, wood, is added. China and other cultures also replace air with metal as one of the five elements. Where cultures vary is on the degree of importance they attach to these elements and the in-

The Republic of Korea's flag, carried by traditional dancers in Seoul, South Korea, in 1995, has as its central element the yin and yang symbol—the blending of opposites such as strong and weak, positive and negative—found in Asian cosmologies. The flag also includes four trigrams (arrangements of solid and broken bars) that represent heaven, earth, moon, and sun, from the I Ching *(Book of Changes).*

fluence they see them exerting on the human world. The Javanese, for example, believe that individuals require a sufficient quantity of each element in order to maintain balance in their lives. This view rests on the broader Javanese belief that the universe is composed both of individual organisms and the natural universe, with the former a miniature version of the latter. Thus, for the Javanese, water, air, fire, and earth are the basic elements of both the physical universe and each living organism.

The third general commonality across cultures is a belief that certain features of the universe are polluting. Pollution in this sense refers not just to polluting physically but also or only to polluting ritually in that contact with the polluted substance, object, or person will disrupt the natural order of relations among elements of the universe. To maintain this order, special rules exist to prohibit contact with polluting substances. Hindus believe that cattle and cattle products are polluting and those who work with cattle and leather are considered to be untouchable—outside the four-level hierarchical structure of Hindu society. Jews and Muslims believe that pork is polluting and a taboo exists on its consumption. Gypsies consider the body below the waist and bodily functions as polluting and attend to such matters with considerable ritual. Gypsies also find contact with non-Gypsies polluting and thus minimize such contact. And in traditional Polynesia chiefs occupied a special social category and they as well as objects and places associated with them were taboo to commoners.

Western Cosmology

From the viewpoint of Western science the visible universe consists of stars, galaxies, planets, asteroids, and comets. Earth is part of the Milky Way galaxy, which contains approximately 100 billion stars, as well as the sun, eight other planets, moons, asteroids, and comets. The age of the universe is placed by astronomers at from 10 billion to 20 billion years, with the majority favoring a figure of about 12 billion years and the theory that the universe came into existence at once, through a "Big Bang." The Judeo-Christian perspective is set forth in the Book of Genesis in the Bible in the story of creation, which left man in charge of the world, superior to other living things, and subject only to God.

One key feature of the Western conception of the universe is a dualism in which various phenomena are placed in contrasting pairs. These include light-dark, sacred-profane, animate-inanimate, living-dead, body-soul, and nature-culture. In addition to their being contrasting, some of these pairs are often seen in terms of superiority-inferiority, with light being better than dark, sacred better that profane, and living better than dead. And other pairs such as animate-inanimate, body-soul, and nature-culture are seen as mutually exclusive alternatives. A second feature of Western philosophy and science is a basically linear view of time and the relationship between the components of the universe. That is, attempts to explain features of the universe or events usually cite one factor or set of factors as the cause and another factor or set of factors as the effect, rather than conceptualizing the supposed causes and effects as part of a broader, more complex pattern of interrelationships.

Non-Western Cosmology

As noted above, there is much variation across cultures in how the origin and structure of the universe is conceptualized. At the same time, however, there are some cross-cultural patterns that do apply to many cultures and that differ markedly from Western conceptions. First, in many cultures people customarily feel a oneness and closeness with nature different from the more distant human-nature relationship characteristic of the Western World. Second, in many cultures no sharp distinction or no distinction at all is made between the natural world and the supernatural world, and the distinction between humans and animals is less clear than in the West. For example, the Tlingit believed that spirits inhabited all features of the environment—lakes, streams, trees, rocks, mountains, birds, fish, the sun, the moon, and so on. Humans could use these resources if they took care of them, respected the spirits that inhabited them, offered the appropriate prayers before hunting or fishing, and took only that which would be directly consumed. Failure to live by these rules and rituals could lead to punishment by the spirits in the future. In addition, Tlingit would interact with their environment through rigorous physical activity, fasting, meditation, and deep thought about nature.

This example from the Tlingit points to a third major feature of non-Western conceptions: nature itself or all the spirits who inhabit and embody natural features control the environment. Humans, unlike in Western cultures, are permitted to exploit nature to meet their material needs only with the permission of supernatural forces; failure to follow proper rituals and the abuse of nature brings with it the risk of supernatural punishment.

A fourth and final feature is that most non-Western dualisms such as life-death or animate-inanimate do not always imply contradiction or exclusiveness as in the West. Instead, as discussed above, for many cultures like the Tlingit,

the natural and supernatural are not seen as distinct entities and in many cultures physical death and life are not distinct as the soul may live on—either on earth or in another world.

To give some sense of the complexity of ideas about the universe across cultures as well as variation across cultures, the following are summaries of the cosmological systems or some central aspects of these systems in four cultures: Chinese, Hopi, Iroquois, and San.

Chinese Cosmology

Traditional Chinese cosmology is one of if not the most complex set of ideas about the origin and structure of the universe. The system is so complex that most Chinese in pre-communist China could not understand it and thus had to rely on ritual specialists for interpretation and application in everyday life. In quite simplified form, four major elements of Chinese cosmology are Tao, Yin and Yang, the Five Elements, and the Forces of Nature. Tao (also called the Way, Ch'i, and the Vital Force) is the force behind the physical universe and the source of all life forms. Tao exerts its influence through the two forces or principles of Yin and Yang. Yin is negative, passive, weak, destructive, dark, cold, humble, soft, and feminine. Yang is positive, strong, active, hot, light, dry, hard, and masculine. At a philosophical level, Yin and Yang are harmonious forces whose continual interaction produces the five elements—wood, fire, earth, metal, water—whose interactions in turn pro-

The Chinese Universe

Feature	Wood	Fire	Earth	Metal	Water
Seasons	spring	summer	late summer	autumn	winter
Directions	east	south	center	west	north
Colors	green	red	yellow	white	black
Tastes	sour	bitter	sweet	acrid	salty
Virtues	benevolence	wisdom	faith	righteousness	decorum

duce all features of the universe. The outcomes of the interactions of the Five Elements are determined by two additional concepts. First, the laws of causality and opposition that influence the interactions of the Five Elements: "Wood produces Fire, Fire produces Earth, Earth produces Metal, Metal produces Water, Water produces Wood, and second, that Fire opposes Metal, Metal opposes Wood, Wood opposes Earth, Earth opposes Water, and Water opposes Fire." (McCreary 1983: 59) Second, each of the Five Elements is associated with components of the physical, social, and moral orders of the universe as indicated in the chart on page 48 (Ibid.: 60).

Daily life in traditional China was governed by the idea that human beings are a product of the forces of nature. Thus seasons are governed by the "breath" or life force of nature, and people must locate their homes and burial places in accord with natural forces reflected in the landscape. Making these decisions correctly took much knowledge and skill, and geomancers, persons who could reckon the forces of "wind and water," were consulted for their expertise.

The Iroquois Cosmos

The Iroquois, who now live mainly on reservations in New York, Wisconsin, Oklahoma, and Ontario, were the inhabitants of what is now much of New York State, as well as parts of Canada and Pennsylvania and Ohio, prior to European settlement. They subsisted through a combination of hunting, gathering, and farming, and their conception of the universe reflects these subsistence activities and is a clear example of the meshing of the natural and supernatural worlds that is common in non-Western cultures. The Iroquois cosmos contains three layers, with the spirit forces in each ascending layer having broader power and dominance over the forces in the layers below. Spirit forces in the same layer have relatively equal power.

While most of these spirit forces are self-explanatory in terms of the physical features of the universe they are part of, four require further clarification. The Four Beings (also called the Four Angels, Four Messengers, or Four People) are supernatural forces responsible for supervising the spirit forces of the Sky. Handsome Lake refers to the Seneca prophet of that

The Iroquois Cosmos

Spirit Forces beyond the Sky				
		Creator		
Four Beings				Handsome Lake

Spirit Forces in the Sky				
Wind	Thunderers	Sun	Moon	Stars

Spirit Forces on Earth				
People	Earth	Grasses	Fruit	Trees	Water
	Animals		Birds		Our Sustenance

name who, in the years of dislocation in the early 1800s, played a central role in stabilizing Seneca society through the Code of Handsome Lake, a set of rules that helped stabilize Seneca society following the displacement of the American Revolution. The Thunderers are spirits responsible for supervising activities on earth and for keeping the monsters contained beneath the earth. And Our Sustenance refers to the Iroquois dietary staples—corn, beans, and squash.

Visually, the Iroquois cosmos can de depicted as a flat earth surrounded by a sky dome sitting on the back of a turtle, with the Tree of Life above the Sky Dome.

The San Universe
The San are mainly a hunting and gathering people of southwest Africa. The following cosmology is that of the G/wi San hunter-gatherers of Botswana. The G/wi believe that the world was created by the supreme being, N!adima, who also owns the earth and is free of control by other supernaturals or humans. Why N!adima created the world is unclear, although it was not for the benefit of humans. For the G/wi, the universe is a place of order, is a self-regulating system controlled by N!adima, and has three levels: Sky Country, Land, and the Underworld. Humans know little about the Sky Country and the Underworld other than that the former is occupied by supernatural forces and the latter by monsters and the spirits of the deceased. N!adima and his wife live in the upper reaches of the Sky World. The G/wi live on the land, are alone in the universe, and derive security from the order created by N!adima and by reliance on other G/wi. In general, however, it is up to humans to use their own skills and knowledge to cope with the daily problems of living. In addition to the G/wi, other features of the human world are the land itself, other human beings, animals, and plants. The G/wi have little interest in the land beyond their immediate environment, although they believe it is largely unchanging and stretches for some finite, though undetermined, distance. The G/wi social world is centered on the individual, with relationships conceptualized as a series of concentric rings of categories of individuals progressively more distant socially from the individual, who is in the center of the circle. Animals are N!adima's creations so they must be respected and killed only for food or in self-defense. Plants are a lower form of life—without motion, thought, or sensation—and thus not entitled to the same treatment as animals.

The Hopi Universe
The Hopi are an agricultural people currently living on a reservation in northeast Arizona, who themselves and whose ancestors have continually inhabited the southwest for several thousand years. The Hopi worldview rests on two basic principles—the bipartite universe and a system of correspondence among elements of the universe. The Hopi bipartite universe is based on a belief in a dual division of time and space and is reflected in dualisms of the upper world of the living-the lower world of the dead, light-dark, day-night, and east-west. These pairs, however, are not seen as being in opposition or as contradictory but as reverse elements in an ongoing system of alternation and continuity in the universe. The appearance of the sun in the east each morning, its movement across the sky, and its disappearance in the west at night is the most obvious and predictable of this pattern or alternation and continuity in the universe. For the Hopi, the most important element in the universe is water, which when combined with Mother Earth is the essence of all things. Virtually all Hopi rituals are in some way about rain. The Hopi world is ordered by a system of correspondences in which animals, plants, features of the weather, etc., are ordered in accord with space, time, color, and numbers. This elaborate system serves as a guide in rituals, which are generally performed four or six times, in accord

with the importance attached to the four cardinal directions (northwest, northeast, southwest, southwest) and the additional directions of above and below. Prayer is the primary means through which the Hopi move between the human and supernatural worlds, with prayer seen as a form of reciprocity in which spirits are expected to respond by providing the asked-for assistance. In essence, the Hopi believe that if one feeds the spirits ritually, the spirits will feed the Hopi, generally by providing rain to make the corn grow.

See also ANIMISM; GEOMANCY; PURITY AND POLLUTION.

Basso, Keith H. (1970) *The Cibecue Apache.*

Brennan, Richard P. (1992) *Dictionary of Scientific Literacy.*

de Laguna, Frederica. (1972) *Under Mount Saint Elias: The History and Culture of the Yakutat Tlingit.*

Fenton, William N. (1962) "This Island, the World is on the Turtle's Back." *Journal of American Folklore* 75: 283–300.

Foster, Michael K. (1974) *From the Earth to Beyond the Sky: An Ethnographic Approach to Four Longhouse Iroquois Speech Events.*

Hieb, Louis A. (1979) "Hopi World View." In *Handbook of North American Indians. Vol. 9. Southwest,* edited by Alfonso Ortiz, 577–580.

Jenness, Diamond. (1922) *The Life of the Copper Eskimos.*

McCreary, John L. (1974) *The Symbolisms of Popular Taoist Magic.*

Malefijt, Annemarie de Waal. (1968) *Religion and Culture: An Introduction to the Anthropology of Religion.*

Rowe, David N. and Willmoore Kendall, eds. (1954) *China: An Area Manual.*

Silberbauer, George B. (1981) *Hunter and Habitat in the Central Kalahari Desert.*

Waters, Frank. (1963) *Book of the Hopi.*

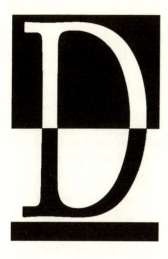

DIVINATION Divination refers to beliefs and practices whose purpose is to enable humans to communicate with the supernatural world so that humans can obtain information that foretells the future or explains past or present events. The activities humans in most societies are interested in foretelling or explaining are often very important ones such as the success of a crop or hunting expedition, where to build one's house, where to bury one's ancestors, happiness in marriage, the identity of a criminal, and the reason for illness or death. Thus, it is not surprising that divination is a cultural universal and takes a very wide variety of forms across cultures. In fact, since any object, action, or event can be used for divination so long as the individual believes that the object, action, or event has divinatory power, the variety of forms divination may take is limited only by the human imagination. Divination differs from other forms of religious activity in that the goal of divination is limited to acquiring knowledge about the intentions of supernatural beings and how those intentions will affect humans. Unlike other religious activities such as prayer, offerings, and sacrifice, divination does not include activities designed to influence the supernatural. However, divination may be accompanied by such activities. For example, it is common in many African cultures for divination activities to be followed immediately by a sacrifice in order to influence the supernatural.

As noted above, divination takes many forms, which has led experts to develop classification systems of divination practices. The oldest such system, which dates to Plato and is still in use, draws a distinction between ecstatic and nonecstatic or inductive forms. In ecstatic forms the diviner is in contact with the supernatural world and serves as a messenger between the supernatural and human worlds. Ecstatic divination generally takes place while the diviner is in a trance or through dream interpretation. In nonecstatic forms knowledge is acquired through observation or human action designed to elicit knowledge from the supernatural.

A more comprehensive classification system distinguishes among intuitive, possession, and wisdom divination. Intuitive divination involves observations and insights that tell the individual something about the future. Possession divination involves indirect communication with the supernatural and takes two forms. First is possession of nonhuman agents, known as augury, in which supernatural knowledge is communicated through the actions of nonhuman agents. Examples include the movement of the stars, the movement of flames in a fire, throwing stones or bones, the flow of water or swelling of waves, the shape of cracks in the soil, the flight of birds, and the occurrence of unusual events such as earthquakes or lightning storms. Second is possession through humans and includes body movements, ordeals, dream interpretation, seances, prophecy, and possession trance. The third form of divination—wisdom divination—involves human activity with the express goal of obtaining messages from the supernatural that

53

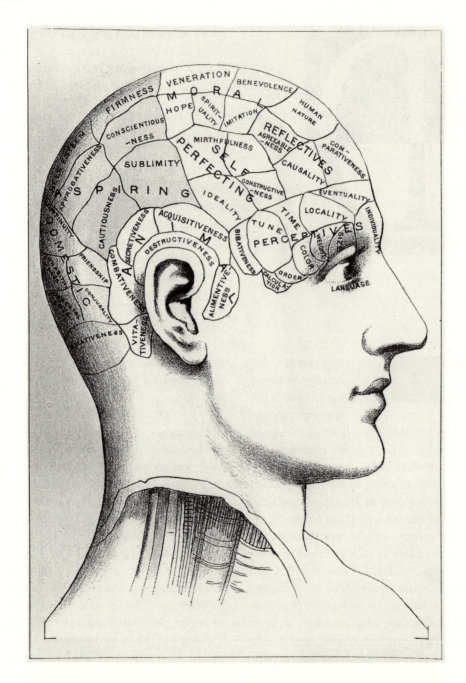

Divination, beliefs and practices to enable communication with the supernatural, has three major forms, including wisdom divination based on interpreting parts of the human body. Study of the human skull to determine behavior and character is called phrenology. This drawing shows areas of the skull that determine such aspects of behavior as combativeness (behind the ear) and individuality (just above the nose).

foretell the future or explain the past. These include interpreting the heavenly bodies (astrology), the earth (geomancy), the human body (somatomancy)—including the hand (palmistry or chiromancy), liver (hepatoscopy), and head shape (phrenology)—and systems of numbers or values (numerology and *I Ching*).

A third classification system is based on the communicative role of divination in human-supernatural interaction. From this perspective, all divination methods can be placed in three general categories: (1) without human experimentation, (2) involving human experimentation, and (3) verbal communication. Divination without human experimentation requires the diviner to interpret supernatural signs and includes astrology, augury, somatomancy, and dream interpretation. In divination with human experimentation, the diviner takes an active role in seeking answers from the supernatural. Actions may include reading natural signs such as animal entrails or bones, inspecting human organs, casting objects such as bones, sticks, or stones, and conducting ordeals. Verbal communication with the supernatural involves possession trance and dream interpretation.

With an activity so common as divination it is difficult to determine why all cultures use divination. It is likely though that in all cultures divination, by providing information about supernatural intent, serves the purpose of reducing environmental uncertainty and thereby lessening stress by giving people a sense of greater control of their world. Divination also plays an important role in the community as well. In communities that lack leaders or have weak leadership, divination may serve as a mechanism of social control by providing answers to questions and direction for future action. In addition, diviners are often people wise in the ways of individuals in their community, and they may interpret supernatural messages in ways that resolve conflict and create community solidarity.

Divination also enables people to act as a group when the information the group is acting upon is believed to be supernatural in origin and therefore reliable. Finally, divination may play an economic role in some cultures. For example, among the Naskapi in Canada decisions about where to hunt are based on scapulimancy—the reading of cracks in burnt animal shoulder blades—which results in widespread hunting and prevents overhunting of territories that have yielded well in the recent past.

See also ASTROLOGY; DREAMS; GEOMANCY; POSSESSION AND TRANCE.

Encyclopedie de la Divination. (1965).

Malefijt, Annemarie de Waal. (1968) *Religion and Culture: An Introduction to the Anthropology of Religion.*

Matthews, John. (1992) *The World Atlas of Divination.*

Moore, Omar K. (1957) "Divination—A New Perspective." *American Anthropologist* 59: 69–74.

Park, George K. (1963) "Divination and Its Social Contexts." *Journal of the Royal Anthropological Institute of Great Britain and Ireland* 93: 195–209.

DREAMS

All people dream and in all cultures people are interested in what their dreams mean. In many cultures the experiences a person has while dreaming are considered to be the same as the experiences one has while awake. And in many cultures the experiences of dreams are more complex as people believe that dreams have both manifest and latent elements. The manifest element is the content of the dream as it is remembered by the dreamer. The latent element is the underlying meaning of the dream, which is symbolized by objects, words, events, actions, and people in the manifest element. Thus the manifest content has meaning in and of it itself, but also is symbolic in that the elements of the dream symbolize the latent meaning. This means that the dreamer or an expert must interpret the dream in order to uncover the latent meaning. While in all cultures people are interested in interpreting their dreams, the level of interest varies widely across cultures. At one extreme are cultures like the Yir Yoront in northern Australia, who have only passing interest in dreams and see dreams as having little import for day-to-day activities. At the other extreme are some cultures like the Cuna in Panama, who place great value in the meanings of dreams. For the Cuna, dreams foretell the future, explain illness, and provide valuable information. Thus, every dream is the subject of discussion and interpretation and religious specialists are used to interpret dreams. When a Cuna is ill, a dream can identify the cause of the illness. For example, a dream of a spot where the individual was shortly before taking ill indicates that his soul was taken at that spot and still remains there. A healer can then be consulted to contact the spirit world to arrange for the return of the soul. The Cuna also learn from their dreams: some who speak Spanish attribute their linguistic ability to dream experiences, while others' dreams of certain animals result in the creation of their spiritual songs, which facilitate contact with the spirit world. As in many other cultures, the Cuna also believe that dreams foretell the future. Some of these dreams foretell misfortune. For example, a death in the family is foretold by dreaming about losing a tooth, about snakes, or about the house falling down. Other dreams foretell good luck, as in dreaming about a person who is away or about finding silver coins, which foretells success in fishing.

As Cuna dream interpretation suggests, in most cultures there are indigenous systems of dream interpretation based on the symbolic meanings of elements of the manifest dream. For example, the Melpa of New Guinea recognize a standardized list of dream symbols that relate to death, gifts of pork, repayments, and sex and reproduction, a sample of which are:

Symbol	Meaning
Harvesting cucumbers	Death of a sick relative
Killing a cassowary	Death of own chief
Killing a small rat	Death of one's pig
Digging up sweet potatoes	Unexpected gift of pork
Someone brings grass	Unexpected gift of pork
Walking into forest	Requests to pay debt will be denied
Seeing people of junior tribal section	Return of gift will be delayed
Seeing people of senior tribal section	Return of gift will be made soon

As this example suggests, what people dream about and dream symbolism are often culture-specific and thus interpretations require both knowledge of the language spoken by the dreamer and the cultural context of the dream. An association between digging up sweet potatoes and a gift of pork would have no meaning in modern Western societies, but for the Melpa both items are of considerable importance. There is also variation among individuals in a given culture concerning the content of their dreams. Across cultures, one major difference is between the dream content of men and women. An analysis of 549 dreams from 75 cultures indicates that women, but not men, dream often about mother, clothes, and the female figure; men, but not women, dream often about weapons, coitus, death, and animals; and both women and men dream about spouse, father, children, and home.

From the viewpoint of religion, dreams are significant in many cultures because they either represent activities of the soul, which receives communications from the supernatural world or leaves the body while the person sleeps, or they are messages sent directly to the dreamer by the gods or spirits. Thus, in many societies, dreams are a major means of communication between humans and the supernatural world. Because they serve as a channel of communication with the supernatural world, dreams serve to foretell the future, explain the past and present, and in vision quests they provide individuals with access to supernatural power. Dreams also are significant in many revitalization movements, as the prophet often receives his or her apocalyptic message via a dream that is interpreted as a message from a god or spirit. The belief that dreams represent the activity of a soul that leaves the body during sleep or direct communication from the supernatural world are common across cultures. While in some cultures only one or the other belief is found, among the Iroquois of New York State and the Iban of Indonesia both types of dreams are recognized.

The Iroquois developed a highly sophisticated theory of dreams that recognized many of the key elements of the psychoanalytic theory of dreams developed by Sigmund Freud hundreds of years later. The Iroquois understood what we now call the conscious and unconscious features of the mind, with the latter thought to represent the wishes of the soul. They also believed that dreams had manifest and latent elements and were symbolic representations of wishes and fears that needed to interpreted in order to be fully understood. They understood that the repression of unconscious wishes could produce both physical and emotional distress and that the best way to prevent or relieve the distress was to satisfy the wish. The Iroquois had two types of dreams. Symptomatic dreams for the Iroquois were ones that set forth wishes or fears of the dreamer's soul, such as wanting to buy a dog, participate in war, avoid being tortured, be reunited with a deceased relative, or commit adultery. These wishes were satisfied through direct action such as going to war or buying a dog or through community rituals in which the wish was granted or granted symbolically. The wishes of the individuals in each Iroquois community determined to some degree the ritual calendar, as ceremonies were conducted throughout the year to fulfill the wishes of community members. The individual dreamer, community members, and ritual specialists participated in interpreting the dream.

The second type of Iroquois dreams were visitation dreams in which a supernatural being such as Tarachiawagon (the Iroquois culture hero) communicated directly with the dreamer. The message communicated was often a wish of the spirit that called for a personal transformation by the dreamer or some action by the community. Such visitation dreams were commonly experienced by boys at puberty as part of their vision quest in which they obtained the protection of a guardian spirit. Visitation dreams that called for community action also transformed the dreamer, who emerged as a temporary prophet, adviser, or wise man who directed the community to take action such as waging war, planting crops, or moving the village.

The belief that dreams are messages from the gods is especially powerful for the Iban of Indonesia. For the Iban, dreams are oracles through which they receive messages from the gods that guide Iban behavior. Dreams are both omens of the future and commands from the gods. Information or commands in a dream can cause people to abandon their house or fields, travel to a spot where good luck will be found, divorce a spouse, convert from Christianity, or change their occupation. The Iban believe that while the body sleeps the soul sees, hears, and understands; thereby the dream is communicated from the gods to the soul. The Iban also cite dreams as evidence that the afterworld is populated by their ancestors and that it resembles life on earth. This evidence comes from dreams in which the soul leaves the body and travels to the afterworld and visits with the spirits of deceased ancestors.

As these examples indicate, dreams are a form of divination as they allow one to explain the past and see the future. In comparison to other forms of divination they are especially powerful in that they bring together the mind and body, are rich in symbolism, require the participation of others in the community to interpret the dream, and often involve direct contact with the supernatural world or indirect contact through one's soul.

See also DIVINATION; SOUL.

Colby, Kenneth M. (1963) "Sex Differences in Dreams of Primitive Tribes." *American Anthropologist* 65: 1116–1122.

Gomes, Edwin H. (1911) *Seventeen Years among the Sea Dyaks of Borneo: A Record of Intimate Association with the Natives of the Bornean Jungles.*

Howell, William. (1908–1910) *The Sea Dyak.*

Nordenskiöld, Erland. (1938) *An Historical and Ethnological Survey of the Cuna Indians.*

Strathern, Andrew. (1989) "Melpa Dream Interpretation and the Concept of Hidden Truth." *Ethnology* 28: 301–315.

Wallace, Anthony F. C. (1972) *The Death and Rebirth of the Seneca.*

Eastern Orthodoxy is one of the three main branches of Christianity. The word orthodoxy (literally "right believing") refers to the church's adherence to the Christian faith as defined and described by the seven ecumenical councils from C.E. 325 to 787. For the first one thousand years after the birth of Jesus Christ, Greek-speaking Eastern Christendom played a larger and more influential role than its Latin counterpart based in Rome. The balance shifted, however, in about C.E. 1000 for a wide variety of reasons. Today, there are between 150 million and 200 million followers of the Eastern Orthodox Catholic Church. They are largely located in the Balkans, eastern Mediterranean, and Russia, although there is a growing population in the United States. The church is the second largest in the contemporary Christian world, far smaller than the Roman Catholic Church but larger than any of the Protestant denominations. The Eastern Orthodox Catholic Church consists of a fellowship of fifteen "autocephalous" churches, each headed by a bishop and largely defined by national boundaries. With the decline of communism in Russia and eastern Europe, Eastern Orthodoxy has experienced a revival in recent years.

EASTERN ORTHODOXY

History

The schism between East and West is conventionally assigned to the year 1054. However, the breakup was in the making for several centuries and the split was not officially recognized until the eighteenth century. Historians assign four general periods to the evolution of Eastern Orthodoxy: (1) the three centuries after Jesus Christ up to 312, when the Roman Emperor Constantine converted to Christianity and established a Christian empire; (2) the Byzantine period starting with Constantine's decision to build Constantinople in 330 as the "new Rome" and center of the Christian empire until 1453, when the city was captured by the Ottoman Turks; (3) the Turkish period lasting from 1453 to 1821, the year of the Greek War of Independence; and (4) the modern era from the early nineteenth century to the present. Separate from this timeline starting in about the tenth century was the development and growth of Eastern Orthodoxy in Russia, which was largely removed from the historical developments of its southern neighbors.

Prior to Constantine's conversion, Greek Christianity was largely limited to cities in Greece. Although numerous forms of Christianity developed throughout the Mediterranean area including Egypt, Palestine, and Syria, Christianity enjoyed no recognition from the Roman Empire. Many Christians were persecuted and martyred by the Romans during this time. The situation changed dramatically in 312 with the conversion of Constantine, which in turn led to two other events that profoundly influenced the development of Eastern and Western forms of Christianity. In 330, Constantine declared Constantinople, which was on the site of the Greek city Byzantium, the "new Rome" and the center of Christendom. Constantine built the "Great Church" of the Holy Wisdom (Hagia Sophia), which served as a symbol of God and came to have a major influence on the development of Byzantine practices. The second event was the summoning of the Council of Nicaea, the first of seven ecumenical councils to issue decrees regarding the basic truths of the Christian faith and the administrative organization of Christianity into five patriarchates centered in Rome, Constantinople, Alexandria, Antioch, and Jerusalem. Later councils were held at Constantinople (381), Ephesus (431), Chalcedon (451), Constantinople II (553), Constantinople III (680), and Nicaea II (787). The councils were called to resolve basic issues and controversies regarding different interpretations of the life of Jesus Christ and the Trinity, consisting of God, Jesus Christ, and the Holy Spirit. The decisions made at these events, along with the Old and New Testaments, embody the faith of all Eastern Orthodox worshipers.

The first four councils defined Christ as having two natures—one human and the other the divine God. Although the East Syrian, or Nestorian, church and the Oriental Orthodox Christian church differed in their interpretations and split from the main body of Christendom, the Greek and Latin Christian churches agreed on this interpretation. Points of disagreement, however, began to spring up during the next several centuries. These differences were exacerbated by several geopolitical issues that created dual developments of Christianity that became increasingly difficult to reconcile. The first event was the overthrow of the western Roman Empire with the barbarian invasions of the fifth century. Latin Christianity survived the wreckage and the papacy emerged as its only institutional legacy. This led to a far stronger political role for the church, which eventually came under the influence of the Frankish Holy Roman Empire, a rival of the Byzantine Empire. In addition, the two centers (Rome and Constantinople) be-

came more and more isolated from each other as Slav invasions in the Balkans in the sixth century and the rise of Islam in the Middle East in the seventh century (which resulted in the decline of Alexandria, Antioch, and Jerusalem as Christian cities) made travel between the cities more treacherous. Further, the simple issue of language became a barrier as fewer and fewer people could speak both Latin and Greek. Finally, while the intellectual thought of Eastern Christianity was driven by Greek teachers, Western Christianity came to be dominated by the teachings of Augustine of Hippo. Although the two regions belonged to the same church, they became increasingly remote from each other.

Two issues brought these differences to a point beyond reconciliation. The first was the decision by the Western church to insert the word *filioque* (meaning "from the Son") into the Nicene Creed text, thus stating that the Holy Spirit proceeds from the Father and from the Son. Eastern Christianity holds that the Holy Spirit proceeds from God alone. The second issue concerned the primacy of the pope. While Eastern Orthodox leaders were prepared to recognize the pope, the patriarch of Rome, as the first among equal patriarchs who made joint decisions, they rejected the increasingly forceful claims from Rome of papal primacy. Several attempts were made to reconcile these differences from the eighth through eleventh centuries, but all failed. The most notable failure came in 1054 when discussions broke down between Pope Leo IX and Constantinople Patriarch Michael Cerularios, resulting in the excommunication of Leo IX's representative, Cardinal Humbert, by Cerularios, and the excommunication of Cerularios by Leo. The schism between the two churches reached its nadir in 1204 when the Crusaders sacked Constantinople and placed a Latin patriarch there, an act the Orthodox East never forgave.

While relations with Rome deteriorated, Eastern Christianity expanded its reach northward. Initiated by St. Cyril and St. Methodius in the ninth century, missionaries spread through the Balkans and Russia in search of converts. Key to their success was translating the Bible into the vernacular, thus making Christianity accessible to the general populations and creating distinctively national churches in Bulgaria (864), Russia (988), and Serbia (1220). This was in marked contrast to Rome's decision to keep Latin as the language of the church. The Russian church was centered in Kiev until the fourteenth century when it was transferred to Moscow. The Russian church gained its independence in 1448, and in 1589 the city of Moscow was the first city to earn the rank of patriarch. Concurrent to these developments was the growth of Hesychasm, or spiritualism, among Eastern Orthodox practitioners who sought to engage the divine light, or Holy Spirit, through certain techniques. This movement reached its height in the fourteenth century with the popularity of the Jesus Prayer, a mystical practice in which worshippers invoked the prayer "Lord Jesus Christ, Son of God, have mercy on me" accompanied by breathing techniques and specific exercises to focus concentration.

The Hagia Sophia, Great Church, in what is now Istanbul, Turkey, was begun by Emperor Constantine in the third century in his new capital of Constantinople. Constantine declared his capital, built on the site of the Greek city of Byzantium, as the new center of Christianity, rather than Rome. The basis of Eastern Orthodoxy, the third branch of Christianity, with Roman Catholicism and Protestantism, is in seven ecumenical councils held between C.E. 325 and 787. Ghostly images from a time exposure show the Hagia Sophia, converted from a Christian church to a mosque by Ottoman Turks in 1453; the magnificent building with Byzantine mosaics has been a museum since 1933.

Hesychasm was very controversial and faded in importance during the Ottoman Empire. It was revived, however, in the late eighteenth century and is now a vital part of Eastern Orthodoxy.

Eastern Christianity suffered a severe blow with the fall of Constantinople to the Ottoman Turks in 1453. Up until then Eastern Christianity was both relatively united and closely linked to the political administration of nations. Both of these factors changed. Greece, the Balkans, and the eastern Mediterranean fell to the Turks, while Russia did not. Russian Orthodoxy continued a largely separate course after this point. Further, the Turks, who were Muslim, seized political control. The Turks, however, did retain the patriarchs as "ethnarchs" to oversee religious and civil administration of the Orthodox populations. Thus, Eastern Orthodoxy remained an important influence under the Turks, but at the same time held second-class status. As opposed to Latin Christendom, which went through dramatic doctrinal and spiritual upheaval during this time, Eastern Orthodoxy remained static, more concerned with preserving its existence than seeking dynamic change. As the Ottoman Empire started to collapse in the nineteenth and early twentieth centuries, independent autocephalous churches were established in the Balkans, starting with Greece in 1833. This was followed by Romania (1864), Bulgaria (1871), Serbia (1879), and Albania (1937).

In Russia, by contrast, Christianity flourished. As the country colonized Siberia, the Pacific region, and Alaska, it spread Eastern Christianity to new dominions. Currents of thought from Protestantism and Catholicism influenced the development of Russian Orthodoxy, which served as the country's state church. The Russian Revolution of 1917, however, resulted in the repression of religion. The church was ruthlessly suppressed. Millions of Christians were either executed or imprisoned for their beliefs by the communist government. Meanwhile, millions of Greek Orthodox were uprooted as the result of war between Turkey and Greece. Many Orthodox worshippers emigrated to the United States—already a destination for many Slavic Orthodox Christians in the preceding years. The United States by this time had a large and growing Eastern Orthodox population. When communist Russia entered eastern Europe and the Balkans after World War II, the Eastern Orthodox Church's role in Bulgaria, Romania, Yugoslavia, and Albania was dramatically reduced by repressive and authoritarian governments. Since the downfall of communism in the late 1980s, however, Eastern Christianity has undergone a vibrant rebirth. Eastern Orthodoxy has played an active role in the worldwide Christian ecumenical movement.

Beliefs

Eastern Orthodoxy believes in two states, natural and divine. When God created Adam, man was placed in a divine state in the image of God and was given freedom to chose. When Adam fell from God's grace, he lost his immortality. But with the resurrection of Jesus Christ, who possessed both a natural and divine state, man became capable of liberation from death through deification. Thus, Eastern Christianity attempts to connect people's natural state to God's divine status. The church serves as a communion in which God and man are reconciled and a personal experience with divine life becomes possible. God, however, is unknowable in conventional human understanding. God is seen as a three-part equation, the Trinity of God, Jesus Christ, and the Holy Spirit, all of which are one and the same, yet separate from each other. God has an essence that is unknowable to humans, but God makes himself present to humans through his energies, manifested in the form of Jesus Christ and the Holy Spirit.

Jesus Christ has a divine identity. The Virgin Mary is known as Theotokos ("the one who gave birth to God") and is venerated by Eastern Christians. By suffering death, Christ is also human. But Christ's humanity included God's. Thus the salvation and redemption of humanity can only be accomplished by God, who had brought himself down to experience death, which had held humanity captive. As opposed to western Christianity, which views salvation as a form of divine justice in which Adam's sin is redeemed, Eastern Orthodoxy views salvation as a uniting of the human and the divine to overcome human mortality. Celebrations of the Transfiguration and Ascension ceremonies are extremely important for the Eastern Orthodox because they celebrate humanity deified in Christ. The goal of the Christian life is to participate in the deified humanity of Christ. This is accomplished through the Holy Spirit.

The Holy Spirit is the agent for human redemption. It is a personal force called upon by worshippers in prayer, invocations, and sacramental acts—particularly the Eucharistic bread and wine. The aim of Christians is to acquire the Holy Spirit of God. The Orthodox spiritual father or elder, typically a priest-monk, is believed to be inspired by the Holy Spirit to detect people's needs and give them personal and spiritual guidance. When a person achieves the Holy Spirit, he or she has attained salvation through divine grace. It is up to God whether to grant divine grace, but a person is free to pursue it by embracing, or not embracing, the humanity of Christ's glorified manhood. A person, however, does not earn salvation in the Roman Catholic sense of merit as salvation is God's gift.

Church Structure

The Eastern Orthodox Church is a fellowship of autonomous churches. Unlike the hierarchical Roman Catholic Church, Eastern Orthodoxy consists of fifteen autocephalous churches—the four ancient patriarchates centered in Constantinople, Alexandria, Antioch, and Jerusalem, and eleven others (Russia, Romania, Serbia, Greece, Bulgaria, Georgia, Cyprus, Czechoslovakia, Poland, Albania, and Sinai) that

participate in an ecumenical council. There are also three autonomous churches (Finland, China, and Japan) that are accorded lesser status. Each of the churches is governed by a bishop. Although the four ancient patriarchates, and especially Constantinople, are regarded as the highest, they are all officially treated as having equal weight in the church. Bishops are regarded as the guardians of the faith and the center of the sacramental life of the community. The Orthodox churches have become closely associated with nationalism in their respective countries because of the traditional use of the vernacular in the religion and the resulting identification of religion in the national culture, and because of the churches' historic role in administrative and civil affairs.

Bishops must be unmarried or widowed. In the lower orders of the clergy, priests and deacons are generally married men. Monasticism plays an important role in Eastern Christianity. Monasticism in Eastern Christianity dates back to the fourth century, when contemplative men sought the experience of God in a life of permanent prayer. There have been several monastic currents and trends throughout the history of Eastern Orthodoxy such as the Hesychast tradition that was practiced widely in medieval times and is now in modern Russia. Although it is on the decline, the center of Orthodox monasticism is Mount Athos in Greece.

Practices

Eastern Orthodoxy views the role of the church and its congregation as a local realization of the whole body of Christ. As such, the very act of the faithful congregating for worship is considered a basic expression of the Eastern Christian experience. Thus, the role of the local church and services conducted at the church are extremely important. Orthodox worship has played a critical role in the survival of Christianity during the extended period of Muslim rule. The Orthodox liturgy, sacraments, iconography, and other acts of worship are rich in theology and spiritual significance. Byzantine liturgical tradition is marked by the various cycles of the year. Hymns are designated for different cycles, of which the most important is Easter, which commemorates the rising of Christ. Easter is set for the first Sunday after the full moon following the spring equinox using the Julian calendar. The worship of icons also figured prominently in Eastern Orthodoxy, starting in the eighth and ninth centuries after more than two hundred years of fierce debate that was not settled until the seventh and final ecumenical council (Nicaea II). The councils determined that icons have a value not only for aesthetic reasons, but more importantly serve as a door for the worshiper to connect through communion with the person or scene depicted. The picture of Christ reveals God in his humanity and thus the deified image becomes accessible for those who believe in Christ. This belief helped spur a rich tradition of iconography in Eastern Orthodoxy.

Eastern Orthodoxy recognizes seven sacraments: Baptism, Chrismation, Communion (Eucharist), Holy Orders, Penance, Anointing of the Sick, and Marriage. Each sacramental act is interpreted as a prayer, led by the bishop or his representative, in which the Holy Spirit is invoked. Baptism involves a triple immersion marking the gift of a new life. This is immediately followed by confirmation. The Holy Chrism, a consecrated ointment, is applied to the child by a priest or bishop with the words "the seal of the gift of the Holy Spirit." The Eucharist or Divine Liturgy is the central act of worship at the weekly Sunday service. The priest calls upon the Holy Spirit to make the bread and wine the body and blood of Christ. There are three Holy Orders in which the Orthodox Church recognizes the ordination of the diaconate, priesthood, and episcopate (bishop). Penance is a voluntary act of confession that is periodically renewed. The anointing of the sick is not necessarily for a person who is deathly ill.

It is a form of healing by prayer and is conferred annually in church to the entire congregation on the evening of Holy Wednesday. Marriage is commemorated through a rite of crowning, symbolizing an eternal union that is projected into the Kingdom of God.

In general, Eastern Orthodox worship is based on a sense of awe in the face of God that is paradoxically accompanied with a sense of informality. Unlike Roman Catholicism, which is often highly structured, Eastern Orthodox churches are relatively unstructured in their regular services of worship. Prayer, symbolism, expressions of prostration, the veneration of saints, and fasting play a more significant role in Eastern Orthodoxy than in Western Christian denominations. The high point of the church year is Pascha, or Easter, to celebrate Christ's resurrection, which is also the dominant theme of weekly services, which are held on Saturday evenings and Sunday mornings. Eastern Orthodoxy does not celebrate Christmas. Instead it marks the Epiphany, the manifestation of Jesus Christ, held on January 6. The event marks the baptism of Jesus and the visit of the Wise Men to Bethlehem.

See also ROMAN CATHOLICISM.

Benz, Ernst. (1963) *The Eastern Orthodox Church: Its Thought and Life.*

Constantelos, Demetrios J. (1990) *Understanding the Greek Orthodox Church: Its Faith, History and Practice.*

EVIL EYE

The "evil eye" is the belief that a person can cause harm to another person or their property by simply looking at that person or his or her property. This harm may come in the form of sickness, an accident, or destruction of property such as a valuable pot, burning a house, or killing livestock or crops. A survey of 186 cultures indicates that the belief is present in 36 percent of cultures, although not all people in these cultures believe in the evil eye and believers vary in the intensity of their beliefs. The geographical distribution of the belief is striking. Virtually every culture in India, the Near East, the Middle East, North Africa, much of East Africa, and Europe has or had a belief in the evil eye. It also occurs in much of Mexico, and a similar belief in "bad air" is found in the Philippines. In regions bordering these areas it occurs only sporadically, and elsewhere in the world it is essentially nonexistent. In North America, the belief is found only among members of immigrant groups from the Old World; there was no such belief among Native Americans. This distribution pattern has led some experts to suggest that the belief began in the Middle East or India and spread to other cultures from there. Others suggest that it may have developed independently in a number of places, although the presence of believers in Mexico and the Philippines is most likely due to the Spanish and Catholic influence on the native cultures of those regions. Wherever it began, the belief goes back at least 5,000 years and was incorporated into the three major world religions that developed in the Middle East—Judaism, Christianity, and Islam—although among many followers of these religions today it is considered a superstition.

Wherever people believe in the evil eye, it is almost always linked with envy. People who are wealthy or good-looking are often targets, and the destruction of valuable possessions is a widespread result of "casting the evil eye." Cross-culturally and throughout history, the evil eye belief is found mainly in cultures that produce social and physical goods that can be envied. Thus, it is likely that the evil eye belief emerged following the development of agriculture and settled communities about 7,000 years ago. In these communities, wealth distinctions became obvious and people could well envy the pottery, weaving, metal goods, money, cattle, pigs, sheep, etc., of others. Wealth distinctions were accompanied by status distinctions, meaning that there were also categories of people—royalty, upper classes, high castes, chiefs—who could be envied. Another characteristic of evil eye cultures is a strong belief in a high god active in human affairs. This belief, of course, is a central element of Judaism, Christianity, and Islam.

In a survey of evil eye beliefs and practices in twelve nations, anthropologist Clarence Maloney identifies eight general features of the belief:

1. power emanates from the eye and strikes a person or object;
2. the object is something of value;
3. the destruction or harm occurs quickly without notice;
4. the one casting the evil eye may or may not know that they have the power;
5. the victim may or may not know who cast the evil eye;
6. the belief is used to explain illness, accidents, and other misfortunes;
7. it can be prevented or cured;
8. envy is involved.

Many of these features of the evil eye, and especially the link to envy, are found in the evil eye beliefs of the Kandyan Sinhalese of Sri Lanka. The Sinhalese believe in three related phenomena—evil eye, evil mouth, and evil thought—all of which are believed to be motivated by envy. Harm results from a projection of this feeling of envy onto the person who possesses what the jealous person desires. While the caster of the evil eye may do so without awareness, he or she can be identified by a "greedy stare" or, in the case of the evil mouth, the making of admiring remarks. Harm resulting from the evil eye includes the destruction of crops and livestock, a reduction in the quality of milk or palm sap, skin rashes and other maladies, and more. Evil eye accusations are commonly made, but never directly at the accused; the suspect is often an elderly person, a category of person not allowed to be the object of direct expressions of aggression. The Sinhalese take numerous measures to protect themselves from the evil eye, such as keeping food out of the sight of strangers and placing protective signs, objects, and building screens around construction sites.

Within the context of this general pattern suggested by the Sinhalese experience, there is much variation in beliefs and practices associated with the evil eye in cultures around the world. And there is even considerable variation within cultures from family to family and individual to individual, especially with regard to measures one must take to prevent the power of the evil from affecting oneself or to reverse its effects. As regards the source of the power, common beliefs are that it comes directly from the caster him- or herself, from a certain category of people (the elderly, women, Jews), from a god or supernatural force, from the personal ritual impurity of the caster, from the Devil, or from an evil eye deity. In some cultures it is thought to be always present and always possible, but the consequences are not as serious, and in others it does not exist.

In some cultures anyone is thought capable of casting the evil eye, in others it can be cast only by certain categories of people such those in low castes, strangers, outsiders, religious officials, witches, babies (also a frequent target), and even animals. Similarly, in many cultures certain categories of people are more often the target, especially the wealthy and handsome, the dominant group in the community, women, babies, and the weak. Fruits and vegetables, livestock, crops, houses, and all sorts of material objects are frequent targets.

Given the widespread belief that the evil eye can strike any time an individual admires something about you or something you possess, it is not surprising that thousands of preventive measures are taken to ward off its effects. Incantations are sung, chanted, recited, and spoken to ward off the evil. Amulets in the form of charms, necklaces, crosses, pins, and ribbon, in thousands of varieties are worn on the body or attached to clothing. Often, the object must be a certain color. For example, Muslims believe that the color blue is most protective, while Jews and Christians prefer red. Formulae in the form of ritualized sayings and actions may also be used. And, precautions are taken to avoid an evil eye caster. For example, food is prepared in private, one eats in private, one always walks behind someone suspected of being a caster, and a child is called by the name of the opposite sex to confuse the supernatural force behind the evil eye. Cures also include a wide array of incantations, amulets, and rituals. They also may require the intervention of a professional curer such as a sorcerer, exorcist, or priest.

A variety of explanations have been suggested for the evil eye belief. Most experts believe that any explanation must consider the role of envy since envy underlies the belief in most cultures. Other factors that may play a causative role in some societies include a paranoid view of the world, unexpressed anger and hostility, a projection of one's own envy onto others (I am envious and want to destroy what they have, so I believe they are envious and want to destroy what I have), and childrearing practices that produce adults who need much emotional support from others. Some of these same factors may also explain individual variations in the intensity of the belief among people in the same culture. And in multicultural communities it is often those people who are socially and economically disadvantaged who have the strongest belief in the evil eye.

In many cultures around the world the evil eye belief is now weaker and has fewer strong believers than in the past. Belief in the evil eye lessens when a culture changes in a way that provides individuals with relatively equal opportunity for achievement. For example, the belief is now much weaker or gone altogether in the second- or third-generation descendants of European immigrants who came the United States around 1900. The opportunity for economic success and the American value system that stresses individual responsibility and self-reliance contradict the beliefs that one's status in life can be attributed to the wishes of others and that one is incapable of achieving the same level of status or wealth as others.

Dundes, Alan, ed. (1981) *The Evil Eye; A Folklore Casebook.*

MacDougall, Robert D. (1971) *Domestic Architecture among the Kandyan Sinhalese.*

Maloney, Clarence, ed. (1976) *The Evil Eye.*

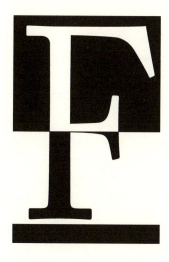

Festivals may be religious or nonreligious, although many nonreligious festivals often include a religious component, such as prayers offered by religious practitioners. Among major types of religious festivals are those that honor deities, spirits, saints, or anniversaries of major events, those associated with pilgrimages or passion plays, and public processions such as parades. Some religious rites that are conducted in private, such as fasting during Ramadan by Muslims, the Passover Seder by Jews, and the Easter or Christmas meal among Christians, are also "public" festivals in the sense that they build a sense of community among adherents who are linked by participation in the activity by time if not by place.

In modern nations, people engage not only in many religious festivals but also in many other types of festivals, including the New Year celebration, national holidays, parades, sports festivals, and folk festivals. Often these types of festivals are integrated into the already existing cycle of annual religious festivals, with the entire community free to participate in the nonreligious festivals, and the members of each religious community participating in its own festivals.

In traditional societies where a clear distinction between the supernatural and natural worlds is often not made, most festivals are mainly religious in nature, although they may also have important social, economic, political, and psychological functions for the participants and community. In cultures where people produce their own food, festivals are generally religious in nature and are also tied to the annual subsistence cycle. For example, the Iroquois of New York State conduct an annual series of thanksgiving ceremonies, during each of which thanks is given to the supernatural beings for what was received in the past and the wish that the supernatural will continue to be benevolent in the future is expressed. The six specific ceremonies

FESTIVALS Festivals are public events created by and participated in by members of a community during which the core values of the community are acknowledged and reinforced. Festivals are closely related to various other group activities with a religious component, including public holidays, feasts, pilgrimages, and rituals such as initiation rites that are held in public and require community participation in some cultures. In terms of the manner in which core values are displayed, festivals can be divided into two categories: (1) rites of intensification or communitas and (2) rites of anti-structure or inversion. Rites of communitas are ones that directly reinforce community values as well as social relations among community members. Most festivals are of this type. Inversion rites are ones that display basic core values and also solidify social relations by allowing for the public acting-out of otherwise unacceptable behaviors. Such rites are less common across cultures, with carnivals being their primary form.

conducted in one Iroquois community are as follows:

January–February	Midwinter Ceremony
February–March	Thanks-to-the-Maple
May–June	Corn Planting Festival
June	Strawberry Festival
August–September	Green Corn Ceremony
October	Harvest Festival

Another example is provided by the Hopi of Arizona who specifically link an annual cycle of nine ceremonies to environmental events that influence the stages of growing corn. As each ceremony precedes the associated subsistence activity by several weeks, it seems that one purpose of the ceremonies is to call on the assistance of supernatural beings in producing a rich harvest of corn. The table below (Bradfield 1973: 185) summarizes the key elements of the ceremonial cycle:

Festivals of Communitas

As noted above, many festivals have, beyond the immediate purpose of providing participants with a pleasurable experience, the deeper purpose of reinforcing a sense of community solidarity. Festivals achieve this purpose by bringing people in the community together both physically and spiritually and also by enabling people to share an experience with the symbols that express the basic core values of the community as understood and shared by its members. Festivals also serve an educational purpose as they are an important tool for introducing children to and teaching them about their culture and its heritage. In virtually all cultures, children from an early age on are expected to be involved in preparing for festivals. Finally, festivals can build a community sense in more practical ways by enabling people to exchange gifts or wealth and by providing an arena for the public display of political alliances. The three examples that follow—of the annual festival cycles in a village in the Serbia region of the former Yugoslavia, a Hindu village in northwestern India, and a Buddhist village in Vietnam—show many of these features of festivals as communitas.

Annual Cycle of
Festivals in Orasac, Serbia

Orasac is a village in Serbia whose residents are adherents of Serbian Orthodoxy, a branch of Eastern Orthodoxy. As the annual festival cycle

Hopi Annual Cycle of Celebrations

Month	Ceremony	Purpose	Agricultural or Climatic Event
Feb	Powa'u	germination	planting of vegetables and early corn
March	Un'kwa-ti	germination	planting of main corn crop
April–June	Kachina dances of spring and early summer	rain	period of drought, followed by onset of summer rains
July	Niman Katchina		corn knee-high
August	Snake-Antelope	rain	ripening of early crops
	Flute		vegetables and early corn ripen
September	Marau		ripening of main corn
	Lako'n		main corn crop ripens

Hindus in New Delhi, India strain under the weight of an image of Durga, the ten-armed goddess of death, during an October (in the Christian calendar) festival celebrating the goddess's victory over evil. Festivals acknowledge and reinforce the beliefs of a particular community and include public religious celebrations such as this.

shows, religion is a major factor in Orasac life and traditional festivals are integrated with Orthodox ones.

The Orasac festivals point to a number of core values in the Orasac community. That nearly all are religious in nature indicates the central role played by Orthodoxy in the community. The celebration of both the major Orthodox holidays and the various saints' and angels' days represents a merging of the world religion of Eastern Orthodoxy with regional and local Christian beliefs and customs. Of much significance in this regard is the celebration of the days of the patron saints of the families and groups of related families in the village. The exchange of visits and food among related families cements kinship ties for the coming year. In addition to spiritual matters, the continuing importance of the environment and subsistence activities in this farming community is also recognized symbolically through the celebration of the coldest day of the year, the first snow, and rites centered on livestock and slaughtering of pigs and sheep. However, these festivals have now merged with religious ones. Finally, the importance of the family is reflected in the mother's and father's day holidays, the blessing of the children, and the involvement of children in all the festivals.

Annual Cycle of
Festivals in Rampur, India

Rampur is a farming village in the Punjab region of northwestern India. The population is mainly Hindu, although as in much of village India, local beliefs and practices within the context of Hinduism are more significant than allegiance to national Hinduism itself.

As with the Serbs, the cycle of Rampur festivals points to the central role played by religion in community life. Only Tij is a secular holiday, and other major Indian secular holidays such as Ghandi's Birthday and Republic Day are ignored in Rampur. Two other features of Rampur festivals point to the localized nature of Rampur Hin-

duism: (1) about half the festivals are ones confined to Rampur or nearby villages and the other half are celebrated throughout much of northern India, and (2) the deities worshipped are mostly local gods and goddess rather than the major deities of Hinduism. This feature of Rampur festivals is typical of many Indian farming villages, which are only marginally integrated into Hindu civilization. Rampur festivals also allow for the public display of daily concerns: food, sickness, and the protection of the deities. These festivals are also mechanisms for building female solidarity, primarily in the giving of gifts to daughters and sisters, although it is not apparent from the information provided above. Finally, Rampur festivals foster solidarity among the women of the village. Most festivals involve cooking, joint singing, and worship by groups of women, as well as the worship of female deities. Additionally, five festivals allow for participation by women only, while none are restricted to male participation only. And in one festival—Holi-Dulhendi—women beat their husbands. As women have little power in daily village life, this emphasis on women suggests that some of these festivals are in some sense festivals of inversion as well as communitas as women are given the opportunity to behave in ways different than what is expected every other day.

Annual Cycle of
Festivals in Khanh Hua, Vietnam

The Serb and Hindu annual festival cycles are ones conducted in communities where the population is religiously homogeneous. Thus, the entire population participates, if they so choose, in all of the festivals, and all people share a common understanding of the meanings and relative significance of the festivals. Many communities in the world are no longer religiously homogeneous and therefore a number of different annual festival cycles exist simultaneously. For example, in the village of Khanh Hua in Vietnam most people identify themselves as Buddhists while a minority belong to four sects of Cao Dai, a religion that developed in the 1920s and is a mix of beliefs and practices drawn from Buddhism, Taoism, Confucianism, Catholicism, and Hinduism, and an even smaller number are Roman Catholics. Each of these groups follows its own annual festival calendar, although the actual ritual activities are much the same, usually taking the form of rituals and prayers in the respective houses of worship.

Buddhist Festivals

Lunar Month	Festival
First Month	Thich Ca Xuat Gia (Buddha's Departure from His Family)
	Thuong Nguon (New Year)
Second Month	Thich Ca Nhap Diet (Buddha's First Mystical Experience)
	Birthday of Quang Am
	Birthday of Pho Hien
	Birthday of Chuan De Phat Mau
Third Month	Birthday of Thich Ca
Fourth Month	Birthday of Nhu Lai
	Birthday of Ho Phap Di Da
Sixth Month	Quang Am Xuat Gia (Quang Am's Departure from Her Family)
	Birthday of Dai The Chi
Seventh Month	Birthday of Dai Tang
	Trung Nguon (Mid-Year Festival)
	Birthday of Nhien Dang
Eighth Month	Quang Am Thanh Dao (Sanctification of Quang Am)
Ninth Month	Thich Ca Co Phat Nhap Diet (Thich Ca's Achievement of Nirvana)
Tenth Month	Birthday of Di Da
	Ha Nguon (End of Year)
Twelfth Month	Thich Ca Dac Dao (Thich Ca Became a Buddha)

The annual festival cycles of the Cao Dai sects contain less events than the Buddhist one and also reflect the syncretic nature of the religion. Syncretism is also reflected in the use of lunar months except for Christmas, which follows the Gregorian calendar. The Ba Chin sect adheres to the following schedule:

Lunar Month	Festival
First Month	Cao Dai (Feast of the Supreme Being)
	Thuong Nguon (New Year)
Second Month	Thai Thuong Lao Quan (Anniversary of a Celestial Deity)
Third Month	Papal Election Feast
Fourth Month	Birth of Thich Ca
Fifth Month	Birth of the Pope
Seventh Month	Trung Nguon (Mid-Year Feast)
Eighth Month	Birthday of Dieu Tri Kim Mau
December 24–25	Christmas

The annual cycle of the Tien Thien sect reflects not just the influence of Buddhism and Catholicism but also the importance of the French-Vietnamese war and thus the mix of secular holidays of national importance with religious ones.

Lunar Month	Festival
First Month	Honoring War Dead
	New Year
Second Month	Feast of Thai Thuong, Supreme Being
Seventh Month	Honoring War Dead
	Trung Nguon, Mid-Year Festival
Ninth Month	Memorial Ceremony for Marshal Duc
Tenth Month	Ha Nguon, End of Year
	Honoring War Dead
25 December	Christmas

This situation is also typical of many communities in the United States where religious holidays are celebrated privately in churches, synagogues, or mosques or at home and community festivals are celebrated in public, often outdoors, with little or no religious content. Some of these public celebrations, such as Memorial Day or the Fourth of July, are explicitly patriotic and nationalistic while others focus on the local community, such as town or county fairs and parades.

Inversion Festivals

Inversion festivals are ones that turn the social order on its head. The key characteristics are that behaviors that are otherwise not permitted are now permitted and encouraged and the festivals are marked by much gaiety, humor, music, dance, and general merry-making. Across cultures, the carnival is the best-known type and most elaborate form of inversion festival. However, such festivals do come in more restricted forms. For example, Halloween and the associated Mischief Night have become inversion festivals in the United States, with children allowed to misbehave by soaping car windows and throwing toilet-paper streamers into trees and also to demand gifts with the admonition "Trick or Treat!" which is a reversal of the daily warning made to children by adults to "Do It or Else!" As noted above, a number of village Hindu festivals contain inversion elements, especially regarding the more public role given women during festivals. Most notable in this regard is the month-long festival of Holi-Dulhendi in which women are the main participants and at the end of which women may beat men. As the women commented: "Men beat women in all the other days of the year, why shouldn't there be a day when the situation is reversed?"

Carnival is the most elaborate form of inversion festival, although carnival in its largest and most dramatic form is confined mainly to the Caribbean and to cultures whose religion is a syncretism of traditional African religions and Roman Catholicism. Carnaval in Rio de Janeiro, Brazil, and Mardi Gras in New Orleans, Louisiana, are the two best known, although similar events are staged in the spring throughout the islands of the Caribbean. Carnivals are massive community festivals in which normal activity

all but stops and the streets are given over to music-making, parades, dancing, and milling about by performers and participant-spectators. Elaborate costumes and masks symbolically represent the desires of the wearer—often a poor or minority member of the community whose aspirations must at other times be kept quiet for fear of threatening those in power. License is given for joking, exhibitionist dancing, ribald or political song lyrics, loud music, and late hours that during the rest of the year are prohibited.

Another type of inversion festival is the ritual of conflict, which is an annual ceremony or celebration during which certain categories of people are expected to speak or act antagonistically toward certain other categories of people. Although these rites have been most extensively studied in Africa, they occur all around the world with some frequency. In a survey of sixty societies, 53 percent had annual rituals of conflict although only 8 percent had them in their full-blown form with actual fighting between adults. These rituals usually take the form of athletic contests, mock battles, relatively harmless attacks against others, pranks, ridicule, and mockery. The people involved are often from different social or economic classes in the society and individuals from the lower of the classes would not normally act antagonistically toward individuals from the superior classes or direct their anger at a person from that class. Thus, the rituals allow for the public display of behavior that is normally controlled and for a reversal of social status. For example, the rites might involve women attacking men as in Rampur, children playing practical jokes on adults as on Halloween, ordinary citizens insulting the chief, in-laws deriding each other, etc. In short, those involved are people who might feel anger at others during the year but are unable to express their feelings due to their subordinate social status.

Annual rites of conflict are of three types: (1) those involving verbal hostility, such as teasing or insulting by adults or aggressive behavior by children; (2) those involving aggressive behavior by adults, short of actual fighting; and (3) those with actual fighting. For example, the Amhara of Ethiopia celebrate the New Year in September when the grain grass begins to mature. As part of the ceremony men engage in mock battles and boys burn scars on their forearms to demonstrate their bravery. Similarly, Tucano men of the Brazilian and Colombian Amazon celebrate their return from the forest with food by whipping each other to see who is the bravest. These rites are so violent that the women and children flee, returning only after the men's cries have subsided.

One of the more dramatic rituals of conflict was the annual Lukang rock fight, which pitted the surname groups against each other in the village of Lukang in Taiwan prior to World War II. On April 5th each year the men in the dozen or so groups would line up around a field and hurl rocks at each other. As they moved toward one another, rock throwing gave way to punching, kicking, and beatings with sticks. Spectators cheered the fighters on and helped patch up the wounded and sent them back into the battle. No one was killed or seriously injured, and no group either won or lost. The purpose was to fight. As one man explained the purpose: "People in those days were quite superstitious, and believed that if blood were not shed during the spring, then there would be bad luck during the rest of the year."

Annual rites of conflict are an emotional safety valve and occur most often in societies where opportunities for the expression of individual freedom are limited. These are societies where communal decision-making governs a wide range of daily activities and where the social order is rigidly maintained by those in power.

Annual rites also occur commonly at harvest time and are especially common in those societies where the harvest ends a period of food shortage and hunger. In these societies the rites tend to be especially violent, which suggests that annual rituals of conflict provide a release for pent-up feelings of anger resulting both from a lack of individual freedom and from the stress accompanying food shortages and hunger.

See also LIFE-CYCLE RITES; PILGRIMAGE; RITUAL.

Birth, Kevin K. (1994) "Bakrnal: Coup, Carnival, and Calypso in Trinidad." *Ethnology* 33: 165–177.

Bradfield, Richard M. (1973) *A Natural History of Associations.*

DaMatta, Roberto. (1991) *Carnival, Rogues, and Heroes.*

DeGlopper, Donald R. (1974) *City on the Sands: Social Structure in a Nineteenth-Century Chinese City.*

Dirks, Robert. (1988) "Annual Rituals of Conflict." *American Anthropologist* 90: 856–870.

Falassi, Alessandro, ed. (1987) *Time Out of Time.*

Gluckman, Max. (1954) *Rituals of Rebellion in South-East Africa.*

Halpern, Joel. (1958) *A Serbian Village.*

Hickey, Gerald C. (1964) *Village in Vietnam.*

Lewis, Oscar. (1965) *Village Life in Northern India.*

Turner, Victor W., ed. (1982) *Celebration: Studies in Festivity and Ritual.*

Wallace, Anthony F. C. (1972) *The Death and Rebirth of the Seneca.*

as more serious adherents than the neighboring Han in southern China.

The origins of feng shui are unclear. Some experts claim that it originated in simplified form among the Mongols and other nomadic peoples north of China in their belief in a "code of the laws of nature and the harmony of man with nature." The Mongols, for example, required that nobles and lamas make camp upstream or uphill from commoners so as to avoid the latter ritually or materially polluting the former. It then diffused to China during the period of frequent and often violent contact between the nomads and the Han dynasty beginning about 206 B.C.E. and lasting to C.E. 8. During this period the more elaborate form of feng shui developed and was called by a number of names, including *khan yu* (heaven and earth) and *ti li* (influences of the earth). Feng shui means "wind and water," the symbolism of which is discussed below. The underlying principle of feng shui is found in ancient Chinese writings, perhaps the oldest of which states:

> By looking up, in order to contemplate the constellations, and by looking down to examine the influences or laws of the Earth, Man may understand the explanations of mysterious and intelligible matters. (de Groot 1912: 287)

The origin of the name, feng shui, is unclear, but in one version it is attributed to the spring and summer winds that bring the monsoon rains needed for raising crops. In another view, "wind and water" is seen as referring to all features of the environment that influence the currents of the winds and the flow of the waters. In this sense, the features of the environment are not just the physical features observable by the five human senses but also unobservable forces in the earth and universe.

In Korea, feng shui is called *pangsu* or *chigwon* and flourished during the Koryo period (935–1392). It remains of considerable

GEOMANCY Geomancy is the art and/or science of site selection. Geomancy is a generic term, referring to a number of related practices and beliefs, all having to do with using knowledge of features of the natural environment in order to select sites for human use—communities, buildings, and graves. The emphasis is not on observable physical features of the environment in and of themselves, but, rather, on unseen forces in the earth and universe that must be utilized in order to achieve harmony with nature. In the past, the term was used interchangeably with *feng shui* (or *fung shui* or other variants) the traditional Chinese method of site selection. Feng shui is still used in modern China, although it and other religious and cosmological beliefs and practices have been restricted in the communist era, and also in Korea, Hong Kong, Singapore, and Japan, where it is called *hogaku.* It is practiced in China by the principal ethnic group, the Han, and by other peoples such as the Miao, Hakka, and Zhuang, to whom it diffused from the Han. Earlier in the twentieth century the Miao were described

importance today and, as in China, is used in selecting sites for both buildings and graves. Hogaku (directions and corners) in Japan is used mainly for placing buildings, but it is also consulted for guidance when marrying, moving, and traveling. Geomancy has been brought to the West by some in the New Age movement and by some environmentalists. In the Western context it used almost exclusively in site selection and building orientation; there is little interest in its use for grave site selection, as ancestor worship is not a component of modern Western culture or religion.

There are two major approaches used in geomancy. In one, the geomancer reads and interprets environmental features and their relationship to the five elements (wood, fire, earth, metal, and water) in selecting a site. In the second, the geomancer relies heavily on the geomancy compass in order to measure the celestial orientation of the site. The two approaches are not mutually exclusive, and both are commonly used in the same community. In China and Korea a geomancer is a man (almost all are men) of considerable reputation and influence and is consulted by those who can afford his services in all matters requiring the selection of building and burial sites and the best time to build structures or bury the dead. Some geomancers may also be involved in selecting the best day for a wedding.

The practice of feng shui is a product of the traditional Chinese cosmology and the multiplicity of religious systems that required specialists to interpret the cosmology and apply it to daily life for the commoners as well as the wealthy and powerful. Geomancers, along with fortune tellers and diviners who used scapulimancy and milfoil (divining with the yarrow plant), were one category of such specialists. Feng shui is one component of traditional Chinese folk religion, which differed over time and across regions but is considered a system of religious belief and practice distinct from the major Chinese traditions of Confucianism, Taoism, and Buddhism. Among the key beliefs that feng shui draws upon or is integrated with are a belief that the earth is a living organism, a belief in the duality and opposition of elements in the universe (especially the forces of yin and yang), and ancestor worship and its elaborate associated funerary customs. Most important is the belief in the earth as a living organism with internal channels, whose locations and points of convergence are beneficial for human beings; these channels can be blocked, thereby disrupting the harmony of the universe. The geomancer's special gift is the ability to identify these channels and to use that knowledge to determine the best location for a building site or grave. In his work he is guided by printed instructions, intuition, knowledge of the landscape, the hidden meanings of visible natural features, and the ability to use a complicated compass to divine if a site is suitable. A suitable site is one where the characteristics of the inhabitant (often reflected in his or her date of birth), the nature of the site, and the heavenly bodies are in harmony in space and over time. Thus, feng shui is used to select a site for a house or other building and the grave or tomb site for a deceased relative. Such matters are of considerable importance as the use of a suitable site will bring prosperity to the individual or his family while the wrong site can bring disaster; in fact, poverty or disasters are often blamed on the location of an ancestor's grave or tomb in a site that ignores the forces of feng shui.

However, alterations to the adjacent environment can reduce or destroy a site's suitability, meaning that the geomancer's work does not end with the selection of a site, as he may also be employed to correct a feng shui that has gone awry because a neighbor has dug a grave nearby, or a stone has been moved, or a nearby hill cleared of trees or mined. Thus, any change in the physical landscape at or near the site—and this is especially true for tombs and graves of ancestors—can cause a suitable site to be viewed by its owners as no longer suitable. The worst offense is the digging of another grave near the first one. Such a grave will cut off the underground channels and cause harm to the ancestor's soul, thereby interfering with the ancestor's ability to provide assistance to his living descendants.

Geomancers are called upon to help restore the suitability of the site or to negotiate a settlement when the disruption is caused by the acts of other persons. However, since both parties to the dispute may have made their site choices on the basis of feng shui, both are reluctant to change their sites, resulting in threats, violence, court battles, and sometimes vandalism of the graves. In addition to disputes over graves, such conflicts also concern villages sites and, between neighbors, building sites and additions to existing buildings that alter the physical landscape. In feng shui, any alteration to the physical landscape alters the flow of unobservable forces and may disrupt the harmony of the elements that make for a suitable feng shui. Thus, the frequent and often intractable conflicts.

Although described here as a religious practice, geomancy does not exist apart from social, political, and economic considerations in Chinese and other societies. First, it is important to note that not all Han Chinese, Koreans, Miao, and others believe in feng shui. In these societies and Japan as well, as many people see geomancy as a quaint folk custom out of place in the modern, secular world. And even in rural communities only some believe, while others are uncertain and still others do not believe at all. And even among believers, feng shui may be but one of a number of factors mentioned as an explanation for a family's economic success, with other factors such as individual ability, fate, and moral qualities given equal or even greater weight.

From the perspective of social stratification in rural communities, feng shui can be interpreted as a belief system that tends to reinforce the status quo—that is, the wealth of some families can be attributed to the beneficial effects of feng shui, while the poverty of other families can be similarly explained as a consequence of their less-than-suitable feng shui. In this regard, the feng shui of ancestors' graves and tombs is especially important, thus the frequent disputes noted above. Such a belief system both frees humans from bearing direct responsibility for their own status and places the responsibility on forces beyond their complete understanding and direct control. Since wealth can buy the services of the best geomancers and the poor often cannot afford their services at all, the belief system is self-perpetuating over the generations. But, because in this context feng shui is a cause of one's status, it can be the source of conflict in communities as different families desire the best sites for their ancestor's graves and tombs. As noted above, even the slightest alteration to a site or land adjacent to it may disrupt the feng shui, lead to conflict, and require the services of a geomancer to rectify the situation. Some experts suggest that geomancers are expert at exploiting such situations for their own financial gain. While this may or may not be true, it is clear that feng shui is a source of conflict in many communities and that geomancers play a major role in conflict management and resolution. Thus, feng shui may serve as a vehicle through which conflicts over land rights and wealth can be voiced and resolved indirectly, thereby mitigating the more prolonged conflict that might result if the actual issues were faced openly.

See also ANCESTOR WORSHIP; DIVINATION.

Friedrich, Paul, and Norma Diamond, eds. (1994) *Encyclopedia of World Cultures. Vol. 6. Russian and Eurasia/China.*

de Groot, Jan Jacob Maria. (1912) *Religion in China: Universism. A Key to the Study of Taoism and Confucianism.*

Harrell, Clyde Stevan. (1983) *Belief and Unbelief in a Taiwan Village.* `

Kalland, Arne. (1996) "Geomancy and Town Planning in a Japanese Community." *Ethnology* 35: 17–32

Knez, Eugene I. (1970) *Sam Jong Dong: A South Korean Village.*

Lattimore, Owen. (1941) *Mongol Journeys.*

Pennick, Nigel. (1979) *The Ancient Science of Geomancy.*

Rossbach, Sarah. (1984) *Feng Shui.*

Walters, D. (1991) *The Fengshui Handbook.*

Wang, Hsing-ju. (1948) *The Miao People of Hainan Island.*

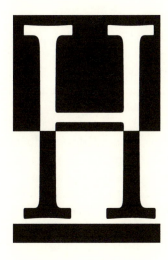

sands of different religious groups that have evolved in India since 1500 B.C.E. More than 98 percent of Hindus live in India with the vast majority of the other Hindus being Indian immigrants, or descendants of Indians, in other parts of the world.

History

The word *Hindu* comes from the Persian word *Hind,* the term used to describe the region around the Indus River in northern India. Civilization flourished in this region starting in about 2500 B.C.E. In around 1500 B.C.E., migrating groups of people from central Asia passed through the Himalayas and settled in India. Known as Aryans, they were fair-skinned and came to dominate the Indian subcontinent for the next thousand years through a network of village communities. They developed the caste system of social organization and used the Sanskrit language. With little or no opposition, Hinduism developed its basic patterns, including spiritual practices, forms of worship, and religious concepts. In addition, many of the Hindu texts were written during this period. Because there was no central authority, however, Hinduism developed in a haphazard way. Many communities came to believe in their own gods and followed very localized beliefs, a trait that continues to this day.

The first great challenge to Hinduism in India came at around 600 B.C.E. when some ascetics challenged the authority of the ruling priests. The most significant of these challengers was Siddhartha Gautama, the Buddha, who went on to found Buddhism. The rise of challengers to Hinduism prompted a reaction from Hindu leaders, who devised new doctrines, most significantly the *ashrama.* India's long period of development free from outside sources was briefly interrupted by Alexander the Great's army, which invaded India in 326 B.C.E., but was supplanted ten years later by the Maurya Empire, which ruled India for almost two hundred

HINDUISM

Hinduism is not a unified, coherent religion, but rather a collection of many related religious beliefs and practices that are accepted within the framework of Hindu society. Having evolved for more than 3,000 years and with more than 750 million followers, Hinduism embraces an extraordinarily complex system of rituals, cults, institutions, practices, and doctrines. A Hindu may be a monotheist, polytheist, or atheist. Hindus may attend temple, follow strict standards of conduct, and practice religious rituals, but these are not a requirement. Hinduism's wide religious umbrella includes everything from animal worship to mysticism to profound theological doctrines.

In many ways it is easier to say what Hinduism is not, rather than what it is. There is no single scripture such as the Bible, but rather thousands of collections of writings and teachings. Although most Hindus believe in gods, there is no single explanation for who or what they are. In fact, there are believed to be more than one million gods in Hinduism. *Hindu* is a catch-all term that includes most of the thou-

years and tolerated diverse religions. From the decline of the Maurya Empire in the second century B.C.E. to the rise of the Gupta Empire in the fourth century C.E., Indian society was disrupted by a series of invasions. Contact with outside societies, however, led to the spread of Hinduism beyond local limits and led to its widespread influence. Several sects had followings throughout India, including the Vaishnavites, Shaivites, and Shaktites. The brahmin caste's status rose significantly during this era as well. Hinduism spread even further during the Gupta Empire (fourth to sixth centuries) to southeastern Asia and Indonesia (the people of Bali still follow a distinctive form of Hinduism).

Hinduism continued to evolve in India for the next several centuries, unchallenged by outside influences and gaining further dominance over Buddhism. This came to an end in 1021 when the Muslim Mahmud al-Ghazni invaded northwestern India, introducing the powerful influence of Islam to the subcontinent. Islamic rulers established a single administrative center for northern and central India in Delhi. The Mughals eventually conquered all of India in the sixteenth century. Muslim leaders took different approaches to Hinduism. While some tolerated the local religions, others persecuted Hindus and destroyed Hindu temples. Muslim control, however, did not arrest the development of Hinduism. In many cases, attempts were made to merge elements of the two religions into new faiths, such as Sikhism. The emperor Akbar attempted in the late sixteenth century to create a single all-embracing religion for India. Efforts to fuse the two religions ended with the advent of the British Empire in the nineteenth century.

By then Christianity had become known. Portuguese missionaries introduced Christianity to India in the early sixteenth century. They were followed by Protestant and Catholic missionaries from the Netherlands, England, and France. Relatively few Hindus converted to Christianity, but many Christian ideas came to influence new Hindu sects. Ram Mohun Roy founded the Brahmo Samaj in 1828 based on the teachings of Jesus Christ as the route to peace and happiness. Later in the century, Sri Ramakrishna founded the Ramakrishna movement, which saw all religions as valid and eventually opened centers in Europe and the Americas. Christian ideas influenced many Hindu leaders, including Mahatma Gandhi, who advocated passive resistance to British rule, also known as *satyagraha*. Gandhi first developed his belief in nonviolent opposition to oppression and unfairness while living in South Africa at the turn of the century. He returned to India during World War I and applied his ideas against British laws there, eventually helping lead to the withdrawal of the British Empire from India in 1947. Gandhi, the great practitioner of revolutionary change through peaceful actions, was assassinated while praying shortly after Indian independence. Perhaps the most familiar fusion of Hindu-Christian beliefs in the United States is the Hare Krishna movement, founded in 1965 by Swami Prabhupada. Its goal is to spread Hindu beliefs to the Western world.

The cross-cultural influences of modernity have placed pressures on many traditional aspects of Hinduism in India. The traditional subservient role of women has lessened. The election of a woman, Indira Gandhi, as prime minister helped accelerate improved conditions for women in India, lifting constraints on women to pursue careers. The pressures of modern urban lifestyles have led to a relaxing of some religious rituals. In addition, the rigid caste system has started to erode as important Hindu leaders, including Mahatma Gandhi, criticized its exclusion of "untouchables" from basic rights and freedoms. Thus, while thousands of tribal Hindu villages still perform rituals unchanged since ancient times, other Hindu communities keep evolving new and different beliefs and practices. This constant change, however, is itself something of a tradition for Hinduism.

Texts

There are two categories of Hindu scriptures: *sruti* and *smriti*. Sruti literally means "hearing." It is the term used for texts that describe eternal knowledge as revealed to Hindu seers (*rishis*). This knowledge has been passed down through the generations by brahmin priests. The most important sruti texts include the Vedas, the Brahmanas, the Upanishads, and the Aranyakas. Smriti refers to traditional knowledge. These texts include the Epics, the Code of Manu, and the Puranas.

The Vedas were written between 1500 and 800 B.C.E. They consist of four collections (the Rig-Veda, the Sama-Veda, the Yajur-Veda, and the Atharva-Veda). The Vedas include about one thousand hymns to different gods, rhythmic chants, and descriptions of sacrificial rituals, magical spells, kingly duties, incantations, and other ritualistic practices. The Brahmanas were written after the Vedas. They consist of an enormous body of writing that describes ritual practices and the mystical meanings of various rites. The Aranyakas (also known as the Forest Books) are very esoteric descriptions of the nature of humanity and the world. They are intended for religious aesthetes who lead secluded lives in the forest and cannot participate in ritual sacrifices. The Upanishads offer the basic philosophical framework of Hinduism. They represent the Vedanta (culmination of sacred knowledge), providing information about the oneness of the universe and how to achieve that knowledge through self-consciousness.

The smriti writings include some of the great Indian literature. The Epics include the Ramayana and the Mahabharata. The Mahabharata is the longest epic in world history and includes three very popular Hindu stories, including the Bhagavad-Gita, or Song of the Lord. The story is a dialogue between a warrior and the Blessed Lord Krishna, disguised as a charioteer. The tale describes the Path of Devotion as the route to liberation from rebirth. The other great Epics tale is the Ramayana, the tale of a prince called Rama who is exiled to the forest for fourteen years after a feud with his half-brother and mother. Rama's wife, Sita, is kidnapped by a wicked demon. Rama's friend Hanuman, a monkey, succeeds in finding Sita and reuniting the husband and wife. All three of the main characters have been deified by Hindus. The Code of Manu is a book of sacred laws. Marriage laws, dietary codes, ethical standards, criminal and civil laws, and the duties of the castes are listed in the code. The Puranas are considered the scriptures of the common people. They include ancient stories, the genealogy of the gods and past kings, and descriptions of the universe.

Hindu scriptures describe a remarkable, complicated mythology. The intertwined stories of thousands upon thousands of deities are intended as lessons in religion, love, history, philosophy, sex, psychology, art, science, and other issues. Broadly speaking, there are two categories of mythology: those that were raised in the early phases of Hinduism or are strictly told in isolated communities in India, and mythological stories that are told throughout the Indian subcontinent and that have gained widespread acceptance.

Beliefs

As stated before, Hindus hold a wide variety of beliefs, and not all of them are consistent. There has, however, been a general evolution of Hindu thinking. Early Hinduism, known as Vedic religion, stated that there were several gods associated with natural orders. At the top of the celestial deities were Varuna, Mitra, and Vishnu. Varuna was conceived as the creator of the universe. As the sky god, he protects moral action and maintains order in the cosmos. Mitra, the god of the sun, is a benevolent and omnipresent force that brings prosperity to people, animals, and vegetables. Vishnu is the third god and is able to appear to people in many different forms, or *avatars*, including the divine Lord Krishna.

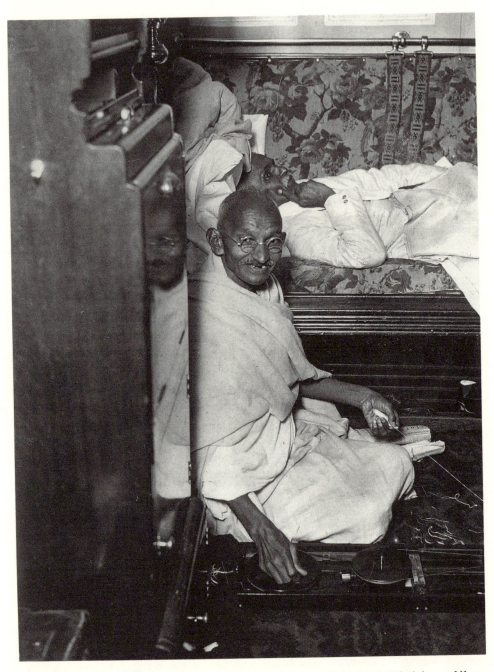

Hindu Mohandas Karamchand Gandhi spins thread aboard a ship in 1931. Hinduism, while not a unified, coherent religion, is an assemblage of religious beliefs, practices, and doctrines with more than 750 million followers. Gandhi lived a simple and ascetic life while advocating civil disobedience through passive resistance, the Hindu concept of satyagraha, *as a tactic in India's stuggle for independence from British rule, which was finally successful in 1947.*

Vedic gods also included atmospheric deities such as Indra, the thunder god that wages war, as well as terrestrial deities. Agni, the fire god, was a terrestrial deity who is closely linked to the sacrificial fire that is a critically important symbol in Hindu worship. Other Vedic gods are called upon for a variety of purposes: healing the sick, marriage ceremonies, patrons of knowledge and language, fertility, prosperity, happiness, and many other uses. Sex figures prominently for many of the gods, as does violence. The deity Kali, for example, is depicted drinking blood and wearing a necklace of human skulls. She is also connected in Hindu mythology to the founding of Calcutta.

The Vedic religion developed an increasingly complicated and diverse system of sacrifices as well as a class of priests that pushed the spiritual limits of the human body in the quest for transcendental knowledge. Many practices developed, especially rituals emphasizing sacrifice by fire, which came to dominate Hindu religious ceremonies. For Hindus, sacrifice became a vehicle for understanding reality and not simply a ceremony. Specific spoken passages, known as mantras, often accompanied the rituals. The *mantras* became critically important elements in understanding reality, or the truth. Similarly, the truth could be realized through a person's unspoken words to himself through thought. The notion that the truth could be realized through the sounds of mantras themselves and/or through a person's own thoughts gave rise to the concept of there being a unity, or a One. The presence of a One meant that Hindus no longer thought of gods as being "creators." The gods were part of that One, as is everything else in the universe. Some Hindus came to believe that the One came about through a massive human sacrifice, thus making the act of sacrifice a creative act. Others believed that before there was the present universe, there was a formless entity known as Tad Ekam, or That One. In this pre-universe state there was neither darkness or light, life or death, but rather a great cosmic reality that was beyond human senses. Because of the existence of a universal One, there are many different avenues for realizing its presence. A person can achieve the quest of knowledge of the universe, creation, and human beings through the performances of rituals or mental meditations.

Out of these concepts grew the principle of Brahman-Atman. The doctrine looks upon individuals as part of a greater whole. The self becomes merged into the One. Like other eastern religions, this doctrine attempts to explain the unexplainable. Brahman pervades the universe in a way that transcends space and time. It is both the external world and the inner world of all beings. The Atman represents the unseen inner soul of everything, living and inanimate. Atman is Brahman and Brahman is Atman. The idea is described in the expression *tat tvam asi*, meaning "That art thou." The Upanishads offer several analogies in nature to demonstrate the concept. "As bees . . . make honey by collecting the juices of trees located at different places, and reduce them to one form [honey]; and as these juices have no discrimination to say: 'I am the juice of this tree' or 'I am the juice of that tree' . . . Now that which is the subtle essence—in it all that exists has self. That is the True. That is the Self. That art thou." (Chandogya Upanishad VI.9.1–2) Thus the doctrine of Brahman-Atman merges the human soul as being the same as the Absolute. And because a single person is in fact part of a larger Absolute, the soul of that person never ceases, even after death. The soul simply comes back to the external world in a different form. Those who cannot fully grasp this Absolute Reality, Hindus believe, are destined to an unending pattern of rebirths and reincarnations.

The process of reincarnation or rebirth is known as *samsara*. Samsara is a perpetual series of rebirths in which a soul takes on any form of life (vegetable, animal, or human) in each birth. The process has no beginning and for most individuals no end. *Karma* determines the form of an individual's rebirth. A person's karma is determined by his or her conduct in life. Every action and thought in a present life dictates what form that person will take in his or her new life. A person's present life is the result of past actions and thoughts. Thus, Hindus do not believe that a person's fate is determined by gods or bad luck, but rather by the good or bad deeds of past lives. This concept helps justify the Hindu caste system, which labels a person's status according to his or her birth.

The Hindu caste system is the religion's most distinctive quality. This social stratification of society based on birth is called *varna,* which literally means "color." The system is very complicated, but in its most general form consists of five major social categories: brahmin, kshatriya, vaisya, sudra, and chandala (or "untouchable"). In the traditional system, brahmins are the highest rank. They are the priests and the spiritual and intellectual leaders of Hindu society. They study Hinduism, perform rituals, teach, and officiate at religious ceremonies. Next are the kshatriyas, the rulers and warriors who protect and promote the material well-being of society. The farmers, merchants, and others who contribute to society's economy are the vaisyas. The sudras are the laborers and servants who supply the menial labor for the upper three ranks. The fifth category emerged over time. The "untouchables," or chandalas, were considered to be so low in status as to be outside the caste system. They were excluded from all rituals and in some parts of India were banned from public. They often had to identify themselves as untouchables so that those of higher rank could avoid being near them. Modern sensibilities have to some extent lessened the stigma of being an untouchable. Nevertheless, the rigorous adherence to the caste system made it so that each class established its own rules and customs, many of which persist in modern life.

Part of achieving good karma requires following the Hindu doctrine of *ashrama* (stages of life), which applies to males in the upper three ranks. All males go through four stages of life: youth (*brahmacarin*), adulthood (*grihashta*), middle age (*vanaprastha*), and old age (*sannyasin*). The first stage begins with a ceremony between the ages of eight and twelve in which the boy becomes a full-fledged member of his caste. He becomes the disciple of a *guru* (teacher) who instructs the youth until he is between twenty and twenty-four years old. The next stage, adulthood, requires the young man to lead an active married life. He should fulfill with vigor three ideals in particular: observing religious duties, accumulating wealth, and enjoying pleasure (this includes sensual pleasure). Hindus do not look down upon the accumulation of wealth or the pursuit of pleasure. However, it is understood that as satisfying as these pursuits may be, they are far less important than spiritual pursuits, which are part of the quest for liberation from the cycle of rebirth.

The third stage begins when the man's hair starts to turn gray or when he has his first grandson. At that point he is meant to leave home (accompanied by his wife if she chooses) and enter the forest to pursue a life of meditation and reflection. The goal of living this hermit-like life is to detach oneself from everything in the world to which he had previously been attached. When he is ready to do this, he enters the fourth stage of a renouncer and leads the life of a wandering ascetic. He becomes a homeless nomad, free from all material desires and possessions. His aim is to reach the Brahman-Atman state of self-realization and thereby break the continuous chain of rebirths through a final emancipation (*moksha*).

Because of the concept of universal unity, Hindus believe there are many paths (*marga*) to moksha. They are broken down into three general categories: *karma marga, jnana marga,* and *bhakti marga.* The first, karma marga, is the vigorous fulfillment of social obligations, rites, and ceremonies. This path involves sacrificing to deities and ancestors, a reverence for the sun, vigilance of the hearth fire, and strict observance of a host of ceremonial duties, social rules, and dietary laws as described in the Code of Manu. These rites include the *shraddha* rite, a domestic ceremony honoring ancestral spirits. The practice involves a regular offering of food (often *pinda,* rice pressed into a cake) and memorial prayers. The role of women within this code is to humbly serve men. Women are given a subservient position to men in Hinduism. A good woman, according to Hindu doctrine, worships and serves her husband faithfully no matter what he does.

The jnana marga (path of knowledge) is the route for the more intellectually inclined. Its role is for the man to reach emancipation through rigorous mental effort. These aspirants cultivate control over their senses to free their minds of clutter to a state of perfect concentration and inner calm. Through uninterrupted contemplation, the person hopes to release the Truth of Brahman-Atman. Achieving this goal takes intense self-discipline and patience. Hindus have recognized six systems for the path of knowledge. They are based in varying degrees on the study of the external world; the recognition of true knowledge over false knowledge through the senses; testimony; comparison of facts and inference; insight into the difference between a person's soul and his matter; a person's ability to gain control over his breathing and physical body through yoga; the observance of ceremonies; and a self-identification of the self and the One. Yoga can play a critical role in this path. Through physical self-discipline and controlled breathing, Hindus say a person can gain control of his senses. In turn, he can pass through a series of stages ending with a state of unimpeded concentration in which there is no difference between the object of thought and the mind itself. The goal is to suppress the normal activities of the mind and reach a state of complete freedom from earthly matters.

Those who decide against these two paths have a third option, the bhakti marga (path of devotion). This is the most popular path for Hindus to take. It involves the passionate love of a god in which the person surrenders his entire self to the deity through acts of devotion and worship. Fear, punishment, and reward cannot be the inspiration for those who follow this path. Rather the driving force must be for the sake of loving the deity itself. The path is described in the Song of the Blessed One, a poem that is written in the form of a conversation between the warrior Arjuna and his charioteer Krishna, who is in fact the human form of the supreme deity, Vishnu. "Fix your mind on me, be devoted to me, worship me, adore me, and to me you will come." (Bhagavad-Gita IX. 33–34)

Hindu Sects

There are thousands of different Hindu sects. The vast majority of these sects are folk versions of Hinduism that are closely linked to Indian tribal religion. The lower castes often restrict their religious practices to deities that exist in trees, water, and other natural elements. They frequently turn to astrology and occult practices. Ritual purification, charms, and traditional local customs play a far more significant role in their lives than the doctrine of Brahman-Atman. Black magic, exorcism, the worship of snakes, and ritual nudity are all elements of the many different brands of folk Hinduism that can be found throughout India, particularly rural areas. Many women worship snakes to enhance fertility, and many households adopt a single god as their household deity. According to Hindu tradition, there are about one million of these deities. Journeys to sacred places such as temples, Harwar in the Himalayas, the Bay of Bengal, and the Ganges, the most holy of rivers, also play a major role in folk Hinduism. Though not limited to folk Hinduism, the worship of cows is also a significant part of a Hindu's life. Cows are treated as deities. Villages use cow dung for fuel, disinfectant, and medicine.

In this vast array of gods, three stand out for millions of Hindus. Collectively, they are known as the *trimurti,* the three deities who represent Absolute Reality. Shiva is known as the Destroyer and has a complex, seemingly paradoxical character. He is the god of death and destruction, but also the god of reproduction and dance. His dichotomous character, which is also described as ceaselessly active and eternally restful, is considered to represent two aspects of one nature. The followers of Shiva are known as Shaivites. They call their deity Mahadeva, meaning Great God. The second of these gods is Vishnu, the Preserver. He is a humane god of benevolence and love. Vishnu has appeared on earth nine times to help preserve and restore humanity. Followers believe he will appear one last time to bring the world to an end. His previous appearances have included stints as Krishna and as the Buddha. Adherents to Vishnu are generally monotheistic. The third god, who is the oldest and least popular of the three, is Brahma, the Creator, from which both society and nature have been derived.

Shatism and Tantrism emphasize physical exertions and rites to achieve mystical goals. Tantrism uses yoga and ritual practices to achieve transcendental knowledge of the Absolute. Followers of Tantrism use many different methods to reach this goal, ranging from self-torture to elaborate exercises aimed at awakening the female energy in a person's body. The shati cults transcend time and space through rituals of lust as a way to be released from the unending cycle of reincarnations. Their ceremonies include ritual copulation as a sacred path for experiencing the divine process.

Hindu Practices

Hinduism places a great deal of emphasis on ritual observance. Possessing all the knowledge in the world and doing many good deeds will have no effect without proper observance of Hindu ceremonies. The list of practices, like the number of different sects, is almost limitless. Nevertheless, some broad generalizations can be made.

Ritual purification plays a major role in Hindu life. Only those who cleanse themselves are eligible to achieve Absolute Knowledge. There are two kinds of physical purity, internal and external. They can be achieved through washing and bathing, and through the natural functions of the body. Yoga exercises and purification formulas and acts can contribute to a person's internal purity. Devotional services are supposed to be observed every day for gods, ancestors, seers, animals, and the poor. There are many different ways to carry out these rituals, including tending to a sacred household fire, the recital of mantras, meditation, yoga exercises, and the recitation of texts. In modern times, however, many people (particularly city dwellers) have not been able to fulfill these requirements on a daily basis. As a result, they tend to fulfill them on a once-a-week basis at local temples. Pilgrimages to sacred places also play a critical role in Hindu practice. There are thousands of sacred sites throughout India.

Hundreds of festivals are held to observe sacred occasions. They are held to honor the births, deaths, victories, and other significant events of Hindu heroes and gods. Many festivals are seasonal. Festivals can be observed through worship, the offering of gifts, drinking, games, fairs, chants, bathing, gambling, the lighting of lamps, and many other acts. One of the more significant religious festivals is the Divali (Cluster of Lights), a four- or five-day event celebrated in October or November to commemorate the actions of several gods, including Shiva and Vishnu. This festival consists of the lighting of lamps, gambling, worship, fasting, and finally a visit by Hindu males to a female relative to receive dinner and offer gifts. Another Hindu festival is the Holi, a carnival-like celebration held in February or March when bonfires are lit to burn evil demons symbolically.

See also ASCETICISM; PURITY AND POLLUTION.

Garg, Ganga Ram. (1992) *Encyclopedia of the Hindu World.*

Stutley, Margaret, and James Stutley. (1977) *Harper's Dictionary of Hinduism: Its Mythology, Folklore, Philosophy, Literature, and History.*

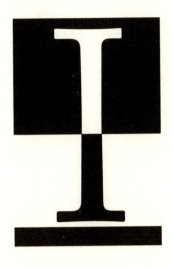

With well over 900 million followers, Islam is the second-largest religion in the world behind Christianity. While Islam began in and is associated with the Middle East, its reach is worldwide. The countries with the four largest Muslim populations are India, Bangladesh, Pakistan, and Indonesia, none of which are in the Middle East. The Arabic term "Islam" means "submission," and the term "Muslim" means "he who submits." Thus, *Islam* refers to the religion and *Muslim* to its followers. In Islam, the most important aspect of life is submission to the will of God (Allah) as interpreted by the prophet Muhammad. It is an all-encompassing worldview that determines an individual's personal conduct in all matters. Islamic tenets are closely associated with political rule and have played a major force in driving Islamic history and contemporary events.

Historical Development

Muhammad is the last and most important prophet in Islam. Born in about C.E. 570 in Mecca, Muhammad led a relatively uneventful life as a member of the local Qurayish tribe and as a merchant and husband until 610 when God revealed himself to Muhammad in a cave outside Mecca. At first Muhammad was unsure about the revelations, but further messages from God, sometimes speaking through the angel Gabriel, convinced him and his family members that he had received the "Revelation of the Words of Allah" and the "Call to Prophecy." He attempted to preach God's message to his fellow residents in Mecca, most of whom rejected Muhammad's claims. The governing powers became increasingly frustrated and threatened by Muhammad. Muhammad's powerful uncle, Abu Talib, protected Muhammad from persecution, but when he and Muhammad's wife died in 619, Muhammad and his followers faced intense hostility from the government. Invited by a delegation from Yathrib to settle a local dispute about 250 miles to the north, Muhammad finally left Mecca in 622. This is known as the Hijra or the year of emigration, and marks the first year in the Muslim calendar. The Muslim calendar uses lunar months of twenty-nine or thirty days (and is about 11 days shorter than the solar year).

Muhammad achieved success in Yathrib, quickly establishing himself as a leader of the agricultural community. He rapidly gained an intensely loyal following. The city became known as Yathrib, City of the Prophet (Medina an-Nebi) or simply Medina. Feeling threatened by Muhammad's growing power, Mecca, then a prosperous trading center, attacked Medina without success. Muhammad, in turn, conquered Mecca and unified Arabs for the first time. He successfully redirected allegiance from localized tribes to Islam. He established a government based on the laws of Allah, which called for a community (*umma*) governed by the word of God in which all men are equal but all are subservient to God. All government institutions, including the army, are meant to serve Allah and implement his laws. Man's role is to apply the laws as described by the Quran, the word of

Allah as described and recorded by Muhammad, and the *hadith,* an extensive collection of traditions, opinions, and decisions laid down by Muhammad during his tenure as leader.

When Muhammad died in 632 a schism occurred as followers were divided over who should succeed him to power as the *caliph* (leader of the Muslims). Most Muslims chose to follow Abu Bakr, a son-in-law and longtime follower of Muhammad. But a different contingent thought Ali, also a son-in-law and a cousin, was the rightful heir. This early divergence is the root of the Muslim split into Sunni Muslims (who followed Abu Bakr) and Shiite Muslims (who gave their allegiance to Ali). Ironically, Ali later became the third caliph. Despite a rapid succession of caliphs due to assassinations and internal division, the Arab Muslims embarked on the successful conquest of neighboring empires and territories. As they spread their power, they compelled people to convert to Islam, often upon penalty of death. The first four caliphs, known as the Four Rightly Guided Caliphs, spread Islam to the entire Arabian peninsula and what is modern-day Syria and Egypt, and a new capital was established in Damascus. By 750, under the leadership of the Umayyads—a hereditary line of Sunni caliphs—Islam had spread to all of North Africa, modern-day Spain (where their conquest was stopped in a major battle with the Franks commemorated by Europeans in the *Song of Roland*), the Persian Empire, and as far east as India and Central Asia.

The Umayyads were ousted from power in 750 by a group of Persians who considered the Umayyads to be Arab, as opposed to Islamic, leaders. The new leadership, known as the Abassids, established a new capital in Baghdad and continued the work of the Umayyads in strengthening the Islamic empire. The Abbasid period lasted until 1258 and marked the era of greatest power and influence by a single Islamic empire. Baghdad became the greatest cultural center of the Islamic world, and perhaps the

entire world, during the ninth and tenth centuries. Rivalries between Arabs and Persians, however, eventually festered allowing the entry of a third group, the Turks, who came to dominate the empire by way of their military power. The eastern lands of the Islamic world collapsed in the thirteenth century in the face of the Mongol invasion in 1258. A period of turmoil ensued in the unconquered portions of the Islamic empire until the middle of the fourteenth century, when the Turkish tribes rose to power and established the Ottoman Empire. The Ottoman sultan became the caliph and ruled over territories that stretched from Spain to North Africa to the Arab Near East and eventually the Balkans. The boundaries of the Ottoman Empire were in a state of constant flux; starting in the eighteen century they began to shrink as western European nations gained the upper hand. The Ottoman Empire came to an end after World War I. In 1924 the Turkish National Assembly abolished the institution of the caliphate, thus ending a 1,300-year tradition. Although there have been periodic and scattered attempts by various Muslim leaders to reclaim that role, no single leader has been acknowledged by the Islamic community.

In the meantime, the influence of Islam continued to spread as traders, merchants, and travelers introduced the religion to East Asia, East and West Africa, and Indonesia. Islamic communities evolved in very different ways in different parts of the world. In India and other parts of South Asia, for example, Muslims were much more accommodating of other religions than in the Middle East, where Islam was the dominant religion. There is now considerable diversity in many aspects of Islam throughout the world and the nature of the religion varies in some respects from society to society. Cultural groups that follow Islam range in size from close to 150 million Arabs with many subsects to very small ethnic groups such as the Wayto in Ethiopia whose total population is about two thousand.

Gabriel, angel of God (Allah), flies above the Prophet Muhammad, whose interpretation of God's will is the foundation of Islam. Muslims, adherents of Islam, number more than 900 million, making Islam the second-largest relgion after Christianity.

With the expansion of European influence in the late-eighteenth century, the influence of Islam declined, causing a great deal of resentment and bewilderment on the part of Muslims who equated success in battle with divine assistance from Allah. Not coincidentally, Islamic countries have tended to be underdeveloped Third World countries in recent times. Much of the frustration with this status has resulted in conflicts with Western ideologies, concepts, and countries that are sometimes manifested through Islamic fundamentalism, which harks back to the origins of Islam. However, not all Muslim ethnic conflicts involve fundamentalism. Secular Muslims find themselves in ethnic conflicts in Bosnia, Georgia, Azerbaijan, the Philippines, India, Sri Lanka, Israel, France, Nigeria, and even in northern Europe and the United States, where anti-Muslim, anti-Arab feelings have developed for a variety of reasons.

The fundamentalist movement, which is centered in the Middle East, strives to replace secular governments in Islamic nations through elections, but fundamentalists have also resorted to terrorism, assassinations, and riots. The movement is in large part a reaction to growing Western influences in the Islamic world. As a result, the rhetoric stresses anti-Western, anticolonial, and anti-imperialism themes and is aimed at institutions, individuals, and governments that are believed to be influenced by the West. In some nations, the struggle is seen as a holy war of good versus evil.

Religious Beliefs

Despite the extremism of some fundamentalist groups, the principle message of Islam is one of peace and submission to the word of Allah. There are three essential elements of Islam. The first is acknowledgment that Allah revealed his will to Muhammad and that his words, spoken in Arabic, are recorded in the Quran. Although God had selected ninety-nine prophets prior to Muhammad to act as messengers of his will (including Adam, Abraham, Moses, most of the Hebrew prophets, and Jesus Christ), over time the message was misinterpreted. Abraham is considered the father of the Arabs through his son Ishmael. The father and son built the House of God at Mecca (the Ka'aba), which serves as the destination for all Muslims and is what Muslims face when they pray. Jesus is acknowledged as a messiah but not as the Son of God. While the Old and New Testaments are considered important by Muslims, they are seen mainly as interesting stories.

The second element is the confessional (*shahada*) that there is only one God who "does not beget or is begotten . . . and there is like unto him no one." This is why the notion of Jesus as the Son of God is blasphemous, although Muslims do believe in the virgin birth of Jesus. Muslims do believe, however, that there are other supernatural creatures, such as angels and the Devil (Iblis). To be recognized as a Muslim historically, all one has to do is recite the Profession of Faith: "There is no god but God, and Muhammad is the Messenger of God" (*La 'ila 'illa Allah, wa Muhammad rusuul Allah*).

The third aspect of Islam is the obligation of duties that must be performed in order to enter paradise. God keeps a tally of a person's good and bad actions in the Book of Deeds. On the Day of Judgment, the person's final destination—heaven or hell—is determined. These duties are known as the Five Pillars of Islam. No matter what the sect, place of residence, or ethnic group, all Muslims accept these duties. They are:

1. The shahada confessional acknowledging that there is only one God.
2. Prayer, or *salat*, which is a supreme duty to pray five times each day at the first light, noon, in the middle of the afternoon, at last light, and dinnertime. This is flexible, however, depending on a person's physical fitness and whether circumstances allow time for each of the prayers. If a person misses one of the times for prayer, he or she can make it up with short prayers at other times of the day. The prayers are offered in the direction of Mecca. The prayer involves a cleansing process, which is why Muslim mosques usually have water available. If no water is available, a person can use sand. This is also the origin of the prayer rugs that many Muslims use when praying to Mecca. Friday is the Islamic holy day and is marked by community prayers, with all males and older females in the mosque. Prayers are made directly to Allah as Muslims do not believe in the use of intermediary religious specialists. Prayer leaders, known as *imams*, are respected members of the community who lead the gathering in fulfilling the obligatory prayers. The senior leader is expected to give a sermon, which may be a call for action, reading from the Quran, or a lecture. There are no requirements to be an imam, although it expected that the person be well educated.
3. Almsgiving, or *zakat*, involves the voluntary contribution of money for the poor. Volunteer charity is considered a way of improving one's chances of entering heaven. Service and charity are ways in which to purify oneself of wealth and greed and level the differences in people's wealth or poverty.
4. Fasting, or *sawm*, during Ramadan, the ninth month of the Muslim year, demonstrates a person's faith through personal sacrifice. Ramadan commemorates the anniversary of when the Quran was revealed to Muhammad. Among other things, Muslims are not allowed

to eat, drink, or engage in sexual activities from dawn to dusk during Ramadan. Muslims must also avoid evil thoughts and words during Ramadan and be especially kind to the destitute. At the conclusion of Ramadan, the *Id al-fitr*, the most important Muslim religious holiday, is celebrated for several days.

5. The pilgrimage, or *haj*, to Mecca is expected of all Muslims, but only if health and circumstances allow. The pilgrimage should take place during the lunar month of Dhu'l-hijjah. The event signifies a return to the center of the Islamic universe and the origin of humanity. God forgives the sins of those who perform the haj, which includes circling the Ka'aba, specific prayers and motions, and a sacrifice. In many cases, people who cannot afford to make the journey will assist another person in the community to make the journey on his or her behalf. Millions of people arrive in Mecca each year to fulfill this obligation, which is considered a crowning moment in a person's religious obligation. Upon arriving in Mecca, a Muslim enters the Ka'aba barefoot and walks around it seven times, each time pausing on the southeast corner to kiss or touch the stone. The pilgrims then commemorate the search of Hagar (the mother of Ishmael) for her son by walking back and forth across a nearby valley seven times. The final climactic ritual is a fifteen-mile trek on foot to the Mount of Mercy east of Mecca, where pilgrims stand before God from noon to sunset in a state of meditation. After spending the night there, they return to Mecca for a three-day feast.

It is also possible to make a lesser haj to Mecca at a different time of year or to the two other Islamic holy sites in Medina and Jerusalem. Jerusalem is considered a sacred city because of its role as the city of prophets in the Old Testament and because Muhammad had a dream in which he rode the angel Gabriel's horse to Jerusalem to view the afterlife. The Dome of the Rock on the Temple in Jerusalem marks the site where Muhammad ascended into heaven. Originally, Muhammad designated Medina as the focal point for Muslim's prayers, but when Christians and Jews in the city refused to acknowledge Muhammad as the prophet, he changed the site to his native city of Mecca.

6. There is a sixth duty, often considered one of the pillars, called *jihad*, or exertion in the way of God. Whenever a Muslim protects the faith, overcomes nonbelievers, or purifies the actions of a nonbeliever, he has performed jihad. Those who die in the act of jihad are assured a place in heaven. A common misinterpretation of jihad is that it means "holy war." Although serving as a soldier of Islam is one way to fulfill the jihad duties, there are many other ways for a Muslim to preserve and establish order in Islamic society.

Religious Texts

The most important Islamic document is the Quran, the written version of the will of Allah as described to Muhammad. Written in Arabic, it is considered to be impossible to translate it accurately into other languages. Even though the stories and words can be imparted in other languages, the subtleties of the true meaning are lost in translation. The Quran, which means the Reading, consists of 114 chapters that cover a wide range of topics from ethics to metaphysics.

Its influence on Muslim thought, expressions, and conduct is enormous. It includes ethical and legal teachings, a sacred history with many parallels to the Christian Bible, discussions of the human soul and a person's spiritual life, and prayers for Muslims to repeat. It has historically been used as a literary style guide and grammatical text. The study of the Quran served as the impetus for the formation of some of the world's oldest universities, which proved to be the most advanced and sophisticated centers for learning of their time. The Quran is so sacred that it serves as the central presence for all Muslims.

The second important text in Islamic law (known as Shariah or the path) is the *sunna,* a collection of *hadith,* traditions and sayings assigned to Muhammad by other people. The Hadith describe many of the daily requirements and rituals of Islam, often in great detail. Other important scriptures include the opinions of jurists written down in *qiyas.* The fourth source of Islamic law is *ijma,* the consensus of a group of judges (*ulama*) representing a community. The ulama serve as judges for interpreting the Shariah. Not all the laws and rituals described in the Quran and other scriptures require the same level of observance. In fact, Islam acknowledges five categories of obedience. They are obligatory (for matters such as prayer), desirable (such as the ritual sacrifice of animals), optional, objectionable (slavery, for instance), and forbidden (including incest and drinking alcohol). Because of the breadth of laws and categories of observance, there are a wide number of different interpretations of the Shariah, which has often led to splits and conflicts between different Muslim groups.

There are four primary schools of Shariah representing different interpretations of the Quran and the Hadith. They are the Malaki, which depend upon the consensus of the community and dominates northern Africa; the Hanafi in Turkey, which use analogy for ortho-dox teaching; the conservative interpretations of the Hanbali between Syria and Egypt; and the more widely accepted Shafi'i in Syria and Egypt.

Sects

Almost immediately after Muhammad died, Muslims split into different sects. The main source of conflict was over succession of leadership. One group of dissenters called the Kharji (from the Arabic word for rebel) broke off from Islamic leadership and stressed three principles: adherence to Islam meant the aggressive pursuit of jihad through military expansion; any person who committed a grave sin and did not properly repent was stripped of Muslim status; and leadership should be open to any person with a righteous character. The Kharji did not last long, but had a significant impact on Islam.

The two main Islamic sects today are the Sunni and Shiite, each of which have numerous subsects. The Sunni constitute close to 90 percent of the Muslims in the world. The root of dispute that led to the split took place upon Muhammad's death, but also includes matters of religious authority. The Sunni believe that the Muslim leader can only come from the Qurayish tribe and hence trace their line of succession to Abu Bakr. Religious authority, the Sunni say, stems from sunna, or tradition, and ijma, or scholarly agreement, and is the basis of Islam.

Shiites—who are mainly in Iran—maintain that divine leadership can only pass to direct relatives of Muhammad and thus consider Ali as the Prophet's rightful successor. Shiite religious authority rests with an imam, an infallible interpreter of Islamic doctrine and rituals, to whose pronouncements all Shiites must adhere. Most Shiites also believe that there have been twelve imams since Muhammad, and that one more is still due to arrive, who will mark the end of the world. There are several Shiite subsects, many of which offer different interpretations of, or place special emphasis on, the imams.

Sufism is a mystical movement within Islam and was the main group responsible for spreading Islam beyond its political boundaries in Africa and Asia as they were able to easily absorb local customs and beliefs. In the same way, however, superstition and occultism gradually crept into different aspects of Sufism, which evolved into several different forms. There are now about seventy Sufi orders. The common threads of Sufism are the belief that the truth can only be found through personal experience culminating in union with god, that Sufi masters known as *shaikhs* are to be honored and achieve the status of saints after death, and that celibacy is preferable to marriage. The group got its name from a coarse woolen mantle, known as a *suf,* that its early practitioners wore and has since become a distinguishing feature.

Observances and Festivals

There are four solemn observances that all Muslims must perform during their lifetime. The first takes place seven days after birth, at which time the parents name the child, cut the baby's hair, and offer an animal sacrifice in which the meat from the animal is given to the poor. The second is the circumcision of boys, usually done by the age of four. The third event is the marriage, which is considered a contractual affair in which the bridegroom promises money, animals, or goods to the bride's family in return for her joining his family and raising his children. Traditionally, a Muslim man is allowed to marry four wives provided he treats them all equally, although this practice has fallen out of favor and most Muslims are monogamous. Although the position of women in Islam is inferior to men, historically Islam actually elevated their standing in most areas, including Arabia, where female infanticide was rampant and mistreatment common. The fourth observance takes place at death when the body is washed in water by a person of the same sex and buried on its right side facing Mecca.

There are two main festivals in Islam. The most significant is the Festival of Sacrifices that takes place at the conclusion of the pilgrimage to Mecca. Every Muslim is expected to sacrifice an animal as a re-creation of Abraham's decision to sacrifice a sheep instead of his son to God. After the feast is over, families go to the tombs of their relatives to lay palm branches on the grave and distribute alms to the poor. The other major festival celebrated with feasts is the Id al-fitr, or Festival of Fast Breaking, that takes place at the conclusion of Ramadan. The event includes three days of feasting and concludes at sunrise on the fourth day when the men assemble in the mosque for prayers. Later, families and friends visit each other to exchange gifts, often candies and cakes.

Ahmad, Imatiaz, ed. (1981) *Ritual and Religion among Muslims in India.*

Encyclopedia of Islam. 2d ed. (1954–).

Esposito, John L. (1995) *The Oxford Encyclopedia of the Modern Islamic World.*

Glasse, Cyril. (1989) *The Concise Encyclopedia of Islam.*

Weekes, Richard V., ed. (1984) *Muslim Peoples: A World Ethnographic Survey.*

duism, renounced his family and wealth, and left his wife and child to join a group of wandering ascetics who followed the rule of Parshva. Mahavira soon became disillusioned with his companions and struck off on his own to practice extreme asceticism and *ahimsa*, or noninjury to other living things. His regimen included traveling naked, tearing at his hair and beard, and visiting different regions during periods of extreme heat and cold. To avoid killing insects inadvertently he would not walk on roads during the rain, and swept the path in front of him when it was dry. He was joined for many years by Goshala Makkhali, who was the head of another sect called the Ajivakes. The two, however, later went their separate ways because of a disagreement on the nature of karma. He refused excessive contact with other people to avoid forming attachments and quashed all sense of desire for earthly pleasures. After twelve years Mahavira reached a state of *moksha* where he was released from the bonds of rebirth. He then devoted his time to preaching and teaching his beliefs.

Many people were impressed by the strength of Mahavira's convictions and his beliefs and he developed a following that flourished for several centuries through oral tradition. In the third century B.C.E. his teachings were written down, but disagreements led to some divisions in Jainism. Nevertheless, the religion was favored by many rulers in India for many centuries. In the twelfth century, however, the religion went into decline after the Muslim invasions. It has enjoyed periodic resurgences in popularity since then. Most Indian cities still have Jain communities today. The religion has been very influential in Indian art, literature, and philosophy.

JAINISM

Jainism comes from the word *jina*, which means "conqueror," and refers to the desire to conquer a person's own *karma* and reach the goal of self-liberation. Founded in the sixth century B.C.E. in reaction to Hinduism, Jainism is the oldest ascetic religious tradition. Jainism is an ethical belief system and focuses on the moral life of the individual. There are about three million followers, with the vast majority in India, although there are small communities in Great Britain, eastern Africa, and North America. The religion's influence in India is disproportional to the number of followers as many Jains are leading members of the Indian business community.

Historical Development
Mahavira ("great hero") is considered the founder of Jainism. The second son of an Indian ruler, Mahavira (599–527 B.C.E.), along with other religious dissidents, objected to the expanding caste system and deities associated with Hinduism, the established religion of the time. When he was thirty years old Mahavira rejected Hin-

Texts and Sects
For close to three hundred years the Purvas, the early sacred literature, were memorized by leading monks. Bhadrabahu was the last person to retain this information in his head, and when he died in about 300 B.C.E. a council was called

to re-create the text. Two factions, however, disagreed on the text. The Digamaras dismissed the Purvas as being distorted from their original meaning and wrote new texts that were subsequently revised six hundred and eight hundred years later. The canon consists of two major works that discuss the doctrines of karma and passions that hold down a person's *jiva*, or soul. The Svetambra scriptures include forty-five Agamas (texts) that discuss the rules of asceticism, the origin of the universe, doctrines on astronomy, and other views.

The main differences between the two sects concern the role of women and the issue of nakedness. The Svetambaras (white-clad), who dominate in northern India, allow the wearing of garments and admit women. The Digamabaras (sky-clad), who dominate in southern India, prescribe total nudity in the pursuit of extreme asceticism, exclude women from temples, and believe that only men can attain total liberation. Over the centuries other sects formed as a result of differences over issues such as the worship of idols and the use of temples. While some Jains practice idolatry and build elaborate temples, others reject these customs entirely.

Practices and Beliefs

Jains believe that twenty-three Tirthankaras (prophets) preceded the appearance of Mahavira, the last of the prophets. The Tirthankaras

Jainism, the oldest ascetic religious tradition, was founded in the sixth century B.C.E. An ornate Jain Temple in Calcutta, India, includes buildings, gazebos, and a pool.

achieved liberation of their souls through meditation and self-denial. They taught the method of salvation before departing from their mortal bodies. Jainists worship the Tirthankaras as a way to commemorate the paths they took to liberation. Mahavira rejected the notion of deities and worship of idols. He believed that the path to salvation lay in one's own destiny and that there should not be a distinct priestly class, only people who can help describe the route to self-liberation.

The underlying principle of Jainism is that all living things have an immortal soul (jiva) that should strive to be liberated from matter (ajiva). The jiva is reincarnated after death but it is almost always held down by karma—a form of matter that clings to the jiva through desires (both good and bad) in present and past lives. To free the soul of karma a person must perform austerities to achieve a state of desirelessness in which the karma is stripped away. The route to achieving this goal is described by Mahavira as the Five Great Vows:

1. Renouncing the killing all living things and denying the right of others to kill. Known as ahimsa, this involves taking extraordinary steps to make sure that one does not intentionally or inadvertently kill any living thing. Jainists often strain water before drinking it, wear masks to prevent accidentally swallowing insects, and refuse to eat meat or work in any job, such as being a butcher, soldier, farmer, or fisherman, that may contribute to the death or harm of others. Jainists also refuse to participate in the sale or manufacture of weapons, alcohol, or drugs.

2. Renouncing all vices associated with lies arising from fear, laughter, anger, and greed.

3. Renouncing all forms of stealing and refusing to accept anything that is not given freely.

4. Renouncing all sexual pleasures, including the acknowledgment of the sensuality of women, whom Mahavira described as "the greatest temptation in the world."

5. Renouncing all forms of attachment that cause pleasure or pain, love or hate, and encouraging others to do so.

By cutting oneself off from earthly attachments, a person's soul can be liberated from the karma that binds it in a state of constant reincarnation. Through extreme asceticism a person can shed past karma. When a soul goes through the process of rebirth it carries the karma with it. If the karma is light, the soul will rise to higher levels of existence, but if the karma is heavy it will descend into lower levels of existence. There are three main steps in reaching the highest level of self-liberation. The first involves accepting the truth of the twenty-four Tirthankaras; the second is gaining knowledge of the path to self-liberation; and the third is following that path. The relatively few souls that find self-liberation break the cycle of rebirth and rise to the top of the universe where all the released souls (*siddhas*) dwell. All siddhas are identical and exist in a blissful state of spiritual omniscience.

Because Mahavira's doctrines were extremely severe for all but the most serious disciples, a less restrictive code of conduct was allowed for ordinary people. This includes ahimsa, never lying or stealing, limiting one's material wealth and needs, giving excess wealth to charity, meditating, going through special periods of self-denial, spending some time as a monk, being chaste, and giving alms to monks and ascetics. Jains are widely respected in India because of their adherence to this code of conduct. Ironically, the code that was prescribed as a route through poverty and asceticism has contributed to making Jains one of the wealthiest classes in India. Jains are major contributors to and organizers of charity, welfare, and cultural organizations in India.

Jains believe that the universe is eternal, with neither a beginning nor an end. There is no god, although there are the consistent elements of soul, matter, time, space, and motion. Time is seen as a wheel with twelve spokes that are divided into two cycles. Six ages create a rising cycle when humans progress in stature, happiness, and knowledge. The remaining six ages are of a descending cycle in which there is a deterioration of these conditions. Together, the two cycles make a single rotation of time.

Over the centuries, many Jains adopted some customs of their Hindu neighbors. Many people consider themselves both Hindu and Jain, often turning to Hinduism for domestic rites associated with birth, marriage, and death.

Dundas, Paul. (1992) *The Jains.*

Jaini, Padmanabh S. (1979) *The Jaina Path of Purification.*

JUDAISM

Judaism is a relatively small global religion with less than 20 million followers worldwide. The numbers, however, belie its significance as Judaism provided the philosophical and historical foundation for two of the world's largest religions—Christianity and Islam.

Judaism rests on the belief that there is one all-powerful God with whom all Jews have a personal relationship that is enacted through individual conduct. It represents the hallowing of life for the glory of God, and in return God has selected Jews as his chosen people. God has re-vealed himself through the prophets and great events, meaning that historical events are seen as crucial guides to the development and meaning of their religion. The primary Jewish scripture, the Torah, devotes large sections to the recording of history.

Historical Development

The history of Judaism dates back to about 2000 B.C.E. when the ancestors of modern Jews were one of several nomadic tribes in northern Arabia under the patriarch Abraham. God promised Abraham and his descendants that they would be given a permanent home in the area that is now Israel. The Jews roamed the entire region with relative freedom for several centuries until they were enslaved by Egyptian pharaohs. In the thirteenth century B.C.E. Moses emerged as a leader to guide the Jews out of enslavement and back to the promised land, which had since become occupied by the Canaanites. Moses, who had been born a Jew but was raised in the Egyptian royal family, received from a burning bush in the desert a message from God to lead the Jews back to Israel. The pharaoh rejected Moses' pleas to let the Jews return to Israel even after Egypt was struck by nine plagues from God. God's tenth and last plague struck and killed the first-born son of all Egyptians, but passed over the Jewish sons. The pharaoh, whose own son was killed, finally let the Jews depart.

Moses led the Jews through the Sinai Desert and at Mount Sinai climbed to the top of the mountain to meet with God, who initiated a covenant with the Jewish people that consisted of the Ten Commandments. Because the covenant was made with the Jewish people, and accepted by the Jewish people, all Jewish descendants are bound to the covenant. The commandments are the basic ethical code that Jews follow. The commandments include pronouncements not to kill, commit adultery, steal, bear false witness, use the Lord's name in vain, worship any likeness of God, or covet one's neighbor's possessions or wife. In addition, God invoked Jews to worship him as the sole god, honor one's father and mother, and keep the Sabbath as a day of rest once a week. So long as the Jews abided by the commandments, God (who was called Yahweh) would protect them and assure them of prosperity. But even in the Sinai the Jews were polytheistic and Moses fought a losing battle to keep them focused on worshipping the single god Yahweh. As punishment, God delayed the Jews' arrival in Canaan for forty years.

The Jews finally crossed the Jordan River under the leadership of Joshua. But their arrival coincided with the arrival of the Philistines, a seafaring people who also envisioned their future in the land occupied by the Canaanites. The three groups struggled for domination for more than two hundred years until King David prevailed and established a Jewish kingdom. His son Solomon built a great temple in Jerusalem. Before long, however, the kingdom collapsed and divided into two parts. In both of the divided kingdoms Jews strayed from worshipping only Yahweh despite the pleas of the Jewish prophets who condemned the occultism and illicit behaviors of their brethren. The prophets took on the responsibility for the character of the Jewish religion. They equated human conduct with ethical principles and moral obligations, these being more important than fulfilling religious ceremony. They stressed the inward quality of religion as a personal relationship between the individual and God, a merciful and just deity.

In the sixth century B.C.E., the ruling Babylonians exiled the Jews three times, the most important of which took place in 587 when the Babylonians destroyed Solomon's Temple. These exiles marked the beginning of the Diaspora, the scattering of Jews throughout the world. With the loss of the Temple, Jews adapted to their new circumstances by meeting in synagogues (the Greek word for meeting place) under the religious leadership of rabbis, who served as teachers. Seventy years after the Temple was destroyed, Persian King Cyrus allowed the Jews to return to Jerusalem and a new temple was built. Under the leadership of Nehemiah and Ezra a Jewish theocratic state was created in the fifth century B.C.E. that ruled according to the dictates of the Torah. It was during this time that many of the diverse practices of the Jews were consolidated into a single religion whose focus was on the one and only Jewish God, although some Jewish beliefs were influenced by Persian beliefs regarding angels, good and evil, and the existence of hell. In addition, the concept of the Holy Spirit as an ethical principal that holds the world together took root.

In 332 B.C.E. Alexander the Great conquered the region (then known as Palestine) and brought with him Greek civilization. The Jews adapted to the changes reasonably well until the reign of King Antiochus IV (175–164 B.C.E.), who prohibited Jews from possessing copies of the Torah, practicing circumcision, and keeping the Sabbath. He tried to force Jews to worship the Greek god Zeus at the Jewish Temple. An elderly priest called Mattathias sparked a revolt by killing a Greek commissioner who commanded him to sacrifice to Zeus. Under the leadership of Mattathias's son Judas Maccabaeus, the Jews reconquered Jerusalem. This era lasted for another century before the Jews yet again were split by acrimonious feuds. Asked by the Jews to arbitrate their difference, the Roman general Pompey entered Palestine in 63 B.C.E. and quickly occupied Palestine as a Roman district.

Several different Jewish groups evolved during the Roman occupation, including the Essenes, a monastic group that practiced nonviolence. They preached that the world of light would prevail over the world of darkness. Jesus Christ is believed to have been a member of this group. The Dead Sea Scrolls (the oldest-known copies of the Torah) are believed to have been written by them. Another, less peaceful Jewish sect were the Zealots, who opposed the Romans and preached an aggressive military stance. After years of repression, the Jews revolted against Rome in C.E. 66 but were put down in brutal fashion. Jerusalem was destroyed and the Temple burned to the ground. The rebellion ended when a band of Zealots committed mass suicide at Masada rather than surrender to the Romans. The Jews were exiled from Palestine and scattered throughout the Mediterranean lands.

The center of Jewish life shifted westward to Spain for several centuries until the Muslims conquered the region in the eighth centuries. When Christian rule returned to Spain in the fourteenth and fifteenth century the Jews were expelled. By this time they were scattered throughout Europe and under constant threat of persecution in most European and Islamic countries. In 1555 the Pope authorized the containment of Jews in ghettos and placed tight restrictions on their activities. They became subject to uprisings known as *pogroms*. Nevertheless, they developed new languages such as Sephardim (a mix of Hebrew and Spanish) and Yiddish (a mix of Hebrew and German), and kept the Jewish traditions alive in the hope of God fulfilling his promise to restore them to their promised land. In the eighteenth century, a mystical movement known as Hasidicism erupted among eastern Europeans. By the end of the nineteenth century most of the restrictions placed on Jews in Europe had been removed.

Also in the nineteenth century, a group of Jews were influenced by the nationalism that was sweeping Europe. Under the leadership of Theodore Herzl, the Zionists were convinced they would never be treated justly in Europe and advocated the creation of a Jewish nation. When World War II broke out in Europe, Nazi Germany systematically killed six million Jews in concentration camps. Known as the Holocaust, the genocide convinced the rest of the world to allow the Jews to establish their own country in former British Palestine in 1948. After a brief but victorious war with Arab Palestinian residents and Arab neighbors, the Jews established Israel as a religious state. Hundreds of thousands of Jews from Europe, the United States, the Arab world, Russia, and Ethiopia have since emigrated to Israel. The largest concentrations of Jews are in the United States (6 million), Israel (more than 4 million), and the former Soviet Union (1.5 million), but there are also substantial Jewish populations in Western Europe, Canada, South Africa, Argentina, and Brazil.

Texts and Beliefs

The Jewish Bible (known as the Old Testament by Christians) outlines the central components of Jewish beliefs. The Bible (which means books in Greek) consists of three main sections: the Torah (Law), Neviim (Prophets) and Kethuvim (Writings). These writings, which are supplemented by a collection of more modern writings called the Talmud, describe Jewish tradition, laws, priorities, religious ceremonies, and codes of conduct.

The Torah consists of the books of Genesis, Exodus, Leviticus, Numbers, and Deuteronomy and is considered the most significant scripture. Tradition holds that Moses wrote the Torah, but scholars believe it was written over the course of several hundred years. The Torah describes the relationship between God, the universe, and human beings. God is the creator of "the heavens and the earth." He is holy and represents moral perfection. He is a personal God who made humans in his image—not physically, as God does not have a physical being, but spiritually. God is just and merciful, but he is also jealous and will punish the grandchildren and great-grandchildren of miscreant Jews. But those who keep the commandments and love God will be rewarded with his benevolence in the form of mercy and grace. In contrast to Christianity

Judaism, whose followers number fewer than 20 million, provides a philosophical and historical foundation for Christianity and Islam, two of the world's largest religions. A Jewish rabbi reads the Torah, a scrolled manuscript that describes the relationship between God, the universe, and humans in a drawing by Onorio Ruofolo.

choice that Jews made as autonomous individuals capable of free will. The purpose of a Jew's life is to serve God by showing humanity to others. It is a way of life in which no amount of confession of faith can itself make a person fulfill his or her religious obligations. According to a well-known Jewish story, when asked by a non-Jew how he could convert to Judaism, the Jewish scholar Hillel told him: "What is hateful unto you, do not do unto your neighbor. The rest is commentary—now go and study."

The second section of the Bible is the Prophets, which consists of the Former Prophet books of Joshua, Judges, Samuel, and Kings, and the Latter Prophet books of Isaiah, Jeremiah, Ezekiel, and the Twelve minor prophets. They describe the history of the Jews from their settlement of Canaan to the rise and fall of the Jewish kingdom and the series of prophets who followed. The Prophets expand on the importance of Jewish moral and ethical conduct. Kings, leaders, and people who obey God's dictates in their daily lives are rewarded, and those who stray are condemned. "I hate, I despise your feasts, and I take no delight in your solemn assemblies," Yahweh states in Amos (5:21-24). "But let justice roll down like waters, and righteousness like an ever-flowing stream." Obedience to God's dictates is rewarded and deviations are punished.

The third section, known as the Writings, includes the book of Psalms, Proverbs, Job, Song of Solomon, Ruth, Chronicles, and several other books. It takes a different, more humanistic and contemplative approach to the same issues confronting Judaism. The stories reflect the daily contradictions a person faces in trying to lead a faithful life. The story of Job, for example, confronts the paradox of how a good person often suffers in life while a wicked person appears to prosper. Job is an extremely pious and faithful follower of Yahweh but loses his home, family, and health. Others determine that Job must be a sinner, and Job declares that Yahweh is in fact

and Buddhism, which subscribe to asceticism, the Jewish God seeks his followers to live a life of reverence and piety in which they elevate their actions to the highest standards that reflect their divine image.

A Jew is free to choose what actions he or she takes, but God holds the person accountable for the course that is chosen. The Jewish people were not simply chosen by God, they were the only ones to accept the conditions that God set forth to them in the Torah. God's acceptance of Israel, therefore, does not come out of some arbitrary favoritism, but rather through the

unjust. The message of the story is that true faith does not require material success because God's rule is incomprehensible to humans.

Similarly, the Book of Ecclesiastes faces the always perplexing issue of the meaning of life. In Ecclesiastes 1:2–4 the king of Jerusalem, Koheleth, proclaims: "Utter futility! Utter futility! All is futile. What real value is there for a man in all the gains he makes beneath the sun? One generation goes, another comes, but the earth remains the same forever." No matter what a person does in life, whether he is prosperous or poor, wicked or good, generous or selfish, death is the common fate of all. By confronting questions such as this, the text challenges the long-held tradition that God controls everything. The answer, according to other texts in the Writings, lies in the pursuit of knowledge and wisdom. "Happy is the man who finds wisdom, the man who attains understanding. Her value in trade is better than silver, her yield, greater than gold," states Proverbs 3. The quest for knowledge described in the Bible is often credited with the traditional Jewish love of learning. To this day, Jews have higher education levels than their contemporaries throughout the world.

After the Bible, the next most important writings for Judaism are the Talmud, a collection of commentaries and traditions, and the Midrash, a series of interpretations of scripture. The two are often considered as recordings of the oral version of the written Bible. Both these collections are studied in Judaism to supplement the knowledge imparted in the Bible. A series of other noncanonical writings were written during the two centuries bracketing the life of Jesus Christ. These materials included histories, psalms, philosophical treatises, and apocalyptic literature describing catastrophic wars, the coming of the Messiah, the resurrection of the dead, and a final judgment of all humanity. These works were an important influence in both Judaism and Christianity, but they eventually fell out of favor.

Sects

Throughout the centuries Judaism has encompassed many different interpretations of its religion. At the time of Jesus Christ, several different sects existed. During the Diaspora, as Jewish groups became scattered and isolated throughout the Western world, various versions of Judaism evolved, including the Sephardism of the Iberian Peninsula, Ashkenazic Jews in eastern Europe, Arabic-speaking Jews in the Middle East, and distinct groups in the Caucasus region of the former Soviet Union, India, and elsewhere.

In the United States there are four main variations of Judaism. Orthodox Jews strive to adhere as closely as possible to biblical laws. This includes eating only kosher food, observing the Sabbath, and having the sexes sit in separate areas in the synagogue. Conservative Jews are not as strict in their adherence to biblical regulations. Synagogue services are held in English as well as in Hebrew. They apply a more objective approach to the study of the Bible. Reform Judaism applies a much less rigorous application of biblical Jewish duties and hold services on Friday nights. Men and women may sit together and do not have to cover their heads. Mordecai Kaplan founded Reconstruction Judaism, a recent movement in the United States that views Judaism not simply as a religion but as a unique culture that encompasses art, music, literature, and other nonreligious aspects of Jewish history.

Jewish communities elsewhere, such as in China, India, Yemen, Asian Russia, and Ethiopia, have practiced forms of Judaism that include ceremonies and observances that date back to ancient times.

Religious Observances and Festivals

A major ritual is the *bris,* the circumcision of male babies. This is an external symbol of a Jew's commitment to Judaism. Boys, and more recently girls in Reform congregations, fulfill a religious obligation when they are thirteen through the bar mitzvah (or bat mitzvah for girls) in which they are recognized as adults responsible for fulfilling the obligations of Judaism. Jewish marriage vows are made under a canopy, representing the bride and groom's home, and are concluded by the couple sharing wine as a representation of their common destiny. Although mixed marriages are permitted, Jewish men are strongly encouraged to marry Jewish women as in Jewish tradition a child takes his or her faith from the mother. When a Jewish person dies there is minimal ritual save for a seven-day mourning period called *shiva*, during which the bereaved remain at home and hold daily services.

The Sabbath, or day of rest, is observed from sundown on Friday evening to dusk the following day. Depending on the Jewish group, restrictions are placed on what a person can do during the Sabbath. Synagogue services are held on the Sabbath. The two most important holy days are Rosh Hashanah, celebrating the New Year each fall with ten days of penitence, and Yom Kippur, meaning Day of Atonement, held at the end of the ten-day period. Yom Kippur involves a day of praying and fasting that includes confessing all of a person's sins and shortcomings and seeking forgiveness. Yom Kippur is followed by Sukkot, a traditional harvest festival of thanksgiving. Hanukkah, a secular festival, is celebrated during twelve days in December to commemorate Judas Maccabaeus's battle of liberation in 165 B.C.E. Passover is a major eight-day festival held in early spring to mark the anniversary of the flight from Egypt under Moses.

Cohn-Sherbok, Dan. (1992) *The Blackwell Dictionary of Judaica.*

Werblowsky, R. J. Zwi, and Geoffrey Wigoder, eds. (1986) *The Encyclopedia of the Jewish Religion.* Rev. ed.

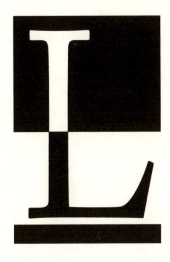

public recognition. In most cultures, each of these stages—and especially the incorporation stage—for all types of life-cycle rites are marked by religious activity. While religious activity is often an important element of these rites, it is important to remember that they are not simply religious observances that are quickly forgotten once the ceremony is over and the participants have departed. Rather, they are often events for the family and the community and serve significant social, political, and economic functions. A number of different life-cycle rites are discussed below, with examples of their variations across cultures provided. First, however, the life-cycle rites celebrated in two cultures—the Zuni of New Mexico and the Berbers of Morocco—are summarized to give a broad view of the flow and cultural context of these rites, which are typical of such rites in many other cultures.

The Zuni are a Native American agricultural people of central New Mexico who live mainly in one village and subsist primarily through the growing of corn and raising of livestock, activities supplemented in recent years by employment as wage laborers and production of art for the tourist and collector's trade. Zuni life-cycle rituals are relatively few and austere, save for the initiation process for boys, which lasts several years. Zuni life-cycle rites and rituals begin during pregnancy, when the expectant parents alter their behavior to protect their unborn child. Believing that "like causes like" the expectant parents avoid death—mothers avoid looking at dead bodies and fathers stop hunting. Additionally, ritual activity may be used to influence the birth—pregnant women stop cooking foods that might produce twins, which are considered bad luck; if a male child is preferred, a boy is made to attend the birth because his presence might help produce a son. After a boy is born, he is touched by a woman from his father's clan, thereby making him a member of that group. Magical beliefs and the sexual division of labor determine the disposal of the

In nearly all cultures, birth, marriage, and death are marked by ritual observances that include not just the individual who has been born, been wed, or died but also members of his or her family and the community. In addition, in many cultures other significant transitions in the individual life cycle such as becoming an adult or reaching the age of religious maturity are also marked by rituals. As a group, these types of rites are called rites of passage, rites of intensification, or crisis rites.

While there is much cross-cultural variation in how these rites are carried out, all involve the individual passing through the stages of separation, transition, and incorporation. In the separation stage the individual is removed from one social environment—at birth from the womb, at marriage from the natal home, and at death from the natural world. During the transition stage, the individual enters the new life stage and learns the behaviors now expected of him or her. And in the incorporation stage the new social role and status of the individual is given

umbilical cord: "that of a girl is buried under a grinding stone, where she must spend many hours grinding corn as a mature woman; that of a boy is buried in the corn field, where he must till the crops." (Leighton and Adair 1966: 61) On the eighth day after the birth, the infant is taken outside, corn meal placed in its hand, and the women in attendance enter into prayer:

> In your thoughts (may we live)
> May we be the ones whom your thoughts
> will embrace
> For this, on this day
> To our sun Father.
> We offer prayer meal,
> To this end:
> May you help us all to finish our roads.
> (Ibid.)

Zuni fear of witches is manifested in their child-rearing practices and various magical means used to protect infants—from birth an ear of corn is kept next to the infant, turquoise and flint are placed in cradles, and charcoal is rubbed on an infant's chest so witches cannot see his heart.

At age six for some boys and perhaps as late as ten or eleven for others, initiation into the Kachina society (religious society) begins. The first initiation rite is a week-long process involving the entire village and takes place once every four years. Each boy is assigned a ritual father, women prepare food, ritual specialists pray, and the boys are ritually whipped in public by masked dancers. The boys are then isolated in the *kiva* (underground ceremonial chamber) for four days, where they fast and are instructed in the ways of the Kachina society. Upon emerging, they are ritually bathed in yucca suds to purify them. This stage of the rite is meant to provide the boys with a religious identity, the whipping is meant to purify them, and not as punishment. Several years later, they go though the final stage of the initiation process with the key element being another whipping. The initiates are then allowed to whip some of those who had whipped

them and to dance with the masked dancers; this right makes them full members of the religious community.

Zuni marriages are made with little ritual, perhaps because they are brittle and divorce is common. If the couple decides to marry after a courtship, the boy gains the girl's father's permission and sits through a lecture on correct behavior; the couple then begins sleeping together. An exchange of small gifts between the families completes the process.

As with birth, death rites reflect concern about the evil work of witches and, in fact, all death is attributed to witchcraft. Zuni death rites also reflect beliefs in the afterlife and the continuing role of the deceased in the lives of the living. The body is dressed for burial and adorned with jewelry so that the spirits can dress well when they return to earth. Corn meal is sprinkled in the house, with black meal spread with the left hand to ward off evil. The body is then buried in the cemetery, with the head facing east so that it can view the Kachina Village to the west. All of this, however, does not end the fear of witches, and they are commonly believed to tunnel under the grave to steal the jewelry.

The Berbers are the indigenous people of North Africa, who now number several million and are Muslims. The following information pertains to the Berbers of the agricultural community of Aith Waryaghar in Morocco. The major Berber life-cycle rites center on birth, naming the infant, circumcision of boys, marriage, and death. Berber birth rites mirror the same concerns shaping Zuni rites—protecting the child from evil and influencing subsequent births. Immediately after the birth the placenta is buried to keep it away from dogs whose eating it will cause the mother to become infertile, a boar's tusk necklace is placed around the infant's neck to ward off the evil eye, and salt on a knife is placed beside the bed to ward off evil spirits. For seven days the mother and infant are secluded to keep them away from these evil dangers. The arrival of twins is considered lucky, and the seclusion period is extended to sixty days, as the fear of harm increases. The birth is marked for the community by the father, who sacrifices a hen if it is a boy and a rooster if it is a girl. Boys are preferred and girls are prohibited from chewing squash seeds as Berbers believe this will cause them to have only female children. After a birth, the midwife cuts the umbilical cord of a female infant with a sickle to make sure the next child will be a boy.

The first major rite in a Berber's life is the naming ceremony after seven days. The father chooses the name and all relatives gather for a two-day ceremony that opens with the sacrifice of a sheep or goat and prayer and is followed by feasting, shooting off of firecrackers or rifles, and the placement of a red flag on the roof to announce the naming of a boy. Naming ceremonies for girls are less elaborate and rarely last the full two days.

Although not required by Islam, all Berber boys are circumcised between the ages of three months and four years. The operation is performed by a barber who specializes in circumcisions and the boy is brought to the barber and attended to by his father. Women are never present, although they give the child money after the rite and rejoice at its successful completion. For the Berbers, circumcision is a marker of male identity and perpetuation of the male line, and fathers view their circumcised sons with much pride. At the father's choosing, it may or may not be celebrated by a family feast.

Marriage is the major life-cycle ritual for the Berbers. It begins with the arrangement of the marriage itself, with the mothers of the young man and woman first discussing the matter informally and then the father of the man visiting the father of the woman in a series of visits to arrange the marriage, agree on the amount of brideprice to be paid to the bride's family, and

then the drawing up of the marriage document according to Islamic law. This ends the Islamic, social, legal, and economic requirements and the three-day marriage ritual (*dhamghra*) begins. Marriages are usually held in the early fall after the harvest is in and for several months are the main social and ritual activities for neighboring communities as people go from marriage ceremony to ceremony. The rituals cover five days as follows:

Day One ("little henna")

- The groom's father and his unmarried sister bring food to the home of the bride. They dine with the bride's father and unmarried sisters, who sing and dance.
- An unmarried sister of the groom rubs henna on the palms of the groom and an unmarried sister of the bride rubs henna on the palms and feet of the bride.
- The groom consults a religious specialist at the mosque who writes a charm that will help him perform on the marriage night.
- The groom spends his time with other men, who engage in ritualized chanting and prayer.

Day Two ("big henna")

- Henna is applied to the groom and bride as on the first day.
- The groom's wedding party returns home.
- Both families continue to feast at their homes, with their relatives and friends.
- The groom spends his time with other men, who engage in ritualized chanting and prayer.

Day Three

- The marriage document is signed and legalized if this has not already been done.
- The musicians arrive at the groom's house.

- Relatives and friends of the groom arrive at the groom's house for the ceremony and all give small monetary gifts to the groom's father to help pay for the wedding.

- The bride dresses in special ceremonial dress, including an arc of twined grapevine on her head, and is veiled.

- The groom's father sends a mule to the bride's house.

- The bride's unmarried sisters and friends dress in ceremonial costumes and dance in the courtyard.

- The bridal party departs for the groom's house. The party includes the bride, her brothers, her unmarried sisters, and friends. Her parents remain at home and do not attend the feast at the groom's house.

- The bridal party arrives at the groom's house where they are greeted by the groom's mother, who offers a mix of wheat and sugar, which the bride throws in three directions.

- The bride's brother carries her to a room in the house, where she waits for the groom.

- Unmarried women enter the room with the hope of increasing their chances of marrying soon.

- The groom enters the room and the bride and groom go through an elaborate ritual of removing her veil and grapevine arc.

- The groom leaves the room and is greeted and beaten by his friends.

- The bride is attended by her friends and now puts on the clothes and wears the braids of a married woman.

- The groom sits silently while his friends dance, conduct rituals, and contribute money to help pay for the wedding.

- From the afternoon of Day Three until 10 or 11 A.M. of the next day the guests talk, dance, and sing.

Day Four

- After all the guests depart the groom enters the bride's room and pays her attendants, who then leave.

- The groom's mother cooks the couple breakfast and then leaves.

- The couple spend the day together and then during the night have sexual intercourse.

Day Five

- The next morning a female relative of the groom displays to all who want to see the bloody, white cloth proving that the bride was a virgin and the groom leaves the house to be congratulated. If the bride was not a virgin the groom will most likely send her back to her father and demand repayment of the entire brideprice.

Berber death rites adhere more closely to Islamic rules than do birth and marriage rites, which reflect pre-Islamic beliefs and practices. An individual is buried in a shroud shortly after he or she dies—usually the same day if practically possible. The washing of the body, placement in the shroud, transport to the cemetery, digging of the grave, and position of the body are all attended to with much concern for the proper procedure and ritual behavior. The body is always buried with the face toward Mecca. The burial, attended only by men, is followed by food and prayer at the home of the deceased. For a widow, other ritual acts are required at three days and forty days after the death and perhaps a final one sometime later in the year.

The Berber and Zuni life-cycle rites both point to a central feature of all types of rites in most cultures—rites tend to be most elaborate when they are of significance for the entire family or entire community, not just for the individuals involved. For the Zuni, the male initiation rights are most important because of their role in making boys into men and in perpetuating the Zuni way of life. For the Berbers it is the marriage rite that is the most significant, because marriage unites families and villages, involves substantial transfer of wealth in the form of the brideprice payments and the cost of the rite, and concerns the public display of family honor in the requirement that the bride be a virgin.

Birth and Childhood Rites

In all cultures, birth is a significant event for the parents, the family, and the community. Thus, it is not at all surprising that in all cultures attempts are made to control pregnancy and birth through ritual activity. The purpose of the rites is to ensure that the newborn is healthy, to protect it from harm, and in some cultures to encourage some types of births, such as that of boys and to prevent others, such as that of twins. Also associated with birth are rites for activities that provide the child with a social identity, such as naming, baptism, circumcision, and its first haircut. Birth rites or ritual activities associated with birth often begin before the actual birth and take the form of taboos that restrict the activities of the pregnant woman. In most cultures women are required to refrain from certain activities, to behave in certain ways, and to eat certain foods and avoid others. Additionally, in many though not all cultures, women are expected to end sexual activities at some point during pregnancy. These restrictions or prescribed behaviors are not rites but rather magical attempts to influence the pregnancy in desirable ways. Across cultures, they are engaged in by millions of women, their husbands, and other family members every day.

Birth itself in most cultures is accompanied by magic and ritual usually meant to protect the infant and the mother and to help it enjoy a healthy and productive life. Among the Zuni and Berbers, magic and ritual is used to protect the infant from harm caused by others—witches, evil eye, and malevolent spirits. In some cultures the primary concern is the loss of the infant's soul and the illness or death that might result. In some cultures, such as the Aranda in Australia, the soul of the infant is thought to be not yet firmly fixed and thus must be protected from harm. Among the Tzeltal of Guatemala the concern is a spirit stealing the soul, so a ritual is performed as early as possible to join the soul to the infant's physical being.

Naming—sometimes accompanied by a naming ritual—is a common social feature of the birth process across cultures. In 60 percent of cultures, children are named within the first nine days after birth and in most states in the United States, infants must be named within seven days. In those cultures where naming is delayed it is usually because parents want to wait to make sure the infant survives or because they fear evil forces and thus conceal the infant's arrival by not identifying it with a name or perhaps mis-naming it. For example, the Central Thai name their infants within a few days of birth, but do not call them by their given names, instead using terms of endearment such as "mouse," "red," "fatty," and so on. These names are used to confuse evil spirits who will not try to eat the children if they think they are animals. Although all children are named, only in 53 percent of cultures is a formal naming ritual used. For example, the Dogon of Mali consider naming a matter of considerable community importance and the ceremony is conducted with all members of the kinship group in attendance. It is the responsibility of the senior man in the group to assign names and he often names infants after himself, with the designations, the first, second, third, and so on. At the other extreme are cultures like the Central Thai, where naming is done by the parents, grandparents, or godparents, perhaps with advice from an astrologer but without ritual or ceremony. Unlike the Dogon, names are not important to the Central Thai, and a

דע לפני מי אתה עומד

Many cultures have ritual observances to mark significant life-cycle moments such as births, deaths, marriages, and coming of age. Judaism marks a boy's thirteenth birthday with a bar mitzvah, which recognizes that he is now able to be a responsible member of the religious community. Stephen Bernstein's bar mitzvah, held in Frankfurt, West Germany, in January 1947, was perhaps the first to be held in a defeated Nazi Germany following the end of World War II.

child's name might be changed when it becomes ill or when it is registered with the government. And, as noted above, the Central Thai use nicknames, not given names, for children up to the age of fifteen. In some cultures, the naming customs may be established by religious authorities. For example, Jews customarily name children after a deceased but not a living ancestor and Roman Catholics are expected to pick

names from a list of saints approved of by the Church. As with other life-cycle rituals, naming rituals are found in cultures where the community, not just the individual or family, is involved in the naming process.

In some cultures rites are used to mark development stages in the child's life. These rites often involve changing the child's physical appearance through body piercing and, more commonly, through the first cutting of the child's hair. The Central Thai pierce girls' ears when they are one week old and at one month of age all infants have their hair cut for the first time in the *konphomfaj* (hair shaving ritual):

> It is believed that the hair with which all children are born ... has been contaminated by fluids at birth. Once shaven, the child is purified and can begin life with a fresh start. Anyone, except the parents, is eligible to do the shaving. An astrologer chooses the auspicious day and the hour for the ceremony. One, three, or five monks are invited to recite the *chajamonkonkhatha* blessing on the eve of the auspicious day. On the following morning, the monks are invited for an early breakfast. After the shaving, the relatives may present the parents with small gifts of money, cloth, and bracelets. A bracelet is put on the child's wrist. . . . Another holy string is attached from the wrist or bracelet to the Buddha on the altar. The monks hold the string and recite a chant which blesses the child and wishes it good health and prosperity. (Kaufman 1960: 145)

For the Santal of India, the first haircut is also associated with ritual pollution but is part of a much more complex rite involving haircutting, naming, and the preparation of various potions and their application to the house and village where the child was born in order to clean them ritually so that members of the community can again pray there.

In rural Taiwan, the first haircut and a second ritual bath are at twelve days: "In the water are placed two eggs and a stone, to make the baby's face 'as pretty as an eggshell' and his head 'hard as stone,' which means, in this context, wise." (Diamond 1969: 31)

For the Aymara of Bolivia, the haircut ceremony is performed apart from the Roman Catholic rite of baptism, with both enmeshed in the *compadrazgo* (patron-client) system that creates important and life-long social, political,

and economic bonds between the child and the godparents and the parents and godparents. At the haircutting rite, the godparents are expected to host a feast in their home and provide all the food, drink, and music and new clothes for the child.

In some cultures there are other rites used during infancy and childhood that focus on the individual's religious and social identity. These rites often take place in sequence over a period of years, with the first rite marking membership in the religious community followed by a period of several years during which the child is educated in religious belief and practice and then a final public rite in which the child becomes a full member of the community. The final rite often requires that the child engage in behaviors allowed only to full members of the religious community. For the Zuni discussed above and other Pueblo groups in the Southwest, the male initiation rite is of this type as the boy progresses through the three stages and becomes a member of the religious society. Although there are variations across denominations in Christianity, the pattern is found in the sequence of baptism, religious education, and then confirmation, as indicated by the Highland Scots (Parman 1972: 166):

> Most children are sent to Sunday school, and all are baptized. In baptism, fathers stand with the children, promise to raise them in the church, and set a good example for them. Baptism must precede Communion, the ceremony by which a person becomes a full member of the church. Baptism signifies membership in the community, the village qua-congregation. "Somehow you're not really legal until you've been baptized." Some feel that the child's soul may be endangered if he should die without baptism, although this idea is discouraged by the church.

In many cultures whose religion has been influenced by the Roman Catholicism brought to the New World by the Spanish, baptism is also the occasion for the establishment of the compadrazgo relationship. Compadrazgo involves the godparent-godchild relationship as well as the co-parent relationship between the godparents and parents. As in Spain and elsewhere, godparents are a backup set of parents who will assist in the religious education, look after the child's welfare, and adopt the child if the parents die. The co-parent relationship is one of reciprocal respect and obligation and requires a certain degree of formality as well as the performance of certain obligations, such as attending family ceremonies and paying for the funeral when the other dies. The co-parent also can play an important social, political, and economic function as a family can increase its social standing by retaining a godparent from a higher social class and a godparent can build a political network by having many godchildren and co-parent relationships.

Initiation Rites

Initiation rites are ceremonies that mark the transition from childhood or adolescence to adulthood. Initiation ceremonies occur in about 55 percent of cultures. Some cultures have rites only for boys, others only for girls, and others for both. Rites for girls are more common, although rites for boys are more elaborate and dramatic and more often take the form of community rites. While rites vary in many details across cultures, there are also a number of commonalities:

1. respected elders in the community officiate;
2. parents play no role in the initiation of their children;
3. one phase of the rite involves education and training in cultural rules and in tasks associated with either men or women;
4. all those of the appropriate age must complete the rite;

5. the rite is a group event and the focus is the group of initiates, not any single initiate;
6. rites are same-sex only and the opposite sex is barred from participating in and observing many aspects of the rite.

In addition, in 65 percent of cultures the rites include activities that cause physical pain to the initiates, such as circumcision, clitoridectomy, scarification, whipping, fasting, sleep deprivation, isolation, cold baths, body piercing, and tooth extraction.

As with life-cycle rites in general, initiation rites across cultures follow the pattern of separation, transition, and incorporation. Typically, the initiate leaves his parents' home and lives with the other initiates, either in a ceremonial structure or in a location away from the village. During the transition period in some cultures, as with the Zuni described above, the initiate is instructed in the ways of being an adult by the elders and participates in various rituals. In many cultures the exact content and nature of the education and rituals are kept secret. In other cultures the initiate engages in adult activities to prove that he is now an adult. For example, Jivaro boys in Ecuador at age sixteen go into the forest, kill a tree sloth, and shrink its head. Two ceremonies are held marking his new status as an adult and he may then wear the headpiece of men and marry. Initiation into the community as an adult takes place in a community ritual. In many cultures initiation means that the individual's status has changed in a few days or weeks from that of child to that of adult and that they may now marry, have children, hunt, and participate in ceremonies.

In some cultures the central event of the boy's initiation is circumcision, although not all cultures practice circumcision and in some like the Berbers it is performed earlier in life as a separate ceremony. In the Sudan, a Teda boy ready for circumcision picks a married couple to serve as his sponsors. The circumcision takes place outside a special hut and is attended by the male sponsor, who performs the operation, other men, and uncircumcised boys. After the procedure the group returns to the hut, the boys play music, and the boy's father visits, telling him "Fortunately you are a man now." After seven days of seclusion and more ceremonies in the hut, the boy emerges to be greeted by his female sponsor who proclaims: "There is a man, there is a man." A feast is then held in his honor and he is given gifts, after which he returns to the hut for three more days of rest and then another seven days of healing at home. He is then a man and can kill animals and have sexual intercourse with women.

Initiation ceremonies for girls are usually associated with the first menstruation and often involve the girls being secluded for the duration of their period or longer and being required to restrict their normal activities in various ways. The Chippewa in the Great Lakes region typically secluded girls for four to ten days in special wigwams in the woods built by the girl, her mother, and her grandmother. The girl was considered ritually polluting and was forbidden from coming into contact with men, eating food in season, or touching a baby. While secluded she sewed and gathered firewood, two activities she would regularly engage in as a woman, and was instructed by her mother. When the seclusion ended she bathed, washed her clothes, and was honored at a feast marking her new status.

In some cultures in Africa, female initiation ceremonies center on the mutilation of the female genitals, although, as with circumcision, in some cultures the mutilation takes place much earlier in life apart from any ceremony. These operations have become highly controversial and are very likely on the decline in many cultures.

Related to initiation rites are the vision quests that adolescents venture on in some cultures, especially American Indian groups in North America. These quests, however, are not always associated with a change in social status and their main purpose is for the boy or girl to acquire a guardian spirit who will protect and help him or her for the rest of their life.

Social scientists have devoted much attention to explaining the presence of initiation rites in some societies and their absence in others. Explanations of other major rites such as birth and marriage rites have drawn less scholarly attention, as they are found in nearly all societies, making it impossible to compare societies where they occur with those where they are absent. Explanations for female rites, which often center on menstruation, point to the role in women in society, their relative status vis-à-vis men, and the notion in some societies that women are polluting, especially while menstruating. To some extent, female rites and especially rites where girls are caused pain seem more common in cultures where the power of women is low and where men fear that they will become ritually polluted through contact with menstruating women. Painful initiation rites, for both girls and boys, are part of a more general cultural pattern that favors the use of physical violence in many types of relationships. Painful initiation ceremonies for boys, including circumcision, have generally been explained as a sociocultural mechanism used to inculcate masculine personality traits and behavior in boys who, because of close contact with their mothers and limited contact with their fathers, have grown up with the female identity. The Zuni rites described above fit this model as boys spend much time with their mothers and other women until the completion of the initiation rite, when more time is spent with men. Puberty rites may also serve to teach boys to be compliant in cultures where boyhood aggression is uncontrolled. These explanations assume that the dramatic and traumatic rites and community involvement will reverse boyish behavior that is not considered appropriate for men. An alternative explanation suggests that such rites have less to do with altering unacceptable behavior and are instead motivated by a desire to create solidarity among men and are therefore found in societies where men must work closely together. Again, the Zuni fit this pattern as men must cooperate as members of the Kachina societies, in agricultural work, and as members of the community.

Marriage Rites

Marriage is a cultural universal and marriage rites a near universal, as there are only a few cultures where a simple announcement that the couple has married is all that is required for the marriage to be recognized as legal. Although not all ceremonies are religious, in most cultures religion plays a role and prayers, sacrifices, offerings, and magical practices are common features of most ceremonies. Even in societies such as the United States where a religious rite is not legally required, such rites are nonetheless the norm. In the United States, 80 percent of couples are married in religious ceremonies and many justices of the peace or other officials who perform nonreligious marriage ceremonies often incorporate religious elements such as blessings or readings from the Bible into the ceremony. Marriage ceremonies are common across cultures for four major reasons:

1. the presence of family and friends provides emotional support for the bride and groom at a major transitional point in their life;
2. the rite gives public recognition to the marriage and the new status of the individuals as adults in the community (in cultures where marriage is not considered a marker of adult status, marriage rites tend to be minimal);
3. the support and financial investment of their families indicate interest in the couple producing children;
4. rites mark the importance attached to the often substantial wealth exchanged

between families at the marriage of their children.

Marriage rites among the Zuni and Berbers described above are examples of the two extremes that such rites take across cultures. Although the couple engages in ritualized courting behavior, the Zuni marry without formal, public ceremonies. For the Berbers, marriage is marked by an elaborate, expensive, extended ceremony that involves the entire community. Across cultures, marriage ceremonies tend to be more elaborate when considerable amounts of property are exchanged at marriage, as is the case with the Berbers. Berber marriage takes place only when the fathers of the bride and groom agree to a brideprice to be paid by the groom's father to the bride's father. While the Berber ceremony is elaborate, in other cultures ceremonies are even more elaborate. Among the Kwakiutl of Alaska, the traditional rites began a year before the actual ceremony for the marriage of a chief's daughter. During this year the suitor might give the girl's father as many as two hundred woven blankets to ensure that the girl was not promised to another man. The ceremony itself was attended by all the members of the groom's and bride's tribes, who joined together at the girl's village. The chief of each tribe made a speech and the groom's family presented as many as one thousand additional blankets to the bride's father. As each blanket was counted, the leader of the bride's family said "walk with this" to remind the groom that he was walking into their community to take a daughter in return for the blankets. The following day some blankets were returned to the groom who gave them to the bride's kin at an elaborate celebration. The women were then invited to a feast given by the groom's brother's wife and the bride and groom ate together for the first time.

In addition to brideprice, as among the Kwakiutl and Berbers where the groom's family pays the bride's family, wealth can be transferred at marriage through dowry, where the wife brings wealth with her or through the exchange of gifts or gift-giving.

In some cultures, the marriage partners come from different villages or kinship groups that are often hostile to one another. In these situations, the marriage ceremony might include some sort of ritualized mechanism for the open expression of hostility between the groups. For example, the Pukupuka of Oceania have insult contests in which the two kin groups hurl insults at each other and the bride and groom, and Hopi women from the bride's and groom's families insult each other and smear each other with mud.

Death Rites

As with all types of life-cycle rites, death rites involve transitions in status for the individual who has died, his or her family, and members of the community. For the deceased, the rite in nearly all cultures involves movement from the world of the living to the world of the dead. Toward this end rituals are followed carefully to ensure that the deceased reaches and enjoys a happy existence in the world of the dead. The motivation for ensuring the well-being of the deceased is two-fold. First, it reflects real concern for the soul of the deceased. Second, it reflects in many societies a belief that spirits of the dead can influence the living and that if the spirits fail to reach the afterworld or are unhappy there, they will make life unpleasant for their descendants on earth. For some of the survivors, the rite often involves a transition in their social roles and statuses in the family and the community: a son may now become head of the family, a daughter the head of the household, a wife a widow who must marry her deceased husband's brother. A member of the village council may now become the community leader, the heads of the village kin groups may now compete for village leadership, and the kin group may have to decide on the disposition of the property of

the deceased. In some cultures, however, the line between the world of the living and the dead is blurred; after death the deceased is defined as an ancestor who continues to influence the lives of his living descendants. In these cultures, such as China and Korea where ancestor worship is an important aspect of traditional religion, funeral rites include additional rituals designed to make the deceased an ancestor. These rites are often spread over one or more years and the position of the grave and the body in it are important considerations. All of this ritual activity is meant to smooth subsequent relations between the deceased ancestor and his living descendants. And, of course, ritual worship of ancestors continues in the home and community as a regular activity.

Across cultures, death rites serve a number of functions:

1. disposal of the body and other physical objects associated with the deceased;
2. provision of material and emotional support to the survivors;
3. public announcement of the death;
4. public recognition of the new status of some of the survivors;
5. rule setting for the appropriate mourning behavior and period of mourning;
6. renewal of ties among family and community members;
7. affirmation that the family and community will survive despite the death of one of its members.

Perhaps the two most striking features of death rites across cultures are that (1) in nearly all cultures substantial numbers of people attend the rites, and (2) in 75 percent of cultures it is customary to have a final funeral rite that occurs at some time after the first rite. In some cultures the final rite takes place later in the year as part of a community rite for all those who died in

the previous year, in other cultures there is a series of rites culminating in a final rite, and in
others there are two rites with the second ending the formal mourning period.

While there is much variation across cultures in the details of death rites, there is also
some commonality as the body is always disposed
of in some way, the immediate family is always
involved in the rite, the supernatural is invoked,
there is community involvement, a religious specialist conducts the rites, rituals are followed
carefully, there is a defined mourning period, and
there is considerable individual variation permitted in mourning behavior.

Death rites among the Chippewa of the
Great Lakes region display many of the general
features of death rites across cultures. Immediately after death the body was washed, dressed
in fine clothing, and adorned with beads, with
the hair braided. His or her face, moccasins, and
blanket were painted in brown and red designs
to assist him or her in joining the "dance of the
ghosts where the northern lights are shining."
The body was laid out and buried with a few
objects of personal value and other objects that
would be needed on the four-day journey of the
soul to the hereafter:

> My father was buried with his jackknife and
> pipe, the Grand Medicine Man who bur-
> ied him requesting this and saying that his
> soul might crave those articles and not leave
> at once for the Hereafter.

The death rites were conducted by members of
the deceased's Medicine Society, who comforted
the family and spoke to the spirit of the deceased,
advising it on how to have a safe trip to the hereafter. Communication with the spirit often began with a statement such as "Your feet are now
on the road of souls. . . ." The body was then
wrapped in birch bark or placed in a wood coffin and set in a shallow grave. Relatives danced
around the grave and it was then filled, with food

placed on it and a fire kept burning for four
nights. The fire was to assist the spirit in keeping warm and cooking food; additional food
placed on the grave was allowed to be taken by
the poor, relatives, and friends for their own consumption. The body was generally placed with
the feet to the west, the direction of the soul's
journey. The grave was then covered with bark,
cloth, or a small shelter and food placed there
periodically, including the first harvests of maple
sap and berries. A clan totem was placed on the
grave upside down as a marker of both death
and the deceased's clan identity.

While certain ritual behavior was required
of all mourners, there was much freedom for
individuals to express their personal grief: some
cut themselves, others wailed loudly, and others
wailed not at all. Widows and others who chose
to do so publicly displayed their status as mourners for one year by wearing old clothing, cutting
their hair short or wearing it unbraided, and
painting their face black. Once a year a ceremony
of "restoring the mourners" was held and those
in mourning were comforted and given gifts and
brightly colored objects, terminating the mourning period. Close relatives might also elect to
keep a "spirit bundle" of the deceased, which at
its center contained a lock of hair cut from the
deceased wrapped in birch bark to which other
objects such as blankets, moccasins, and beads
might be added over the course of the year. Such
bundles were more often kept by women for a
deceased child or husband. They were un-
wrapped one year after the death at a feast and
the core of hair and birchbark wrapping buried
next to the grave of the deceased.

See also ANCESTOR WORSHIP; FESTIVALS; MAGIC;
TABOO

Alford, Richard D. (1988) *Naming and Identity:
A Cross-Cultural Study of Personal Naming
Practices.*

Barry, Herbert III, and Alice Schlegal, eds. (1980) *Cross-Cultural Samples and Codes.*

Broude, Gwen J. (1994) *Marriage, Family, and Relationships: A Cross-Cultural Encyclopedia.*

———. (1995) *Growing Up: A Cross-Cultural Encyclopedia.*

Buechler, Hans C., and Judith M. Buechler. (1971) *The Bolivian Aymara.*

Child, Alice B., and Irvin L. Child. (1993) *Religion and Magic in the Life of Traditional Peoples.*

Densmore, Frances. (1929) *Chippewa Customs.*

Diamond, Norma J. (1969) *K'un Shen: A Taiwan Village.*

Cohen, Yehudi A. (1964) *The Transition from Childhood to Adolescence: Cross-Cultural Studies of Initiation Ceremonies, Legal Systems, and Incest Taboos.*

Gennep, Arnold Van. (1960 [1909]) *The Rites of Passage.*

Hart, David M. (1976) *The Aith Waryaghar of the Moroccan Rif.*

Kaufman, Howard. (1960) *Bangkhuad: A Community Study in Thailand.*

Leighton, Dorothea C., and John Adair. (1966) *People of the Middle Place.*

Levinson, David. (1989) *Family Violence in Cross-Cultural Perspective.*

Levinson, David, and Martin J. Malone. (1980) *Toward Explaining Human Culture.*

Levinson, David, and Marilyn Ihinger-Tallman. (1995) "Marriage Ceremonies." In *Encyclopedia of Marriage and the Family,* edited by David Levinson, 466–468.

Parman, Susan M. (1972) *Sociocultural Change in a Scottish Crofting Township.*

Paulme, Denise. (1940) *Social Organization of the Dogon (French Sudan).* Translated from the French for the Human Relations Area Files.

Rosenblatt, Paul C., R. Patricia Walsh, and Douglas A. Jackson. (1976) *Grief and Mourning in Cross-Cultural Perspective.*

Skrefsrud, Lars O. (1942) *Traditions and Institutions of the Santals: Hororen Mare Hapramko Reak' Katha.*

Although magic is universal, there is no general agreement among experts about how precisely to define it. In general magic refers to appeals to supernatural beings or forces in order to produce some earthly result desired by the person making the appeal. The basic function of magic is to provide individuals and groups with greater control of their social and natural environments. Thus, magic is most important in cultures, or in situations, or to individuals, who have little direct control over their environment. For example, Trobriand Islanders in Melanesia fish in lagoons and on the open sea. Lagoon fishing is safe and somewhat predictable, thus magic is not used to help produce a safe and productive outing. Ocean fishing in canoes is dangerous and uncertain, thus these trips are attended to with magical appeals for supernatural protection and assistance. Similarly, in many cultures magical rituals before going to war are designed to bring victory, magical acts accompanying the planting of crops are designed to bring a plentiful harvest, and the placement of magical objects near a loved one is designed to bring marriage. The use of magic for these and thousands of other purposes across cultures implies a cause-and-effect relationship. The person using magic believes that the supernatural can cause the effects he or she desires. However, this belief is rarely absolute, as people in all cultures know that factors other than supernatural ones also influence the outcome they desire. For example, farmers planting corn know that the temperature, soil conditions, amount of rain, condition of the seed, insect damage, and numerous other factors influence the success of their crop. The use of magic thus complements the human control of these other factors in assuring a rich harvest. This widespread view and use of magic is exemplified in the modern world by the behavior of professional athletes. While they are aware that it is their own skills and abilities relative to the skills and the abilities of their opponents that produce success or failure, many athletes routinely engage in magical rituals in order to gain divine support. These include the wearing of amulets and talismans, touching parts of their bodies in ritualized sequence, wearing the same piece of clothing during a winning streak, and so on. In common with individuals in many societies, these athletes engage in magical behavior not because they believe that the supernatural causes their success or failure but because they are looking for any possible assistance in dealing with uncertainty and difficulty.

Since the late 1800s, magic has been compared and contrasted with religion and science. The nineteenth-century theorists who wrote about magic in non-Western peoples considered it inferior to both religion and science as they then existed in Europe. Magic was labeled as traditional, prescientific, prelogical, and irrational and was seen by some evolutionary theorists as a precursor to first religion and then science as a system of thought that explains the universe. This view persists in modern society, where magic is often equated with superstition and viewed as apart from and inferior to organized religion. Still, the rites of all world religions involve magic and many adherents of world religions engage in magical behavior. However, magic in the Western world is no longer as important as it once was, although the revival of astrology in the twentieth century and the New Age movement suggests it has hardly faded entirely. Magic began to decline in Europe in the seventeenth century as rationality, science, industrialization, and democracy changed the basic nature of relations among people and between humans and the natural environment, providing humans with more control over their own lives. Thus, as daily uncertainty declined, magic became less important. However, magic often did not disappear entirely, and in many cultures adherence to a world religion is often accompanied by the survival of many traditional magical beliefs and practices. This pattern of magic and religion existing side-by-side is typical of many peoples who have been converted to Christianity, such as the Serbs in the former Yugoslavia. Most Serbs have been adherents of Serbian Orthodoxy, a branch of Eastern Orthodoxy, for centuries. Still, hundreds of years later, especially in rural communities, numerous traditional beliefs and practices survive, occasionally integrated into Serbian Orthodoxy, but more often separately. Many rural Serbs, for example, believe in *bajanje*, the exorcism of evil spirits; *vracanje*, the practice of divining the cause of illness; *lecenje*, the use of healing herbs; *caranje*, casting and removing spells; and *gatanje*, fortune-telling. They also assign special religious significance to certain caves, trees, and springs. However, these activities are usually engaged in by individuals acting outside the context of organized Orthodoxy and are considered separate from one's beliefs in God, salvation, mortal sin, and the various rites associated with Orthodoxy.

Although it is clear that magic is not religion and religion is not magic, it is nonetheless difficult to distinguish completely between the two, in part because all religions contain some magic. Efforts to distinguish between magic and religion focus on the following: (1) magic is based on the belief that supernatural beings are amenable to human influence, while in major religions supernatural beings are separate from and uninvolved in the daily lives of humans; (2) magic is purposeful in that individuals engage in magic to gain immediate benefits, whereas religion is concerned with larger issues and religious rituals are concerned with broader issues of faith and spirituality and the individual's place in the religion; (3) magic is individual, whereas religion is communal; (4) magic is concerned with relationship between humans and the natural environment, whereas religion is concerned with relations among humans. However, it is often impossible to sort out these distinctions in the actual religious practices found in many societies.

Magic is also compared with science and is considered to be different from science in three important ways. First, science is ultimately concerned with explaining the universe. Magic is less concerned with ultimate explanations than with producing immediate results. Second, science is considered to be rational, while magic is considered to be irrational, as evidenced by the fact that many people continue to engage in the same magical acts even in the face of much evidence that the magic often fails. Third, science is about verifiable truth, that is, science produces knowledge by submitting ideas to careful testing that is likely to prove them wrong if they are in fact wrong. Magic does not employ such testing or verification.

Magic takes a variety of forms across cultures, with distinctions between individual and group magic, magic carried out by anyone, and magic performed by ritual specialists such as shamans and sorcerers, white (beneficial) magic and black (harmful) magic, and contagious or imitative magic. Contagious magic is based on the idea that an objec, once in contact with another object, will continue to be spiritually tied to that object even after they are separated. The use of a person's hair or fingernails in healing rituals, divination, or casting of evil spells on that person are examples of contagious magic. Imitative magic is based on the idea that acting in ways similar to what is desired will produce the desired result. For example, dipping a sinner in water will wash away the sin.

Magic almost always involves the use of ritual—that is, the performance of a prescribed series of tasks. Performing the ritual in exactly the correct manner is often an essential requirement of magic, and when magic fails the practitioner may be accused of shoddy ritual performance. While rituals vary in their content and performance across cultures, there is also considerable similarity in the basic procedures used. Kapauku shamans in New Guinea use a variety of techniques and objects, all of which are found in other cultures as well:

1. plants with supernatural powers;
2. offerings of items thought to be desired by the supernatural;
3. manipulating fire;
4. applying water; and
5. prayer asking for aid.

Magic can be applied to any aspect of the human situation. However, across cultures a number of concerns are most often addressed by magic.

Love Magic
Love magic, or what may be better labeled relationship magic, refers to magic used to cause someone to fall in love with one, to ensure a partner's fidelity, to cause a reconciliation, or to punish an unfaithful partner or their lover. For example, Goajiro girls in Colombia wear a charm that will attract a wealthy man, Balinese men

seek to attract a woman by thinking about her and calling her name, Cuna husbands in Panama use a love potion to patch up a quarrel, and Aymara men and women use charms to drive off undesirable suitors. Love magic may serve some important practical purposes in the 80 percent of societies where it is practiced. First, these societies are mainly those in which sex is frowned upon and where people are often anxious to talk about sex or openly express sexual desires. Magic provides a way of dealing with this anxiety by dealing with sexual urges in an indirect manner. Second, people are often aware that another person is directing love magic at them, and thus it is a way for two people to communicate their feelings to each other without directly facing the threat of rejection.

War Magic
War magic is used to produce victory in battle, to provide warriors with traits such as bravery that will make them victorious, or to make them impervious to injury. Kapauku warriors, for example, lick and rub a polished stone or a green branch over their bodies to prevent an evil spirit from entering a wound and causing illness. To them, magic cannot prevent being wounded, but it can prevent illness and death. For the American Indians of the Plains in the 1800s raiding other groups for horses and glory was an important activity for men and was accompanied by much magical ritual. For the Pawnee as well as other groups, carrying a medicine bundle—a leather pouch filled with herbs with magical power—provided protection in battle. The Pawnee also carried mescal beans, which they called "horses" and assured that the warrior would capture horses from the enemy. And before battle, roots were chewed and spit over men to make them brave and healthy. Pawnee magic was considered so powerful that enemy groups such as the Omaha sometimes saw the Pawnee warriors themselves as magical:

The Maha (Skidi Pawnee) do not lose courage; their warlike virtues are so great that one brave is often seen setting out by himself to go five and six hundred miles away to steal horses at the hazard of his life, for all the nations are at war with his tribe. Dark stormy nights are the ones the Pawnee choose by preference to attack. They can warn one another by imitating the cries of wild animals, and also create anxiety among the horses and cause them to stampede; so the Osage claim the Pawnee are sorcerers whose medicine can make nights darker, attract storms, put the warriors to sleep, and stampede the horses. . . . One of them enters the camp of the enemy alone and without trying to hide his coming into it. He strokes the horses and, of course, does not arouse any suspicion; he cuts the tethers and the reins; then, suddenly jumping on a fast horse, he gallops away uttering his war cry, while the horses scatter on the prairie, where the Pawnee will soon capture them. On other occasions, if all the warriors are asleep, he crawls into a lodge and silently kills and scalps a brave, whose horses he steals afterwards. (Weltfish 1965: 327)

Economic Magic

Economic magic is both an individual and a group activity in many cultures. It takes a number of forms to encourage a rich harvest or hunt, to protect crops, to increase one's wealth, and to control the natural environment, most importantly rainfall. The Tiv of Nigeria use magic to establish markets for a number of groups. The markets were originally established by sacrificing a slave or a dog from each of the Tiv groups participating in the market. The marketplace was then marked by a special tree that could be moved when the market was moved. The magic not only created the market but also helped cement relations among the groups and created a locale in which differences could be discussed and settled peacefully. Rain magic, both to cause rain and to cause it to stop, is probably the most common form of economic magic across cultures. To bring rain, the Santal of India make sacrifices, but they also engage in ritual behaviors: women and girls plaster the dance floors and courtyards with cow dung, women are made to remove any ropes they may have tied on the roof, and oil or food stored in the wrong way or place is rearranged. These actions are meant to ensure balance among humans, nature, and the spirit world, which will then produce rainfall. Magic is often used by hunters or ritual specialists to improve the hunt. For example, the Tiv of Nigeria use magic to reverse a hunter's bad luck. A black line is drawn with charcoal on the hunter's body; when he washes it off, he also washes "away the mental blackness, which had formerly prevented him from seeing or hitting the game."

Black Magic

Black magic is magic used to cause evil to a person, often illness or death or the failure of a crop. In many cultures, it the fear of black magic that causes people to use magic to protect themselves or to prevent the black magic from having its harmful effects.

Protective Magic

Protective magic is used to thwart the evil intentions of another person. The Central Thai, for example, protect their rice fields with emblems of spirits that will drive off those who seek to damage the young plants or steal the ripe ones. Similarly, the Bemba of East Africa worry about the work of those who use black magic to take all the nutritional value out of their harvest of millet. They protect their harvest with charms, by mixing in some of the previous season's harvest, by conducting the appropriate agricultural rites, by smoking the grain with smoke "medicine," and, if they are Christian, by crossing themselves before harvesting the grain.

Counter and Preventive Magic

Counter and preventive magic is used when one fears that another person has attempted to use magic to cause harm. Among the Kapauku, a shaman will be employed before the victim falls ill and will attempt to drive the spirit from the victim's body and the victim will also make a donation of pig meat to the community.

Curative Magic

Curative magic is used by shamans and other healers to cure sickness; in many societies this means reversing the effects of black magic.

See also ASTROLOGY; DIVINATION; PURITY AND POLLUTION; RELIGIOUS SPECIALISTS; RITUAL; SHAMANISM; TABOO.

Bohannan, Paul, and Laura Bohannan. (1957) "Tiv Markets." *Transactions of the New York Academy of Sciences,* Series II, 19: 613–621.

Broude, Gwen J. (1994) *Marriage, Family, and Relationships: A Cross-Cultural Encyclopedia.*

Culshaw, W. J. (1949) *Tribal Heritage: A Study of the Santals.*

Evans-Pritchard, E. E. (1950) *Witchcraft, Oracles, and Magic among the Azande.* 2d ed.

Filipovic, Milenko S. (1954) "Folk Religion among the Orthodox Population in Eastern Yugoslavia." *Harvard Slavic Studies* 2: 359–374.

Frazer, James G. (1880) *The Golden Bough: A Study in Magic and Religion.*

Kemp, Phyllis. (1935) *Healing and Ritual: Studies in the Technique and Tradition of the Southern Slavs.*

Malefijt, Annemarie de Waal. (1968) *Religion and Culture: An Introduction to the Anthropology of Religion.*

Malinowski, Bronislaw. (1935) *Coral Gardens and Their Magic.*

Murie, James. (1914) *Pawnee Indian Societies.*

Pospisil, Leopold. (1958) *Kapauku Papuans and Their Law.*

Textor, Robert B. (1973) *Roster of the Gods: An Ethnography of the Supernatural in a Thai Village.*

Weltfish, Gene. (1965) *The Lost Universe: With a Closing Chapter on the Universe Regained.*

MANA

Mana is a word (with various spellings) and a concept indigenous to societies in Polynesia and Melanesia that was later applied, often erroneously, to other cultures around the world. It is closely related to the equally indigenous concept of *tapu,* which in its Anglicized spelling (taboo) has also been widely applied to the religious systems of cultures around the world. Mana was first brought to the attention of the Western world by missionaries working in Melanesia whose descriptions were exaggerated by others to the point that mana was defined as a spiritual or mystical substance distributed throughout the world that might be housed in spirits, humans, or physical objects. Thus, it was a very powerful, impersonal form of supernatural power that was held by some experts to be a basic characteristic of all non-world religions (those specific to one culture) that stood in opposition to the highly personal nature of supernatural power in Christianity and other world religions. Research in Polynesia and Melanesia half a century later proved that the early missionary reports were in error and that interpretations based on them were serious misconceptions of what mana means to Polynesians and Melanesians.

Mana is now understood to be a state of being in which a person, place, or object is temporarily or permanently under supernatural influence. Mana comes from the gods and spirits and flows directly to humans, places, or objects. It does not float freely in the world nor is it transferred from objects to humans. And with the exception of first-born children in Polynesian royal families who inherit mana from their fathers (although it arose first from the gods), it is not passed among humans either. People who have mana are usually individuals of considerable personal achievement and thus it is warriors, leaders, artists, and priests who often have mana. Mana was an important state for rulers in Polynesian societies whose lives were separate from the commoners they ruled. For example, chiefs in Tikopia had special relations with their ancestors and the gods that enabled them to provide for the economic and health needs of their subjects. Tikopians believed that the relative success of a chief in these endeavors was a reflection of his mana. The chief received his mana as follows: "The gods take and place it on the head of him who has asked for the mana to be given to him."

While leaders were the possessors of mana in many Polynesian and Melanesian cultures, its meaning and uses were broader as indicated by the role of mana in traditional Lau Fijian society. The Lau chief, because of his ties to the ancestors and their spirits, had the most mana. It was held in his head, which was so sacred that it was taboo—that is, the chief's head, comb, and headrest could not be touched by anyone else. Mana was available to the people from the greatest spirit, the Kalou. It was the responsibility of the priest to bring offerings of fruit, palm wine, and cooked food and to pray to the Kalou in the Nggara Kalou (Cave of the Spirit) to obtain mana (reflected in success and avoidance of difficulty) for the community. Before war, a priest would pray to bring mana to the weapons. Victory or defeat were attributed to the relative strength of the gods and their mana. In addition to the priest, each clan prayed to their ancestor spirits for mana for the clan. The rank of each ancestor spirit was based on the relative success of their clans. Thus, the mana-giving power of each ancestor spirit determined its rank in the pantheon of spirits. Finally, there was a

secret cult of young men, each capable of contacting a guardian spirit and obtaining mana, whose influence was reflected in such personal achievements as developing a new dance, recruiting new members to the cult, or predicting the future.

Under the influence of Christian missionaries, the traditional meanings of mana disappeared or were revised to fit the new social and religious order. Today, mana is now also used in some cultures to refer to personal power, which may be supernatural, such as the mana of a clergyman, or secular, such as the mana of a government official.

See also TABOO.

Child, Alice B., and Irvin L. Child. (1993) *Religion and Magic in the Life of Traditional Peoples.*

Firth, Raymond. (1939) "The Analysis of Mana: An Empirical Approach." *The Journal of the Polynesian Society* 48: 483–510.

Levy, Robert I. (1973) *Tahitians: Mind and Experience in the Society Islands.*

Thompson, Laura. (1940) *Southern Lau, Fiji: An Ethnography.*

MEDITATION

In the Western world, meditation refers to a peaceful state of mind achieved by performing various focusing techniques or rituals. Although its genesis in ancient Asian religions such as Buddhism and Hinduism is acknowledged, it is usually used as a relaxation technique separate from any body of religious belief and practice. In Asian religions, meditation is a means of expanding consciousness and becoming closer to the supernatural world. Within the Judeo-Christian tradition, practices such as chanting, singing, and repetitive prayer are used in a similar way, although they are a means to an end, not an end in and of themselves. In the Asian meditative traditions, the supernatural is experienced as within as well as outside an individual. In Western traditions, God is generally experienced as outside of us, as someone to pray *to*.

Meditation is most closely associated with Hinduism and Buddhism, although there are major variations within and between these two traditions as to the meaning, techniques, and purposes of meditation. As with other practices in Hinduism, meditation takes a variety of regional forms, although it is often engaged in by Hindu ascetics as a mechanism for achieving salvation. An example of one specific form of Hindu meditation is Kundalini meditation practiced both in India and Tibet. It is based on the belief that all people have divine energy, or *kundalini*, suppressed in our bodies. This energy, coiled at the base of the spine, is believed to be a tremendous power, and it is released through the practice of meditation. It is usually experienced as radiant warmth and light, and can sometimes overcome a practitioner. Traditionally, a student who wished to learn this meditation would renounce the world and, under the guidance of a teacher called a Master, engage in strict and lengthy meditation practices. He (most students, until recently, were men) would leave his family, and any aspirations for a career or family would be left behind. He would become a monk, devoted to the goal of union with God that comes with the unblocking of the kundalini, or life force.

Of all the Asian religions, meditation is most highly elaborated in Buddhism, and while there are variations across the types of Buddhism and across communities, many of the key features of Buddhist meditation are found among the Central Thai and among Sinhalese Buddhists in Sri Lanka. Meditation exists in Buddhism as a primary means of reaching *nirvana*, the final goal on the eight-fold path to enlightenment. The eight states of being associated with the path run from mortality to meditation to wisdom. The Central Thai use two forms of meditation—*samadhi* and *vipassana*. Central Thai samadhi meditation is similar to Sinhalese *bhavanaya* meditation. These forms of meditation are forms of mental purification that ultimately lead the practitioner to salvation. They are practiced by monks who isolate themselves from society, engage in highly ritualized behavior, enter trance states, rely on intuitive thinking, and clear their minds so that they may enhance their powers of understanding. For the Central Thai these powers include:

> the powers to be manifold, to pass through solid objects, to travel through the earth, to walk on water, to fly, and to travel through all the heavens. Besides "magical powers" there are other powers of the divine ear, the ability to hear all sounds in both heaven and on earth, the powers of the divine eye, to see the fate of others in heaven or hell or to see anywhere, and the powers to know the minds of others, and to remember former existence. (Van Esterik 1978: 48)

The second Central Thai meditation approach is called vipassana, which was borrowed from Burmese Buddhist meditation and is especially popular as an alternative to the rigorous samadhi approach among lay persons in cities. This is a less rigorous, more intellectual, and more rapid approach to achieving nirvana. Some practitioners of this approach dismiss samadhi not just because of its practical limits but also because they question the ability of humans to actually achieve the powers listed above. The vipassana approach relies heavily on intuitive thinking and understanding and emphasizes the mind-body relationship.

Although they vary in many ways, Asian meditative practices often include the following common characteristics:

1. a calm environment, with silence or simple rhythmic sound;
2. an attempt to quiet daily thoughts and emotion and quell "busyness";
3. a belief that by stopping the flow of rational thought and normal mental activity, a state of passive awareness can be achieved;
4. a belief that by achieving this passive awareness, doors to higher consciousness can be opened;
5. learning the method from a Master.

Meditation Techniques

Whatever the goals, there are similar techniques used in both Asian traditional meditation and Western adaptations and approaches, and all use one or more of the following techniques:

1. Mantra or sound
2. Focus on breathing
3. Moving meditation
4. Visual meditation
5. Guided meditation

The various methods used are points of mental focus, so that the falling away of everyday thoughts and emotions can occur. The mind may stray from the focus, but is continually re-

Sufi Muslims, an order of Islam, the Mevlevi dervishes from Turkey dance at the 1971 World Islam Festival held in London. Such repetetive movements as this whirling dance lift the participants out of ordinary consciousness, an objective of meditation.

turned. Eventually what is left is the point alone: the sound, the breath, the image, the motion, and then that begins to slowly dissolve. When the mind is empty, and there is no grasping onto any thought or sensation, a person experiences a flood of relaxation, often accompanied by a sense of warmth and light. There is generally a feeling of well-being and increased energy. With repeated practice, states of higher and more expanded consciousness may be achieved.

To allow the conscious mind to release its hold, a person generally closes his or her eyes, or focuses them on a fixed point, and is either seated or lying down. The traditional Asian posture is called the lotus position, with the legs crossed and hands resting in the lap, or with palms facing upward while resting on the knees. The spine is held very straight with the top of the head pulled upward toward the sky. The chin is in. This can be an uncomfortable pose at first, but the spine is straight to allow for an unimpeded flow of the life force, and the legs are crossed to contain it in a closed system. Often, the tips of the index finger and thumb are pressed together in each hand to further complete the "circuit." Once the posture is assumed, the points of focus are brought in, and the practitioner begins to allow his thoughts to disappear.

In vocal meditation, a sound is repeated over and over as a way of blocking conscious thought and moving from the rational mind to passive awareness. In traditional meditation, a *mantra*, the Sanskrit word for "thought form" is used. A mantra is a word or words, usually having a religious significance, that is given to the student. Traditionally, the belief is that a particular mantra resonates in a special way for that student, and is therefore not to be shared with anyone else. The word's resonance is often to a particular deity, and is believed to assist in the person's connection to the life-force. One of the most commonly used mantras is "Om," which is believed to be the universal sound from which all other mantras spring.

Modern Forms and Uses of Meditation

Modern practitioners of meditation, especially in the West, may not renounce the world, gain supernormal powers, or seek salvation, but by practicing meditative techniques daily they may achieve some aspect of this experience. It is generally not as profound or life-consuming—or it may be, depending on the person's goals and the length of time they engage in the practice. Meditative techniques are used in the West as complements to psychological and medical treatments, since relaxation is one of the best-documented effects of the practice (relaxation has been proven to aid the body and mind in healing). Other people may meditate to reduce stress and to feel more relaxed and energized.

Transcendental meditation (TM), a method developed for modern life, is derived from Hindu meditation. It was developed by the Maharishi Mahesh Yogi, who brought it to the United States in the 1960s. TM is taught by the International Meditation Society and can be mastered in four days. One does not have to believe in any spiritual or religious doctrine, but the concept of the secrecy of the mantra is maintained. The mantra is given to the student in a special spiritual ceremony called the *puja*.

In her research on meditation, clinical psychologist Dr. Patricia Carrington discovered that some TM meditators who had shared their mantras found that they had all received the same one, and that TM mantras are often assigned on the basis of age. TM teachers report that there are 16 mantras regularly used. In Clinically Standardized Meditation (CSM), developed by Dr. Carrington, students are allowed to choose their own mantra.

Breathing meditation also has its roots in Indian philosophy and religion. *Pranayama* is the Sanskrit name for the life force, and it is also the name for the yoga of breathing. In pranayama, a devotee sits in the lotus position and, using one of the many forms, fixes his or her awareness on the sensation of breathing. Eventually the breathing becomes automatic, as the body and mind relax. There are many types of pranayama, including the alternate breath, in which the practitioner inhales in a particular way, holding one nostril closed, then opening it for the exhale. Use of the throat in *ujaya* breathing imitates the relaxing sound of ocean waves. Another technique is the cleansing breath, during which the lips are pursed on the exhale for a forceful expulsion of the breath. Practitioners experience a sense of wholeness and peace from the practice.

A Harvard Medical School cardiologist, Herbert Benson, researched meditation techniques to determine their use as tools to combat heart disease and developed a breathing meditation technique he called "Benson's Method." Using the focus on simple breathing as his starting point, he added the repetition of the word "one" to his instructions to his students, thereby mixing breathing and vocal meditation.

Other forms of breathing meditation include the Japanese-based *Zazen*, a strict and rigorous discipline from Chinese Zen Buddhism. Students are not allowed to move while meditating and are forced to ignore any and all distractions, including insects, numbness, or any painful sensation within or outside of the body. They sit in the lotus position, their eyes open and focused on a spot a few feet in front of them. Often an unanswerable riddle, called a *koan*, is offered by their teacher. "What is the sound of one hand clapping," goes one popular koan. Again, there is a mixture of the two techniques, with the goal of derailing conscious thinking so that the divine energy can enter the body and mind.

An example of a moving form of meditation is the ecstatic dancing of the whirling dervishes of the mystic sect of Islam, the Sufi order. In this repetitive group twirling, dancers are lifted out of ordinary consciousness. Another type of moving meditation is called Tai Ch'i, from Chinese Taoism. In this meditation, a series of slow and meditative martial arts postures are strung together into a form that is repeated over and over. Relaxing into the movement, with practice, allows release of the life force, or *ch'i*.

Not all moving meditation uses the whole body. A simple moving meditation was described by Dr. Carrington as follows:

> Sit with a pillow on your lap so that your hands are resting comfortably on the pillow and cup your hands together in a "prayerlike" position with fingers lightly touching. Then gently open your palms while still keeping their lower edges resting against the pillow and in contact. Now once again bring your palms together so that all fingers touch lightly, returning to the position. . . . This meditation consists of opening and closing your palms over and over again, gently and easily. . . . Use as little energy as possible for this exercise and let your motions be easy and rhythmic. (1977: 81)

Traditional visual meditation includes use of a *mandala,* or spiritual painting:

> In Sanskrit, the word mandala literally means the "centerpoint." And, in fact, spiritual meditation is largely based on holding your attention on one point over a period of time, while also expanding your consciousness to include the whole that surrounds the centerpoint. . . . These paintings offer a calm, clear path to finding one's visual center, and to expanding one's mind in all directions around the centerpoint. (Selby 1992: 68).

In another, more simple visual meditation, a natural object is placed at eye level a few feet away from the meditator. A candle is often chosen, but a plant, a flower, or any other pleasing object can be used. While sitting comfortably, the meditator rests her eyes on the subject, but instead of consciously focusing, she lets the object slowly enter the awareness. Periodically, the attention is taken away from the object to a more distant place in the room. It is then returned. Each time, the meditator becomes more absorbed in the object until conscious attention falls away. In *tratak* meditation, from Hinduism, one stares unblinkingly at a flame until the eyes tear.

Guided meditations involve the gentle, calm voice of someone telling a detailed story, praying, or repeating inspirational messages. A guided meditation may involve asking meditators to imagine that they are in a relaxing place, like the beach or in the woods. There may be a very detailed description of the place or the journey to the place, which allows the meditator to relax deeply in this imaginary state. He may be led to some point of catharsis or be given directions to increase self-love and love of others. These meditations may be goal-directed, suggesting self-esteem or some other positive psychological state.

See also ASCETICISM; BUDDHISM; HINDUISM.

Ames, Michael M. (1964) "Magical-Animism and Buddhism: A Structural Analysis of the Sinhalese Religious System." *Journal of Asian Studies* 23: 21–52.

Arguelles, Jose. (1992) *Mandala*.

Carrington, Patricia. (1977) *Freedom in Meditation*.

Elliot, C. (1969) *Japanese Buddhism*.

Selby, John. (1992) *Kundalini Awakening: A Gentle Guide to Chakra Activation and Spiritual Growth*.

Van Esterik, John L. (1978) *Cultural Interpretation of Canonical Paradox: Lay Meditation in a Central Thai Village*.

Watts, Alan. (1957) *The Way of Zen*.

Yogananda, P. (1946) *Autobiography of a Yogi, Self-Realization*.

MISSIONS

As applied to religious activity, the term *mission* has a variety of meanings. As used in reference to Christianity and in its most general sense it refers to the goal of creating a world in which all people are Christians. In a more limited sense, it can also mean a specific missionary initiative (such as the mission to the Huron), a specific site of missionary activity (such as San Juan Mission), or a specific missionary organization (such as the New Tribes Mission).

Individuals who work toward converting others who are adherents of a religion different from their own or nonbelievers are called missionaries or missioners. In some religions, such as Islam or Pentecostal Christianity, all believers are also missionaries, as an expected activity of adherents of these religions is the conversion of nonbelievers. In some other religions, such as Mormonism, some members must devote a period of time (usually two years) to missionary activity. In most Christian denominations the missionary role is a special one occupied by religious specialists such as ministers, priests, brothers, sisters, and lay missionaries. All missionaries have a "calling" to do this work and many receive special education and training. Within the general missionary role there is further task specialization, with some missionaries performing ministerial work and others teaching, providing medical care, community and economic development assistance, or administrative work. In some locales today, and more so in the past, a single missionary performed all or many of these tasks alone. Some missionaries operate independently, although the majority are supported by a central church organization, a free-standing mission organization, or even a single congregation. The majority of missionaries come from cultures different than the one in which they work. In recent years, however, there has been a trend toward utilizing indigenous peoples as missionaries to their own people.

While all major religions seek converts to some extent, interest in missionary activity and its effects has been mostly centered on the Christian mission. This is mainly because the Christian mission has been closely tied to Western colonial expansion for over 500 years. Interest in the missionary aspect of the spread of other religions, such as Buddhism from South Asia to East Asia and Islam from the Arabian Peninsula to North Africa, Central Asia, and Southeast Asia, has been much lower, although their spread certainly resulted in part from missionary activities.

Missionaries are often in competition with one another. It is not unusual to find Catholic, various Protestant denomination, Mormon, and other missions represented by missionaries working in the same region or with the same cultural group. For example, in northern Nigeria in the 1970s, Islamic, Catholic (Dominican), and Protestant (United Mission Society) missioners vied for converts among the local ethnic groups. The Muslims enjoyed a number of advantages, including residence among the local population, a lifestyle more like that of the local population, support from the Nigerian government, and the backing of the Islamic Hausa, the dominant ethnic group in the region. Thus, conversion to Islam was more common, with entire villages most likely to covert to Islam while only extended families converted to Protestantism and only individuals to Catholicism. Similarly, in Alaska, the Russian Orthodox Church was the primary mission among the Tlingit until the sale of Alaska to the United States in 1867 and the arrival of American missionaries. When the Russian traders left the region, the Orthodox Church was the only Russian institution remaining and it gradually lost influence, concentrating its efforts on a few larger communities. It continues to exist, however, as a native Orthodox church

with Tlingit clergy, liturgy in the Tlingit language, and local parishes operating to meet the needs of the communities they serve. A similar situation obtains in Orthodox Eskimo and Aleut communities, which have been more resistant to American missions such as that of the Moravians than the Tlingit. As in the Tlingit situation, missionaries from different faiths or denominations not only work at the same time in one place but often follow each other over time. For example, Latin American groups were heavily missionized in colonial times by Roman Catholic missionaries. In recent decades, as Catholic missionary activity has decreased, many converts have converted again, this time often to Pentecostal Protestantism, whose expressive style, emphasis on miracles, and encouragement of lay ministers makes it congruent with local cultural traditions.

As discussed below, while missions are found around the world, not all regions have been equally responsive to Christian missionary efforts or even to the presence of missionaries. The goal of missionary work is the conversion of the targets of the work to the religion of the missionary. Missionaries, of course, see this change as beneficial both to individual converts and the culture as a whole, while critics of missionary activity see such activity as mainly harmful or destructive of indigenous cultures.

The strategies and techniques used by missionaries vary widely over time and from situation to situation. Two strategies with major implications for ethnic relations are indiginization and contextualization. Indigenization refers to an approach in which the Gospel is presented in a way that can be best understood by indigenous peoples. One major aspect of indigenization is the translation of the Bible into indigenous languages, a task that dates to the beginnings of Christianity. Today, the Bible, the Gospels, and other religious documents have been translated into several thousand languages.

Another form of indigenization is to present elements of Christianity in a way that fits with existing beliefs and symbols in the indigenous culture. For example, Catholic missionaries to the Tupi-Guarani in Paraguay and Brazil in the 1660s called the Christian God Tupa, after the local supernatural responsible for thunder, lightning, and rain, and called the Devil Yurupari or Giropari, after the names of harmful local forest spirits. Similarly, a common missionary practice has been to incorporate indigenous dance and music into Christian ceremonies.

Contextualization is a rather new development and is seen by missionaries as moving beyond indigenization. Contextualization requires a consideration of the Bible, the indigenous religion, the indigenous culture, and then a fitting of elements of the religious message to elements of the indigenous culture. It also takes into consideration the reality that cultures vary both internally and over time and that much of the stimulus for cultural change is external to the culture. Thus, a contextual approach might involve the building of an impressive church for use by a wealthy, powerful elite alongside the use of Biblical passages in indigenous healing ceremonies by other members of the same community.

The variation among missionaries was in the actual impact they had and how they pursued their goals. In South America, missionaries were an integral component of many pacification efforts, the first step in what became the wide-scale exploitation of indigenous peoples, the conquest of their territory, and the displacement and disappearance of many. In Africa, where European settlement was not a goal, missionaries were participants in the indirect-rule strategy as recruiters and educators of indigenous peoples to perform administrative and clerical work in the colonial regimes. In North America, as elsewhere, the role of missionaries was determined to a large extent by the goals and colonization methods of the nations that supported or allowed for their work. Thus, there was considerable variation in these matters. For example, Catholic missionaries in the Southwest were part of the Spanish conquest of the region and allowed (and were the victims themselves of) torture and killing in the name of conquest and conversion. In southern California, many indigenous peoples were forced to live at the local missions, forced to wear European-style clothing, forbidden to speak their native languages, and performed forced labor. In New Mexico, the Spanish presence led to the establishment of Catholic churches at nearly all pueblo communities, but conquest and conversion were often incomplete and today many Pueblo groups such as the Taos are both Catholics and adherents of their traditional kiva-based religion. In the Northeast, early missionaries often seemed as interested in "civilizing" the indigenous peoples as in converting them and many encouraged permanent settlement, intensive agriculture, formal education, and trade with white settlers.

Modern Mission Activity

Contemporary Christian missions fall into five major categories. Evangelical missions cross-cut denominational differences and institutional structures and include a wide range of missionaries who all believe in the following: (1) acceptance of the Scripture as the word of God; (2) belief in the atonement of Jesus Christ; (3) a saving experience with the Holy Spirit; (4) proper use of the sacraments; and (5) a calling to convert non-Christians. Conciliar missions are missionaries sent out by churches who are members of church councils such as the World Council of Churches. Missionaries working in this tradition stress an ecumenical perspective with an emphasis on building unity among the churches, missions to the poor and people in Western cultures, contact with non-Christians, and applying the Gospel to everyday life. The Roman Catholic mission, as defined since the Second

Vatican Council (1962–1965), emphasizes salvation in the context of human history and local culture, with an emphasis on work with the poor, the building of local communities, and an increasing role for lay missionaries. Pentecostal and charismatic missions are perhaps more personal than the others in that adherents are empowered and guided directly by the Holy Spirit as evidenced by speaking in tongues or the receiving of gifts. Spirit baptism enables each believer to act as a witness, minister, and missionary and thus is one major factor in the widespread appeal of Pentecostalism. Finally, there are missionaries from religions considered to be non-Christian (at least by mainstream Christian missionaries) such as the Church of Jesus Christ of Latter-Day Saints (Mormons), Jehovah's Witnesses, the Unification Church, and New Age churches, which also seek adherents (often on a large scale) throughout the world.

In terms of current goals, Christian missionaries divide the world into three major regions: (1) "Those Who Call Themselves Christians" (the New World, western Europe, southwestern Africa, and Australia and most of Oceania); (2) "Have Heard, Limited Response" (the former Soviet Union, China, East Asia, Central and East Africa, and parts of South Asia); and (3) "Least-Evangelized World" (North Africa, Middle East, Central Asia, South Asia, and China). Thus, those parts of the world with the fewest Christians and a history of resistance to missionary work are those where other religions such as Islam, Hinduism, or Buddhism are sufficiently established to combat missionary activity or where the national governments such as those in China and the former Soviet Union banned or restricted missionary activity. For this reason, the largest concentrations of missionaries today are found in nations considered to be in the Christian world—Brazil, Colombia, Ecuador, France, Germany, Kenya, Mexico, and the Philippines. At the same time, some nations in the unconverted world also have sizable missionary activity, including Japan, Indonesia, and Papua New Guinea.

The total number of missionaries in the world is unknown and because of the proliferation of missionaries operating on their own or with support of a single congregation or educational institution, they can not be counted accurately. A recent count of what may be called mainstream Protestant missionaries found that there were 41,142 supported U.S. missionaries in 1992, down from 50,500 in 1988. In addition, there were 5,210 Catholic missioners from the United States, including priests, brothers, sisters, and lay missioners. When we add to these figures the sizable numbers of Mormon, Jehovah's Witnesses, Unification Church, and other missionaries overseas, missioners operating out of other nations such as Great Britain, and missionaries working in the United States it becomes obvious why mission activity is a major form of ethnic relation around the world. The majority of missionaries are engaged in evangelism but sizable numbers are also involved in health care, education, development projects, child care, and other activities.

One major issue facing missionaries today is their relationship to indigenous peoples, some of whom were the objects of missionary activities during colonial times in the past. Some missionaries take the position that economic development will inevitably impact these peoples and therefore change the lives of indigenous peoples around the world. And they argue that allowing missionaries to arrive first and prepare these peoples for Western contact and the changes it will bring is more humane than allowing first contact to be with developers, land speculators, miners, farmers, ranchers, etc., whose interest is either in taking the land or exploiting the labor of indigenous peoples. These missionaries see themselves as cultural brokers who assist in planned change. This view contrasts with that of others who either question whether large-scale change is always the fate of indigenous peoples or see missionaries as participants in the development effort.

Other missionaries—seen as radical by many—work with previously colonized peoples and see their role as righting the wrongs of the past and protecting and advocating for indigenous rights today. For example, in Brazil a new mass was celebrated in 1979, entitled "The Mass of the Land without Evil." The mass condemns colonialism, depicts the traditional Indian culture as damaged theologically by missionary work, and presents indigenous culture as a route to salvation and a better world. In some nations, not only missionaries but also community religious leaders such as priests and ministers are now among the leading advocates of indigenous rights and often find themselves in conflict with national governments who had supported missionary and religious activity in the past.

One of the key issues facing missionaries in the past and today is how effective they are in winning converts. That is, how deep is the devotion of the converts to their new religion? It seems that unless the indigenous religion is destroyed completely, the typical result of missionary activity is nominal adherence to the new religion with some elements of the traditional religion incorporated into it or continuing to exist apart from it. For example, in Taos, New Mexico, Roman Catholicism and the indigenous religion exist side-by-side and the community houses both a Catholic church and underground ceremonial chambers, where traditional ceremonies are held. And among the Wolof of Senegal, who are mostly Muslims, elements of their traditional religion such as a belief in malevolent spirits, witchcraft, shamanism, healing, and a circumcision ceremony exist alongside Islam. In addition to combining elements from different religions, missionary activity also sometimes results in indigenous beliefs being redefined to fit the new religion. For example, the Zande of northern sub-Saharan Africa now equate their high god, Mbori, with the Christian God and have redefined ghosts of ancestors from being benevolent to being equivalents of Satan. In Africa, the introduction of Christianity ultimately led to the development of hundreds of independent churches, all based on elements combined from the indigenous religions and Christianity. For example, among the Zande, diviners have been redefined as prophetesses of the Zande Christian Church and now counsel parishioners as well as continue to identify witches.

Barrett, David B. (1994) "Annual Statistical Table on Global Mission: 1994." *International Bulletin of Missionary Research* 18: 24–25.

Bowden, Henry W. (1981) *American Indians and Christian Missions: Studies in Cultural Conflict.*

Burridge, Kenelm. (1991) *In the Way: A Study of Christian Missionary Endeavours.*

Gillies, Eva. (1995) "Zande." In *Encyclopedia of World Cultures. Vol. 9 Africa and the Middle East,* edited by John Middleton and Amal Rassam, 397–400.

Neill, Stephen. (1986) *A History of Christian Missions.* Revised for the Second Edition by Owen Chadwick.

Phillips, James M. and Robert T. Coote, eds. (1993) *Toward the 21st Century in Christian Mission.*

Rathburn, Robert R. (1976) *Processes of Russian-Tlingit Acculturation in Southeastern Alaska.*

Richardson, Don. (1988) "Do Missionaries Destroy Cultures?" In *Tribal Peoples and Development Issues: A Global Overview,* edited by John H. Bodley, 116–121.

Salamone, Frank A. (1974) *Gods and Goods in Africa.*

Shapiro, Judith. (1987) "From Tupa to the Land without Evil: The Christianization of Tupi-Guarani Cosmology." *American Ethnologist* 14: 126–139.

Siewert, John A. and John A. Kenyon, eds. (1993) *Mission Handbook: USA/Canada Christian Ministries Overseas.*

MONOTHEISM AND POLYTHEISM

Monotheism and polytheism are terms used by theologians, social scientists, and others to categorize religious systems. The basic distinction between the two is that in monotheistic religions people believe in one god who has created and rules or oversees the universe. In polytheistic religions people believe in two or more gods who rule different domains of the universe. Additional features of the god in monotheism are that he is perfect, immanent in the world, and eternal, that he transcends the supernatural and natural worlds, and that he has unlimited and uncontested power that is not shared with other supernatural beings. In polytheism, gods are not immanent in all aspects of the world nor do they have unlimited, uncontested power. In between monotheism and polytheism are religious systems that fall in the category of religious belief called theistic dualism. In theistic dualism, there is one high god as in monotheism, but evil intentions are disassociated from the high god and attributed instead to another supernatural being who stands in opposition to the high god. The notion of theistic dualism appears in some forms of Christianity with evil personified in the form of Satan; however, it is questionable whether Satan is an equal of God because (1) he may be conceptualized as merely symbolizing sin rather than being a true supernatural being comparable to God, or (2) he may be created by God for the purpose of expressing evil and sin. Also reflecting both monotheistic and polytheistic beliefs are the religions of some hunting-gathering peoples and many cultures in Africa in which there is a high god who created the universe, but the god then became uninvolved in life on earth while various other gods or spirits take an active role in human affairs. For example, the San peoples of southern Africa believe in a creator god who then removed himself from worldly events, an overseer god who manages life on earth, and ancestor spirits who influence the lives of their living relatives. Similarly, the Mossi of Burkina Faso believe in a creator god no longer involved in human affairs, two superior gods who control soil fertility and rainfall and whose assistance is sought through periodic rituals, and kin group ancestor spirits who look after the interests of the living members of their kin groups.

Across cultures, three major forms of monotheism may be identified. First, monarchic monotheism in which (1) one high god rules two or more superior gods who have less power and usually were created by the high god, or (2) the high god is pitted in battle against an evil god or force. The latter form is more common and is found in Zoroastrianism and some forms of Christianity, Judaism, Islam, and Hinduism. Second, emanational mystical monotheism in which (1) a high god is approached through the worship of a multitude of gods, or (2) the high god is conceptualized as embodied in the world. Examples of the first form are found in Hinduism and Buddhism where Vishnu and Buddha, respectively, can be worshipped through lesser gods or under different names. The second form is found in Sikhism in which God is seen as present in all of the world and through a cycle of death and rebirth believers seek to become one with him. Third is ethical monotheism in which a high god designs the moral order for

*Renaissance artist Albrecht Dürer's 1513 engraving "The Knight, Death, and the Devil"
includes theistic elements of Christianity. Death carries an hourglass and rides with a
knight while Satan, a horned and cloven-hoofed creature, follows on foot.*

life on earth, judges his human subjects, and communicates through prophets, events, and written texts. Judaism, Christianity, and Islam are of this type, although all three in the past and in some beliefs and practices today display features of other forms of monotheism as well.

Polytheism takes two major forms across cultures. First, there may be a pantheon of superior gods, each with a name, distinct persona and appearance, and responsibility for one specific domain of the universe. The Saami of northern Scandinavia had a pantheon of eight superior gods, each responsible for some feature of the universe of importance to the Saami:

- Tiermes, God of Thunder
- Paive, God of the Sun
- Mano, God of the Moon
- Biegolmai, God of Wind
- Leibolmai, God of Hunting
- Sarakka, Uksakka, and Juksakka, Goddesses of Childbirth

In the second type of polytheism, there is a high god who created the universe but is not now involved in the world of humans and a pantheon of superior gods, each responsible for specific domains of the universe. The Nzema, an Akan group in Ghana, practice this type of polytheism. Edenkema, their high god, created the world, all humans, and all other gods and spirits. Immediately below Edenkema are the sky god, Nyamenle, and the earth goddess, Azele, the wife of Nyamenle. Beneath these three gods are hundreds of other gods and spirits, all created by Edenkema, ruled by the three highest gods, and inhabiting the earth.

One of the most intriguing questions about monotheism and polytheism is why different cultures developed these different conceptions of the supernatural world. The idea once popular in the social sciences, that monotheism was the basic form of religion and that polytheism represents a divergent form of belief, is no longer

believed to be true. Instead, following the assumption that the world of the supernatural is modeled on the world of the believers, it seems that monotheism and polytheism vary across cultures in accord with variations in social organization. Polytheism is found in societies that are reliant on agriculture for subsistence and whose population is stratified into a number of distinct groups on the basis of occupation and social status. Thus the social organization of the gods—multiple gods, each responsible for one domain—reflects the social organization of the world of the believers. This pattern is typical of many of the ancient civilizations, such as Greece, Egypt, Japan, and China, which were polytheistic. It is also typical of those contemporary non-Western cultures that are polytheistic. Monotheistic societies are similar to polytheistic ones in the reliance on agriculture, but a key feature of their social organization is a hierarchy of sovereign social groups such as villages, kinship groups, and families, one of which exerts some control over the other groups. In monotheism, the single, all-knowing, all-powerful high god occupies the same structural position as the ruling sovereign group and apparently serves the same function—to provide order and unity among the sovereign groups.

See also SUPERNATURAL BEINGS.

Davis, William D. (1974) *Societal Complexity and the Nature of Primitive Man's Conception of the Supernatural.*

Grottanelli, Vinigi L. (1969) "Gods and Morality in Nzema Polytheism." *Ethnology* 8: 370–405.

Karsten, Rafael (1955) *The Religion of the Samek: Ancient Beliefs and Cults of the Scandinavian and Finnish Lapps.*

Silberbauer, George B. (1981) *Hunter and Habitat in the Central Kalahari Desert.*

Skinner, Elliot P. (1989) *The Mossi of Burkina Faso: Chiefs, Politicians, and Soldiers.*

Swanson, Guy E. (1968) *The Birth of the Gods: The Origin of Primitive Beliefs.*

MORMONISM

Founded in western New York State in the 1830s, Mormonism represented a radical departure from traditional Judeo-Christian scriptures. Although the New and Old Testaments play a major role in its religious doctrine, the scriptures are supplemented by the Book of Mormon, which describes Jesus Christ's activities in the Western Hemisphere after crucifixion, including his gospel teachings and the institution of a new church. Mormonism developed in relative isolation in Utah during the nineteenth century and remains a dominant religion in that state and other sections of the Rocky Mountains. Membership extends throughout the United States and many nations around the world, where people have converted to Mormonism in response to a large and active Mormon missionary initiative.

Mormonism claims to have more than five million followers, with the vast majority belonging to the Church of Jesus Christ of Latter-Day Saints, based in Salt Lake City, Utah. The church and its members dominate the Utah economy and hold considerable sway in surrounding states such as Nevada, New Mexico, Idaho, and Arizona. There are substantial populations in such western cities as Los Angeles, San Francisco, and Portland. The church has recently broadened its reach by sending missionaries to Asia, Latin America, and Africa. Splinter Mormon groups include about 200,000 members—mainly in the Midwest—with the largest of these being the Reorganized Church of Jesus Christ of Latter-Day Saints in Missouri.

Mormonism places a heavy emphasis on the family and communal living under the authority of the church, as well as education, work, and personal development and a strict code of conduct that discourages activities that would interfere with those goals. The term Mormonism is applied to the Church of Jesus Christ of Latter-Day Saints and such splinter groups as the Reorganized Church of Jesus Christ of Latter-Day Saints.

Historical Development

The church was founded by Joseph Smith, Jr., known as "The Prophet," in 1830 during the time of the Second Great Awakening. Several new religious sects such as the Shakers, Campellites, the Oneida Community, and the Mormons were forming at that time. They all placed a renewed emphasis on New England Puritanical beliefs in reaction to the rapid changes in the industrial economy and an increasingly pluralistic society. Mormonism was the only one to survive and prosper into modern times.

Smith first received divine guidance, as an adolescent in 1820, not to join any of the existing denominations. For the next decade visions were revealed to Smith, convincing him that he was chosen to restore the true church of Christ, which had been corrupted during the course of history. An angel directed Smith to a set of golden records buried in a hill near his parents' farm. With divine assistance, Smith translated the records and published them in 1830 as the Book of Mormon. Shortly afterwards, Smith officially organized his new church in New York State on April 6, 1830.

Saying that God had given him and his colleague Oliver Cowdery divine authority through John the Baptist and the apostles, Smith struggled to form his church. The first settlement was established in Kirtland, Ohio, where the first Mormon temple was built in 1836. The group soon moved to Independence, Missouri, and then across the Mississippi River to Nauvoo, Illinois. By the early 1840s the church had attracted several thousand converts, including a large contingent from Great Britain enticed by Mormon missionaries. However, the group was also wracked by internal and external conflicts. Members and nonmembers grew increasingly alarmed at some of Smith's practices and beliefs, which included men having several wives, baptism of the dead, and man's capacity to achieve divinity through obedience to Mormon principals. On June 27, 1844, a mob killed Smith and his brother Hyrum.

Brigham Young, one of Smith's loyal followers, soon took over the leadership of the Mormons and led most of the Mormons on a migration to the Great Salt Lake in 1847, leaving behind a group of the more traditional Mormon believers who rejected some of the more radical beliefs. Those remaining in the Midwest became the Reorganized Church of Jesus Christ of Latter-Day Saints with headquarters in Independence, Missouri.

Young established a self-sufficient community in the region called "Deseret" stretching throughout much of the West. The federal government, however, rejected Mormon claims of a kingdom and established the Utah Territory in 1850 with Young as the governor. When Young died in 1877 there were more than 100,000 Mormons and they were the dominant group in Utah and parts of several neighboring states. Tensions, however, continued between Mormons and their neighbors. Toward the end of the century the U.S. government passed several laws designed to restrict the Mormons' financial influence and the more objectionable aspects of the religion.

By 1900, the church made several concessions to non-Mormon, or "Gentile," society, including the renouncement of a religious kingdom and forbidding the practice of polygyny. Relations between Mormons and their neighbors have remained peaceful throughout the twentieth century even as the size of the Mormon population increased many times over.

Texts and Beliefs

Mormon scriptures consist of the Bible and the Book of Mormon, often called the Mormon Bible by Gentiles. The Book of Mormon records the sacred history of three pre-Columbian migrants in the New World—including the ancestors of the American Indians—between 600 B.C.E. and C.E. 421. It also proclaims the teachings of the prophets as described in the Doctrine and Covenants and the Pearl of Great Price. According to the text, Jesus Christ came to the New World after his crucifixion to teach the gospel and instituted a church. Mormons believe that Jesus will return to rule the earth and that there is a three-person Godhead. They subscribe to the immortality of the human spirit and salvation through repentance of sin, baptism, and proper behavior as described in a strict code of conduct. There are some disagreements between the different sects regarding the interpretation of the scriptures and the degree of literalness that should be applied to the texts.

Ceremonies and Practices

Religious services involve prayer, singing, and blessing, with a heavy emphasis on the belief that "worship is the voluntary homage of the soul." Baptism and marriage ceremonies are considered especially important. Individual prayer is a central portion of many Mormons' lives. Only Mormon males may serve in the priesthood. There is no professional priesthood, but "worthy" practicing males may become priests when they are twelve years old or older. An Aaronic, or lower, priest serves as a deacon, teacher, and priest during his teenage years. Melchizidek, or upper, priests are "worthy" adult men who may serve as an elder, on the Council of the Seventies, or high priest.

The authority of the church is based on a complicated hierarchy that places the First Presidence at the top (the president and two counselors). The first president holds office for life and is considered the successor to Joseph Smith, Jr. He carries the title "prophet, seer and revelator." Beneath him in the hierarchy is the Quorum of the Twelve (Apostles) and then the First Council, or the Council of the Seventies. When the first president dies the senior member of the Quorom of the Twelve succeeds him.

Mormons place a high premium on family solidarity, which is expressed through theological and institutional practices. Temple ordinances for both the living and the dead are intended to bind families through sacred covenants. Only Mormons who live by the Mormon rules of conduct are allowed to enter the temple to take part in these rituals and ordinances. The rules of conduct include acceptance of dress codes, abstinence from tobacco, alcohol, coffee, and tea; and adherence to strict sexual morality codes. Only a relatively few fundamentalist Mormons continue to practice polygyny, and those who do are subject to excommunication. Wives are expected to stay at home to raise the family and husbands are meant to provide for the family through work.

The church sponsors an extraordinary number of auxiliary social organizations, such as the Young Men's Improvement Association and the Young Women's Improvement Association, designed to maximize an individual's potential within the context of the Mormon community. These organizations serve the very young to the very old and serve as stimuli for social and economic success among Mormons in the world at large. This is especially apparent in the Mormon emphasis on education. Brigham Young University is the largest church-affiliated university in the United States. Mormons are believed to have the highest percentage of college graduates among all religions in the United States. Although Mormons consider themselves part of mainstream society in the United States, their self-identity as Mormons takes precedence.

Ludlow, Daniel H., ed. (1992) *Encyclopedia of Mormonism.*

Shipps, Jan. (1984) *Mormonism: The Story of a New Religious Tradition.*

Talmage, James E. (1976) *A Study of the Articles of Faith: Being a Consideration of the Principal Doctrines of the Church of Jesus Christ of Latter-Day Saints.* 51st ed.

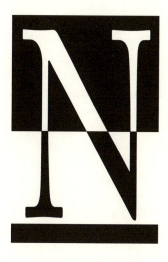

and Hinduism, from ancient civilizations such as the Mayan and the Celtic, from Native American cultures (particularly those of the Southwest and Great Plains), and from non-Western indigenous peoples. Some of these inspirations, especially the environment and holistic health movements, have in turn been influenced by the New Age. Some members of the cultures the New Age draws from object to the use of their traditions in the New Age, especially Native Americans who are offended by the use (or, in their view, misuse) of their traditional religious beliefs and customs by non-Native peoples.

Because its beliefs and customs are collected from other cultures, the New Age movement represents the first attempt in human history to peacefully integrate the beliefs and customs of many different cultures to form a multicultural global community. Among the core values guiding this global community are holism, a oneness of humans with nature, one universal set of religious beliefs, peace, harmony, and an orientation to the future. Some adherents of the New Age work actively toward creating the New Age by serving as guides or by leading growth or healing events, while others are simply waiting for the New Age to arrive.

For the individual seeker of the New Age, personal transformation and a deepened sense of spirituality can be achieved in a wide variety of ways. These include maintaining or improving one's health through acupuncture, chiropractic, myotherapy, bodywork, shiatsu, and homeopathy; becoming more intimate with nature by communicating with plant spirits, taking nature walks, and herbology; broadening and strengthening one's relationships by examining codependent patterns, telepathic communication, and encounters with ancestors; understanding one's self better through spiritual healing, recovered memory, yoga, or meeting one's inner child; deepening spirituality through creation spirituality, tarot, channeling, Eckankar,

NEW AGE The New Age is an international social movement that began in the early 1970s. The merging of ideas from Asian religions and Western interpersonal psychology in the 1970s is often cited as the defining event of the movement. Spirituality and individual personal growth and transformation are the key elements of the movement. While the movement incorporates religious objects and rituals from a variety of religions, both worldwide and traditional, adherents of the New Age do not see it as a religion in of and itself. Rather than stressing the religious elements, adherents are more interested and involved in the "spiritual" essence of the movement.

The New Age has clear links to social movements preceding it, including the Beat generation of the pre– and post–World War II eras, the Hippie subculture of the 1960s and 1970s, the peace movement, and the environmental movement. In addition, the movement incorporates ideas and practices from alternative medicine such as homeopathy and Ayurvedic healing, from Asian religions such as Buddhism

Buddhism, Dharma, and vision quests; and relaxing through crafts, living theater, wearing crystals, drumming, and burning incense. These activities are but a few of the hundreds available to New Age seekers.

The number of people who associate themselves publicly with the New Age probably numbers several hundred thousand. As the New Age is deeply personal for many adherents and the movement lacks a central structure or formal network, the movement provides few employment opportunities or localized New Age communities, making it difficult to live an exclusively New Age lifestyle. Thus, most adherents selectively incorporate those elements of the New Age that are meaningful to them into their own lives. In this sense, for most adherents the New Age is about the freedom of self-expression—especially the freedom to add nontraditional but personally meaningful and fulfilling elements to their lives. Although demographic information is lacking, it seems that most adherents are white and most are women, although men are prominent in the movement as gurus, educators, healers, guides, and writers.

Perhaps because the New Age is ultimately about personal transformation and growth, there is no centralized New Age organization or leadership nor any set of core religious beliefs that adherents must follow or rituals that must be performed. There are some New Age intentional communities whose members seek to live a communal New Age lifestyle and numerous centers devoted to various New Age activities. Particular locales associated with the New Age include Salem, Massachusetts; the Berkshire region of western Massachusetts; Santa Fe, New Mexico; Woodstock, New York; Boulder, Colorado; Santa Cruz, California; Totnes, England; Katmandu, Nepal; and various locations in India. These locales are important to adherents because they provide a "spiritual essence" not generally experienced in other locales. In these and other communities with many New Age adherents, local institutions reflect the New Age. For example, churches might revise their ritual to include New Age prayers or ceremonies or emphasize peace and nature. Similarly, the local economy will support commercial establishments and services specifically for the New Age market.

Melton, J. Gordon, Jerome Clark, and Aidan A. Kelly. (1990) *New Age Encyclopedia.* 1st edition.

The New Age Catalogue: Access to Information and Sources. (1991).

Autonomic ordeals are ones where the outcome is determined by the involuntary reactions of the participants to painful or dangerous stimuli. The reactions are usually physiological responses to painful or dangerous situations as the ordeals often involve burning, scalding, bleeding, or drowning. Through modern science we now know about the physiological components of these ordeals, but in societies where they are customary it is supernatural power rather than human physiological reactions that are believed to cause the outcome.

Autonomic ordeals were common in medieval Europe and often involved fire and heat, water, and direct appeals to God. For example, an individual was judged guilty if his hand was burned after immersing it in boiling water or carrying a red-hot piece of iron. In water ordeals, the guilty were thought to float and the innocent to sink. These tests were not especially reliable. Direct appeals to God were more contests than ordeals, for the innocent party was the one who could stand longest in front of a cross with his hands upraised. Ordeals faded from use in Europe when they were replaced by more rational legal procedures such as trials and the use of evidence.

A cross-cultural survey of ordeals in 150 cultures in more recent times indicates that autonomic ordeals are used in 26 percent of cultures. Ordeals are not distributed uniformly around the world. Rather, two-thirds of societies with ordeals are in sub-Saharan African and no native North or South American culture is known to have ever used ordeals. Ordeals are usually the method of final resort, called for by those in power only when other methods of resolving a dispute or discovering the facts have proved fruitless. The Rundi of Zaire are a society that traditionally made heavy use of ordeals in judicial proceedings. The preferred ordeal was by poisoning in which the accused was forced to inhale a poisonous powder mixed with water and

ORDEALS The ordeal is a custom that demonstrates the close relationship between religion and other institutions of society in many cultures around the world. Ordeals link the legal system to religion; in some societies, in the past and today, ordeals are used to identify criminals and settle disputes.

Ordeals are used to determine guilt or innocence by submitting the accused to painful or dangerous tests. The underlying belief is that the tests are controlled by supernatural beings who will intervene to protect the innocent from harm and allow the guilty to suffer. Thus, failure to pass the test proves guilt. In addition to these types of ordeals, there are other types, including those where the outcome is based on chance or the knowledge or skill of the participant as well as those used as part of initiation rites or to prepare men for combat. Ordeals that are part of initiation rites or that prepare men for combat are often religious in nature as surviving the ordeal or resisting bodily injury are often interpreted as signs of supernatural power.

tobacco. The mix causes some to have seizures and hallucinations, proving their guilt. Those who confess immediately are administered an antidote that reverses the effects of the poison. Other ordeals include ingesting materials that will cause sickness such as cow dung or certain plants, immersing a hand in boiling water, sitting a person in a basket into which others thrust spears, and more benign methods that do not subject the accused to harm. The severity of the ordeal often reflected the severity of the wrong being investigated. Thus, not all were as harsh as those just described. For example, the Dogon of Mali determined if a boy stole sorrel by tickling along the spine of his back with a stick of straw. If he cannot control his laughter, he is considered guilty. These ordeals are now customs of the past among the Rundi and Dogon and in Africa in general. They were banned first by the European colonial powers who instituted their own legal systems, which have now been replaced by the legal systems of the African nations.

Little is known about why some cultures use ordeals and others do not, although it is clear that they fall into disuse when a formal legal system becomes the primary means of settling disputes in a society. In Africa and medieval Europe it seems, though, that ordeals occurred mainly in societies where the political leadership was weak, the group was fragmented into a number of different subgroups such as kinship groups, and there was a strong belief in the supernatural. In this context, ordeals allowed the weak leadership to maintain control by appealing to a higher authority in judicial decision-making.

See also ASCETICISM; POSSESSION AND TRANCE; RITUAL.

Griaule, Marcel. (1938) *Dogon Games.*

Pagès, G. (1933) *A Hamitic Kingdom in the Center of Africa: In Ruanda on the Shores of Lake Kiva (Belgian Congo).*

Roberts, John M. (1967) "Oaths, Autonomic Ordeals, and Power." In *Cross-Cultural Approaches,* edited by Clellan S. Ford, 169–195.

Teksbury, William J. (1967) "The Ordeal as a Vehicle for Divine Intervention in Medieval Europe." In *Law and Warfare: Studies in the Anthropology of Conflict,* edited by Paul Bohannan, 267–270.

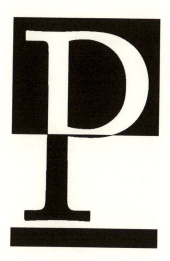

(called charismatic) may still retain their affiliation with a Catholic or Protestant denomination, but attend Pentecostal prayer services. But many independent churches that are Pentecostal in character have sprung up all over the world.

History

Pentecostalism traces its origins to a day, some time after the death and resurrection of Jesus Christ, when Christ's disciples were believed to have been visited by God in the form of the Holy Spirit. Here is the Biblical description of what is believed to have happened that day in C.E. 34.

> And suddenly a sound came from heaven like the rush of a mighty wind, and it filled all the house where they were sitting. And there appeared to them tongues as of fire, distributed and resting on each one of them. And they were all filled with the Holy Spirit and began to speak in other tongues, as the Spirit gave them utterance. Now there were dwelling in Jerusalem Jews, devout men from every nation under heaven. And at this sound the multitude came together, and they were bewildered, because each one heard them speaking in his own language. And they were amazed and wondered, saying, "Are not all these who are speaking Galileans: And how is it that we hear, each of us in his own native language? . . ." And all were amazed and perplexed, saying to one another, "What does this mean?" But others mocking, said, 'They are filled with new wine.'" (Acts 2:2–13)

This sense of being overpowered by a force greater than oneself, which causes a sense of ecstasy and oneness with God, is known as the baptism of the Holy Spirit. It is repeated in congregations all over the world for the more than 400 million Pentecostal worshipers.

What the early members of the church experienced was recorded in the New Testament. In a letter of St. Paul to the Corinthians (I

PENTACOSTALISM Christianity has evolved and split over the centuries, when believers in the divinity of Jesus Christ differ as to the "correct" meaning of his life and ministry. Early writings about Christ and the experiences of his disciples in the New Testament of the Bible can be interpreted in many ways. The controversies have been both about doctrine, what a church teaches, but also about corruption and scandal, as when Martin Luther challenged the hierarchy of the Roman Catholic Church and led the Protestant Reformation.

Many sects of Protestantism have emerged, some varying only in emphasis on a small area of belief. But there have always been Christians who believe that a person does not need the structure of a church or a priest to be the intermediary in the experience of God-given grace. They believe that the true Christian experience lies not in memorizing prayers and following rules but in this direct experience of God. Pentecostalism is in many ways more of a movement than a denomination. Some Pentecostals

Corinthians 12: 7–11), Paul outlines the gifts of the Holy Spirit that were received that day:

> To each is given the manifestation of the Spirit for the common good. To one is given through the Spirit the utterance of wisdom, and to another the utterance of knowledge according to the same Spirit, to another faith by the same Spirit, to another gifts of healing by the one Spirit, to another the working of miracles, to another prophecy, to another the ability to distinguish between spirits, to another various kinds of tongues, to another the interpretation of tongues. All these are inspired by one and the same Spirit, who apportions to each one individually as he wills. For just as the body is one and has many members, and all the members of the body, though many, are one body, so it is with Christ.

Of these, speaking in tongues (also known as glossolalia) is the gift most associated with Pentecostalism, followed by healings and prophecy. The gift of speaking in tongues was originally thought to be the utterance of another language, which would help the disciples take the words of Jesus Christ to other parts of the world. Although, over time, claims have been made to this effect, most speaking in tongues today is an unintelligible form of direct communication with God—an emotion-filled expression of prayer. No scientific study has ever determined that a real language, previously unknown to the speaker, is being spoken. Today speaking in tongues is not as important: "For them, the issue is not tongues, but the fullness of life in the Spirit. The gift of tongues is a manifestation of this fullness and is only one of a number of possible manifestations. [They] are more concerned with tongues as a gift of prayer." (Erling 1973: 95)

Speaking in tongues created controversy from the beginning. Passers-by thought the disciples were drunk, the level of emotion and praise was so high. But subsequently there were questions about what really happened when one spoke in tongues and what it meant. For example, does that mean one is chosen, closer to God than someone else? Apparently there was some arrogance on the part of some who received these gifts, and that arrogance was recognized as not the spirit of love that was taught by Christ. In any event, after the third century C.E., little is heard about the practice until the eighteenth century. At the turn of the twentieth century the practice gained a strong hold.

In the United States, at about that time, there was more than one movement back to the roots of Christianity. Mary Baker Eddy resurrected the idea of returning to "primitive" Christianity by restoring spiritual healing as a component of Christian belief. In the 1870s she formed the Church of Christ, Scientist, and the "science" was the metaphysical belief system that allowed for physical healing through prayer. They believed in the inherent ability of anyone to surrender to God's goodness through prayer and in that process cast out illness.

Later came the so-called "Holiness" churches, an outgrowth of the Methodists, who believed in a "second blessing" in the form of a visitation by the Holy Spirit. The first blessing was believed to be the experience of conversion. In the second blessing, paralleling the experience of the disciples at the Pentecost, a person is strengthened and transformed. Conflicts arose among the believers: Did the second blessing represent a complete cleansing from sin? Would it have to be proven by supernatural signs?

On New Year's Eve, in 1900, a female participant at a Kansas Bible College led by Charles Fox Parham was prayed over and suddenly began speaking a foreign language. It was reported at the time that she spoke Chinese, and she was unable to speak English for three days. Parham and his students were bowled over by the display and took it as a sign from God. The students fanned out over the Southwest, spreading the word of the second blessing by holding prayer meetings. Part of their appeal was their preaching that the second blessing was a sign that the end of the world was near. Those who followed them believed that all of the signs laid out in the Bible for the end of the world were present and that to receive the second blessing was to be saved for all eternity. The San Francisco earthquake of 1906 added to the feeling that the end was coming.

The movement grew in urban centers, where industrialization was creating disruption in the natural flow of people's lives. Many, especially immigrants, were experiencing poverty and the stress of the impersonal nature of work. Those attracted to the movement were not a part of the power structure and some were suspicious of the formality and hierarchy of traditional Christian churches. They were often desperate for miracles of healing in both the physical and the financial realms, and this contact with the Holy Spirit may have seemed to hold out the promise of miracles. Everyone was an equal in discovering the indwelling power of the Holy Spirit.

The participation and leadership of women was notable in this resurgence. This factor, plus the inclusion of ethnic minority groups, was seen by some as proof of the workings of the Holy Spirit in its inclusiveness and diversity.

In 1906, in Los Angeles, a black preacher named William Joseph Seymour joined a mission opened by Julia W. Hutchins. He had gained his knowledge about the coming of the gifts of the Holy Spirit by sitting outside of classes at Parham's college. A Ku Klux Klan sympathizer, Parham would not allow Seymour in the class. After Seymour arrived in Los Angeles, he preached at the mission for a time, but no one had yet spoken in tongues. Then one of his parishioners had a dream in which he believed that the Apostles had come to him and told him how to speak in tongues. He and Seymour prayed the following night, and soon many participants, including Seymour, were speaking in unknown tongues, praising God.

The word spread and soon the group founded a church on Azusa Street in Los Angeles. On April 14, 1906, the first service was held. The church grew. Black and white, poor and rich, praised God together in music, prayer, and praise. Intercession was made on behalf of the sick. Parham was invited to come, and distressed at the integrated environment and effusion of praise, he condemned the ministry. But visitors to the Azusa mission took the experience they found there around the nation and the world in a short time. Other women were prominent in the movement in Los Angeles. Aimee Semple McPherson had a tabernacle from which she presented dramatic interpretations of Bible stories and used the performing arts to preach the teachings of Christ.

Ethnic and doctrinal differences soon splintered the Pentecostals. All originally believed in the three acts of grace: conversion, sanctification, and baptism in the Spirit. But by 1916, there were three basic groups: Finished Work or Baptistic Pentecostals, Second Work or Wesleyan Pentecostals, and Oneness or "Jesus Only" Pentecostals.

The Finished Work Pentecostals believed that conversion and sanctification were a single act of grace. The Assemblies of God, created in 1914, became the first Finished Work denomination.

The Second Work or Wesleyan Pentecostals held to the three acts of grace. They became the Church of God in Christ, the Church of God, and the Pentecostal Holiness Church.

The Oneness, or Jesus Only, Pentecostals resulted from the Finished Work controversy over the proper water baptismal formula and the nature of God. Oneness believers said that the idea of a triple Godhead—Father, Son, and Holy Ghost—was simply different titles for the same God—Jesus Christ. The interracial Pentecostal Assemblies of the World was formed in the

Midwest. White Oneness Pentecostals formed the United Pentecostal Church.

From the 1920s to the 1950s many disputes arose in Pentecostal churches: how much structure would there be in the churches; how would the church be governed; what exactly did they believe? One issue was that of having to prove that one had spoken in tongues before being accepted into a church. And then there was the kind of praise that was more like circus sideshow entertainment. Some "cults" included snake handling and other exotic practices that did not cast a favorable light on the Pentecostals. The term "holy rollers" comes from the practice some groups had of rolling in the aisles of the church. Though these practices were not endorsed by the larger Pentecostal congregations, it brought ridicule from mainstream churches.

Holiness preachers continued to preach during the 1950s. Numbers remained smaller in Pentecostalism because of the prerequisite of speaking in tongues. A Pentecostal Holiness preacher from Oklahoma, Oral Roberts, became the most prominent Pentecostal in the United States. He subsequently encouraged a wealthy Pentecostal from California to found the Full Gospel Business Men's Fellowship. The group introduced many people to the Pentecostal movement and became instrumental in promoting the growth of Pentecostalism during a 1960s revival.

In the 1960s, the gift of speaking in tongues was experienced by Episcopalian minister Dennis Bennett and ushered in what is called the New Pentecostalism. Bennett began holding prayer groups in his congregation, which later led to his dismissal from his parish. National publicity resulted and, in a short time, midweek prayer groups grew up in many different denominations across the country.

Both newer Pentecostals and those from the turn of the century accept the Bible as their main source of information and inspiration. They be-lieve that Jesus was both man and the son of God. They also believe that Jesus Christ will come again—bodily—as the day of judgment nears.

Contemporary Pentacostalism

Some of the characteristics of the most recent resurgence of Pentecostalism are as follows:

1. Most do not require speaking in tongues as a prerequisite for joining.
2. There are many upper-class members as well as those from more disenfranchised groups.
3. Some Pentecostals form communal living arrangements.
4. The meetings are informal in style and dress. They often incorporate music, and time is left to minister to the individual needs of members.
5. The tone is one of joy and praise.
6. Many teenagers and young adults are involved.
7. The moral code of the older Pentecostals, which rejected smoking, dancing, and using makeup, is more relaxed.

Here is the point of view of one of the first ministers to introduce charismatic gifts into his congregation: "The Christian religion is essentially an experience—a personal experience of God. Theology and doctrine are simply an explanation of that experience. Many people know something about the doctrine, but have never really had the experience. So, of course, their religion is dry, formal, powerless. It has no life, no zest, no sense of reality." (Christensen 1954: 49)

Speaking in tongues in some Pentecostal services takes the following form: "Sometimes virtually the entire congregation does it all at once, and the sound is like small waves of murmurs and gentle sighs, mounting into billows of muffled vowels and muted consonants. Sometimes it begins as a tiny trickle, grows into a roaring cascade, then wanes again into a rustle. Sometimes it is a single person who stands and, for thirty seconds or so, rarely more, speaks clearly discernible but incomprehensible syllables. Sometimes this is followed by an interpretation by another person, sometimes not. Sometimes it happens with music, a polyphony of tones and vocables but with no recognizable words. Sometimes the speakers sound anxious or urgent. More often they sound joyful, thankful or serene." (Cox 1995: 85–86)

Pentecostalism is one of the fastest-growing international religious movements today. In the years between 1985 and 1990, Baptist, Methodist, Presbyterian, and Roman Catholic churches in the United Kingdom all lost members. During the same period, independent, mostly Pentecostal and charismatic churches gained nearly 30 percent. In Italy, Pentecostals are the largest non-Catholic religious group. Scandinavia, France, Belgium, and Switzerland have Pentecostal congregations, as do many countries in Eastern Europe.

Pentecostalism continues to appeal to the poor and politically disenfranchised. There are four types of Pentecostalism in Asia, Africa, and Latin America: (1) mission churches established by European and North Americans; (2) charismatic movements in traditional denominations; (3) independent offshoots of the mission churches; and (4) indigenous beliefs that, while they include the idea of spirit baptism and speaking in tongues, may also include non-Christian elements such as polygamy and ancestor worship. In a recent three-year period in Brazil, over 700 new Pentecostal churches were formed; there are now more Pentecostal pastors than Catholic priests. Colombia and Argentina have large numbers of Pentecostals. In South Africa, Zaire, Ghana, and Nigeria, Pentecostals number in the millions, with large numbers in other African countries.

In Korea, the former Soviet Union, and China churches are springing up. The only area that has resisted Pentecostalism is the Islamic Middle East. The total number of Pentecostals worldwide in the mid-1990s is estimated at 410 million, with growth of 20 million new members per year.

The growth of Pentecostalism is an example of the search for passion and emotion in what many believed is a dead and unresponsive Christianity. Many believers thought there was a missing element in Christianity—that of direct experience with God.

See also REVITALIZATION MOVEMENTS.

Christensen, James B. (1954) *Double Descent among the Fanti.*

Cox, Harvey. (1995) *Fire from Heaven: The Rise of Pentecostal Spirituality and the Reshaping of Religion in the Twenty-first Century.*

Erling, Jorstad, ed. (1973) *The Holy Spirit in Today's Church: A Handbook of the New Pentecostalism.*

Glock, Charles Y., and Robert N. Bellah. (1976). *The New Religious Consciousness.*

Mills, Watson E. (1985) *Speaking in Tongues: A Guide to Research on Glossolalia.*

PILGRIMAGE

A pilgrimage is a type of religious journey. An individual who makes a pilgrimage is called a pilgrim. The destination of a pilgrimage is a place that is believed by the pilgrim and other adherents of a religion to have a special, sacred quality. Often the place is a shrine, that is, a place associated with a particular supernatural being, a supernatural event such as a miracle, or a sacred personage such as a saint. The reason an individual makes a pilgrimage is to become physically, emotionally, and spiritually closer to the supernatural world. There may be other purposes as well, such as asking for forgiveness or assistance, seeking a cure for an illness, meeting a religious obligation, enhancing one's reputation as a devout adherent in one's home community, and the more worldly purpose of participating in a journey to a distant and exciting place. Some experts view pilgrimages as rites of passage, as the pilgrim leaves his or her community, joins a community of fellow pilgrims (Geoffrey Chaucer's *Canterbury Tales* has much about this aspect of pilgrimage), is emotionally and spiritually changed by the religious experience, and then returns home with a redefined status in the religious community. While all of this is true of many pilgrimages, what is most significant about pilgrimages for most pilgrims is the deep and very personal emotional and spiritual nature of the experience. Of course, the reasons people make pilgrimages vary both from person to person, and one person may have different reasons for making different pilgrimages or even different reasons for making the same pilgrimage at different times.

Pilgrimages are a feature of all major world religions and there are tens of thousands of pilgrimage sites around the world with millions of people making pilgrimages each year. Many pilgrimages are to major sites, such as those by Muslims to Mecca, Medina, and Jerusalem; Jews to Jerusalem; Hindus to Banaras and Mount Kailas; Shinto to Ise; Christians to Rome, Jerusalem, and Lourdes; and Buddhists to Lumbini, Bodh Gaya, Sarnath, and Kusinara. Although each of these, just a few of the major pilgrimage centers, draw millions of pilgrims every year, an even greater number of pilgrims around the world travel each year to tens of thousands of local and regional pilgrimage sites.

Types of Pilgrimages

Pilgrimages fall into a number of types. Archaic pilgrimages, like those to Jerusalem, Canterbury, and Mecca, are ones that are made to sites that were pilgrimage centers before the emergence of the world religion that came to use the site as the destination for pilgrimages. Often, as is the case with Christians and Muslims who pilgrimage to Jerusalem, the beliefs associated with the original pilgrimage have disappeared or have merged with the religion whose adherents now use the site for their own reasons. Prototypical pilgrimages are ones established by the founder of the religion or by early adherents of the religion. These include Mecca for Muslims, Rome and Jerusalem for Christians, Jerusalem for Jews, Banaras and Mount Kailas for Hindus, and Bodh Gaya and Sarnath for Buddhists. High-period pilgrimages are mainly Christian ones that developed in medieval Europe when travel to Jerusalem, then controlled by Muslims, was impossible for European Christians. The pilgrimage was centered around a shrine dedicated to a specific holy personage, such as a saint or the Virgin Mary. Marian pilgrimages are probably the most common type of high-period pilgrimage and many such shrines have been founded in recent times. Often, the town where the shrine is located becomes a pilgrimage center, with associated businesses, beggars, and fairs. These types of pilgrimages and pilgrimage sites were transferred to the New World by Roman Catholic missionaries and settlers and many contemporary pilgrimages of regional or local form are of this type. For example, Lourdes in Litchfield, Connecticut, was built by priests and brothers between 1954 and 1958, using a postcard photograph of the shrine in Lourdes, France, as their model. The final type of pilgrimage is the modern pilgrimage, which emerged only in the last 200 years and is characterized by the establishment of apparitional pilgrimage centers and the use of modern forms of transportation to reach those centers.

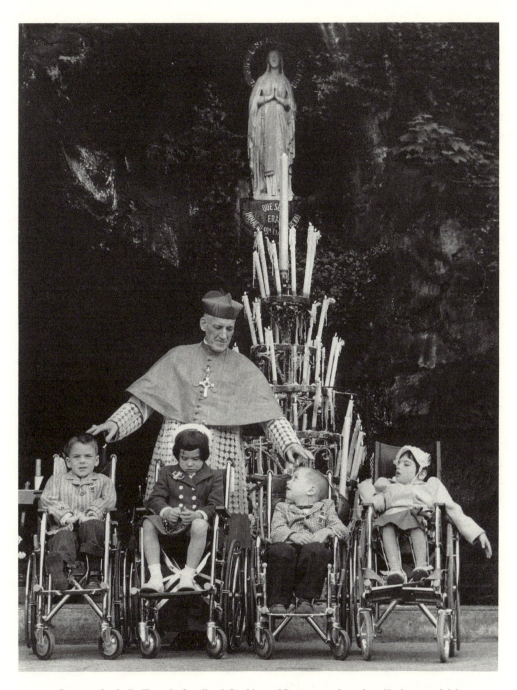

Roman Catholic Francis Cardinal Cushing of Boston conducted a pilgrimage of sick American children to Lourdes, France, in 1961. Pilgrimages, religious journeys, can be to a shrine associated with an event or supernatural being. Lourdes has been a destination for Roman Catholics and others since 1858 who believe that an illness or condition may be cured by the intervention of the Virgin Mary, Mother of Jesus.

In addition to these types, pilgrimages may also be classified as major, regional, or local. Major pilgrimages are ones like those to Jerusalem by Christians, Jews, and Muslims, which may be made at some time by any adherent of the faith, and which, even if not required, are a goal for all adherents. Regional pilgrimages are ones made mostly by people living in a particular world region, either because the pilgrimage site marks a person or event of regional significance or because the site was established as a regional pilgrimage center. For example, the Bom Jesus de Lapa pilgrimage site in Bahia, Brazil, draws pilgrims from all of Brazil; during the pilgrimage season the town is transformed into a pilgrimage center with much social, economic, and religious activity directed toward the needs of the pilgrims. A local pilgrimage is one to a site located in or near the community of the pilgrims. For example, Kurds in the Middle East are Muslims and therefore are expected to make a pilgrimage to Mecca at least once during their lives. But, as with other religions, in many communities local pilgrimage sites are also established. The community of Rowanduz, for example, has six such sites at the graves of important Muslim religious leaders in the community that people may visit and ask for assistance:

1. Shaykh Piri Mawili near the village of Kani Kah. Shaykh Piri Mawili is said to have lived about two hundred years ago, "in the time of Kor Pasha."
2. Shaykh Sa'idi Galikarak near the village of Karak. The shrine is said to be very old, dating perhaps from the time of the Islamic conquest.
3. Shaykh Saran in the village of Saran itself. Shaykh Saran is said to have died about fifty years ago.
4. Shaykh Usu Shaykhan on the road to Kawlok. "No one knows how old it is, but it is very ancient."

5. Shaykh Muhammad or Shaykh Balik, the second most famous shrine in the district, at Hajji Umran.
6. Shuwani Shaykh Muhammed or Shuwani Mala, "The Shepherd of Shaykh Muhammad. (Masters 1953: 313)

Shrines and Pilgrimage Centers

Nobody knows how many shrines and pilgrimage centers there are around the world, but they number in the tens of thousands and certainly more than one hundred thousand if all local sites are included in the count. A particular place can become a shrine for any number of reasons:

1. relics associated with a supernatural being or sacred person are found or stored there;
2. a miracle took place there;
3. a supernatural being or sacred personage appeared there (apparitional shrine);
4. a physical transformation of a natural object such as a stone or tree took place there;
5. an event that led to the salvation of a religious community took place there;
6. a major community event occurred or occurs there;
7. a sacred personage was born or died or is buried there;
8. there is a feature of nature, such as a mountain, cave, or river, believed to have supernatural power or meaning;
9. it is an already important place of religious activity such as a temple or monastery;
10. adherents chose to build a shrine there.

A shrine is a place where a supernatural being or a sacred personage is acknowledged, honored, and worshipped. The being or personage is usually represented by a relic associated with him or her or a statue of him or her. Shrines are especially common in cultures that practice ancestor worship, and there are often shrines in each home and in village shrine halls where ancestors are worshipped. Pilgrimages to ancestor shrines are not common because people live in or near the village where the shrines are located. However, descendants who have moved away may journey back to the village or to ancestors' graves to pay homage to them. Shrines, are, of course, a major feature of world religion pilgrimages and most pilgrimage sites center on a shrine. Lourdes of Litchfield, for example, contains three shrines—the central and largest one of Mary and smaller ones of Saint Joseph and Saint Jude.

Shrines that are frequently visited by large numbers of pilgrims or are the focus of large-scale pilgrimages often become pilgrimage centers. These centers provide a wide range of services and products to the pilgrims who arrive throughout the year or during pilgrimage seasons. These centers also often become the locale for festivals on festival days that are the high point of the pilgrimage season.

As a place that draws devout adherents, pilgrimage centers often provide a range of religious services to pilgrims. For example, the pilgrimage season at Lourdes in Litchfield, Connecticut, is from May until mid-October, although the shrine may be visited on any day of the year. During pilgrimage season mass is conducted daily (except Mondays) at 11:30 A.M., Rosary at 11 A.M. on Wednesdays and Fridays, and 3 P.M. on Sunday is set aside as Holy Hour. In addition, events are scheduled throughout the season to celebrate Roman Catholic and secular holidays and attend to the special needs of pilgrims, including the following:

April 29	Solemn Feast of St. Louis de Montfort
May 7	Feast Day of Blessed Marie Louise of Jesus
May 12	Special Blessing for Mothers
	May Crowning of the Statue of Blessed Mother
May 16	Ascension of Our Lord
May 19	Annual Blessing of Motorcycles
May 26	Pentecost Sunday—Anointing of the Sick
May 27	Memorial Day Mass
June 2	Trinity Sunday
June 9	Corpus Christi Prayers
	Exposition of the Blessed Sacrament and Procession
June 16	Special Blessing for Fathers
	Special Collection to Benefit Birthright of Torrington
June 23	Anointing of Sick
July 4	July 4th Mass
July 28	Anointing of Sick
August 12–14	Triduum in Preparation for the Feast of the Assumption
August 15	The Solemnity of Our Lady's Assumption
August 23	Family Night
August 25	Anointing of Sick
September 2	Labor Day Mass
September 20	Family Night
September 22	Anointing of Sick
October 20	Mission Sunday
October 27	Harvest Dinner to Benefit Montfort Community Ministry at the Shrine

Pilgrimages in Indigenous Cultures

As noted above, pilgrimages are a feature of world religions. These types of pilgrimages are not a practice common to indigenous religious systems. This is mostly due to three factors. First, in most indigenous religious systems no clear distinction, or no distinction at all, is made between the supernatural and the natural worlds. Much of what people come into contact with in their daily lives is sacred or has a spiritual dimension. And, while there is a gradient of "sacredness" to different places or objects, there is often no categorization of places as either sacred or secular. Thus, the notion of a shrine as a sacred place completely separate from the secular places of the everyday world is absent. Second, most indigenous cultures have small populations and live in a relatively small geographical area. Thus, they would not establish pilgrimage sites in some distant place. While pilgrimages as defined here are not found in indigenous societies, some such societies do regularly engage in travel for religious purposes. Travel on vision quests to sacred places or to encounter supernatural beings and soul travel are two common forms of religious travel. In some cultures, people regularly engage in collective travel to sacred places that in some ways are similar to the pilgrimages of world religions. For example, the Huichol of northern Mexico make an annual journey to Wirkuta, the sacred peyote land in the San Luis Potosí Desert, where through peyote-induced hallucinogenic trances they communicate with their gods. And each August, as part of the boys' vision quests, the Taos of northern New Mexico travel to the sacred Blue Lake in the Sángre de Cristo Mountains. The location is so sacred to the Taos that no non-Indian has witnessed the ceremony conducted there in the twentieth century, and the Taos waged a 65-year battle with the federal government to regain control of the land, a battle they finally won in 1971. While Huichol and Taos religious travels resemble world religion pilgrimages, they also differ in important ways—both are part of the annual cycle of religious observances, both are mandatory for all or select members of the community, and both have a community-defined purpose that benefits the entire community, not just the pilgrims themselves. Thus, the elements of individual choice and individual purpose characteristic of world religion pilgrimages are not as important, although the actual experience is as personally meaningful for all pilgrims, regardless of their religion.

The mandatory, collective nature of indigenous pilgrimages is clear in the annual "Pilgrimage for Spruce" of the Hopi of Arizona. For the Hopi, the spruce is a sacred plant because it "has the magnetic power to bring in the clouds and moisture" and water is especially important for growing corn in the desert region where the Hopi live. Thus, spruce twigs are worn by all ritual dancers and are required at some rituals. The Hopi and other Indians attending the ceremonial dances take twigs home to plant in their fields to attract rain. The Pilgrimage for Spruce is undertaken by one man accompanied by two other men who are to protect him from supernatural evil he may encounter on the journey. The journey is to Kisiwu (Spring in the Shadows), a spring located in a cave forty miles to the northeast, a three-day trip by foot. Once near the cave, the men approach and enter while carefully following the required rituals and looking for signs of how much water will fall in the next year as well as signs from the supernatural as to whether or not they are pleased by the ritual objects the Hopi clans have made and sent for presentation. The men then pick two spruce trees from the ridge above the cave:

"We pick a good-sized one about two and a half feet high, one with needles that show it is a male tree. We then look carefully for another which has the female needles. Picking them up gently after they are cut, we put our arms around them and take them to our bosoms, for we know that we are bringing their kachina spirits into our village, and the kachinas who participate in the ceremony are the spirits who bring rain. . . . It is the spirits of the spruce, the clouds, and the rain who give this life to us, you understand. So we offer our prayers again to the male and female branches, and we invite all the spirits to our village to take part in the ceremony." (Waters 1963: 202)

Upon returning to the village, the spruce branches are distributed to the clans, ceremonially welcomed to the village, and then used in the dance ceremonies meant to bring rain and a rich harvest in the coming season.

While this Hopi journey is meant to benefit the entire community and is taken by only three men selected for the task, their ritual behavior differs little from that of many pilgrims who are adherents of world religions. The pilgrimage may be long and difficult, and even if modern transportation is used may be costly in time and money. To experience the full effect of the pilgrimage and to please the supernatural beings, the pilgrim must travel the correct route and adhere to the required ritual behavior while traveling to and at the pilgrimage site. Prayers are said and an offering made and upon returning home additional prayers may be said and offerings made to help secure the objectives of the pilgrimage. The pilgrim experience of a traveler to Santeria de Chimayo, a Roman Catholic healing shrine in northern New Mexico, provides an example of typical pilgrimage behavior. The pilgrim flew by airplane from Connecticut to New Mexico and traveled to the shrine by car in order to obtain divine assistance in curing an aunt who had been diagnosed as terminally ill with cancer. The pilgrim arrived with a small, plastic zip-lock bag and a pre-posted express-mail envelope addressed to her aunt. In the sanctuary, she scooped soil from the small hole in the ground containing the healing soil into the bag, offered a prayer, made a monetary contribution to the shrine, and then attended an outdoor mass in the grove behind the church. She then drove to the nearest town and mailed the soil in the envelope, again praying for its safe journey to her aunt. After a week of vacation, she returned home, prayed and lit a candle at her parish church for her aunt and attended mass the next Sunday. Thus, while there are sociocultural differences between religious journeys, the personal behavior and experiences of the pilgrims is much the same across cultures.

See also FESTIVALS; LIFE-CYCLE RITES; MAGIC; SOUL; VISION QUEST.

Bhardwaj, Surinder M. (1973) *Hindu Places of Pilgrimage in India.*

Bodine, John. (1979) "Taos Pueblo." In *Handbook of North American Indians,* edited by Alfonso Ortiz, vol. 9, 255–267.

Gross, Daniel R. (1971) "Ritual and Conformity: A Religious Pilgrimage to Northeastern Brazil." *Ethnology* 10: 129–148.

Kamal, Ahmad. (1961) *The Sacred Journey.*

Khanna, Ashok, and Pramesh Ratnakar. (1988) *Banaras: The Sacred City.*

Kollek, Teddy, and Moshe Pearlman. (1970) *Pilgrims to the Holy Land.*

Masters, William M. (1953) *Rowanduz: A Kurdish Administrative and Mercantile Center.*

Myerhoff, Barbara. (1974) *Peyote Hunt: The Sacred Journey of the Huichol Indians.*

"Pilgrimage." (1987) *Encyclopedia of Religion,* edited by Mircea Eliade, vol. 11, 327–354.

Turner, Victor W., and Edith Turner. (1978) *Image and Pilgrimage in Christian Culture.*

Waters, Frank. (1963) *Book of the Hopi.*

POSSESSION AND TRANCE

Possession and trance are two altered states of consciousness commonly used across cultures as a means of communicating with the supernatural world. While in modern nations techniques such as hypnosis, meditation, and mood-altering drugs are used for recreational purposes, in most traditional cultures, use of such techniques and others to induce possession or trance are nearly always religious in nature. While possession and trance are not major elements of contemporary world religions, beliefs in spirit possession are found in Islam, Hinduism, Judaism, Roman Catholicism, Pentecostal Christianity, and the New Age movement.

Altered states of consciousness are states of human experience in which one's perception, memory, sense of time and space, body image, etc., differ from what is typically experienced while one is awake or sleeping normally. Such states may be induced psychologically (by hypnosis, for example), physiologically (by sleep deprivation, for example) or pharmacologically (by hallucinogenic drugs, for example) and can take place in a variety of culturally institutionalized ways such as in certain forms of dreaming, visions, ecstasy, fire walking, snake handling, speaking in tongues, out-of-body near-death experiences, channeling, and possession by an external force such as spirit or ghost. Altered states of consciousness are a cultural universal (although not all people in all cultures experience them) and possession and trance are elements of the religious systems of 90 percent of cultures, with some cultures having only trance, others only possession, and still others both. Despite much research, little is known about the neurophysiological basis of altered states of consciousness although most experts now agree that altered states of consciousness are complex phenomena that result from the interaction of physiological, psychological, cultural, and social factors. In addition, it is also clear that the experience of an altered state both at the individual and cultural levels varies widely from person to person and culture to culture and that the experience is molded by a variety of individual and cultural factors.

Trance

Trance is a psychological state in which an individual loses contact with most of his or her external world, forgets the past, and often does not remember what transpired during the trance. Trance induced by hypnosis or by the use of hallucinogenic drugs are the two most common forms in Western societies, where trance is typically not linked to religion. In traditional societies trance may be induced by mind-altering drugs, rhythmic activities such as repetitive drumming, physical deprivation such as fasting, or by dream activity and often takes the form of soul travel in which the individual's soul leaves his body and travels to an encounter with supernatural beings such as spirits or ghosts. Trance is not distributed equally around the world, is experienced more often by men than by women, and is found most commonly in East Asia and among the traditional hunter-gatherer cultures of North and South America and Siberia, where in the latter it is often a component of shamanism and religious healing.

In rural Taiwan, soul travel is undertaken by a shaman who, with the assistance of chanting assistants, causes his soul to leave his body and travel to the *yin* land, where contact is made with deceased ancestors of friends and relatives, usually to check on their condition. While the shaman's body remains on earth and visible to others, the absence of his soul is marked by odd behavior. There is always the possibility that his soul will become lost and have trouble finding its way back to his body. If this happens, a Taoist priest is employed to unite soul and body. Chinese shamans practice another form of soul travel in which the soul leaves the body and is replaced by the spirit of a god. Acting as a medium, the god then speaks through the shaman and anyone present may make inquiries about any matter. People know that a god's spirit is in the body because the shaman's personality changes to that of a god—proud, in control, knowledgeable, and compassionate. During these seances, a shaman might cut himself and write charms with his blood, although it is claimed that no physical wounds result, suggesting that injury is caused by wounding the soul, not just the body.

Among Native Americans of the Plains, visions during a trance state were an important part of the Ghost Dance ceremony and revitalization movement. Among the Pawnee, people danced over a four-day period, usually from mid-afternoon to midnight each day. Trance was induced as follows:

> As each song was sung, the circle of dancers, holding hands, moved clockwise through one complete circuit, returning to the original starting point. This is determined by the main singer's position: he begins at the west and finishes at the west. . . . During the dancing period of the day, the dancers could carry out as many songs as they wished; there was no special number. The singing was initiated and led by the seven crow-feathered singers, and the others joined in. While the dancing went on, some "hypnotizers" would dance inside the circle directly in front of individuals they wished to throw into a trance, using feathers or other objects to focus and fix the eyesight of the subject, thus transfixing them. Usually the subject fell when he or she was touched with the object used. When individuals fell into a trance, they were laid down and the others continued to dance. (Lesser 1933: 80)

While in the trance state the individual had a vision during which, guided by an eagle or crow, he traveled to the world of the dead where all deceased Pawnee lived as they did in the past, before Pawnee culture was disrupted by Europeans settlers.

The individual focused on one aspect of traditional life, such as the buffalo hunt or dances, and upon awakening wrote songs, designed costumes, and made other objects that told of these old Pawnee ways. As part of the Ghost Dance revitalization movement, this form of trance served to provide information about the traditional culture that the people sought to revive.

As noted above, another route to a trance state is through the use of mood-altering or hallucinogenic drugs, use of which was especially common among Native Americans in the southwest United States and tropical South America. The use of peyote, a mild mood-altering drug, for example, is a sacrament of the Native American Church today, although its use has been curtailed by court cases brought by the U.S. government. In South America, drugs are used to induce a trance so as to communicate with the gods and spirits. Among the Yanomamö of Brazil, shamans inhale a drug when they want to communicate with the spirits so that they can bring harm to an enemy or cure the sick. In a trance, the shaman chants to the spirit, asking for his assistance. When curing the sick, he seeks to force the spirit who has entered the patient's body to an arm or leg; he then sucks it out, discarding it by vomiting or spitting it out.

Possession

Possession, or possession trance or spirit possession as it is often called, differs from trance in that the body is taken over—possessed—by a spirit. It also differs from trance in the types of cultures where it is found and in the people involved. About 50 percent of cultures have a belief in possession, and most of these are found in Oceania or sub-Saharan Africa or are African-American groups in the New World that practice syncretic religions such as Vodou (also voodoo or vodoun), Santería, and Candomblé. Most of these cultures are ones whose traditional economy was based on horticulture. Again unlike trance, those subject to spirit possession are usually women and the spirits who possess them are usually male. Additionally, possession is often a group activity (in some cultures there are possession cults and in others possession is a public event).

In some cultures, and especially in world religions such as Judaism and Christianity, possession is equated with possession by an evil spirit and thus is always considered harmful and therefore feared, although many other aspects of the possession are typical of possession beliefs in general. An example of possession as always harmful is the *dybbuk*-possession of traditional Jewish communities in nineteenth-century Europe and the Middle East. Dybbuk is derived from the Hebrew word for "to stick," and refers to the spirit of a deceased evil male that enters the body of a woman in order to escape the state of limbo in which it is forced to live. Dybbuk-possession was considered a disease and its major symptoms were aggressive behavior, obscene speech, convulsions, speaking in tongues, and amnesia following the episode. As the spirit preferred to remain in the woman rather than return to limbo, his removal required an exorcism, performed in the synagogue by a rabbi. The exorcism involved identifying the spirit, discussing the conditions for its departure, and agreeing to the route of its exit from the body.

In other cultures some spirits are seen as helpful and possession is voluntarily sought in order to seek the help of these spirits. For example, the Central Thai believe that possession can both be harmful and helpful. When a person is possessed by the ghost of a deceased relative that wants to communicate some message, no attempt will be made to exorcise the ghost

and it will be allowed to depart when it chooses. The view that possession can be beneficial is especially elaborated in cultures in sub-Saharan Africa and in African cultures in the Western Hemisphere.

In some cases, the behavior of the person possessed by a specific spirit is highly stylized, as among the Vodou spirits in Haiti (see below).

In many cultures, spirit possession is considered a major source of illness and a ritual healer is employed to identify and remove the spirit. For the Central Thai, spirit possession by ghosts of the dead can be both helpful or harmful and full or partial. In full possession, the individual is able to communicate the messages of the spirit by both physical gestures and speech. In partial possession, communication is by gesture alone. Not all spirits are capable of possessing a human and not all Central Thai are subject to possession. Those most susceptible to possession are women with "hot hearts," that is, they are often lonely, depressed, and suffer from psychosomatic symptoms such as headaches. When possessed they convulse, make strange sounds, utter strange words, thrash about, feel hot, and display marked mood swings. This behavior, typical of possession in many cultures, is often described in psychological terms as a disassociative or hysterical state. While possessed, the woman often (as is common in many other cultures as well) identifies with the male spirit possessing her and speaks like a man and behaves like the deceased person the spirit rep-

Vodou Spirits in Haiti

Spirit	Powers	Behavior of Possessed
Legba	Guardian of crossroads	Carries cane and limps
Damballa	Cures serious illnesses	Rolls on the ground, drinks too much, and is violent
Saint John	Causes earthquakes	Drinks too much and is both aloof and friendly
Adjasou	Makes water rise in springs	Excitement
Maitresse Mombu	Causes heavy rain	Dances and eats food off the ground

resents did, such as drinking heavily, cursing, or being violent. In those cases where the possession is seen as an illness rather than a friendly communication from a deceased ancestor the services of a healer are needed to end the possession and cure the patient. The healer's first task is to determine if it is a case of full possession or some other disorder. The healer then must determine the identity of the ghost, which is accomplished by rituals that arouse the ghost in the patient's body, close off passageways out of the patient's body, and interview the ghost to learn its identity and plot the exorcism to remove it. One common result of this procedure is to cause the patient to become actively possessed, which provides the healer with valuable information about the ghost's identity. The healer then chooses from any number of techniques that he thinks will serve best to drive the ghost out the patient's body, usually through the soles of the feet. These techniques include fooling the ghost by offering the patient a ritually treated cigarette or betel to chew, inducing a ghost the healer controls to enter the patient's body to drive the possessing ghost out, brushing the ghost out by brushing the patient's body from head to toe, or beating the patient with a switch to drive out the ghost.

Possession among the Amhara of Ethiopia is seen as a major cause of illness, especially illnesses whose major symptoms are unusual behavior. As with the Central Thai and most other cultures, it is Amhara women who are most often possessed. The illness is often cured by female *zar* doctors who lead zar cults, the activities of which center around the healing and support of its possessed members. The zar doctor's primary qualification is that she is susceptible to possession but, unlike her patients, has learned to control powerful zar spirits whom she can call on to help remove the malicious spirits that possess her patients. The genesis of the zar spirits as an evil force are explained by the Amhara as follows:

the 'zar' spirits originated in the Biblical Garden of Eden at the same time man was created. They assumed physical form when Eve began to bear children. Eve is believed to have had 30 children. One day, when God the Creator came to visit, and began to count the children, Eve (evidently fearing the evil eye), hid the 15 most beautiful ones. God, being all-knowing, realized this, and became angry. As punishment, he decreed that the 15 hidden children always remain hidden, invisible, night creatures, for all eternity. The present-day zar spirits are believed descended from them. (Messing 1957: 599)

The Amhara have a large pantheon of zar spirits, some of which are listed below along with their major characteristics (Messing 1957: 617–626):

Some Zar Spirits of the Amhara

Wädaj (Lover)
Sex: male
Power: subordinate to powerful zars
Social Status: unclear
Regional, Religious, or Ethnic Affiliation: Muslim
Personality: fickle and promiscuous
Totemic Symbol: qat leaf
Attributes: possessor of women

Aweliya
Sex: male
Power: great
Social Status: high
Regional, Religious, or Ethnic Affiliation: unlimited
Personality: tough, can be made protective, generally irascible
Totemic Symbol: lioness, female elephant
Attributes: possessor of the chief zar doctor in the region

Mälak (Angel)
Sex: male
Power: medium

Social Status: medium
Regional, Religious, or Ethnic Affiliation: Coptic Christian
Personality: mystic
Totemic Symbol: horse
Attributes: appears in dreams in the shape of a horse

Abba Yosef
Sex: male
Power: great but vulnerable to Coptic influence
Social Status: medium
Regional, Religious, or Ethnic Affiliation: Coptic Christian
Personality: very jealous, purist
Totemic Symbol: none
Attributes: causes miscarriages in married women out of jealousy for husband and as "purist"; can be restrained by wearing amulet of *däbtära*

Barya (Slave)
Sex: male
Power: sometimes great
Social Status: low
Regional, Religious, or Ethnic Affiliation: from Negroid Sudanese people and has come to wreak vengeance for the enslavement of his people by the Amhara
Personality: evil, very stubborn, never protective; at most agrees to plague the patient less; sometimes attacks in group, led by their chief, Legewon (Like a Tornado), who has red eyes
Totemic Symbol: tornado
Attributes: causes epilepsy, especially in men, whom he prefers to possess; the convulsions are his orgies; he is vulnerable to spellbinding formulae of *däbtära*.

Rahelo
Sex: female
Power: very great, chief female zar
Social Status: high

Regional, Religious, or Ethnic Affiliation: Christian, yet was married to a Muslim
Personality: evil, never becomes protective
Totemic Symbol: lemon tree
Attributes: causes miscarriages, preferably in rich or noblewomen, for she is a snob; amulets and formulae of *däbtära* may have power against her

Aynä Tela (Shadow Eye)
Sex: female
Power: medium
Social Status: low
Regional, Religious, or Ethnic Affiliation: none
Personality: evil, never protective, but not very powerful when alone: parasitic zar, waiting for the spoils left by other zars
Totemic Symbol: none
Attributes: general troublemaker; tries to prevent patient from entering trance properly, confusing the diagnosis, confusing other zars when about to reveal their names; likes to attack men that have been attacked by other zars and thus weakened

The illnesses caused by zar spirits are mainly ones whose major symptoms are odd behavior by the afflicted individual. For women the most common zar disorders are assuming a male identity and behaving like a man; regression to infantile behavior such as baby talk, asking for gifts, and prancing about; and depression. For men the most common disorders, which occur less often than female ones, are behaving like a woman, inflicting physical injury on oneself, and epileptic seizures.

Treatment is conducted by the zar doctor within the context of the zar cult, a group of patients previously cured by the zar doctor that now regularly meets to prevent new zar attacks and also to assist in the treatment of new patients. Treatment takes place at night when the zar spirits are active and involves diagnosis (identification of the zar spirit possessing the patient), negotiation with the zar to persuade it to leave the patient, and the cult relationship that provides protection from subsequent attacks. The setting is the doctor's hut, with incense burning and the assembled cult members talking quietly, drumming, and chanting. Each member then performs her "gurri" dance "when the spirit moves her." The dance, which lasts for twenty minutes, progresses from rhythmic movement of the shoulders while seated to broader movements while standing to twirling about until the dancer collapses to the floor. The patient then dances herself, placing herself in a trance in which the zar spirit possesses her but is also accessible to the doctor. Diagnosis then begins and the manner of subsequent dances by the patient provides the doctor with clues to the identity of the zar. The doctor then questions the patient, announces the identity of the zar, and begins discussions with the zar toward the end of enticing it to leave the patient's body. This generally requires finding out what has offended the zar, how he would like to be compensated, and what compensation he would like in the future to keep him from possessing the patient again. Payment of compensation, such as the sacrifice of a sheep or an offering of vegetable water, is then arranged, the patient pays a fee to join the zar cult, and the illness is cured.

Possession trance is found across cultures in its most highly elaborated form in some New World African-American religions, including Vodou in Haiti, Santería in Cuba, and Candomblé in Brazil. These are all syncretic religions, as they are based on a mix of beliefs and practices drawn from indigenous African religions and Roman Catholicism. While each religion differs from the others in some ways and there is internal variation in belief and practice within each religion, most of the basic features of possession trance are exemplified by the Candomblé religion of Brazil.

Although the possession trance of these religions often draws much of the attention of outsiders, it is important to remember that they are but one aspect of these religions and that individuals who are capable of being possessed are but one religious functionary. Candomblé activities are based at *seitas* (cult centers), which contain the *terreiro* (temple grounds) and *franquai* (sacred groves). Within the terreiro are the *barracao* (sacred dance hall), *camarinha* (sacred room for the initiates), the *pegi* (sanctuary for the fetish stones of the deities), special huts where some deities live, and living quarters for the priest and his or her assistants. The key supernatural beings are the *orixás,* deities who personify some aspect of nature and are capable of possessing humans, through whom they then communicate. The key religious specialists are the priests (male—*pae de santa;* female—*mae de santo*), their male assistants (*ogans*), assistants who perform sacrifices (*achôgun*), and those individuals capable of being possessed by an orixá, the *filha de santo.*

Each orixá is identified by name and personal characteristics, usually including a distinctive call that announces his or her arrival in the body of a filha de santo. Some major orixá from the nearly one hundred associated with this particular cult are listed below.

Some Major Gods of the Gêge-Nagô Cult of Candomblé

Xangô
Sex: male
Personification: lightning
Fetish: meteorite
Insignia: lance, hatchet
Sacred Foods: cock, turtle, he-goat
Dress: red
Beads: red and white
Bracelet: brass
Sacred Day: Wednesday
Call: *hay-ee-ee*

Ogun
Sex: male
Personification: war, iron
Fetish: hoe, anvil, scythe, spade, shovel, sledge
Insignia: lance, sword
Sacred Foods: he-goat, cock, oxhead, guinea hen
Dress: all colors
Beads: all colors
Bracelet: bronze
Sacred day: Tuesday
Call: *guara-min-fo*

Oxóssi
Sex: male
Personification: the hunt
Fetish: bow and arrow, clay skillet, stone
Insignia: bow and arrow, hunting bag, powder horn, oxtail
Sacred Foods: sheep, cock, maize
Dress: green, yellow-trim
Beads: green
Bracelet: bronze
Sacred day: Thursday
Call: bark like a dog

Omolú
Sex: male
Personification: pestilence
Fetish: *piassava* with *buzios*
Insignia: lance
Sacred Foods: he-goat, cock, *acassá*, popcorn, *orôbô*, maize with *azeite de dendê*
Dress: red, black
Beads: red and black, red and white
Bracelet: cowries
Sacred day: Monday
Call: *ha*

Exú
Sex: male
Personification: evil
Fetish: clay, iron, wood
Insignia: unknown

Sacred Foods: "eats everything that is edible"
Dress: red, black
Beads: red, black
Bracelet: bronze
Sacred day: Monday
Call: unknown

Yemanjá
Sex: female
Personification: salt water
Fetish: sea shell
Insignia: fan, sword
Sacred Foods: pigeon, maize, cock, castrated he-goat
Dress: red, dark blue, rose
Beads: transparent
Bracelet: aluminum
Sacred day: Saturday
Call: *hin-hee-ye-min*

Yansan
Sex: female
Personification: wind, storm
Fetish: meteorite
Insignia: sword
Sacred Foods: goat, hen, *amalda, acarajé*
Dress: red
Beads: red, coral
Bracelet: copper, brass
Sacred day: Wednesday
Call: *hay-ee-ee* (softer than Xangô)

Oxum
Sex: female
Personification: fresh water
Fetish: stone worn smooth by a river
Insignia: fan, looking glass, small bell
Sacred Foods: fish, she-goat, hen, beans
Dress: unknown
Beads: yellow, blue
Bracelet: brass
Sacred day: Saturday
Call: *hmm-hmm*

An individual's first step in becoming a filha de santo is a visit from an orixá, who takes possession of the individual and speaks through her. This is followed by either a long and intense initiation period, a partial initiation, or an initiation conducted on and off over a period of years. In the full initiation, the woman first undergoes a ritual at the seita in which she makes an offering to, and a fetish is secured and prepared for, the orixá. She then discards her clothing and is ritually bathed. The fetish is then placed in the fetish hut, prayers and a sacrifice are offered, the initiate's head is shaved and white dots are painted on her face and skull, and she dances the special dance of her orixá so he "arrives in her head." This is followed sixteen days later by a public ritual and then by six to twelve months of secluded training in the camarinha, where she is instructed by the priestess in religious beliefs and practices. To prove her new status as a filha de santo at the end of the initiation period, she might be required to submit to ordeals, such as swallowing hot candle wax, washing her hands in hot oil, being beaten with thorns, or chewing barbed leaves, without any signs of injury. Once accepted as a filha de santo, she must follow various food and sex taboos, conduct rituals, and wear the appropriate costume on ceremonial occasions in accordance with the requirements of her orixá.

Candomblé possession takes place in the dance hall of the terreiro during ceremonies attended by members of the cult attached to the seita. The filha de santo precipitates possession by fasting, dancing until exhausted in the hot hall, inhaling pungent herbal aromas, and listening to ritual, repetitive drumming. The others present in the hall know that her orixá has "arrived in her head" when she begins to behave strangely and her head, shoulders, and back move in spasmodic movements. While possessed, the orixá speaks through her and talks to the assembled while also answering questions and responding to requests for advice and assistance. The possession is accompanied by elaborate rituals including dancing, drumming, singing, sacrifices, wearing of ritual costumes, and the careful following of required sequences of ritual movement and activity. When the trance ends, the filha de santo has no memory of what took place during it.

While the Candomblé possession serves the same purposes as possession in many other societies—building group cohesion, resolving personal crises, recognizing individual needs—it also serves the important function of maintaining African identity in the New World. This is reflected in the fact that filha de santo enjoy high status in part because of their knowledge of African customs and their personal relationships with African deities, reflected by the custom of placing the ritual clothing, beads, necklaces, and headgear of a deceased filha de santo in the ocean so that they may be "carried by the waves back to Africa."

Role and Function of Possession and Trance

Spirit possession is common across cultures because it meets certain basic societal and human needs. In terms of its function at the societal level, possession seems to help maintain social order in cultures with a rigid structure where most decisions concerning one's life are made by leaders who inherit their positions rather than attain them through more democratic means such as elections. In these cultures—where possession is most common around the world—there is much risk involved in making personal decisions. Thus, allowing a spirit to make that decision for you relieves people of personal responsibility and creates less threat to those in control. At the individual level, possession may benefit individuals in a number of ways:

1. The possessed individual gets much attention from others.
2. Possession by a punishing spirit can alleviate guilt.
3. Abnormal behavior can be attributed to possession or one's susceptibility to possession.
4. Membership in a possession cult may help satisfy needs for nurturance and gratify sexual desires.
5. Possession provides solutions to life's problems.
6. Possession allows a person to switch social roles.

In addition to these basic functions of possession, the examples from cultures around the world discussed above point to a number of common features of possession: women are more often possessed than men; the possessing supernatural being is more often male; although possession may be either harmful or helpful, only select individuals are able to use possession in helpful ways; possessed people often speak differently, act violently, and display a loss of normal control over bodily movement; and possession is often considered an illness that can be cured.

Related Altered States

In addition to possession and trance, in some cultures around the world people are able to alter their normal bodily responses to harmful stimuli in such a way that they suffer no physical harm. This includes not dying or getting ill after drinking poison; not being burned when washing with hot oil or walking on hot coals; not being cut while lying on broken glass or nails; and not being bitten or surviving bites while handling poisonous snakes. These behaviors usually occur in a religious or spiritual context and are meant to create a closer relationship between the adherent and the supernatural world. In some cultures, as with the Afro-Brazilians noted above, the behavior is engaged in mainly by religious specialists as a way of proving their closeness to and special relationship with supernatural forces or beings. In other cultures, anyone may choose to participate. Although none of these altered states are common across cultures, snake-handling and firewalking have drawn considerable interest, perhaps because both are employed in Western as well as non-Western religions or spiritual contexts.

Snakes are a ubiquitous feature of the natural world and difficult to classify in the world of living things as they have no appendages; thus, it is not surprising that they have some role in many religions. The different roles that snakes play in religion are indicated by three cultures, the Cuna of Panama, Nestorian Kurds of the Middle East, and Pentecostal Christians in the United States. The Cuna of Panama pay much attention to snakes and never kill them as they fear it will make them more susceptible to being bitten. Some Cuna are believed to have a special susceptibility to being bitten, while others have a special talent for taming snakes. Taming requires knowledge of snakes and recitation of a prayer in which God is acknowledged as the creator of the first snakes and notes how they were born to the Earth Mother, Olotililisop. Curing a snakebite is a job for the magico-religious healer, who protects himself from bites by wearing an amulet of beads in the shape of a snake. To effect a cure, the victim must be treated in a special place and his close family must be present. The healer selects medicines on the basis of the symptoms, which help him identify the species of snake.

Among the Kurds, Nestorian cultists called *darwishes* display their supernatural powers by identifying and handling snakes, by curing others bitten by snakes, and by making and selling charms that protect against snakebites. While handling snakes they are in a trance-like state, a state they also enter when they display their supernatural powers by allowing their arms to be cut but experiencing no pain.

Since the early 1990s, snake handling has been part of church services in some rural Pentecostal Christian churches in the southern Appalachians and the neighboring Midwest. The rationale for Pentecostal snake handling is as follows:

> acquisition of various spiritual gifts conferred upon believers by the Holy Ghost is, next to salvation, the most important religious goal in the life of a church member. These gifts, referred to as "the fruits of the spirit," constitute proof that a communicant has been saved, is living in a state of holiness, and enjoys a personal relationship with God. They include speaking and interpreting "unknown" tongues, serpent and fire handling, strychnine drinking, miracle working, casting out devils, the discerning of spirits, prophecy, and healing by prayer and the laying on of hands. Individuals manifesting one or more of these gifts are said to have "the power," and communicants afford special deference and respect to those with the greatest power. It is believed that a devotee's spiritual gifts are great in proportion to his withdrawal from the profane world and his attempt to "live close to the Lord." (Kane 1979: 10)

Toward this end, Pentecostal men catch rattlesnakes, copperheads, and cottonmouths and purchase other snakes, which they handle at church services. Bites are rare considering the number of times a man handles snakes and death from a bite even rarer.

Firewalking has drawn more attention than other "altered state" religious behaviors, perhaps because it is an activity that can be engaged in by anyone, not just religious specialists or devout followers of a particular religion. It is also of significance because of the use of fire, which is associated with rebirth, transition, and purification in many cultures. Two modern firewalking movements—Anastenaria in northern Greece and the American Firewalking Movement associated with the New Age in the United States—display this symbolic role of fire. Anastenaria involves possession trance, appeals to Saint Constantine, singing, dancing, and firewalking, all of which help resolve interpersonal conflicts in the community, cure illnesses, temporarily give women power and freedom they otherwise lack, and build community solidarity. In the New Age American Firewalking Movement, possession is absent, although the walking on hot coals is preceded by meditation, group discussion, and rhythmic drumming that relax the participants. The goal is not the healing of any illnesses but rather giving the participants a sense of achievement and self-control over their own lives.

See also ASCETICISM; NEW AGE; PENTACOSTALISM; RITUAL; SHAMANISM; VISION QUEST.

Bilu, Yorum. (1985) "The Woman Who Wanted To Be Her Father: A Case Analysis of Dybbuk Possession in a Hasidic Community." *The Journal of Psychoanalytic Anthropology* 8: 11–27.

Bourguignon, Erika, ed. (1973) *Religion, Altered States of Consciousness, and Social Change.*

Bourguignon, Erika. (1973) *Possession.*

Chagnon, Napoleon A. (1968) *Yanomamö: The Fierce People.*

Danforth, Loring M. (1989) *Fire Walking and Religious Healing.*

Harrell, C. Stevan. (1979) "The Concept of Soul in Chinese Folk Religion." *Journal of Asian Studies* 3: 519–528.

Kane, Steven M. (1979) *Snake Handlers of Southern Appalachia.*

Lesser, Alexander. (1933) *The Pawnee Ghost Dance Hand Game.*

Masters, William M. (1953) *Rowanduz: A Kurdish Administrative and Mercantile Center.*

Messing, Simon D. (1957) *The Highland Plateau Amhara of Ethiopia.*

Mischel, Walter, and Frances Mischel. (1958) "Psychological Aspects of Spirit Possession." *American Anthropologist* 60: 249–260.

Nordenskiöld, Erland. (1938) *An Historical and Ethnological Survey of the Cuna Indians.*

Pierson, Donald. (1967) *Negroes in Brazil: A Study of Race Contact at Bahia.*

Simpson, George E. (1971) "The Belief System of Haitian Vodun." In *Peoples and Cultures of the Caribbean,* edited by Michael M. Horowitz, 491–521.

Textor, Robert B. (1973) *Roster of the Gods: An Ethnography of the Supernatural in a Thai Village.*

PRAYER

Prayer is verbal communication with the supernatural world and is a component of religion in all cultures. Despite it being so common, prayer has drawn relatively less attention than have most other aspects of religion. This is perhaps because it is so common and also because one form of prayer—personal prayer—often takes place in private and thus is not available to outside observers. Prayer has three major elements:

1. it is a text that is maintained in written or oral form and communicated by speaking;
2. it is an act that includes ritual behavior performed as part of the verbal communication;
3. it is a belief or set of beliefs about the nature of the human and supernatural worlds and the relationship between the two.

While prayer is used by people in all cultures, there is enormous cross-cultural variability in the types of prayers used, the use of personal versus communal prayer, the reasons prayers are used, and the contexts in which they are offered. Across cultures prayer is used to petition, invoke, praise, give thanks, dedicate, supplicate, intercede, confess, repent, and bless. An important distinction with regard to type of prayer is between individual or personal prayer and communal or ritual prayer. Personal prayer is prayer performed by an individual acting alone. It is often spontaneous, emotional, and subject to individual interpretation. Some experts consider it the true form of prayer, while others argue that communal prayer in some cultures—such as the Shakers—can be just as emotional and spontaneous as personal prayer. Communal prayer is performed by individuals in a group and is formalized, repetitive, and symbolic. In cultures with writing, prayers are often kept in written form—written in prayer books, religious texts, prayer wheels, amulets and talismans; carved in stone or wood; and etched into glass. The Hopi of Arizona and some other Pueblo Indian cultures of the American Southwest use prayer-sticks to convey their prayers to the supernatural world. Although the sticks carved from wood with feather and other ritual adornment are unique to these cultures, the use of the sticks is a good example of the use of prayer in many religions:

A man makes a prayer-stick because he wants something good, some benefit.

Feathers are used in prayer-sticks and breath-feathers, because they are *ka-pu'tu,* "not heavy," light; and Cloud, and all the other Chiefs, desire them to make the fringe of feathers with which to decorate their foreheads.

The Hopi barters his prayer offerings with those of chiefs for the benefits he desires to receive from them. He exchanges prayer-sticks and breath-feathers for material benefits.

As sun journeys over the earth, he sees the prayer-sticks and breath-feathers, and comes to them and inhales their essence and takes them. He places them in his girdle and when he goes in at the west to the Below, he gives them, all that he has collected through the day's journey, to Mu'iyinwa. Mu'iyinwa knows all prayer-sticks and breath-feathers, and as he takes them up one by one, he looks at each . . . [and] those that are ill made, or made by men of evil hearts, he casts away, saying: "this one is from a bad man, *ka-ho'pi*, a foolish one." (Bradfield 1973: 432)

As a ubiquitous feature of religion across cultures, prayer is used both alone and in combination with other religious practices. Examples of prayer in these various contexts are provided in a number of articles throughout the volume.

Appleton, George, et al. (1985) *The Oxford Book of Prayer.*

Bradfield, Richard M. (1973) *A Natural History of Associations.*

Clark, Charles A. (1932) *Religions of Old Korea.*

Malefijt, Annemarie de Waal. (1968) *Religion and Culture: An Introduction to the Anthropology of Religion.*

PROTESTANTISM

Protestantism is a broad term used to describe hundreds of Western Christian denominations that have developed since the sixteenth century. More than 500 million people throughout the world are Protestants. Because of the diversity of Protestant faiths it is impossible to give a single accurate and all-inclusive definition other than to say they all fall under the category of being Western non-Catholic Christian faiths. Some Protestant sects decline the label as they do not like to be lumped under the same term as other faiths that they find repugnant. Broadly speaking, however, Protestants emphasize studying the teachings of Jesus Christ, believe in the presence of God's grace to overcome sin and gain redemption, and purport to place a higher priority on a person's individual relationship to God than relying on religious institutions and designated mediators to delegate grace.

Historical Development

All Protestant churches spring from the same event. On October 31, 1517, the disgruntled German monk Martin Luther posted on his chapel door Ninety-five Theses challenging the doctrines and practices of the Roman Catholic Church. A popular uprising ensued in support of Luther's objections known as the Reformation. Though thousands upon thousands of people could agree in their opposition to Catholicism, few could agree on what brand of Christianity was the most appropriate to replace it. Ceremony, true faith, predestination, hierarchy, preaching, the sacraments, baptism, the relationship between church and state, and transubstantiation are just some of the issues that divided Protestants. How these differences unfolded has driven the history and doctrine of Protestantism for the last five hundred years.

The advent of Protestantism led to an irreversible division of Christianity in Europe. Religious and civil matters could no longer be dealt with on a transnational basis as was the case when the pope in Rome sat as the spiritual leader of the Catholic Church. Recognizing the strength of their position prior to the Reformation, the Catholic Church squashed earlier reform movements led by Jan Hus in Czechoslovakia, John Wycliffe in England, and Girolamo Savonarola in Italy. And when Martin Luther made his pronouncements against certain practices—and not Catholicism directly—the church attempted to stomp out the criticism. But this time discontent with the abuses and aloofness of the church was so widespread that entire populations rose in support of Luther and similar criticisms leveled at the church by other reformers such as Huldrych Zwingi in Switzerland and later John Calvin. The church's practice of selling indulgences (essentially buying God's grace through contributions to the church), the placing of a clerical and sacramental system between the individual and his relationship with God, and the outright corruption of some priests, bishops, and the pope created the social context for religious reform.

Protestantism earned its name and official recognition in 1529 at the Diet of Speyer where a gathering of German Roman Catholic princes and the Holy Roman Emperor, Charles V, rescinded a three-year era of tolerance of the reformist religions. The diet termed the movement Protestantism in reference to the protests the religions were making against the Roman Catholic Church.

Protestants wanted a religious system that freed them to be directly responsible for their relationship with God and to experience grace without institutional interference. The source of their inspiration for Protestantism was primarily the New Testament and to a lesser extent the Old Testament. Instead of relying on the pope and the church to serve as the religious authority, the Bible became the central authority. Luther described the Bible as "the cradle in which Christ lives." One of Luther's most significant actions was to translate the Bible into the vernacular to facilitate a person's ability to read and learn from the Bible directly. Thus, the rise of Protestantism coincided with an increase in literacy. Not coincidentally, Protestantism also spread with the invention of the printing press that allowed for much greater distribution of the

texts. A Bible with a chain attached to it became one of the despised symbols of Catholicism as the churches often would keep the handwritten religious texts secure under lock and key.

Early Protestantism took two general forms. The conservative reformers hoped to reform the church without creating a break with Rome or their own Christian tradition. But the Roman Catholic Church excommunicated even the most moderate reformers and they soon found themselves in the same position as the radical Protestants who sought to break away from Catholicism. Both groups turned to the New Testament, and particularly the writings of Paul, for guidance in establishing new churches and building an administrative structure. While some groups such as the Anglicans in England continued the tradition of bishops, others such as the Calvinists established an order of lay leaders, and yet others such as the Anabaptists insisted on local leadership from within individual congregations.

While all Protestant groups denounced Catholic sacraments, there was widespread disagreement on whether to practice sacraments, and if so, which sacramental acts to continue and whether to change the way they were performed. The more conservative Protestants such as the Lutherans often altered the sacraments in relatively minor ways, while the more radical sects frequently abandoned sacraments such as baptism and communion entirely. Disagreements on these issues among Protestant sects often caused as much bitterness among Protestant groups as they did against Catholicism.

The Reformation affected every European country, each in its own way. In the German states where Lutheranism took root, horrific civil wars ensued for 150 years. Scandinavian countries such as Sweden and Denmark adopted Lutheranism to the point that they became the state religions (although, ironically, Luther was one of the few early Protestants to advocate a

Members of the Roman Catholic hierarchy at the Diet of Worms (1521) declare Martin Luther, center, a German monk who challenged church doctrines and practices, a heretic. Christianity's division between Catholicism and Protestantism led to civil wars and great unrest in Europe for years following Luther's challenge and that of other reformers such as Huldrych Zwingi in Switzerland and, later, John Calvin in England.

separation of church and civil authority). In England, Henry VIII supplanted the pope's leadership and placed himself as the head of a new Anglican Church that at first instituted only minor changes, but was later confronted by more radical Protestants in the seventeenth century, culminating in the English Civil War. Switzerland served as the center of the austere and doctrinaire Calvinist sect. The minority French Protestants known as Huguenots found themselves engaged in a bloody civil war with French Catholics until the Edict of Nantes of 1598, when they were able to earn toleration. The Irish remained Catholic as a way to distinguish themselves from the hated English. In Austria and Bohemia (now the Czech Republic), Protestants and Catholics wrestled for control until the end of the Thirty Years War in 1648, when the Catholics prevailed. Even in Italy, the home of Roman Catholicism, a minor Protestant movement took hold.

As these examples illustrate, Protestantism played a major role in the rise of nationalism as different countries adopted new religions as a way to either wrest control from Rome or identify themselves as nations. After nearly 150 years of wars, massacres, and acrimony, the two religions had pretty much established their areas of influence in Europe. One of the tenets of Protestantism, however, is *ecclesia reformia semper refromanda,* or "there is also room for more reform." Thus, Protestantism continued to find itself in a constant state of flux, the subtleties of which have been incredibly complicated.

Nevertheless, some major currents emerged. By the end of the seventeenth century many Protestant sects such as Lutheranism and Calvinism had been established with definitive doctrines. But in almost every Protestant country, renewal movements were also established, such as the Puritans in England and the Piests in northern Europe, both of which pushed the boundaries of Protestantism even further and sometimes bordered on mysticism. This era was followed by Rationalist Protestantism in the eighteenth century, when philosophers such as Gottfried Wilhelm Leibniz, Immanual Kant, and other Enlightenment thinkers incorporated natural laws into Christianity. This resulted in a tempering of passions over doctrinal issues and instead focused on the benevolence of God, the capability of man, the need for tolerance, and the importance of morality. It was out of this brand of Protestantism that many of the principles such as freedom of religion and the separation of church and state were established and incorporated in the United States by the new government in the late eighteenth century.

The evangelical movement in the late eighteenth and early nineteenth century was a reaction against this more intellectual form of Protestantism. Usually conservative in their theologies, evangelical Protestant leaders (most prominently John Wesley, founder of Methodism) emphasized the life and works of Jesus Christ. Evangelical leaders revived hymnals as a source of inspiration for followers. The evangelical movement persevered through the nineteenth century and remains a potent force today, particularly in the United States, even in the face of the secularism and ecumenism that came to dominate Western societies in the twentieth century. Ironically, the very nature of Protestantism has helped drive secularism. By calling into constant question the "divine rights" of kings and monarchs, church hierarchy, and the role of

church in civil affairs, Protestantism has in many ways pushed religion out of the realm of public affairs where it once played a central role. The relationship of Protestantism to the secular world has become a major issue in its own future. At the same time, the divisions that once drove Protestant sects into bitter and bloody conflict have fallen by the wayside with the rise of the ecumenical movement, which has seen the formation of international Christian organizations such as the World Council of Churches. Increasingly, Protestant groups have come to focus more on what binds them together as adherents to the principles of Christ than on what separates them.

Concurrent to these changes was the rapid spread of Protestantism from northwestern Europe to the rest of the world, especially English-speaking America. As northern European nations and England built worldwide empires in the eighteenth and nineteenth centuries they also brought Protestant missionaries who both converted indigenous peoples and saw to it that the colonists remained true to their Protestant backgrounds. The Anglican church alone spawned close to twenty denominations, including the Episcopal Church in the United States, the Church of Australia, and the Archbishopric of Jerusalem. Protestantism has to a large degree shaped modern attitudes toward the economy, natural resources, and capitalism. Philosopher Max Weber attributed the roots of capitalism to Calvinist influences in his controversial book *The Protestant Ethic and the Spirit of Capitalism*. While few people today link Calvinism to the birth of capitalism, the Protestant sense of calling has often been applied to its followers, who seek to prove to themselves and others their own worthiness or sense of grace in the workplace.

Texts

The central text of all Protestant sects is the Christian Bible, consisting of the Old and New

Testaments. Protestants look to the stories of the Bible, especially the New Testament, as the source of their faith. The Old Testament is the Jewish Bible. The New Testament includes twenty-seven writings, the most significant of which are the four Gospels (Matthew, Mark, Luke, and John), which describe the life and teachings of Jesus. Other writings include the Epistles of Paul, the Acts of the Apostles (which describe the history of early Christian missionaries), and Revelation, a visionary description of God's final triumph. Several other Protestant works have been written to supplement the Bible by the different sects to clarify their own doctrines and set forth practices. They are far too numerous to list but include works such as the Anglican Book of Common Prayer, the Presbyterian Forms of Prayer, and Luther's Formula Missae (Formula of the Mass).

Beliefs

Although Protestantism incorporates a wide diversity of views that evolved over its factionalized history, some broad statements can be made about Protestant beliefs. All Protestants embrace the lessons of Jesus Christ and believe that grace can be achieved through faith. To varying degrees, Protestant sects believe that a person's own conduct determines his own fate, although some believe that whether a person is graced to enter the kingdom of God is determined even before birth. Unlike the Roman Catholic and Eastern Orthodox churches, Protestants maintain that the Bible is the only source of authority and that the Holy Spirit—and not the church—enlightens those who read and study the Bible. The role of the church in most Protestant sects is to facilitate a person's relationship with God and to instruct followers on the teachings.

Because Protestantism was formed as a reaction against Catholicism, it is simpler to distinguish its Christian beliefs by how it differs from Catholicism and Eastern Orthodoxy than to attempt to define what it is. Protestants reject the following principles that the other two major Christian branches uphold: prayers offered to saints, the succession from Jesus to the apostles to the popes, hierarchical structure, systems of priesthood, intercession for the dead, and transubstantiation (the belief that the wine and bread eaten at the Last Supper was turned into the body and blood of Jesus Christ).

Practices

Most Protestant churches hold weekly gatherings on Sunday for their congregations to worship God. The structure of these services, however, varies widely. While some churches, such as the Anglican, have carefully prescribed rituals consisting of the singing of hymns, recital of passages, the execution of specific rituals, and a sermon all under the direction of a minister, others such as Quaker services have very little structure, consisting of observations and thoughts from members of the congregation under the supervision of a lay leader. Similarly, Protestant branches have different ceremonies commemorating different parts of people's lives. Most Protestant churches, however, have specific services to mark the birth of a child, marriage, death, and the induction of clergy members.

The two most important festivals for Protestants are Christmas and Easter. Christmas, held on December 25, celebrates the birth of Jesus Christ. Preceding Christmas is Advent, which marks the beginning of the ecclesiastical year four Sundays before Christmas. Easter commemorates the crucifixion and Resurrection of Jesus Christ. It is celebrated on the first Sunday after the first full moon following the vernal equinox (March 21). Some Protestant groups observe Lent, a solemn period of fasting and prayer prior to Easter. Most Protestant groups also mark two days following Easter, Ascension Day and Pentecost Sunday.

See also CHRISTIANITY; JUDAISM; ROMAN CATHOLICISM.

Cobb, John B., Jr. (1960) *Varieties of Protestantism.*

Léonard, Émile C. (1965–1968) *A History of Protestantism.*

Marty, Martin E. (1973) *Protestantism.*

PURITY AND
POLLUTION

In all cultures there are customary beliefs that allow people to distinguish between objects, places, events, and people that are considered to be unclean and those that are considered to be clean. Some of these beliefs and the rules of behavior based on them are, of course, utilitarian, as they mark unclean items such as a polluted well or spoiled food that might be physically harmful. However, in all cultures people also categorize phenomena as ritually pure or polluting. The idea that certain items are ritually unclean is always accompanied by the notions of pollution and contagion. That is, people who come into contact with the item can themselves become ritually polluted. These beliefs are accompanied by religious and other behavioral requirements that serve to minimize contact with ritually polluting objects, places, events, and people. As contact with these items is believed to cause illness, misfortune, or even death, there is much reason for following the proper behavior required to avoid contact with them. In addition to the religious nature of beliefs and behaviors involved in ritual purity and pollution, such customs also often have a powerful sociopolitical component, since classifying certain categories of people as pure or polluting influences the role and status of those people in society. As discussed below, ideas about ritual purity and pollution are markers of in-group versus out-group identity in some cultures and also

play a role in many societies in male-female relations. Across cultures there is enormous variety in the nature and number of items thought to be polluting. In addition, an item might be polluting temporarily or permanently or only at certain times. For example, in many cultures menstruating women are thought to be polluting to men and their contact with men while they are menstruating is banned or restricted. At all other times, however, they are not thought to be polluting and contact with men is allowed.

Social scientists have devoted considerable attention to explaining purity and pollution. In one view, as discussed below, rules governing pollution and purity are interpreted as a mechanism that serves to mark and reinforce social boundaries between people or certain categories of people. Another explanation, also discussed below, focuses on the role of power in purity and pollution, especially in regard to male-female relations. A third explanation focuses on the universal human need to classify items into clear categories. From the perspective of purity and pollution, in this interpretation, items that do not fit neatly into classification schemes are classified as polluting. For example, bodily fluids are considered to be polluting because they are neither wholly within or outside the human body. This same interpretation can be used to explain the use of purification rituals such as baptism in ceremonies that mark a change in a person's social status. The use of a purification ritual marks the transition across one status boundary to another and thereby removes any ambiguity about the individual's status and role in the community. A fourth set of possible explanations emphasizes the practical effects of classifying items as pure or polluting. One possible effect is protecting human health. For example, one interpretation of the Jewish classification of pork as polluting and unfit for human consumption is that in ancient times pork was unclean and caused disease; thus classifying it as polluting was a public health measure. Another practical explanation for purity and pollution focuses on the economic value of the items so categorized. In this view, items of little economic value—such as insects in Western cultures—are classified as unclean because they are not likely to be used anyway. Conversely, items of high economic value may be classified as pure as a way of protecting them from overuse. For example, Hindus in India are prohibited from eating cattle, the theory goes, because they are more valuable economically for their dung, which is used for plastering buildings and fuel, and as draft animals than as food. Another practical interpretation focuses on the widespread belief that female sexual organs and fluids are polluting to men and the practical value this belief will have on controlling population in societies that are threatened by overpopulation.

Purity, Pollution, and Social Boundaries

Perhaps the two most complex systems of purity and pollution around the world are the Hindu caste system in India and the Gypsy *marime* system. Both of these systems concern the classification of entire categories of people as either pure or polluting and, as such, reflect and reinforce social boundaries and power relations in Indian and Gypsy societies.

For some two thousand years Indian society has been organized on the basis of caste. A caste is a particular type of social group into which members are born, remain for life, and marry within. The castes are ranked in a hierarchy of status. In India, Hindu castes, in addition to these basic characteristics, are also occupational groups. The ranking of the thousands of occupational castes of India rests on Hindu beliefs about ritual purity and pollution. The basic rationale for the caste system is set forth in Hindu religious texts, which established the four general caste categories: Brahmans

(priests), Kshatriyas (warriors and rulers), Vaisyas (landowners and traders), and Sudras (farmers). A fifth category, the Harijans (untouchables), are technically outside the caste system. The status of each of these five categories as well as the thousands of occupational castes subsumed under them and distributed throughout rural India are predetermined by the innate abilities and behavior of their members. Members of each caste are believed to be born with the physical and mental abilities appropriate for the work performed by their caste. During their lifetime, they are expected to perform the work of their caste and to behave in the required manner. Proper behavior means that the person will move to a higher caste in the next life, improper behavior that the person will move to a lower caste in the next life. Thus, one's current status is determined by one's behavior in a previous life. The ritual rank of each caste is based on its occupation, with each occupation ranked on a scale of ritual purity-pollution. Brahmans are the ritually purest, with each Brahman child inheriting its purity from its parents. The untouchables, as their names implies, are the most polluted as their work can involve disposing of cattle and working with leather. Other highly polluted people include launderers, fishermen, and oil-makers because each takes another life, and palm wine tappers and prostitutes because each performs work for money that stimulates the senses. Leaving this work to lower castes protects the ritual purity of the higher castes and protects their rebirth.

This system of ritual purity-pollution is maintained across Indian communities and over time by extensive rules that govern behavior between members of different castes. Much of this activity, both by Brahmans and others, is designed to maintain Brahman purity. For example, virtually no one may touch a Brahman, clean non-Brahmans may enter the home of a Brahman but not the kitchen, and polluted non-Brahmans may not even enter the house. The Brahmans themselves maintain their purity by eating a vegetarian diet, avoiding contact with lower castes, following rigid rules governing personal hygiene and eating, respecting family members, and regularly engaging in religious activities.

A core element of the belief system of Rom Gypsies throughout the world is the notion of marime, a complex concept that depending on the context means defilement, impurity, shamefulness, pollution, and rejection. Marime is used by Gypsies to order their physical and social worlds, manage male-female relations, maintain distance from outsiders, and maintain order within the group. Unlike the caste system in Hindu India, marime is not linked to the formal religious system, as most Gypsies have traditionally adhered to Roman Catholicism, some follow Eastern Orthodoxy or Islam, and in the last decade significant numbers have been drawn to Pentecostal Christianity. Within the family and the local group, marime focuses on the human body. The upper half, especially the head and mouth, is considered to be ritually pure while the lower half, and especially the female genitalia, menstrual blood, and anything associated with birth, are considered polluting or marime. Much ritual activity is devoted to keeping the two spheres separate. The hands, which move between and thereby cross the boundary between the clean upper and marime lower body, are frequently washed, always before cooking or handling religious objects. Items that come into contact with the different body regions are kept clean and stored separately. Newborn infants and the mother—because of involvement with the female genitalia—are considered especially marime and are isolated for days or even weeks before allowed normal contact with men. As regards relations with non-Gypsies, these are restricted to economic matters only, as all non-Gypsies are considered to be marime and

the source of disease. Gypsies feel comfortable and safe only at home in the company of other Gypsies. Violation of marime rules are a major source of community disruption and violators are subject to a trial that may result in temporary or permanent isolation or expulsion from the community, for both the violator and his family.

For Gypsies and people in many societies the female genitalia, menstrual blood, and birth are considered polluting for men. While in the majority of societies some restrictions are placed on menstruating women to keep them apart from men, in Gypsy communities the restrictions on male-female contact are far more pervasive. It is marime to touch women's undergarments, to sit on a toilet seat used by a woman, to have a woman sit on a man's lap, to see the genitalia of a woman who is not one's wife, to engage in sexual intercourse while the woman is menstruating, to engage in oral sex, and to touch any objects associated with birth. Gypsy men go to considerable lengths to avoid these sources of marime—they might sleep in separate beds while their wife is menstruating, prefer that birth takes place in a hospital, never live on the first floor to avoid women being above him on the second floor, avoid having a woman step over him or his possessions, and ride only in the front seat of cars while women ride only in the rear seat. While these beliefs and restrictions on women suggest a considerable degree of male control of female sexuality, Gypsy women can and do use the marime status of their genitalia to control men. By lifting their skirt and exposing their undergarments or genitalia they make marime and shame a man who has abused or disgraced them. This shame and the subsequent punishment meted out by the community extends not just to the man but also to his family. Thus, their marime status can be a powerful weapon for women in Gypsy society.

This pattern holds in other societies as well where women, their genitalia, or their sexuality is considered polluting to men. Among the Zulu of South Africa, pollution (*umnyama*) is a spiritual force that makes a person susceptible to disease, brings bad luck, and makes the polluted person unpleasant and poor company. Some forms of pollution are contagious, others are not. The two most powerful sources of pollution are birth and death, with women, as the sex that gives birth and as the sex with the role of chief mourner at funerals, being the source of the pollution. In order to maintain their purity, women and adolescent girls must complete various rituals and obey various behavioral prohibitions. As with the Gypsies, the Zulu conception of female pollution, while on the surface suggesting male dominance, also reflects the power of women in Zulu society. The Zulu are patrilineal (they trace kin ties only through the father's line) and polygynous (a man can have more than one wife at the same time). In this situation, wives are a key social bridge in the community as they link families (the one they were born into and the one they marry into) and also the children in the family who have different mothers and the same father and are, therefore, half-siblings. Thus, as with Gypsy women, Zulu women are a powerful force for social stability and control.

To take a third example of the tie between beliefs in female pollution and female power, we can look at the rural Taiwanese. In these communities menstrual blood is considered to be especially polluting and contact with it will interfere with one's ability to interact with the gods. However, menstrual blood is also believed to create babies, and blood in general is considered to be a powerful fluid. Thus, the production of menstrual blood is a powerful possession of women that is needed by men who wish to produce males heirs. This power is used by women in their early reproductive years to establish independence from the mother-in-law and their husbands and to gain control of their homes and their families.

In addition to these situations, ritual purity and pollution may be related to social relations and power in other ways. For example, in some cultures in Oceania, such as the Maori of New Zealand, kings in traditional times were thought to have such a high state of ritual purity that they were not permitted to touch a commoner nor to even touch everyday objects for fear of ritual pollution. These dramatically different rules of behavior for the royalty versus the commoners helped maintain distance between the two and reinforced the authority of the rulers.

See also ASCETICISM; HINDUISM; TABOO.

Ahern, Emily M. (1976) "The Power and Pollution of Chinese Women." In *Studies in Chinese Society,* edited by Arthur P. Wolf, 269–290.

Douglas, Mary T. (1966) *Purity and Danger: An Analysis of the Concepts of Pollution and Taboo.*

Gough, Elizabeth K. (1969) "Caste in a Tanjor Village." In *Aspects of Caste in India, Ceylon, and North-west Pakistan,* edited by Edmund R. Leach, 11–60, 147–148.

Harris, Marvin. (1985) *The Sacred Cow and the Abominable Pig.*

Lindenbaum, Shirley. (1972) "Sorcerers, Ghosts, and Polluting Women: An Analysis of Religious Belief and Population Growth." *Ethnology* 11: 241–253.

Miller, Carol. (1975) "American Rom and the Ideology of Defilement." In *Gypsies, Tinkers, and Other Travelers,* edited by Franham Redhfisch, 41–54.

Ngubane, Harriet. (1977) *Body and Mind in Zulu Medicine.*

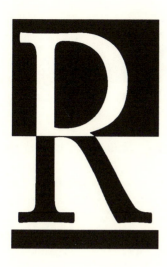

als may be reincarnated as humans or animals. In cultures where people are reincarnated as animals, the particular species is often one of considerable importance to the individual and his or her social group. For example, the Azande of West Africa return to life as an animal (for example, a leopard) that was important to the ancestors and was in turn protected by the ancestors.

In cultures where people believe in reincarnation, the belief usually exists as part of a broader belief system and, thus, makes sense only in this broader context. For example, the Tlingit of North America believe that life is like the curving coast of the sea and that every individual is a reincarnation of a deceased relative on his or her mother's side. Thus, when an old person nears death, the pain is lessened by the knowledge that he or she will return again and the family is comforted by the expectation that the deceased will return as a newborn member of the clan. The same view of the life cycle is applied to animals as well, and fish that are caught one year are expected to be reincarnated as fish and return year after year so long as the fisherman follows the appropriate rituals in burning their bones. For the Buddhist Central Thai, reincarnation takes place within the context of the beliefs indicated by the saying: "Do good and you will get rewards in return; do bad and you will get punishment in return." For the Central Thai, one's current state of physical being is but one in an endless series of reincarnations, with the current state determined by the individual's behavior and status in his or her previous state. Depending on their behavior, the reincarnation can be as a human, animal, subhuman, or deity, and he or she may enjoy a life of richness and happiness or want and suffering. The same view of reincarnation is held by the Taiwan Hokkien who believe that only a very few people go to heaven, the rest being reincarnated into a form (human, animal, plant) and a state of happiness

REINCARNATION

Reincarnation is the belief that the dead return to life in a new physical form. Reincarnation is an unusual, though not rare, belief across cultures. Depending on the survey, a belief in reincarnation is absent in anywhere from 54 percent to 74 percent of cultures around the world. However, while the number of cultures that formally include reincarnation in their belief system is relatively small, the number of people around the world who believe in reincarnation is substantial, when we consider the hundreds of millions of Hindus in South Asia and Buddhists in Southeast and East Asia who believe in reincarnation. In cultures with a reincarnation belief, a person is usually reincarnated in one of two forms: (1) human (the more common form, which occurs in about 20 percent of cultures) where the dead individual returns to life in the physical form of another human being; or (2) animal (the rarer form, which occurs in about 7 percent of cultures) in which the dead individual returns to life in the physical form of a nonhuman animal. In a few cultures, individu-

and fulfillment reflecting their behavior in their previous incarnation. The largest number of believers in reincarnation based on one's past behavior are Hindus in India, who believe that one's soul lives on in a new physical form after death. One's fate (*karma*) is determined by one's performance of appropriate behaviors (*dharma*) in one's previous existence. This belief, a key component of Hinduism, has for several thousand years served as a justification for the Hindu caste system in which individuals and families occupy rigid, hierarchical positions for life.

In some cultures only certain categories of people are reincarnated. For example, the Andaman Islanders of South Asia believed that only a baby who died before the age of two could be reincarnated and then always as the next child born to the mother, a belief reflected in the naming of the new baby with the same name as that previously given the deceased child. In one case, a mother had three children, two deceased and one living, all with same name, reflecting the belief that all three were the same person in three different bodies.

See also BUDDHISM; HINDUISM; JAINISM; SOUL.

Davis, William D. (1974) *Societal Complexity and the Nature of Primitive Man's Conception of the Supernatural.*

de Laguna, Frederica. (1972) *Under Mount Saint Elias: The History and Culture of the Yakutat Tlingit.*

Lagae, C. R. (1926) *The Azande or Niam-Niam.*

Radcliffe-Brown, A. R. (1922) *The Andaman Islanders: A Study in Social Anthropology.*

Swanson, Guy E. (1968) *The Birth of the Gods: The Origin of Primitive Beliefs.*

Textor, Robert B. (1973) *Roster of the Gods: An Ethnography of the Supernatural in a Thai Village.*

RELIGIOUS OBJECTS

In all cultures there are physical objects believed to have some special magical, spiritual, or supernatural quality that play a role in the religious system. Across cultures, religious objects are of three general types—amulets, talismans, and fetishes. Amulets are objects that are believed to ward off harm to the person who wears or displays the object. Talismans are the opposite, as they are objects that are believed to bring good fortune. A fetish is an object that is believed to be connected to a spirit, ancestor, or some other supernatural force and therefore can be used by the owner of the fetish to influence supernatural forces. Fetishes are generally more elaborate, are usually made by humans, and have more innate power than do amulets or talismans.

Because they are found in all cultures and because in all cultures many individuals have their own personal amulets, talismans, and fetishes virtually any object, natural or human-modified, can serve as a religious object. All that is necessary for an object to be considered religious is that someone believes that the object has inherent spiritual or magical power. Often the exact nature of the power is kept secret by the believer, although in most cultures knowledge about the power of some religious objects is shared by all. For example, in the United States everyone knows that many people believe that a rabbit's foot or a horseshoe hung with the open end up will bring good luck.

The role of religious objects in many religious systems is indicated by the beliefs and practices of the Baganda of Uganda. The Baganda venerate four types of religious beings and objects—gods, fetishes, amulets, and ghosts. Fetishes are manufactured by religious specialists and are believed to have supernatural powers that can be used by the purchaser of the fetish to ward off evil or benefit himself. Many fetishes have ghosts associated with them and, like religious

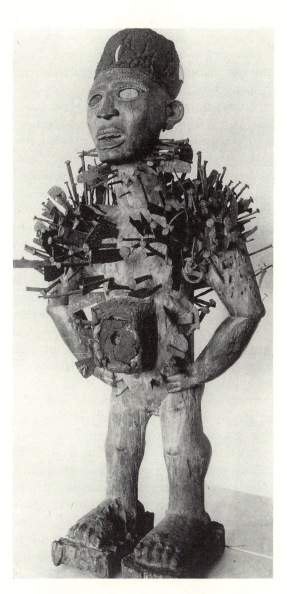

A fetish against illness was collected from Zaire. Such physical objects play a role in many religious systems and fall into three categories: amulets, talismans, and festishes. Fetishes are regarded as connections to a spirit or ancestor or from one supernatural force to another.

objects in many cultures, their power is called upon through incantations and sometimes offerings. Some are thought to be especially powerful and are kept in temples where their powers can only be called upon by certain priests and mediums while others were used only by a king or ruler. Amulets are also manufactured by the Baganda but are used mainly to ward off or cure disease and are not approached through incantations or offerings. As in many cultures, specialists who made amulets and fetishes were kept busy by their clients.

While some religious objects ward off evil or bring good fortune in general, in all cultures there are often many hundreds of objects whose power is thought to be more focused and, therefore, are used by only certain categories of people in specific situations for specific reasons. The Tlingit of the northwest coast of Canada provide an example of this universal pattern. For example, among numerous other amulets, the Tlingit use certain leaves or roots to bring luck in hunting, scratching stones to ward off bad luck, fingernails woven into baskets to bring artistic talent to children, and roots to make oneself wealthy.

While a religious object may simply be an object in its natural, unaltered form, such as a stone, in all cultures objects are altered to turn them into religious objects and in many cultures bear writing, pictures, symbols, and geometric designs that make their meanings clear. For example, the Amhara of Ethiopia wear written amulets hung on cords from their necks or waist; they also wear or hang amulets with scenes such as a cross over the sun and moon, angels with fiery swords, an eye with a red iris, and the six-pointed star. For the Amhara wearing or displaying amulets is an important means of warding off the evil of sorcerers, witches, and casters of the evil eye. Written amulets prepared by scribes often contain the name of or a reference to the person whom the wearer fears is trying to cause him or her harm.

See also EVIL EYE; PILGRIMAGE; WITCHCRAFT.

de Laguna, Frederica. (1972) *Under Mount Saint Elias: The History and Culture of the Yakutat Tlingit.*

Messing, Simon D. (1957) *The Highland Plateau Amhara of Ethiopia.*

Roscoe, John. (1911) *The Baganda: An Account of Their Native Customs and Beliefs.*

RELIGIOUS SPECIALISTS

A religious specialist is an individual who occupies a social role with obligations that are tied to religious belief and activity. In virtually every culture there are some individuals who through some means have access to supernatural power and who use this access to carry out religious practices. These individuals fill the specialized role of magico-religious practitioner and have abilities, knowledge, obligations, and authority that set them apart from other people in the culture. In addition to magico-religious practitioners, there are in many societies individuals who also occupy social roles that are closely tied to religion. These include ascetics, prophets, messiahs, and teachers. It should be noted that in nearly all cultures there are two or more types of magico-religious practitioner. For example, the Ojibwa of North America recognize three types: the healer and charm-maker, the conjuror, and the seer. Larger and more complex cultures have more types of religious specialists than do simpler cultures. Thus, in modern Western cultures, we find all types of religious specialists.

Magico-Religious Practitioners

Across cultures there are three major types of magico-religious practitioners—shamanistic healers, priests, and sorcerers/witches. As the label suggests, shamanistic healers occupy much of their time with diagnosing and curing illness and with divination. Shamanistic healers become shamans through an altered state of consciousness experience. Both altered states of consciousness experiences and shamanistic healers are cultural universals. Across cultures, four different types of shamanistic healers can be distinguished: shamans, shaman/healers, mediums, and healers.

Shamans are found almost exclusively in hunter-gatherer societies and are the oldest form of religious specialist, dating back at least 50,000 years and probably much earlier. Shamans are usually part-time specialists, devoting only some of their time to religious matters and the remainder to other activities, including ones engaged in by all members of the community such as obtaining food as well as serving as the decision-maker for the community. A shaman's status is based primarily on his or her personal characteristics, with many shamans having that set of qualities known commonly as "charisma." Shamans engage in a wide range of magico-religious activities including healing the sick, removing spells, casting spells on enemies, divining to select hunting locales and settlement sites, dream interpretation, and the recovery of lost souls. Shamans do not choose the role for themselves, but instead are selected for the role by the spirits. Such selection is usually indicated by a very serious personal crisis or a serious illness accompanied by a deep spiritual experience involving transport to or communication with the supernatural world. The shaman selectee then undergoes rigorous training for the role, which centers on altered states of consciousness induced by hallucinogenic drugs, sleep deprivation, food deprivation, drumming, chanting, prolonged social and physical isolation, and exposure to the elements. A key feature of the experience is travel to the supernatural world or transformation into an animal, which provides the shaman with the ability to communicate and control the spirits in the performance of his duties.

Shamans among the Chukchee, a formerly hunter-gatherer people of Siberia, displayed many of the salient features of shamanism. The Chukchee recognized three types of shamanistic activity: (1) communication with the spirits, which also included behaviors such as ventriloquism through which the shaman communicated the wishes of the spirit to his human clients; (2) "looking into" or divination in which the shamans asked their clients to organize a ritual in order to influence the spirit to either cause something desirable to occur or to prevent misfortune; and (3) incantations to help or cause harm to others. The Chukchee differentiated between good and bad shamans and the black and red coats they wore symbolized their status. All shamans were part-time specialists who were paid for their services (with reindeer, meat, garments, skins, or symbolic trinkets), but they also had to spend time engaged in nonshamanistic activities such as hunting.

The Chukchee called shamans "those with spirits," and both men or women could be shamans, although women often had less power as shaman power was weak during childbearing years. Shamans were seen as being different than other people—adolescents selected by the spirits as shamans often had a distinctive gaze that allowed them to see the spirits, even in the dark, and shamans in general were nervous and highly excitable. In a form of shamanism called family shamanism, members of a family would seek to contact the spirit world, although their power was far less than that of an actual shaman.

For most Chukchee shamans, the calling manifested itself during adolescence, often as an "inner voice" that bid the person to communicate with the spirits. If the person ignored the call, the calling spirit appeared in some other way, such as through a serious illness. Spirits also appeared as certain animals or as inanimate objects such as rocks or shells; these then become the protector and assistant spirit of the shaman. Once the call was accepted, the individual underwent a several-month period of soul transformation with much sleep, isolation, and perhaps wanderings in the wilderness before he became a shaman. This period is called the period when "he gathers shamanistic power." Older persons more commonly received their calling during a time of major misfortune, such as after the loss of one's family or during a serious illness. Women did not endure the same hardships as men and most of their training took place through dreaming.

Shamans worked by communicating with their spirit. Shamanistic spirits were thought to be shy and reclusive. They would punish the shaman if he behaved inappropriately but would always grant his requests if he obeyed their rules governing appearance, behavior, and the performance of rituals. The drum was the shaman's primary means of communicating with the spirit world and rituals centered on drumming, dancing, and chanting. In addition, the spirit would speak through the shaman and the shaman would perform other acts, such as cutting a sick client. A ritual might last several hours and the shaman was not allowed to show fatigue.

Shaman/healers are similar to shamans except that they are found in large, settled communities, are often full-time specialists, receive special training, and may be organized into professional associations. In a single society, they may also specialize in certain ritual activities, such as agricultural rites, or in the treatment of specific types of illness. One well-described type of shaman/healer is the *zar* doctor found in North African cultures such as the Amhara of Ethiopia. Zar doctors are the leaders of zar cults and treat mental illness, primarily in women although men may also use their services. Zar doctors diagnose and treat the illness and then incorporate the patient into the doctor's zar cult, which provides protection for life. A zar is a particular type of spirit. Zar spirits first appeared in the Garden of Eden. Eve had thirty children and when she tried to conceal fifteen of them from God, he punished her by declaring that all fifteen would be invisible night creatures. Zar spirits are descended from these fifteen children and may be either harmful or benevolent in their relations with humans. Harmful spirits possess humans through magical coitus and cause illness, including mental illnesses such as fatigue, depression, seizures, and mood disorders. All humans are susceptible to zar possession. The difference between zar doctors and others is that the doctors have learned about the spirits and their victims; the doctors can use their possession by their zar spirit to control the spirit and cure others. Doctors treat while in a trance and possessed by their zar spirit. They first diagnose the illness by interpreting the words of the possessed victim, by causing the victim to become possessed again, or by observing the possession as it occurs. Once the doctor determines the reason for the spirit's unhappiness, he or she negotiates with the spirit, which usually results in the patient making an offering through the doctor to the spirit, thus curing the illness. Then the patient is socialized into the zar doctor's cult, which provides life-long protection from the spirit. Cult members attend other patients' treatment sessions, which involve the burning of incense, drumming, poetry recitations, and possession.

Many zar doctors inherit the role from their mothers, or they may claim the status on the basis of having been kidnapped by a zar spirit early in life. In either case, the zar doctor must complete an apprenticeship with an established doctor and at the end receive his power directly from his teacher. Zar doctors are respected members of the community, free from some social obligations required of other people, and often

wealthy. Zar doctors may specialize in treating certain types of illness, or they may gain reputations as being especially skilled at treating difficult cases, such as a person possessed by more than one zar spirit at one time. The zar doctors hold an annual convention, open only to them and their most dedicated cult members, at which new diagnostic and treatment techniques are presented and tested.

A *medium* is a type of shaman/healer whose power comes from possession by a supernatural force such as a god or spirit. Across cultures, the most common function of mediums is divining—predicting the future or explaining the past—although they may also conduct various rituals and cure illness. For the Ganda of what is now Uganda, a medium (*mandwa*) served as the spokesperson for the god who possessed him or her. The person was selected as a medium by a god and identified within the culture as a medium through their knowledge of events or their ability to predict the future. The first possession was called "being married to the god" and subsequent possessions were called "being seized by the head." A female medium was considered to be a wife of the god and had to keep separate from men and refrain from sexual activity. There was generally one medium per temple. The medium became possessed in order to divine by smoking a pipe filled with ordinary tobacco and gazing intently into a fire. While possessed and under the influence of the god he spoke the words of the god, which were interpreted for the Ganda rulers by a priest.

Healers are religious specialists who form a distinct occupational group of high status and considerable influence in their communities. While possession may be involved in achieving healer status, it is not always required, and they cure not through possession but through the use of spells, rituals, and formulae to communicate with the supernatural. Healers are especially common in agricultural communities, where certain individuals may be identified as having powers they can use to cure others. The use of these powers requires knowledge and skills in ritual activities and therefore training, often in an apprenticeship.

Priests are not found in all societies but are found primarily in societies with large settled communities, a subsistence system based on agriculture, and centralized political leadership. In anthropological usage *priest* is a generic term that is used for any individual who is specially trained to conduct rituals in order to communicate with the supernatural world. Thus, Catholic priests, Baptist ministers, and Jewish rabbis are all priests. A person may become a priest because of personal choice or because he or she receives a supernatural calling to devote their life to priestly work. Priests often enjoy high status in their community, although various rules that do not apply to others may shape their appearance and behavior. The influence of priests often concerns both religious and secular matters and they may serve as advisers to political leaders. In addition, they conduct rituals concerning many important matters, such as planting and harvesting, birth, naming, marriage, and death. While priests provide services for individual members of the community, most of their ritual work is for matters of importance to the entire community.

Many of the key features of priesthood are displayed by Buddhist priests in Central Thailand. Buddhist priests and their temples are ubiquitous features of rural Thai life and the priest or head priest is often a central figure—in both religious and secular matters—in the village communities:

> To the layman, the priest in the yellow robe signifies devotion to the highest standard of enduring truth and goodness known in his culture. The village regards the life of the priest as the most complete human response possible to the teaching of the Lord Buddha about the meaning of life and suf-

fering and the achievement of happiness. (Ingersoll 1969: 71).

Buddhist priests serve individuals in their community and the community as a whole. Typically, a community has more than one priest (and sometimes more than one Buddhist sect, each with its own priesthood) organized in a hierarchy of head priest, his deputy, ordained priests, novices, and temple boys. Women may not become priests, although they may become *chii*, a role similar to that of a Roman Catholic nun.

Priests perform a wide range of duties and have little time for other activities. Each day they study, sweep the temple compound, collect rice from villagers, chant in the morning and afternoon, study passages relevant to the priest's discipline, teach, and tend the temple gardens. Weekly they conduct services for the village and provide advice and counsel as required. Every two weeks they are required to confess to each other, and each month they must shave their heads and eyebrows and teach morals to school students. On major holidays they lead processions through the village and rice fields, chant, and engage in ritual bathing. They officiate at all major life-cycle events—weddings, house warmings, ordinations, cremations, and merit making—and conduct rituals in the homes of their temple members. They also conduct rituals to aid the community, most of which involve rainmaking, especially during dry months. Finally, they counsel and advise the villagers, lead community building projects, and liaise with government officials. Some specialize as healers, often in collaboration with ritual healers.

Buddhist priests are required to own and wear special ritual costumes and paraphernalia. They must wear a long skirt and a large robe and may possess only eight essential items—three robes, an alms bowl, a razor, a belt, a drinking cup and filter, and a needle and thread. In reality, priests often own many other items as well, and as residents of the temple compound have access to the best housing, tools, medical supplies, personal care, and food in the village. Priests interact mainly with others in the temple community—other priests, novices, and temple boys.

The rules of behavior are set forth in Buddhist texts and are studied by the priests and taught by the head priest. The major rules are the 227 Patimokkha rules in the Vinayana Pitaka section of the Tripitaka. These rules set forth the restrictions, obligations, and duties of priests in considerable detail. Only men twenty years of age or older may be priests. In order to qualify they must have finished elementary school, have the permission of their parents and the district officer, place their property in care of another, obtain the approval of local priests, be free of debt, and pass a medical exam that shows them free of leprosy, ringworm, boils, tuberculosis, and epilepsy.

The priests learn the rules and tasks of their role in a variety of ways. Perhaps most importantly they have been in regular contact with priests throughout their lives and therefore enter novice status with a relatively full understanding of the role of a priest in the village. The actual learning varies from novice to novice and can involve living in the temple and studying independently, receiving instruction from the head priest, or getting help from a priest as needed. Completion of the learning process and achievement of priest status is marked by a public ordination ceremony.

Sorcerers and *witches* are distinct but related categories of magico-religious practitioners. The basic difference is that witches are believed to have innate supernatural power and that they mostly use that power for evil purposes while sorcerers lack innate power and must appeal to the supernatural for assistance through the use of formulae and ritual. Sorcerers also are not generally believed to be inherently evil or benevolent but instead will work their magic to

suit the needs of their clients. In fact, one major activity of sorcerers is uncovering and reversing the effects of witchcraft. Details on sorcerers and witches are provided in the separate entries on those topics.

Ascetics

Ascetics are individuals who deny themselves the comforts or pleasures of life that are normally enjoyed by others. Asceticism is a common feature of many religions and is viewed by adherents as a sign of an especially high level of devotion. In many religions—such as Catholicism and Buddhism—religious specialists such as priests and nuns are required to follow ascetic rules of behavior such as not engaging in sexual relations, not marrying, living apart from the community, not acquiring personal wealth, and so on. In these and other religions, adherents may or may not be ascetics. For example, in various religious groups in South Asia, such as the Baul, Bengali Shakta, and Bengali Vaishnava, some adherents live a normal lifestyle while others choose an ascetic one. For example, some Bengali Vaishnava live as laypersons and worship in their homes, while others live as monks in a monastery where dietary and ritual pollution rules are strict, and still others live an ascetic lifestyle, either in the woods or in meditation huts. Female ascetics wear white or yellow saris, keep their heads covered, and spend their time praying and chanting.

Prophets

A prophet is a person who receives divine revelations from the gods. The message or messages he receives are usually directives from the gods concerning their displeasure with human behavior and directives that the people change. Thus, prophets are individuals selected by the gods to bring the message of the gods to the people. In order to be successful, prophets must be convincing messengers, which is usually achieved through a combination of personal charisma and demonstrations of their special relationship with the supernatural such as the performance of miracles. Prophets are often the initiators of revitalization movements designed to change the existing social order. Successful prophets whose messages led to the founding of new religions, such as Jesus Christ, Mohammad, and Zoroaster, are called messiahs.

Teachers

In all religions there are teachers—individuals who teach the beliefs and practices of the religion to adherents. In major world religions all adherents are expected to receive religious education, while in other religious systems education may be provided only for religious specialists. Perhaps the best-known religious teacher is the *guru* in Hindu India. In the past, the guru was considered to be his pupil's second father and absolute obedience was required. The guru was believed to be the voice of god (in Hinduism, the god of the specific sect) and one served god through devotion to the guru. Today, the system has changed and education with a guru is no longer required; gurus more often serve as the spiritual and moral leaders of sects or spiritual movements.

See also ASCETICISM; DIVINATION; POSSESSION AND TRANCE; REVITALIZATION MOVEMENTS; SHAMANISM; SORCERY; WITCHCRAFT.

Bogoras, Waldemar. (1904–1909) *The Chukchee.*

Eliade, Mircea. (1964) *Shamanism: Archaic Techniques of Ecstasy.* Translated by Willard R. Trask.

Ingersoll, Jasper C. (1969) *The Priest and the Path: An Analysis of the Priest Role in a Central Thai Village.*

Jenness, Diamond. (1935) *The Ojibwa Indians of Parry Island: Their Social and Religious Life.*

McDaniel, June. (1989) *The Madness of the Saints: Ecstatic Religion in Bengal.*

Messing, Simon D. (1957) *The Highland Plateau Amhara of Ethiopia.*

Roscoe, John. (1911) *The Baganda: An Account of Their Native Customs and Beliefs.*

Winkelman, Michael. (1986) "Magico-Religious Practitioner Types and Socioeconomic Conditions." *Behavior Science Research* 20: 17–46.

———. (1990) " Shaman and Other 'Magico-Religious' Healers: A Cross-Cultural Study of Their Origins, Nature, and Social Transformations." *Ethos* 18: 308–352.

REVITALIZATION MOVEMENTS

The appearance of religious cults or movements is a common and recurring phenomena in human history. Such movements were, in fact, the beginning of major world religions, including Judaism, Christianity, Buddhism, Islam, and Mormonism. Over the past several centuries they have been especially frequent in regions of Western colonization. *Revitalization movements* is the term introduced by anthropologist Anthony Wallace in 1956 as a generic label for a number of different though similar types of social movements. Wallace defines a revitalization movement as "the deliberate, conscious, organized efforts by members of a society to create a new and more satisfying culture." (1956: 279) A plausible alternative term is "justicating movement," which suggests that the common feature of these social movements is that the people are seeking a more satisfying life to which they feel entitled. The terms *millenarian* or *millennium movement* are also used frequently as well, and are especially relevant for the consideration of revitalization movements as a form of religious movement. Millenarian movements have five basic features: (1) they are a collective activity; (2) participants believe that salvation will be achieved in the present world; (3) a belief that the change will occur in the immediate or near future; (4) a belief that the change will be dramatic; and (5) a belief that the change will be achieved with the help of supernatural intervention.

Four types of movements are classified as revitalization movements:

1. crisis cults, which are group responses to a crisis involving activities of a cult;
2. nativistic movements, which involve efforts to revive elements of the indigenous culture;
3. messianic or prophet cults, which feature a messiah's ushering in a new golden age;
4. millennial or chiliastic (Latin and Greek, respectively, meaning 1,000 years) movements, which foretell a period of social and spiritual bliss, not necessarily lasting 1,000 years.

Revitalization movements have been especially common in regions of Western colonization where native peoples were subjugated and their traditional way of life repressed. Since World War I this has been the case in Melanesia. Melanesia is a cultural region of the South Pacific that includes the cultures of the large island of New Guinea, the Bismark Archipelago, the Solomon Islands, Vanuatu, and New Caledonia. Revitalization movements in Melanesia are conventionally called "cargo cults" in reference to the theme prominent in many that Western goods will arrive for local consumption via Western ships and planes. This theme reflects the personal and cultural disorientation that often resulted from colonial contact with the indigenous cultures of the region. Among Melanesian movements are the Milne Bay Prophet cult, the German Wislin movement, the Vailala Madness, the Taro cult, the Naked cult, the Chair-and-Rule and Marching Rule (Masinga) movements, the Tuka cult, the Baigona cult, the Lontis cult, the Markham cargo cult, and the John Frum movement. Cargo cults were so common in New Guinea that they were reported as occurring in remote areas where the people had never met Westerners. These people evidently learned of Westerners and their material goods and the cults through contact with people closer to the coast who had contact with Westerners. Although many of these movements were quickly suppressed by the colonial (mainly English, French, German, and Japanese) governments, some had broader impact. Most notable is the John Frum movement, which began on the island of Tanna in Vanuatu in the 1930s and remains a powerful political force there as well as on other islands.

Revitalization movements have also occurred elsewhere, though not with the same frequency. In Africa, the Congolese Kinbangu cult has been described, although a more common religious response of African peoples to colonial domination was the formation of separatist Christian churches that accommodated traditional beliefs and customs. In the Caribbean, the Rastafarian movement has spread far beyond Jamaica, where it originated. In South America, the Tupi-Guarani Free Land movement has been described in the Amazon region as well as the nineteenth-century movements associated with Venancio Kamiko (Christu), a Baniwa Indian. And, in North America, the American Indian Ghost Dance, the Peyote cult (incorporated in 1918 as the Native American Church), and the Handsome Lake religion of the Iroquois are well documented. Revitalization movements are no longer so common, probably because indigenous peoples are more often now seeking to achieve control over their futures through political action.

Three Revitalization Movements

The descriptions that follow are of three different types of revitalization movements among three different cultures in three different places. They point out the similarities among the movements as well as the variations.

The Rastafari Movement. The Rastafari is a Black Jamaican religious movement that began in the early 1930s. Followers, called Rastafarians, Rastas, or Dreadlocks, now number over 100,000 in Jamaica and include an unknown number of others in the United States, Canada, most other Caribbean islands, many African nations, and Europe. Among the major features of Rastafari is the belief that Haile Selassie, the late Emperor of Ethiopia, is the returned Jesus Christ; that God is black; that all people in the Western Hemisphere of African ancestry must return to Africa; that life in Jamaica is a life in exile; and that marijuana (*ganja*) is a gift from God and is to be smoked as part of religious rituals. Rastafari also includes a strong condemnation of white oppression in the New World, referred to as Babylon. For nonbelievers, Rastafari is most often associated with the dreadlock hair style and

In 1979 Anthony Leroy, also known as Tamara I, left, and Saloman Mu-aa-ya, their hair in dreadlocks, were leaders of the Rastafari Movement. Rastafarians fall within anthropologist Anthony Wallace's 1956 definition of a revitalization movement, which exists when society members decide to "create a new and more satisfying culture."

191

reggae music. Rastafari began in Jamaica shortly after the coronation of Haile Selassie as the Emperor of Ethiopia in 1930. The local conditions setting the stage for the movement were white oppression, poverty, and the philosophy of Marcus Garvey, which stressed black pride. Despite government efforts to control the movement, including the imprisonment of some leaders, the movement grew and expanded and is now a firmly established global religion and political movement.

The Ghost Dance. The Ghost Dance is a well-described American Indian revitalization movement that promised the revival of the traditional culture, the expulsion of Europeans, and the return of deceased ancestors. The Ghost Dance actually occurred twice. It began in about 1870 when Wodziwob, a Northern Paiute man (in present-day Nevada), reported that he had learned through visions and dreams that the Great Spirit and the spirits of deceased ancestors would return, that whites would vanish, and that Earth would become paradise. The major manifestation of the movement was the dance itself, which would cause the visions to come true. The dance was conducted in a circle with an opening left for the returning spirits to enter through, and accompanied by singing, body and facial painting, and the wearing of white clothing. The movement spread west and led to other movements, such as the Earth Lodge cult, Warm House cult, and Bole-Maru cult among groups in Oregon and northern California. In about 1886, the movement reappeared among the Paiute, this time through visions of a man named Wovoka. The message and dance were similar to the 1870 version, but this time the movement spread east and was adopted by a number of Plains groups before largely disappearing. Although the movement was clearly in response to encroachments by white missionaries, settlers, traders, and soldiers, subsequent research has shown that many of the beliefs and the dance itself reflected traditional practices, with the visions about whites disappearing and some Christian elements, such as a belief in salvation, added on.

The Vailala Madness. This movement is one of the first that is well described and also a good example of a cargo cult. The Vailala Madness began among the Orokolo people (a number of related groups) living on Orokolo Bay on the southern coast of New Guinea. The cult takes its name from the mass hysteria that began in about 1919 and manifested itself in people acting giddy, reeling about, and losing control over their limbs. The origins of the cult are traced to an Orokolo man, Evara, who went into a trance, experienced convulsions, and prophesied the arrival of a steamship carrying the bodies of deceased Orokolo ancestors along with Western goods, such as rifles, flour, and tobacco. Followers also experienced trances and had visions of a new world and a new supernatural order integrating traditional Orokolo spirits and biblical figures such as Mary, Noah, and Adam and Eve (the Orokolo had been in contact with missionaries for several generations). Tall poles were erected as radio towers to communicate with the supernatural world, Western-style furniture was set up in the villages, and traditional religious objects such as bull roarers and masks were burned. When the prophesies and various sightings of arriving ships failed to prove true, the movement waned and within a few years traditional practices largely resumed. While the movement itself disappeared, it did have the positive effect of integrating traditional religious beliefs such as ancestor worship with Christianity and served as a means for legitimizing the arrival and continuing influence of Western culture.

The Causes of Revitalization Movements

Social scientists have set forth at least fifteen different explanations for revitalization movements in general or for specific types of movements. What these explanations share is a belief that revitalization movements occur in response to severe stress experienced by members of a society. Among the possible causes of this stress are colonial oppression, the collapse of traditional values, natural disasters such as famine or floods, warfare, and a discrepancy between people's expectations about what they desire and what they can actually achieve. Research shows that revitalization movements, in whatever form they take, do occur following events likely to cause stress. One particular source of stress that seems related to the appearance of revitalization movements is what is called relative cultural deprivation; that is, the relatively recent loss of some important aspect of the cultural system. For example, the near-extermination of bison on the U.S. Plains caused much disruption to the Native American cultures of the region; it was in cultures such as the Arikara, Assinboin, and Teton, who lost their herds late in the nineteenth century, that the Ghost Dance flourished.

However, loss of the resource base, colonial oppression, wars, and famine have been experienced in many cultures and only some develop revitalization movements. Thus, it seems clear that stress alone does not cause revitalization movements; other factors that encourage or allow the development of these movements must already be present. In her research with a worldwide sample of sixty societies, Judith Justinger sorted through a variety of these "predisposing" factors and examined their relationship to the appearance of revitalization movements. She found that revitalization movements are more likely to occur in societies where people believe that life can change for the better, where they believe they can improve their own life situation, where they believe that the distribution of wealth and power can be altered, and where a role for the prophet already exists in the belief system. Thus, contrary to what might be expected, revitalization movements tend to occur more often in cultures with a secular rather than a religious orientation. This, of course, raises the intriguing though as yet unanswered question of why people with a secular orientation seek a religious solution to their problems.

See also PENTECOSTALISM.

Barrett, Leonard. (1977) *The Rastafarians: The Dreadlocks of Jamaica.*

Carroll, Michael P. (1975) "Revitalization Movements and Social Structure: Some Quantitative Tests." *American Sociological Review* 40: 389–401.

Cohn, Norman. (1957) *The Pursuit of the Millenium.*

Justinger, Judith M. (1979) *Reaction to Change: A Holocultural Test of Some Theories of Religious Movements.*

Lantenari, Vittorio. (1963) *The Religions of the Oppressed: A Study of Modern Messianic Cults.*

Lessa, William A., and Evon Z. Vogt, eds. (1965) *Reader in Comparative Religion: An Anthropological Approach.* 2d ed.

Mooney, James. (1965 [1896]) *The Ghost-Dance Religion and the Sioux Outbreak of 1890.* Edited and abridged by Anthony F. C. Wallace.

Suttles, Wayne. (1957) "The Plateau Prophet Dance among the Coast Salish." *Southwestern Journal of Anthropology* 13: 352–396.

Thrupp, Sylvia L., ed. (1970) *Millennial Dreams in Action: Studies in Revolutionary Religious Movements.*

Wallace, Anthony F. C. (1956) "Revitalization Movements." *American Anthropologist* 58: 264–281.

Williams, Francis E. (1923) *The Vailala Madness and the Destruction of Native Ceremonies in the Gulf Division.*

Worsley, Peter. (1957) *The Trumpet Shall Sound.*

Wright, Robin M., and Jonathan D. Hill. (1986) "History, Ritual, and Myth: Nineteenth Century Millenarian Movements in the Northwest Amazon." *Ethnohistory* 33: 31–54.

RITUAL

Experts do not agree on how to define *ritual,* nor do they agree about its role in society. A good deal of confusion about ritual is because ritual behavior is so common and is engaged in by all individuals in a wide range of social, political, economic, and religious contexts. In fact, it is fair to say that no aspect of human behavior and culture is without ritual. As applied to religion—where ritual is equally ubiquitous—ritual can be broadly defined as repetitive, formalized, stylized acts and forms of speech that are engaged in purposively in order to communicate with or become closer to the supernatural world. In addition, ritual in the religious context is cultural behavior, as the meanings symbolized by the ritual behavior are shared by members of the religious community. In fact, one of the major tasks facing individuals who seek to become members of a religious community is learning the expected ritual behaviors, the meanings associated with those rituals, and the correct religious contexts for the use of different rituals. In all cultures, the religious socialization of children focuses on ritual behavior and the rite of passage that marks the achievement of religious majority often requires the successful public performance of the most important rituals such as reading from the Torah in Judaism or taking communion in Roman Catholicism.

Various attempts have been made to classify the hundreds of thousands of different types of rituals engaged in by people around the world. One classification scheme that encompasses the primary forms of religious rituals lists five major types:

1. technological rituals that seek to control the natural environment such as those found in divination and shamanism;

2. harm-causing and curing rituals that seek to injure others, such as those in witchcraft, sorcery, or casting the evil eye, or that seek to prevent illness or misfortune or prevent or cure illness;

3. ideological rituals that symbolize and reinforce group values, such as rites of passage and taboos;

4. salvation rituals that help individuals cope with personal issues, such as possession and trance;

5. revitalization rituals that seek to correct societal problems.

As such a ubiquitous feature of the human experience in general and religion in particular, ritual is covered in numerous entries throughout this volume, with major, formal rituals covered in the articles on Festivals, Life-Cycle Rites, and Pilgrimage.

Crapo, Rickley H. (1990) *Cultural Anthropology: Understanding Ourselves and Others.*

de Coppet, Daniel, ed. (1992) *Understanding Rituals.*

Moore, Sally F., and Barbara G. Myerhoff, eds. (1977) *Secular Ritual.*

Wallace, Anthony F. C. (1966) *Religion: An Anthropological View.*

ROMAN CATHOLICISM

With more than one billion followers, the Roman Catholic Church is the largest branch of Christianity. Catholicism traces its origins to the earliest days of Christianity and has continued its identity as the original interpreter and disseminator of the Christian faith as exemplified by Jesus Christ. The church is highly structured and hierarchical and is uniform in its beliefs and practices. The role of the Roman Catholic Church in Western civilization is impossible to exaggerate. The church's history is integral with European history, and its influence on Western society, art, and thought is deep and widespread. For more than one thousand years, the papacy not only influenced European affairs as a spiritual head, it also had secular control over the papal states in Italy. Starting in the fifteenth century, Catholicism became a driving force in the rest of the world, helping to spur on the colonization of the Americas, Africa, and Asia and influence the spiritual and political development of these lands. The word *catholic* comes from the Greek word for universal, an appropriate term to describe the religion's influence.

History

Roman Catholicism traces its roots to the apostles of Jesus Christ. The Catholic Church evolved out of the early Christian church, a largely underground movement among the lower classes who subscribed to the teachings of Jesus Christ. Christianity struggled through periodic persecutions in the first three centuries C.E. before the Roman Emperor Constantine converted to Christianity in 312 and made it the official religion of the empire. With Rome as the center of the empire, the city played a significant role in Constantine's administration of Christianity. However, in 330 he transferred the center of the empire east to Constantinople, thus sowing the seeds of division in Christianity. Bishops or patriarchs were centered in five cities—Rome, Constantinople, Antioch, Jerusalem, and Alexandria. Officially, all five were given equal status, although Rome was considered the first among the equals.

When Rome fell the political empire collapsed, but the bishop of Rome, or pope, remained as a religious leader. Christian missionaries converted others throughout western and northern Europe, gradually enhancing and expanding the Roman church's influence. At the same time, the growth of Islam led to the isolation of Antioch, Jerusalem, and Alexandria as Christian centers. Although Christianity flourished from the eastern center in Constantinople, Rome was becoming increasingly isolated from Eastern Christianity. Rome and Constantinople gradually split over a variety of doctrinal and political issues, first and foremost being the pope's claim of primacy. The schism is dated as 1054. The division, however, started many years earlier and was not made official until several centuries later.

By the tenth century European Christendom stretching from the western Mediterranean to northern Europe was taking shape. In every European state, the Roman Catholic Church was the official religion. For the next six hundred years the Roman Catholic Church was the dominant religious—and in many ways political—institution in Europe. Monarchs drew their source of "divine right" from the church, which relied heavily on political leaders for its own strength. The papacy spearheaded the fight against Islam with the Crusades, thus galvanizing Christian nations under a common religious cause. The church was also the sole educational source for Europe. Religious universities, scholars, and teachers revived philosophical debates and perpetuated sources of human knowledge. Thus, the Roman Catholic Church claimed a triple source of authority in Christendom: political, religious, and educational. Ironically, while the Roman Catholic Church was expanding its authority in secular affairs, this era also saw the growth of monasticism in which monks cloistered themselves in seclusion. Monasticism flourished as individual Christians sought to seclude themselves from worldly matters and instead pursue religious understanding and prayer. Benedictine monasteries, based on the teaching of Benedict of Nursia in Italy, grew. A spiritual revival took place in the thirteenth century when a number of mendicant orders (Dominicans, Carmelites, Franciscans, Augustinians) rapidly grew as friars lived in monasteries and preached Christianity among the lay populations.

Although belief in and support of Christianity never wavered, several challenges were made during this era to the Roman papacy. In the fourteenth century Christendom split as the French established the Avignon papacy to challenge Rome's dominance. For several years there was open conflict between the contingents and at one point three popes claimed to be the rightful leaders of Christendom. Disputes, however, were resolved and the papal seat was restored to Rome. Corruption, too, sapped loyalties to the papacy and the church. Widespread abuses by priests and bishops caused dissent throughout Europe as did the moral lapses of several popes, most notably the notorious Alexander VI, who was elected in 1492. These problems combined with doctrinal disputes led to periodic calls for reform in the fourteenth and fifteenth centuries. John Wycliffe led an anti-Roman movement in England in the fourteenth century. In the early fifteenth century, the Czech university professor John Hus called for numerous reforms in the Catholic Church. Both of these movements were suppressed ruthlessly, but they proved to be forerunners of the Protestant Reformation of the sixteenth century.

Martin Luther set in motion two hundred years of turmoil when he posted his Ninety-Five Theses in Wittenberg, Germany, in 1517, condemning the practices of the Roman Catholic church. His calls for reform were quickly picked up and followed by thousands of followers and other reformers who challenged the Roman Catholic interpretation of Christianity and the primacy of the pope. The Catholic Church responded to the challenges both with force, culminating in the bloody religious struggles of the Thirty Years' War (1618–1648), and through internal reforms at the Council of Trent (1545–1563). The council took action against the moral corruption that decimated the church's internal hierarchy and set forth its theological doctrines in the face of widespread dissent. Many of the internal reforms involved a hardening of theological doctrine that went a long way toward preserving Catholicism for the short term, but at the same time set in stone a theology that was all but impervious to change for the next several centuries. The Jesuit order that grew out of this Counter Reformation was led by Ignatius of Loyola, who pioneered a renewed religious vigor based on self-sacrifice and will to foster and spread Catholicism both within Europe and abroad.

The Protestant Reformation permanently ended the Roman Catholic Church's total dominance of European spiritual affairs and severely hampered its political control. However, at the same time that the church's European presence waned, new opportunities for spreading Catholicism opened up as explorers discovered new lands filled with indigenous, non-Christian peoples. Catholic missionaries accompanied and encouraged the colonization of foreign lands by Portugal, Spain, and France. Whether by the point of the sword, spiritual inspiration, or political persuasion, Catholic missionaries eventually converted entire populations in the Americas, Africa, and, to a lesser extent, Asia. While some attempts were made by missionaries to blend native beliefs and traditions with Catholicism, these efforts were squashed by Rome, which maintained a rigid stance that favored imposing Catholic beliefs on other nations without compromise.

In the meantime, Catholicism's influence continued to wane in Europe. New scientific discoveries and the Enlightenment of the eighteenth century called into question much of the spiritual authority of the Roman Catholic Church. The French Revolution, which to a large degree represented an assault on the Roman Catholic Church's affirmation of the French

Pope John XXIII, then leader of the Roman Catholic Church, is carried in a procession to St. Peter's in Vatican City to open the twenty-first ecumenical council October 15, 1962. Adherents of Roman Catholicism, the largest branch of Christianity, number more than one billion.

monarchy and aristocracy, nearly brought down the papacy altogether. In 1798, French troops sacked Rome and captured Pope Pius VI. But the papacy survived and its authority was restored. Pope Pius IX (1846–1878) responded to the growing secularism and modernism of the nineteenth century with a series of decrees and actions that formed the modern papacy and placed the church's strength in the Roman pontiff. He called for the first Vatican Council

(1869–1870), which defined the infallibility and primacy of the pope as a religious leader. Not coincidentally, the decree came three months before Victor Emmanuel II destroyed the papal states, thus stripping the papacy of its last vestige of direct secular authority.

Pope Leo XIII (1878–1903) furthered the modern role of the Roman Catholic Church with his emphasis on theological substance and social justice. Known as the "pope of peace," Leo XIII set forth a social philosophy that affirmed political liberalism and democracy, called for national governments to care for the welfare of their citizens, and condemned the exploitative aspects of capitalism (the Roman Catholic Church, however, has always been a firm and determined opponent of socialism and communism). Pope John XXIII (1958–1963) continued the spirit of reform with the calling of the second Vatican Council (1962–1965), which in many ways challenged the decrees of the Council of Trent four hundred years earlier, bringing forth drastic changes, such as the use of the vernacular in the church, greater participation of the laity in worship, and a new ecumenical spirit of cooperation with Protestantism and Eastern Orthodoxy. The council expressed its regret at past anti-Semitism by the Christian community and embraced the notion of freedom of religion. Although the Roman Catholic Church is now divided between liberal reformers and conservatives determined to fight against any further changes, the Roman Catholic religion remains a remarkably unified and influential institution.

Beliefs

Roman Catholicism is based on the idea of faith as revealed by Jesus Christ, the son of God. God—a three-part entity called the Trinity and consisting of God himself, Jesus Christ, and the Holy Spirit—makes his presence and desires known to humanity both through his direct expressions and by evidence that can be discerned through human reason. The Old Testament recounts God's direct interventions and the New Testament describes his expressions through the life of his son, Jesus Christ. How does a person know that this is God's word? Through faith. Faith must be applied to accept God's authority. Man cannot know who God is or what God is doing or why unless God tells him. Reason and rationality can never fully explain the mystery of God in Catholicism. One cannot use human experience alone to describe the supernatural and unknowable authority of God.

The Roman Catholic Church sees its role as fulfilling the commands of the Scriptures and revelations of God. The revelations ended with the death of Christ's apostles. The Roman Catholic Church has inherited the role of the apostles and taken the word of God and interpreted it for Christian worshipers. "He who hears you hears me," Christ told the apostles. Although Protestants objected to the church's role in interpreting the Scriptures, Roman Catholicism claims a traditional role as the exclusive source of understanding the Scriptures. It was the Roman Catholic Church that assigned the importance of the Scriptures in the first place and maintained an oral tradition through the church hierarchy that perpetuated Christ's teachings.

Roman Catholicism believes that man is incapable of goodness because of original sin as described in the Old Testament story of Adam and Eve. Man is stuck in his human condition because of his own failing, not God's. Only God can deliver man from his predicament. God sent his son Jesus Christ to live among humans to reveal grace as salvation. The resurrection of Christ was an atonement for Adam's failure and a triumph over death. Those who believe in Jesus Christ are no longer alienated from God, but are his children and capable of salvation through grace. The presence of grace in man is reflected through faith, hope, and charity, all of which allow him to live the Christian life described and exemplified by Jesus Christ (treat others as they would treat you, refrain from sin, love thy enemy, obey Moses' Ten Commandments as described in the Old Testament). Man is initiated into a life of grace through the sacrament of baptism. The sacraments sustain a person's grace.

Structure of the Church

Roman Catholicism assigns the Roman pontiff, or pope, as the successor of Peter, upon whom Jesus assigned the primacy of the apostles. As such, the pope has absolute supreme jurisdiction over the Roman Catholic church. This authority, however, is tempered by a number of other elements. Tradition plays a major role in determining what a pope does and who is selected to fulfill the role. The College of Cardinals has elected the pope since the Middle Ages and serves as his advisory board. Cardinals, who are ordained bishops, are selected at the personal discretion of the pope. The only authority equal to that of the pope is that of the regional councils of bishops to settle doctrinal disputes, and they can meet only when called by the pope. These councils have only been held twenty-ones time in the entire history of the Roman Catholic Church. The most recent council was the second Vatican (1962–1965).

Bishops serve three roles. Subservient to only the pope, they control their assigned diocese, teach Catholic doctrine, and administer the sacraments. Because of the complexity and weight of these responsibilities, bishops are assisted by priests as officers to administer the duties. Priests typically serve as pastors in parishes. All members of the Roman Catholic hierarchy set themselves apart from the laity in several ways, most obviously in their dress. Perhaps the most controversial distinction for Roman Catholic officers is their vow of celibacy. There is a clear distinction between Catholic clergy and the laity. It is the clergy's job to teach the word of God and administer to the sacraments. The laity's role is simply to accept it.

Separate from this hierarchical structure is a wide range of religious communities that falls within the Roman Catholic Church. These religious communities, many of which cloister themselves in seclusion, have been a part of the church's heritage since the second and third centuries. The communities consist of groups of men and women who pronounce vows of obedience, chastity, and poverty in a common life. The goal of their existence is to live a life of Christian perfection. Historically, these monasteries have proven to be great sources of strength and inspiration for the church. During the Middle Ages, Catholic monasteries preserved writings and were educational centers. In the era of the Catholic Counter Reformation, monastery communities were among the most devoted preachers and missionaries of Catholicism. Religious communities of women were introduced in France with the Daughters of Charity, who vowed to help feed, cloth, and educate the poor and sick, a role that remains the mission of most female communities.

Texts

Roman Catholicism is based on the word of God as described in the Old and New Testaments. Disputes on interpretations have been settled at the twenty-one councils of bishops held periodically over the last sixteen centuries. The church's doctrine incorporates a wide range of theological writings, including the works of Augustine of Hippo and Thomas Aquinas. The basic law of the Roman Catholic Church is the Canon Law, a collection of laws, rules, and regulations accumulated over the centuries. The codification of the various laws was initiated in 1904 by Pius X and finalized in 1918.

Practices

The most important act of worship in Roman Catholicism is the Eucharist at mass, commemorating the Last Supper of Jesus Christ. All liturgies, which follow an annual cycle reenacting the life, death, resurrection, and glorification of Jesus Christ, include the Eucharist. A member of the clergy presents bread and wine as the body and blood of Jesus Christ for worshipers to eat to honor Jesus Christ's sacrifice for humanity. The Eucharist is one of the seven sacraments that Roman Catholics practice to produce grace. The clergy's role in the sacraments is as an agent of the church who facilitates the saving act of God. Only an agent of the church is capable of facilitating the conversion of seemingly normal matter such as bread, wine, and water into sacred objects through blessings, prayers, and recitations. In addition to the Eucharist, the other six sacraments are Baptism, Confirmation, Penance, the Anointing of the Sick, Marriage, and Holy Orders.

Baptism is the sacrament of initiation into the church. A person either immerses himself in water or has pure natural water poured on him. The purpose is to cleanse the new initiate of the sins of his or her past and emerge as a completely innocent person, embraced in the church of Christ. Confirmation, which comes after baptism, is normally applied to adolescents. An oil is applied to the person and the Holy Spirit is called to embolden the recipient with the wisdom and fortitude to live a Christian life. Penance is offered as a way to repent from sins. No quality or quantity of sin is too profound for sacramental absolution. While penance used to typically involve fasting and public humiliation, it no longer requires such stringent atonement. Priests typically administer penance through confessions. Protestant reformers rejected this sacrament, believing that only God can forgive sins. The Anointing of the Sick, or Last Rites, is delivered to a person suffering a serious illness. A clergyman confers it by applying blessed oil to a person's sense organs (lips, nose, ears, hands, and eyes) and reciting a formula. Marriage in Roman Catholicism involves the exchange of consent between the two partners, witnessed by the priest. Before entering into marriage, however, Roman Catholicism calls for a rigorous review and process between the two partners. Sacraments for the Holy Orders pertain to the power given to deacons, priests, and bishops to administer the sacraments.

The two most important holidays celebrated by Roman Catholics are Easter, celebrating the death and resurrection of Jesus Christ, and Christmas, celebrating his birth. Christmas is celebrated on December 25 and preceded by Advent on the four previous Sundays. Twelve days after Christmas, on January 6, Roman Catholics celebrate the Epiphany, representing the baptism of Jesus Christ and the visit of the three wise men to Bethlehem. Easter is celebrated on the first Sunday after the first full moon following the vernal equinox (March 21). Lent, a period of solemn fasting and prayer, is observed prior to Easter. Roman Catholics also observe feasts commemorating saints, and, especially, the mother of Jesus Christ, the Blessed Virgin Mary.

See also EASTERN ORTHODOXY.

Glazier, Michael, and Monika K. Hellwig. (1994) *The Modern Catholic Encyclopedia.*

McBrien, Richard P. (1995) *The HarperCollins Encyclopedia of Catholicism.*

made from plants, or material objects are given to supernatural beings. Animal sacrifice and plant offerings are far more common than human sacrifice, although all forms have been found throughout human history in all regions of the world. Across cultures, sacrifice and offering have a number of basic, common features: (1) they are highly structured, ritual activities; (2) they are symbolic activities, as what is sacrificed or offered is not physically transferred to the supernatural being and may itself represent the human making the sacrifice; (3) they are goal-directed behaviors; (4) they involve a transfer of a physical item to a supernatural being or force; (5) the object sacrificed or offered is a sacred object; (6) in sacrifice, the animal or human must always be living before it is sacrificed.

A common feature of sacrifice and offering is that what is sacrificed is of economic value in the culture in which it is sacrificed or offered. In cultures that make food offerings, it is the staple crops that are chosen. In cultures with animal sacrifice, it is always only domesticated animals of economic importance, not wild animals, that are sacrificed. Human sacrifice has been characteristic of cultures in which humans were an important source of energy. Because valuable economic resources are involved, in many cultures steps are taken to ensure that such resources are not wasted. Thus, it is not uncommon for the people themselves to eat some or all of the animal that is sacrificed. For example, among the Yakut of Siberia, after a cow was sacrificed as part of a shamanistic curing ritual, the animal might be slaughtered and eaten by members of the community. In other cultures sacrifices might be made only by the wealthy, or be delayed, or a less valuable resource sacrificed if the animal to be sacrificed was in short supply.

While sacrifice is, on the surface, an exchange between humans and supernatural beings, it also in many cultures mirrors the social relations among humans. For example, exchange

SACRIFICE AND OFFERING

Sacrifice and offering are related forms of nonverbal communication between human beings and the supernatural world. Both are exchanges of goods meant to influence the supernatural to behave in a way that is beneficial to the humans making the offering or sacrifice. Sacrifice and offering are important elements of Judeo-Christian, Islamic, Hindu, and other major religious traditions and are found in all non-Western cultures. Sacrifice and offering reflect four basic assumptions humans make about their relationship with the supernatural world: (1) supernatural beings can and do influence life on earth; (2) supernatural beings can be influenced by the behavior of humans; (3) giving a desired item to a supernatural being will please him or her and cause him or her to act benevolently toward the person making the sacrifice; and (4) supernatural beings are free to accept or reject the item and help, ignore, or harm humans.

Sacrifice refers to practices in which an animal or human is killed. Offering refers to practices in which no blood is shed and plants, food

relations among humans and between humans and the supernatural of the Subanum of the Philippines are quite alike. Subanum give food and drink to each other in order to gain the help of the other person. They view offerings of food or drink to supernatural beings as being the same type of exchange—giving food and drink will induce the supernatural beings to assist them. In a broader sense, sacrifice and offering, like all forms of community rituals, are community-reinforcing activities, as they bring the community together, require a shared understanding of the meaning and symbolism of the rite, and define the relationship between the human and supernatural worlds.

Animal sacrifice and offering as common religious practices take a wide variety of forms around the world, although they are most common and most elaborated in societies that subsist by raising domesticated animals and agriculture. One such culture are the Garo of India who employ sacrifice in their annual cycle of festivals and to cure disease. The Garo believe that spirits cause disease and that specific spirits cause specific disorders. To cure the disease, the spirit causing it must be identified (the disease symptoms give the key clues to the identity of the spirit) and then a sacrifice must be made in a specific location to that spirit. While the details of the sacrifice—where it is held, what animal is sacrificed—vary from disease to disease, the overall pattern of the ritual is the same:

> Several men spend about two hours building an altar. Most altars are built of bamboo and leaves, but the precise form depends upon the particular spirit to whom the sacrifice is to be directed. Once the altar is built, a ritually skilled man must offer an egg, a chicken, pig, or even a cow, depending upon the seriousness of the disease and the demands of the mite [spirit]. The priest kills the animal in a ritually prescribed manner, and smears blood on to the altar. He recites a number of chants while standing or squat-
> ting before the altar, and usually pours a bit of rice beer upon the ground as an additional offering....the priest inspects their viscera for omens. If the proper portion of the chicken's intestines prove to be filled, for instance, the prognosis is good; otherwise it is bad. . . . There is no ecstasy and sleight of hand, and the sick person is not even necessarily present. When the formalities are completed, the helpers prepare the animal and cook it into a curry. Rice is prepared and all of the helpers share in the ensuing meal. . . . Afterwards the participants go to their own houses. They are not supposed to go to their fields for the whole day, although they may do chores about the house. (Burling 1963, 55–56)

These sacrifices take about two to three hours and hundreds are held in a Garo village each year. As those involved in each ritual are only those close to the sick person, village life is not disrupted in any general way. The Garo find the sacrifices usually work, but if the person does not recover in a few days, another sacrifice will be given to a different spirit. If many people in a village are ill, the men of the village will capture a monkey, ritually display it before each house, and then hang it near a river. Death is attributed to a spirit too strong to be influenced by a sacrifice.

The Garo also use sacrifice to communicate with the spirits who control the food they grow in the fields and the weather. These sacrifices are made as part of the annual ritual cycle, with a goat sacrificed to mark the clearing of the fields and to bring a good crop, and a cow sacrificed when the rice is planted. These sacrifices are made to Saljong, who controls the water and rain and thus determines whether the Garo will enjoy a rich rice harvest.

In East Africa where many cultures subsist in whole or part through the raising of cattle, sacrifice is an important element in the indigenous religions, used in various rituals and often accompanied by prayer and offerings. As many

A Balinese girl carries an offering to a Hindu temple.
Offerings and sacrifices are given to influence supernatural beings.

of these cultures also have strong systems of ancestor worship and centralized leadership, sacrifice is used to communicate with ancestral spirits and to reinforce the control of the chiefs and subchiefs. The Bemba of Zimbabwe employ a number of rituals to communicate with the spirits, including *ulupepa lukalamba* (big offering), which is one of the more important:

> at which offerings of cattle, chicken, beer, hoes, or sloth are made at all the big shrines in the land. This series of rites usually coincides with the first-fruit ceremonies, and in fact it would be difficult to feed a big gathering of officials except at harvest time. The special *ukusumata* (tasting) rite for the Kaffir corn is first performed and the Citikafula, the *mukabilo* in charge of such sacrifices, should be sent with a basket of Kaffir-corn blessed at the relic shrines, and two oxen to the neighboring shrines of Mulenga Porkili and Bwalya Cabala, the first royal ancestress. Here the beasts must be sacrificed and the flour scattered on the ground. This initiates the succession of sacrifices which are to follow. All the *bashimapepo* are called to the capital and are given cloth or chickens to offer at their local spirit centres, and messengers go to and fro between the different capitals to inform the territorial chiefs of the proceedings. They start to sacrifice at the sacred spots in their own districts. Only when the chain of sacrifices is complete the Bemba say "Ulupepo luabuka mu calo" (the sacrifice has risen up in the land). (Richards 1939, 360)

Human Sacrifice

A survey of 107 cultures shows that human sacrifice occurred commonly in 17 percent of cultures and sporadically in 14 percent in the nineteenth and early twentieth centuries. Thus, it was not customary in 69 percent of cultures, making it relatively rare compared to most other forms of behavior that result in death for the victim, such as homicide or capital punishment. A limited form of sacrifice, in which one might cut off a finger or part of a finger, is reported for some Native American groups of the past but is not common today. Around the world, sacrifice was concentrated in cultures in Africa (50 percent of those with human sacrifice) and Oceania (30 percent), for reasons discussed below.

Humans are sacrificed only for the most important requests to the supernatural. Among the Marquesas Islanders in Polynesia these reasons included success in war, to end a drought, to secure a plentiful harvest, to consecrate a new house or canoe, and special events in the life of the chief such as his being ill or departing on a voyage. For the Bambara of West Africa, the reasons were the chief's running short on money, his having problems governing, and a family suffering many deaths. Humans who were sacrificed in most cultures were outsiders such as slaves or war captives or those who did not fit in such as albinos. When members of one's own culture were sacrificed, women and children were more likely to be the victims than were men.

Cultures with human sacrifice were mostly ones with an advanced horticultural economy and political organization—a common type of culture in Oceania and West Africa. In these cultures people subsist primarily on food grown in large gardens and groves, live in large, relatively permanent villages, and are governed by a chief who might be supported by a cadre of public servants. In this type of culture, human labor is the major source of energy used to plant and tend the gardens, build houses, construct tools, and so on. Two indicators of the importance of human energy were the use of slaves and the presence of specialized craftspeople such as potters and leather workers. Thus, when an important request was made to the supernatural, it was often accompanied by a sacrifice of what was most important economically—a human life. It has been suggested that human sacrifice did not occur in other types of societies such as foraging, farming, or industrial ones because in such systems human labor is not such an important commodity. In farming cultures it is food crops that are offered, indicating their economic importance. And in industrial and postindustrial societies, donations of money to support various religious or moral causes have many of the same features as sacrifice and offering, although there is not always the link to the supernatural.

The culture that has drawn the most attention for its use of human sacrifice is the Aztec state of pre-Columbian Mexico. Compared to any other known culture, the Aztec were at the far extreme in the use of human sacrifice and also in the practice of cannibalism. Sacrifice was a central feature of the Aztec religious system, with the human heart and blood believed to be the ultimate source of power for the sun and Aztec deities. During the two annual ceremonial cycles of 365 and 260 days, it is estimated that about 250,000 humans were sacrificed in hundreds of temples throughout the Aztec empire. There were at least 80 such temples in the capital city of Tenochtitlán. The victims were usually warriors captured and kept alive to be sacrificed or enslaved. While a variety of killing methods was used, the preferred method was cutting the victim open on a stone slab, removing the heart into a ceremonial vessel, smearing blood on the carved image of the god, and placing the skull on a skull rack alongside thousands of others. Aztec sacrifice was allegedly accompanied by cannibalism, with at least three of the limbs going to the warrior who captured the victim and the torso fed to animals in the royal zoo.

Various explanations have been suggested for Aztec human sacrifice. Older explanations emphasized the central role of sacrifice in Aztec religion and the elaborate Aztec sacrifice complex that developed around it. This complex included the religious beliefs and myths, the stone temples, ceremonial platforms and equipment such as the skull racks, the sacrifice rituals that lasted three days, the ceremonial cycle, cannibalism, and the warfare that was waged primarily to capture sacrificial victims. Both the archaeological and historical records point to the central role of human sacrifice in Aztec culture.

More recent attempts to explain Aztec sacrifice move beyond the Aztec's own beliefs and the cultural manifestation of those beliefs and cite both environmental and political forces. The environmental explanation suggests that the vitality and survival of the Aztec state may have been threatened by overpopulation because of the limited food resources available in central Mexico. The Aztec lived mainly on foods derived from corn; there was a severe shortage of wild animals to hunt for meat and no domestic food-producing and -supplying animals. Thus, in this explanation, sacrifice is seen as a form of population control (one estimate suggests that 250,000 people or the equivalent of 10 percent of the regional population may have been sacrificed each year), while cannibalism provided protein that could not be obtained from other food sources. The political explanation suggests that sacrifice and cannibalism were but one of a number of political strategies used by the Aztec monarchs to control the noble class and the military. In this view, human sacrifices were a form of wealth given to and consolidated among the nobles, who otherwise might rebel against the monarch. Whatever the causes of Aztec sacrifice and cannibalism, both ended with the Spanish conquest in the sixteenth century.

See also CANNIBALISM; MAGIC.

Burling, Robbins. (1963) *Rengsanggari: Family and Kinship in a Garo Village.*

Dieterlen, Germaine. (1951) *An Essay on the Religion of the Bambara.* Translated by Katia Wolf.

Handy, E. S. Craighill. (1923) *The Native Culture of the Marquesas*. Bernice P. Bishop Museum, Bulletin No. 9.

Harner, Michael. (1977) "The Ecological Basis for Aztec Sacrifice." *American Ethnologist* 4: 117–135.

Malefijt, Annemarie de Waal. (1968) *Religion and Culture: An Introduction to the Anthropology of Religion*.

Price, Barbara J. (1978) "Demystification, Enriddlement, and Aztec Cannibalism: A Materialist Rejoinder to Harner." *American Ethnologist* 5: 98–115.

Richards, Audrey I. (1939) *Land, Labour, and Diet in Northern Rhodesia: An Economic Study of the Bemba Tribe*.

Sheils, Dean. (1980) "A Comparative Study of Human Sacrifice." *Behavior Science Research* 15: 245–262.

Soustelle, Jacques. (1962) *Daily Life of the Aztecs*. Translated by Patrick O'Brian.

SHAMANISM

Shamanism refers to a system of religious and medical beliefs and practices that centers on the shaman, a specific type of magico-religious practitioner. Shamanism rests on the belief that many events on earth are caused by supernatural forces and therefore human contact with and control of the supernatural is necessary to control life on earth. The shaman is the individual who specializes in contacting and controlling the supernatural. Classic shamanism is associated with the indigenous cultures of Siberia and Central Asia and is characterized by the shaman's being a charismatic male, a master of the supernatural spirits, concerned mainly though not exclusively with curing disease, and serving a client base composed of particular families or communities. During the nineteenth and twentieth centuries classic shamanism was severely repressed by the Russian, Soviet, and Chinese governments and in some cultures disappeared, in others survived only in limited form, and in others went underground. Since the mid-twentieth century there has been a revival of shamanism and a broadening of the meaning of the concept to include related magico-religious practices elsewhere in the world. In the former Soviet Union, the end of Soviet rule has led to a revival of shamanism in some Siberian cultures as part of a broader pattern of cultural revitalization. In Korea, where shamanism was also repressed, it has been revived as a marker of indigenous Korean culture, although nearly all Korean shamans are now women rather than men. The conceptualization of shamanism has also been broadened by social scientists and others to include related practices that rely on an altered state of consciousness or possession trance, and thus one now speaks of Cuna, Tibetan, Malay, and !Kung shamans. Some experts argue that many of these other religious healing systems are not shamanism as the key element of shamanistic control of the spirits is missing. In the last several decades, and particularly in the 1990s, elements of shamanism have appeared as an element of the New Age movement, especially such practices as chanting and drumming, which are seen as tools for achieving a deeper state of personal spirituality. The New Age movement has drawn both from classic shamanism and also shamanistic practices among various Native American cultures in North and South America.

Shamanism as a religious healing system has a number of key elements: (1) the shaman himself—his characteristics, initiation and training, and lifestyle; (2) the issues addressed by the shaman; and (3) the séance. The discussion below focuses on these topics, with examples provided from classic Yakut shamanism in Siberia and the broader shamanism of the Tlingit of northwest North America.

The Shaman

Shamans may be male or female, old or young, and benevolent or harmful. The key characteristic is that shamans control supernatural spirits and use that power to cure illnesses caused by these spirits as well as to influence or communicate with the spirits about other earthly concerns such as the weather. Shamans also must be brave, smart, creative, and willing to alter their behavior by honoring taboos required of their status.

The Yakut distinguish between male *(oyun)* and female *(udahan)* shamans and white-creative *(Ajy ayuna)* and black-harmful *(Abasy oyuna)* shamans. The white shaman looks like other people and uses no special means to communicate with the creator spirit whom he asks to help in matters such as infertility. He is incapable of causing harm and of little use in curing illness caused by evil spirits. The black shaman more closely fits the image of the classic shaman—he intervenes between spirits and humans to cure illness caused by spirits. The power of the shamans vary according to the power of the different spirits they control. The black shaman can also compel the spirits to cause others to fall ill. Although he may be consulted for other reasons, the Yakut shaman is mainly involved with curing illness.

For the Tlingit, the shaman is concerned with a broader range of issues:

> The shaman is the intermediary between men and the forces of nature. He cures the sick, controls the weather, brings success in war and on the hunt, foretells the future, communicates with colleagues at a distance, receives news about those who are far away, finds and restores to their families those who are lost and captured by the Land Otter Men, reveals and overthrows the fiendish machinations of the witches, and makes public demonstrations of his powers in awe-

inspiring ways. He is the most powerful figure in his own lineage, or sometimes even in his sib. (de Laguna 1972, 670)

Tlingit shamans may be men or women, although male shamans are more powerful because childbearing saps the strength of women. Shamans are often family heads of close relatives. A Tlingit becomes a shaman by inheriting the status from a deceased uncle (mother's brother) or brother. Going near the body or grave, touching the shaman's masks or drums, or holding a lock of his hair are the primary means by which the spirits of the deceased shaman become one with his successor:

> Infection by the spirit or power of a dead shaman manifests itself as an illness, even in the one who welcomes it. The unwilling recipients of such power "always have the hardest time." This is the way it always starts, until the power is accepted and controlled, "until it starts working right. It bothers them. That's why they call it `anelsin, hiding—it hides inside.'" This is conceived as something actually inside the body. (de Laguna 1972, 674)

Once a Tlingit receives the "call" he must go through a period of training and initiation as "Nobody is born to be an Indian doctor. They got to do certain things." The most important of these "things" is a spirit quest deep into the woods to contact and take control of an animal spirit. On the first quest the new shaman might be assisted by a friendly shaman and relatives. The first quest, lasting eight days, involves fasting, cold baths, and ultimately contact with an animal that appears at the shaman's feet. The shaman then cuts a slice off the animal's tongue, binds it between pieces of wood, and hides it in the woods. The process is repeated on subsequent quests until the shaman feels he has acquired enough power. The soul of the animal then becomes a spirit of the shaman and powerful shamans may obtain as many as eight spirits in this way.

Yakut shamans trace their professional ancestry to the spirits:

> His name was An-Argyl-Ojun. He was powerful and performed great miracles. He raised the dead, and gave the blind their eyesight back. This fame eventually also reached Aj-Toen (God, the Lord). He sent a messenger to the shaman to ask in the name of what god he did those miracles and whether he believed in him, Aj-Toen. An-Argyl-Ojun (the important shaman) replied three times he did not believe in God but performed miracles by his own strength and power.
>
> Aj-Toen became angry at that and ordered the shaman to be burned. As however, Ojun's body consisted of countless vermin, one little frog managed to be saved from the flames. The powerful demons who still give shamans to the Yakuts are descendants of this little frog. (Krauss 1888: 171)

For the Yakut shaman-to-be, the initiation is a public ritual directed by an older shaman on a hill. The public nature of the ritual suggests the role of Yakut shamans in treating all members of the community, while the more restrictive nature of Tlingit initiation reflects that many Tlingit shamans administer mainly to their kin. The Yakut initiate must repeat the shamanic oaths whispered to him by the older shaman. These oaths indicate the type of catastrophes the Yakut feared and the central role Yakut shamans played in curing disease.

> I promise to be a protector of the unhappy, a father of the miserable, and a mother of the orphans. I shall honor the demons who live on the tops of the high mountains, and swear that I shall serve them with all my strength. I shall honor, bow to, and serve the highest and most powerful of them, the demon who commands all demons, the master of the three demon sibs who live on the tops of the mountains; him whom the shamans call Sostuganach Ulu-Toen (the

frightful, terrible one), his elder son Ujgul-Toen (the insane one), his wife Ujgul-Chotun (the insane woman), his younger son Kjakja-Curan-Toen (the loudly speaking one), his wife Kjakja-Curan-Chotun, and their numerous family and servants, through whom they send the people diseases, accidents, breakings of legs, and the podagra. I vow to save those who have been affected by these diseases, by sacrificing a cream-colored mare.

I shall profess and worship, bow to, and serve Ulu-Toen's younger brother, the demon Chara-Surun-Toen (the black raven), his son Alban-Buran-Toen (the resourceful venturer), his daughter Kys-Salisaj (the virgin who walks), who prompts people to commit manslaughter, suicide, and calumny. I promise to help rid these people of their passions by offering the said demons a black horse.

I shall profess, worship, and bow to the demon Altan-Sobiraj-Toen (the brazen basin), his wife Altan Sobiraj-Chotun (the one with the biggest brazen arrow), their daughters Timir-Kuturuk (iron tail) and Kejulgan Darchan (the important, great, lopping woman), who send mankind chronical abscesses. I shall help free the sick by sacrificing some (Arago) liquor, and offering the demons a motley searnew, as a gift of honor.

I shall profess and worship, and bow to the ancestor of these demons who is known as Kjun-Zelerjuma-Sakryl-Chotun (the horrible foe of the sun) who has 52 tables full of holes, and 52 servants. She sends people the passion game and drinking, of robbery, plundering, abject deeds, and suicide. I shall try to heal those who are obsessed with these vices. I shall kill a red-spotted young mare who is an ambler, and twist heart and liver of the mare round my neck; I shall perform shaman magic to propitiate the goddess.

I shall profess and honor the demon above the demons of the six sibs who live in the place where the sinners' souls are sent to; I will bow to the one who is known among the shamans as Talirdach-Tan-Taraly-Toen (he who drags into ruin), his daughters Sorocho-Chotun (the wind-driven female beauty), and San-Chotun, and his countless servants who send men and cattle epidemic diseases. To propitiate them I shall offer them a sorrel-spotted mare.

I shall profess, honor, and bow to the Demon Bor-Malachaj-Toen (deformed earth) and his wife Bor-Malachaj-Chotun who send mankind various diseases and, especially, death. If in a family children should die, I will implore these demons for mercy, and offer them a black cow with a half-white head.

I shall profess, honor, and bow to the demon Archach-Toen (the sick one) and his wife Archach-Chotun, who send mankind consumption. I shall heal the affected by offering a blackish brown cow.

I shall profess and honor the demon Njas-Elju (cart-horse, death) and his wife Yeryk-Chotun (the sick one) who send the people falling sickness and Siberian pestilence. I shall try to heal those who have been affected by these diseases by offering an eelpout and a trout.

I shall profess, honor, and bow to the demon Kytaj-Baksy-Toen who gives the Yakuts resourceful smiths and powerful shamans. When Kytaj, angry with a smith, sends him a disease, I promise to kill a red cow in his honor, to spread the blood over all the forge tools, and to burn the heart and liver to ashes in the chimney. If I should be affected by this disease, another shaman will sacrifice for me and propitiate the demon.

I shall profess, honor, and bow to the daughter of the demon, Tamyk-Chotun (the haughty one). She sends mankind mental diseases of various kinds. Those who have been affected by such disease I shall heal by sacrificing nine ermines, nine snow-weasels, nine fitchews, and nine pigeons; I vow to catch them alive, to adorn them, and to release them entirely.

I shall profess and bow to, I shall honor the shaman woman Tajaktach-Njacaj (the feeble one with the reed), her husband Atyr-Chataj (the eagle) and his countless family and descendants, who send the people oppression of the chest. Those who have been affected by this disease I shall try to save by sacrificing a light-red cow with but one horn.

I shall acknowledge, honor, and bow to the heavenly shaman Kybilyr Ojun (the

white swan), his sister Kytalyktyr-Kyrbyky) (the swan of the acute wings), and their mother Soruktach-Sodor (the charitable ruler), who send the people deafness and every kind of ear disease. Those who have been affected by it I shall try to save by offering a red cow with but one horn *(agar mostach kugas)*. (Krauss 1888, 170)

This oath serves as a "job description" for the shaman as it lists the diseases he is expected to prevent and cure, the spirits involved, and the procedures used to control the spirits.

Once a man or woman becomes a shaman, he or she is expected to appear and behave in ways that mark him or her as different from other members of the community, that reinforce shamanistic powers, and that protect him or her from harm. These include observing food taboos, especially on shellfish, during certain months; sexual continence for long periods; and fasting for days before conducting a séance. The shaman's wife and some relatives might also be expected to honor these taboos and restrictions as well. The shaman also has to obtain and protect his ritual paraphernalia—most importantly the masks that represented the animals whose souls he controls, his drums and rattles. The Tlingit shaman is assisted by others—usually relatives—who sing and drum, bang sticks, serve as subjects for the shaman's display of his power, and interpret the words of the spirit being spoken through the shaman. The assistant's role is not a minor one:

When they become shaman, after they start in, his assistants have to know just what song to sing and how to beat the drum. If they misbeat the drum, the shaman just become normal again. Or, if they sing the wrong song, the same way. Yakut shaman, along with blacksmiths, were the most respected people in the community. Because villages might be far apart, shaman traveled about and were sought after . . . as soon as a shaman arrives somewhere, news of his arrival will be quickly spread over the entire neighborhood. Curious people, and those who hope to be relieved from the ailments will crowd together at the spot to see the shaman and to inquire of him about the future. (de Laguna 1972: 702)

The shaman is seated in the place of honor, will feed, and might demand an offering of meat or sacrifices to the spirits and gifts to himself before conducting the séance.

Séance

A séance is a ritual in which the shaman is possessed by a spirit or travels to the spirit world and serves as a medium of communication between humans and the spirit world. The shamanistic séance is a magical performance in which the shaman uses a combination of his power over the spirits, his knowledge, his physical strength and stamina, his performing talents, and an altered state of consciousness to convince the audience of his powers and to achieve the goal of the séance, which might be simply to demonstrate his powers, to cure a sick person, or to predict the future. Believers in the power of the shaman attribute any success he has to his powers. Skeptics, while admitting that the altered state of consciousness takes place, attribute any success to the placebo effect in which patients get better because they are getting attention and expect to be cured and to the healing-cult, self-help nature of curing séances.

Yakut séances involve soul travel to the supernatural world, communication with evil and benevolent spirits, healing rituals, and animal sacrifice. The shaman, patient, and audience all operate on the belief that healing will result if the spirit responsible for the disease is satisfied with the sacrifice. If the spirit is not propitiated, the shaman can do no more to save the patient. After he is fed and honored and his help requested, the Yakut shaman begins his work of contacting the spirit world. As with all magical rituals, shamanistic séances require that the sha-

man follow the required procedures exactly, as suggested by the following account:

. . . he . . . approaches the fireplace at its front side, throws fat into the fire as a sacrifice for the spirits, grasps the fat smoke with open hands and brings them to his mouth to make believe that he is swallowing them and so gets control over the spirit whom he wants to address with his intercession. Then he takes the drum, sits down before the fireplace on a reindeer skin of good quality, and takes a whip which is adorned with fringes of horse hair and motley rags, or with tails of small game, colored with alder bark. The skin is turned toward the fireplace so that the head is next to it. The shaman now beats his drum and tries to divert the spirits' attention towards himself by sounding a long ay, he yawns devilishly opening his mouth, sounds three times the cry of the ember-goose (cek, cek, cek), apes three times the cry of a stork, three times that of a cuckoo, and three times that of a raven.

Then he calls upon the squint-eyed *(inistjaga)*, deformed *(keltjagjaj)*, lame *(dogolon)* devil *(jugjug emjagjat)* and curses himself by assuring Satan [the evil spirits] of his devotion, promises to be a faithful servant, and asks him to obsess [possess] him. Now he rises, supposing that he now has communication with the devil, that the latter has obsessed him, and that he himself is now in command of the devil's power and might. He calls upon the white bird *(jurjun-as):* May this become my place; may green grass grow on here; I have given myself to your life and blood, of Satan. You root of every evil and mishap *(ytyk eljuterde),* so he continues, you monster of the eight feet, I have joined you, so lend your aid in accomplishing the wishes. I have come from the *sjurdjach-kjaptjach, sjugja-toenton,* the terrible god of the hatchet, and from *kini-sjurgju-jutjanjan-sjurgjuju,* in order to save him by means of the salutary tool. But you, she-shamans of the fiery lashes, who live in the nether world, do not come to the upper world to fight or curse me. I have sat down on the navel of the earth in order to give protection to the sick. I am well aware of my faults, but suppose I were without faults and give way. Your three black shadows, of devil, have come upon me, so I beg you, help me. Look, I am offering you such an animal, so help my misery. (Krauss 1888, 173–174)

Upon returning from his trip to the upper or lower world, the audience questions him about the condition of the patient and the chances of cure. His report is followed by the healing ritual, which may take a variety of forms depending on the illness, patient, and circumstances. A common element is the offering and picking of an animal that will satisfy the spirit who has entered the patient's body and caused the disease. An acceptable sacrifice will cause the spirit to leave and the patient will be cured. One healing ritual takes the following form:

. . . the shaman approaches the patient's couch and cries three time above the head of the latter: Just tell me what kind of sacrificial animal you want; only leave the patient. The spirit who lives in the sick person replies through the shaman: If you offer me a *sadzaga* (a cow with a white-spotted back) or a *bulur* (a dun horse), I shall quit the patient. The animal is offered. For this purpose, ten very small larches and one birch are needed. One larch and the birch are placed before the tent, one behind the other. Nine notches are made into the first larch. The other nine are placed around the first two in a semi-circle. On the southern side they are twisted with a linen cord, which is hanged with motley rags and horse-hair.

The animal to be offered is bound on the tree which has been notched (*salama*); the shaman, going to heaven, addresses Ajtoen asking pity from him. He says: As men feel pity towards the patient, and since the old mothers (*chotottur*) have given back his soul to him (*kul*), accept the animal instead of his soul. After he has cried three times and spat at the animal (the patient spits, too), the animal is allowed to run to the flock. Then the shaman continues: Look here it is, accept it, give deliverance. I have accepted it, the devil replies through the

shaman, and the patient will recover within seven, eight, nine days.

The shaman sings that the devil is at once precipitating into the nether world (*ojbontimirja*) with the ember-goose; there he delivers the animal offered for slaughter. For concreteness's sake the shaman takes a little board (which may be interpreted as a table), carves a round hole in it, puts a bit of meat on it, and throws everything into the fire. Then he lights the mane of a black horse three times, inhales the smoke, and asks somebody of the present to cut the fire below his head, and give him a drink of water and sour milk (*umdan*), of the water of this world. Now he takes three twigs, beats the drum with them, and exercises the last survivals of the devil: Those of you who have fallen from above, go up; those of you who have come from below, go down, you devils! Exhausted by the movements on all sides, and giddy, he sits down, wet with sweat. Occasionally, he is unable with exhaustion to put out his kuma.

Tlingit shamans conduct séances when a spirit approaches them, when they seek the spirits, or to prove their power. Proof of power may be demonstrated before influential men in the community or as a "sales-pitch" before a séance, or in competitions with other shaman. Tlingit séances resemble Yakut ones in the following of magical ritual and possession by communication with spirits but the performances are often far more lively and dramatic. A shaman might lick a hot object without his tongue being burned, carry a hot, glowing log, or be submerged in water in order to bring fish. When he is possessed he makes sounds like the animal whose spirit he controls and acts like the animal, digging like a bear, jumping like a fish, or barking like a dog. Unlike the Yakut shaman, his messages from the supernatural may be vague and confusing and must be interpreted for the audience by his assistants. And, while the Yakut shaman was paid with honor, food, and drink before the séance and perhaps food after, Tlingit séances would be successful only if the shaman were well paid in advance with a valuable item such as a rifle. The importance of payment is shown in the following account in which the shaman acts as a clairvoyant:

> For example, the shaman might "see" that someone was to be drowned, even though this was to happen in Dry Bay and the shaman himself was in Yakutat. The omen would appear to him like a "big hole in the water—*hin kkiwa's*, they call it [water heaven]. Then he will say, "Somebodies going to drown." When this informant was asked if the shaman could save the victim from this impending fate, she said that he could, provided "that they give him something—money," but not if he were not paid. "That's the law. Those *yeks* (spirits) never help without paying, you know. It's just like a show, a movie, you know, that spirit," because a fee is required. (de Laguna 1972, 703)

See also MAGIC; POSSESSION AND TRANCE; RELIGIOUS SPECIALISTS.

Atkinson, Jane M. (1992) "Shamanisms Today." *Annual Review of Anthropology* 21: 307–330.

Balzer, Marjorie M., ed. (1990) *Shamanism: Soviet Studies of Traditional Religion in Siberia and Central Asia.*

de Laguna, Frederica. (1972) *Under Mount Saint Elias: The History and Culture of the Yakutat Tlingit.*

Eliade, Mircea. (1964) *Shamanism: Archaic Techniques of Ecstasy.* Translated by Willard R. Trask.

Harner, Michael. (1982) *The Way of the Shaman: A Guide to Power and Healing.*

Hultkranz, Åke. (1992) *Shamanic Healing and Ritual Drama: Health and Medicine in Native North American Religious Traditions.*

Jochelson, Waldemar. (1933) "The Yakut." *Anthropological Papers of the American Museum of Natural History* 33(2): 33–335.

Kendall, Laurel. (1985) *Shamans, Housewives, and Other Restless Spirits: Women in Korean Ritual Life.*

Krauss, Friedrich S. (1888) *Yakut Shamanism.*

SHINTO

Shinto is the indigenous religion of Japan that has influenced many aspects of Japanese society since ancient times. Shinto, or *kami-no-michi*, literally means "the way of the gods/spirits," which refers to *kami*. Kami is the spiritual or godlike essense that exists in gods, human beings, animals, and even inanimate objects. The world is created, inhabited, and ruled by kami, an indescribable quality that evokes wonder, fear, and awe. Shinto is a collective term covering the hundreds of different national and religious customs used in the worship of kami, largely through prescribed rituals. An important Shinto principle is *saisei-itchi*, which refers to the oneness of religion and government. Because of this concept, which up until recently meant that the emperor was viewed as both Japan's political leader and highest priest, the history of Shinto is very closely tied to the history of Japan as the religion has to a large degree shaped the national outlook and culture.

Historical Development

Shintoism evolved from a multitude of scattered but tightly held communities in ancient Japan. The date of its origins are unknown. It did not even have a name applied to it because it was so pervasive until the sixth century C.E. when Buddhism and Confucianism were brought to Japan from China and a name was needed to distinguish Japanese beliefs and practices from the new foreign concepts.

According to Shinto mythology, Japan and the Japanese people are of divine origin. Three kami originally created a community of male and female kami in heaven. Two of the kami (the male Izanagi and the female Izanami) were crossing a heavenly bridge when Izanagi inserted his celestial spear into the ocean below. When he lifted the spear out of the ocean the drops that fell back into the sea coagulated to form Japan's islands. Izanagi and Izanami went to one of the islands and gave birth to many more kami, whose offspring subsequently became the ruling samurai class. Izanagi also created in an act of purification the moon god Tsukiyomi-no-Mikoto and the sun goddess Amaterasu. Amaterasu later assigned her grandson Ninigi to Japan to bring order to the islands as its ruler. Thus every Japanese emperor was considered a direct descendant of the sun goddess.

Early Japanese religion was unorganized and scattered among the many agricultural and fishing communities that dotted the Japanese islands until the ascent of the Yamato clan in the third or fourth century. The Yamato conquered and consolidated other clans under its rule. Although the clan tolerated local traditions, its belief in the supremacy of the Amaterasu sun goddess eventually took hold throughout Japan, and Yamato chieftains became recognized as both the rulers and chief priests of Japan.

The arrival of Confucianism and Buddhism from China in the sixth century had a profound influence on Shintoism in Japan. But unlike many other instances where the arrival of a new religion led to conflict, the interaction between Shintoism, Buddhism, and Confucianism in Japan was largely—although not exclusively—one of tolerance and harmony. In fact, elements of the three quickly merged. Yamato leaders even sent envoys to the Chinese mainland to study Chinese civilization and identify aspects of it to adopt in Japan. The Japanese took on the concept of an emperor and learned the Chinese monosyllabic language. They also became enamored of many aspects of Confucian ethics, Buddhist religion, Taoist philosophies, Chinese superstition, and the cult of ancestor worship—

all of which were incorporated in varying degrees into Shinto practices. Confucianism was a major influence in Japanese education and legal institutions, and in the relationships between subjects and rulers, and between family members. Confucianism eventually provided a framework for Japanese feudalism and ancestor worship became a key element in Japanese social conduct.

Buddhism was integrated with Shintoism, so much so that many Buddhist temples were built under the direction of Shinto priests and often dedicated in Shinto ceremonies. Within the first century of its arrival, Buddhism had a great influence on the arts, literature, and sciences. It was the dominant religion of the upper classes. A lengthy era of peaceful intermingling of the two religions continued during the Heian period (794–1192), as Buddhism evolved to incorporate many aspects of Shintoism and the worship of kami. Buddhist priests took over many Shinto shrines where Shinto priests were assigned to lesser capacities. A division of responsibility emerged in which Buddhists oversaw the preaching, funeral services, and administration, and Shinto priests oversaw births, marriages, and various religious celebrations and national festivals.

At the same time, however, a new effort was under way by Shinto priests to preserve or heighten the Shinto identity. For the first time, Shinto priests in the eighth and ninth centuries wrote down their oral traditions. And as Buddhism's role in Japanese life grew larger and larger to the point that Shintoism and Buddhism were virtually the same, more and more Shinto priests began to emphasize their native, ancient traditions in contrast to the foreign, more sophisticated Buddhist beliefs. This sentiment first started to emerge in the twelfth and thirteenth centuries with the advent of the Zen and Amida Buddhist sects, and it continued to fester until the nineteenth century. Shinto's tolerance for other religions did have its limits prior to this

Shinto priests participate in a purification ceremony at the Togo Shrine in Tokyo, Japan, in July 1978. Shintoism, indigenous to Japan, did not have a name until the sixth century C.E., when it became necessary to distinguish it from Buddhism and Confucianism introduced from China.

date, however. When Christian missionaries arrived from Europe in the sixteenth century, Shinto priests initially accepted their presence. But as different missionaries arrived preaching loyalty to a pope in far-off Rome, Japanese leaders began to suspect their motives. In 1587 Christian missionaries were banned from Japan and for the next fifty years a series of initiatives was undertaken to abolish Christianity from the islands of Japan.

In 1868 the official tolerance of Buddhism came to an end when Emperor Meiji ascended the throne. He designated Shinto as the national religion and brought most Shinto shrines and priests under government control. A campaign against Buddhism was launched in which estates were seized, temples closed, and Buddhist priests persecuted. The government divided State Shinto into two categories, Shrine Shinto (Jinja) and Sectarian Shinto (Kyoha). All Japanese were required to participate in ceremonies at Shinto shrines as a patriotic duty to pay respect to the emperor. The national government administered and supervised the priesthood, religious organizations, and ceremonies, and taught ancestral Shinto traditions in schools. Acceptance of State Shinto was a test of loyalty to Japan. Although Buddhism and Christianity (starting in the 1880s) were allowed to exist, practitioners had to acknowledge the essential principles of State Shinto: that Japan was divinely created, the emperor descended from the sun goddess, and the Japanese themselves had divine origin. The emperor was considered sacred. In some cases, people subscribed not only to his right to rule Japan but also the entire world. Shinto played a major role in the government's ability eventually to wield enormous political and military power.

State Shinto came to an abrupt end on December 15, 1945, four months after the end of World War II. U.S. General Douglas MacArthur, the supreme commander of the Allied forces of occupation, ordered the Japanese to abolish State Shinto, thus separating the Japanese church and state. In a statement that came as a shock to the nation, the emperor denounced the concept of a divine emperor and the notion that the Japanese are a superior race destined to rule the world. The impact on Shinto and Japan was enormous. An estimated 110,000 State Shinto shrines were cut off from government assistance and forced to rely on volunteer contributions. The entire outlook of the nation and the way it viewed its emperor and itself changed overnight. To this day, religion is separate from the state. Shinto is no longer taught in the schools and freedom of religion is assured. The emperor's role is largely symbolic. He is confined to officiating at traditional ceremonies in the imperial palace. Nevertheless, Shinto continues to be the dominant religion of the nation and plays a major role in the character of Japan.

Religious Beliefs

Shinto traditionally served as the route for understanding the beauty and bounty of nature. Shinto was a path for realizing a person's oneness with nature, seeking to merge with it rather than trying to overcome it. Kami represents the superior object of worship in nature. It does not refer to an Absolute Being that created or oversees the world, but rather to an essence in the universe that creates the wonder of nature. Shinto does not have a system of ethics or morals. Instead, Shinto places an emphasis on ritual and ceremony to express the joyful acceptance of nature. Life and death are viewed as natural processes. The general concept of good and evil does not exist. What is important is ritual, particularly rituals pertaining to purity, which are closely related to an individual's obligations to his superiors—ancestors, the emperor, family, Japan, and Shinto. It is more important for a Shinto to demonstrate loyalty than to do good for others. This expression of loyalty comes in the observance of rituals and taboos. The ultimate act of loyalty in the Shinto tradition is *hara-kiri,* a ritual suicide by cutting one's stomach that is done in a carefully prescribed manner. A person who commits hara-kiri does so to prove his continuing loyalty after having failed to meet the Shinto code of conduct in some other way.

Sects

Shinto is divided into three different categories: Shrine Shinto, Sectarian Shinto, and Folk or Popular Shinto. All three involve the worship of spirit and nature. Shrine Shinto is centered around the more than 100,000 shrines that are scattered throughout Japan. The shrines are operated through voluntary contributions and are run by independent priests. They devote themselves to an incredibly diverse number of objects and deities. During the Meiji era and up to World War II the shrines were under government control and were used as centers of worship for the emperor. Objects of worship today include historical emperors, gods, mountains, birds, snakes, swords, trees, and many other items. The aim of Shrine Shinto is to promote happiness and health, and the practice of traditional rites. There is a very heavy emphasis placed on performing Shinto rituals.

Sectarian Shinto was divided into five categories by the Meiji government (Pure, Confucian, Mountain, Purification, and Redemptive), which included thirteen different sects. All told there are more than six hundred subsects of Sectarian Shinto that fall under the different categories. Sectarian Shinto groups hold regular meetings with large congregations, which are more elaborate ceremonies than Shrine Shinto and often include modern sermons. Sectarian Shinto emphasizes a particular aspect of Shinto. The general characteristics are as follows:

1. Purification Shinto sects perform rites of purification that often date back to ancient times. The ceremonies purify a person's soul, mind, and body from evil. Some of the ceremonies involve cooking rice, proper breathing exercises, and

fire. All Shinto sects place a high priority on purity and the cleansing of pollution, which is why the Japanese are considered to be among the cleanest people in the world.

2. Pure Shinto sects seek to perpetuate the rituals and beliefs of ancient Shinto tradition. They foster nationalism and deplore any foreign influences. Loyalty to the state, charity, and purification are all central elements of Pure Shinto.

3. Confucian Shinto sects emphasize Confucian ethical principles and are considered extremely nationalistic. Members seek inner tranquility through prayer and meditation.

4. Redemptive or Faith-Healing Shinto sects are relatively modern sects that rely heavily on the founders of the sects and their beliefs. They tend to believe in a divine source such as the sun goddess or other specific gods and adhere to a rigorous faith to that source.

5. Mountain Shinto sects assign mountains as the source of kami. They typically build shrines on mountain peaks for the kami and practice elaborate ceremonies on behalf of the kami. Groups frequently climb to the tops of mountains to worship the deities. Mount Fuji and Mount Ontake are the most sacred mountains, and not coincidentally are the most popular.

Folk or Popular Shinto is an extremely diverse and disorganized form of Shinto that frequently involves superstition, the occult, and ancestor worship. Thousands of deities are associated with Folk Shinto. Many households that subscribe to Folk Shinto have rituals that are centered on the *kami-dana* (kami shelf), a small shrine that is used for daily worship and special occasions. Memorial tablets often made of wood or paper are inscribed with the name of an ancestor or patron kami. For special life-cycle events such as births, marriages, and anniversaries, candles are lit and food and flowers are offered by the head of the family while relatives sit on the floor with their heads bowed in respect.

Texts

Because of its diverse and ancient origins Shinto does not have a definitive written text. In the eighth century, however, in an attempt to distinguish Shinto from Buddhism and Confucianism, two ancient histories were written, the Kojiki (Records of Ancient Matters) written in 712 and the Nihongi (Chronicles of Japan) written in 720, to record the oral traditions of Shinto history and mythology. Also written at about this time were the Kogoshui, a history of early Japan, and the Manyoshu, a collection of ancient poems. Two other documents that are considered part of the Shinto scripture are the Shinsen Shojiroku, a comprehensive list of families written in 815, and the Engishiki, relating the codes of the Engi Era written in about 927. These all describe Shinto legends, poems, and ceremonial practices as well as codes for behavior and action.

Festivals

The purpose of all festivals is to express Japanese pride and patriotism. The New Year festival requires much preparation. The house is cleansed of evil influences and the kami-dana is provided with new tablets, flowers, and other items. Special food is prepared and the house is decorated with arrangements of flowers, straw, paper, pine branches, and bamboo sticks. At Shinto shrines bells are rung 108 times to banish evil at the arrival of the new year. The Girls' Festival is held each March 3 to honor family and national life. The Boys' Festival is marked each May 5 for families to announce to the community their good fortune in having male children. Bon is a festival of the dead held in the middle of the year in which souls of dead relatives return home to be fed by their families. When the feast is over farewell fires are lit to light the way for the relatives on their journey home. Several other festivals are held in different parts of the country to mark regional, national, and seasonal events, as well ceremonies to commemorate particular kami.

Picken, Stuart D. B. (1994) *Essentials of Shinto: An Analytical Guide to Principal Teachings*.

SIKHISM

Sikhism has about 18 million followers, most of whom are located in the Punjab region of northwestern India, but many others have emigrated and formed communities throughout the world, especially in North America and Great Britain. Several different Sikh sects have evolved in its five-hundred-year history, but all Sikhs are united in their belief of the one god and in their reverence for the original ten gurus and the teachings from the scripture, the Granth Sahib or Adi Granth. Although scholars often describe Sikhism as a Hindu reform movement or a blend of Hinduism and Islam, Sikhs reject these descriptions, claiming instead that their religion springs from the divine inspirations of Guru Nanak and the nine gurus who followed him.

Historical Development

Guru Nanak (1469–1539) was the first guru and founder of Sikhism. The son of Hindu parents, Nanak was married and had two children before renouncing his family and wandering India in search of truth and wisdom. He studied Hindu and Muslim texts and is believed to have visited Mecca. At the age of about thirty, Nanak received a vision from God while meditating in a forest in Sultanpur, India. God designated Nanak to proclaim him as the True Name. "There is no Muslim and there is no Hindu,"

Nanak announced as part of his doctrine of the unity of Hinduism and Islam. Wearing a mixture of Hindu and Muslim clothing styles, Nanak and his Muslim companion Mardana traveled throughout India preaching. Many people—both Hindu and Muslim—in the Punjab region became followers. When Nanak died in 1539, the first of nine successor gurus, Guru Angad, succeeded him as the leader of the fledgling religious movement.

The gurus consolidated and institutionalized many aspects of Sikhism and shaped a social, political, and religious life for the movement. Guru Angad devised a Punjabi script that was used for writing the Sikh scriptures. The fifth guru, Arjun Dev, compiled Sikh scriptures into the Granth Sahib (Holy Book). He completed the construction of the Golden Temple at Amritsar, which is now the Sikh holy city, and initiated pilgrimages to the temple. When Guru Arjun was killed by the Mughals in 1606 his son, Har Gobind, succeeded him and instilled a sense of Sikh militancy in his followers to protect the expanding religion from outside forces, which in turn exacerbated the persecution by the Mughal rulers. The ninth guru, Tega Bahadur, was beheaded by the Mughals. He was succeeded by the tenth and final guru, Gobind Singh, who greatly strengthened Sikhs by establishing a military defense group known as the Khalsa (the Brotherhood of the Pure) that still remains. Guru Gobind Singh bolstered the political, social, and religious aspects of Sikhism. Shortly before his death in 1708, Guru Gobind Singh declared himself as the final guru and stated that the writings of the Granth Sahib would be the authority from which the Sikh community would be governed.

Sikh warriors were active in the demise of the Mughul Empire in the eighteenth century and were able to carve out a kingdom in the Punjab under the leadership of Ranjit Singh by the end of the century. When Singh, who be-

came the leader of the Punjab region, died in 1839, however, the kingdom soon collapsed and was absorbed by the British Empire. The Sikhs continued their military tradition and became a "military race" in the Indian and British armies. In gratitude for their loyal and courageous service during World War I, the British awarded land to the Sikhs. A series of disturbances ensued, though, and soon the Sikhs became active supporters of Mohandas K. Gandhi's freedom movement. In a tragic irony, Indian independence proved to be disruptive for the Sikhs, who saw their community divided between Hindu India and Muslim Pakistan. Widespread bloodshed forced millions of Sikhs to emigrate to the Indian side of the border where they remain as a major force in Indian politics. The Sikhs continue to be involved in conflict in India, such as the 1984 government attack on the Golden Temple, the 1984 assassination of Prime Minister Indira Gandhi by a Sikh, and the ensuing riots that resulted in the massacre of many Sikhs. An ongoing Sikh separatist movement has as its goal the establishment of an independent Sikh state, called Khalistan (Land of the Pure). Sikhs play a significant leadership role in the public sector and the professional Indian classes.

Religious Practices and Texts

Sikhism is based on a discipline of purification aimed at overcoming five vices: greed, anger, false pride, lust, and attachment to material goods. Successful adherence to the purification discipline allows the person to elevate his or her soul into union with the True God Sat Nam, an omniscient, ever-present, characterless, and infinite being that is the source of all things and is omnipresent. Sikhs worship Sat Nam by striving to act in accordance with the correct values: contentment, honesty, compassion, and patience. At the end of a person's life the tally of good and bad conduct determines the family, race, and character of the person when he or she is reborn as another human being. Those who are selfish and cruel in this life do not go to hell, but rather will suffer in their next existence. Those who act with compassion and honesty will lift the spirit to positions of good standing and high character. The soul develops through countless lives until it becomes united with the infinite One.

The Sikh Holy Book is the Guru Granth Sahib, or Adi Granth. It consists of three principal sections. Similar to the book of Psalms, it is a devotional book. The first is the Japji, which recites the teachings of Guru Nanak. The second is the Ragas (Tunes) with four books. The final section consists of twenty-six books that elaborate on the Ragas. The Guru Granth Sahib is treated with great reverence by Sikhs. It serves as the focal point of Sikh temples where the book is always installed with great ceremony. The book is placed on cushions and covered with elaborate decorations. All who enter an area hallowed by the Guru Granth Sahib must cover their heads and take off their shoes. Worshipers bow before the Guru Granth Sahib. During services, prayers are addressed to the book, which is followed by a sermon, the chanting of hymns, and finally a communal meal. Sikh families set aside a room to hold a copy of the Guru Granth Sahib. Daily readings are part of the obligatory duties of Sikh households and many Sikhs recite verses during their daily activities.

Ceremonies

There are four main life events marked by ceremonies during a Sikh's life: one's naming as an infant, initiation, marriage, and death. The naming takes place soon after the birth of a child. The child is taken to the temple and presented to the congregation. The Guru Granth Sahib is opened at random for a reading. The first initial of the child's name is determined according to the first letter of the first verse on the left-hand page. In the initiation ceremony the child (who is between eight and fifteen years old) becomes a full member of the Sikh religious community. The ritual is a baptismal ceremony preparing the boy or girl to become responsible for abiding by Sikh religious practices. The third major ceremony is that marking one's marriage, which symbolizes the eternal union with the True God, Sat Nam. Marriage hymns describe the human spirit as the bride of the eternal husband. The final ceremony occurs after one's death. After cremating the body a service is held for relatives of the deceased, which is followed by a ceremony at the person's home or at the temple where a continuous reading of the Guru Granth Sahib is held.

Sikhs also ascribe to a series of daily rituals that include a morning bath, meditation, and the reciting of prayers and hymns. There are many different ceremonies held by Sikhs to celebrate the birth and death of the ten gurus, two events to commemorate the deaths of martyrs, and a festival marking the anniversary of the Baisakhi, the date that the Khalsa was founded. Of all these there are five major observances. They are the birthdays of Gurus Nanak and Gobind Singh, the martyrdom of Gurus Arjun Dev and Tega Bahadur, and the anniversary of Baisakhi. These events are marked by forty-eight-hour readings of the Guru Granth Sahib from start to finish.

Sects

There are several different Sikh sects that place different emphasis on the three fundamental precepts of Sikhism: reverence for the ten gurus, the oneness of God, and the divine revelation of the Guru Granth Sahib. Some groups, such as Singh Sabha, promote education to elevate the standing of Sikhs in the world. Another sect, the Nirankari, pursue the worship of Sat Nam in its original pure form. The Udasis, an order of holy men, pursue an ascetic life similar to Jain monks, wandering as beggars. The Sahajdharas reject the use of force. The best-known group in the West is the Singhs, who take their inspiration from the last guru, Gobind Singh. The Singhs adhere to the principles of the Khalsa's Brotherhood of the Pure created to protect Sikhs from persecution. All Singhs are baptized in a special ceremony and carry the distinguishing marks (all of which begin with the letter *k*). They are *kirpan* (a dagger), *keshas* (uncut hair), *kangha* (comb), *kuchka* (a pair of shorts), and *kara* (a steel bracelet worn on the right wrist).

McLeod, W. H. (1990) *The Sikhs.*

O'Connell, Joseph, et al., eds. (1988) *Sikh History and Religion in the Twentieth Century.*

SORCERY

Although some experts treat sorcery and witchcraft as equivalents, they are different phenomena, and in cultures where both occur the people distinguish between them. A witch (a witch is a female, a male witch is called a warlock) is someone who causes harm to another person by simply wishing the harm to take place. A witch has direct access to the supernatural world and can call on the powers of supernatural forces to cause harm to another. Sorcery, on the other hand, requires the use of a sorcerer, who, through his or her knowledge of formulae and rituals, can direct supernatural power. Sorcerers, unlike witches, cannot innately cause supernatural forces to affect the lives of the living as sorcery relies on the use of magical power. For an Ojibwa sorcerer of Canada that power comes from the plants he uses and from the evil spirits whose assistance he has learned to summon, and whom the Ojibwa believe are only too ready to assist him. The Ojibwa believe that these evil spirits seek to reverse the normal course of events and thus the sorcerer must move in ways opposite the normal. When he digs up a plant to make a potion he must first circle it in a counterclockwise direction and when he calls the spirits by invoking the four directions, he must call east, north, west, and south instead of east, south, west, and north, the normal travel route of the sun. The Ojibwa sorcerer has a considerable arsenal of techniques at his disposal, including:

1. Sketch his victim's image on the ground and place his medicine over the place where he wishes him to feel pain. His victim is stricken immediately.

2. Carve a wooden image of his victim and tie it by a thread to a poplar tree. The man will die when the thread breaks and the image falls to the ground.

3. Scratch him with a poisonous spine, *bagamuyak*, imported from the south. Only sorcerers who use these spines know the antidote.

4. Sprinkle medicine in his victim's food, on his clothes, or on the ground where he walks.

5. Mix with evil medicine clippings of his victim's fingernails or hair, shreds of fur from his clothing, or charcoal from his campfire. The Indians, therefore, carry away with them a dead coal wrapped in leaves or bark when they break camp, to retain any soul of the fire in their possession; they preserve the souls of old clothing that they give away by keeping a scrap of its wool or hide; and they burn all clippings of their nails or hair.

6. "Shoot something into his victim's body. To do this he chews with the stick or bone he selects for his missile a leaf of the plant called *zobiginigan*...and shoots the two substances together from his mouth in the direction of the enemy. The leaf acts like gunpowder, propelling the stick or stone over the inter-

vening miles until it penetrates the man's body. A *kusabindugeyu* [seer] may extract it and shoot it back at the sorcerer; but unless it penetrates the marrow of his bones he escapes unharmed. Should it penetrate the marrow, however, the sorcerer becomes crippled for life." (Jenness 1935: 85)

Beyond how direct their access is to supernatural power, sorcery and witchcraft differ in other important ways. First, they are found mostly in different cultures. In a survey of 137 cultures, in 47 percent of people believed that sorcery was an important cause of illness, in 14 percent people believed that witchcraft was an important cause, in 4 percent people believed that both were important, and in 35 percent people believed that neither was important. Second, they are found in cultures in different parts of the world. Belief in witchcraft as a source of illness predominates in cultures near the Mediterranean Sea, while sorcery beliefs predominate in the New World, in Native American cultures in North and South America. Nearly 50 percent of cultures that attribute illness to sorcery are in the New World. Third, they are found in different types of cultures. Beliefs about sorcery as a cause of illness are found mostly in relatively simple cultures—those with no indigenous writing system, small communities, and an economy based on foraging or horticulture. Witchcraft attribution, on the other hand, is found more often in more complex cultures with larger settlements and agriculture. Fourth, unlike witchcraft, sorcery can be used by anyone. A person can become a sorcerer by learning the spells, formulae, incantations, and so forth or can hire a known sorcerer. This suggests that sorcery is more likely to flourish in cultures where people have relatively equal access to the supernatural world. This is more typical of relatively simple cultures where there is less social inequality in all spheres of life. Fifth, witchcraft causes

only harm while sorcery can be used to cause harm, to cure, or to benefit others in various ways. Thus, a witch might cause someone to fall ill or die because witches are intrinsically evil, but to cause harm a sorcerer must do so intentionally. While attention is often called to harm caused by sorcery, it seems that sorcerers in most cultures also use their skills to do good as well as evil. Some of most sorcerers' work centers on treating illness, rather than causing it. This is especially true in cultures where sorcery is believed to be a major cause of illness, as sorcery is also the major way to cure illness. Sorcerers who cure are usually called medicine men or shamans.

Sorcery is found primarily in cultures that rely on coordinate control to maintain social order and that do not have agencies of superordinate control. Coordinate control means that conflict is resolved through the direct action of the persons involved such as through retaliation, apology, or avoidance. Superordinate control means that social order is maintained through the actions of culturally recognized authorities such as a council, a chief, or courts. Sorcery acts as a coordinate control in that it causes individuals to pause before causing harm to others for fear that the other person will retaliate by using sorcery to cause them to become ill, have an accident, or even die.

An example of the fear that the threat of sorcery causes is provided by the Toba of Argentina, where sorcery is practiced both in the rural and urban communities. The Toba believe that a sorcerer can cause death through the use of contagious magic, which involves the ritual treatment of physical objects or items associated with the victim—sweat on pieces of clothing, urine, hair, a cigarette butt, and so on. The object is mixed with other objects of magical importance and then burned or buried, causing the victim to become ill and eventually (usually within a month) die. Death is usually inevitable, although the victim can undo the magic by finding a shaman who can "see" the person causing the victim to fall ill. Additionally, a person dying from sorcery can get revenge by identifying the person causing his death just before he dies and when he dies knowing that his death will be avenged. Given the wholesale pattern of aggression and counter-aggression sorcery can cause, it is not surprising that the Toba and other cultures prefer to emphasize the beneficial effects of sorcery and use it to cause harm very selectively. In most cultures, the threat of sorcery is enough to maintain social order.

Persons who practice sorcery are called sorcerers. However, the methods used by the sorcerer may also be used by other religious or healing specialists in the community. For example, the Aymara of Peru recognize six different types of specialists, all of whom use magic to influence the supernatural world: magician, sorcerer, doctor, diviner, chiropractor, and midwife. Similarly, witches and sorcerers among the Lozi of Africa use many of the same techniques to do their work, although sorcerers must learn the techniques and the harm they cause is often less than that caused by witches. Across cultures, sorcerers achieve this status in a number of ways including inheriting it, choosing it, or through supernatural direction. Relatively little is known about the training of sorcerers or the specific methods they use, as in nearly all cultures people do not usually admit to being sorcerers. In all cultures, however, men (sorcerers are almost always men) must learn how to use magic, usually by serving an apprenticeship. The Lozi are not sure how a person becomes an apprentice, but many believe that consulting a sorcerer is probably the first step. For a fee the apprentice then learns the trade of Lozi sorcery. Lozi sorcerers rely on three forms of magic. First, they use familiars, that is, carved representations of the souls of the deceased. The souls are obtained magically, by raising the body from the grave, bringing it back to life, and killing it again. Upon the orders of the sorcerer, the familiars travel about and kill the intended victim with a small

knife held in the left hand. Second, Lozi sorcerers rely heavily on *siposo*—invisible missiles shot at the victim. Many Lozi wear needle charms to protect themselves from the effect of such missiles. Third, sorcerers use charms that are placed over or under the intended victim in order to kill, bring on illness, or cause a miscarriage. A magical tortoise shell and iron point are favored charms, although they are not as effective as the first two methods as they must be placed very close to the victim to work properly.

See also EVIL EYE; SHAMANISM; SUPERNATURAL EXPLANATIONS FOR ILLNESS; WITCHCRAFT.

Jenness, Diamond. (1935) *The Ojibwa Indians of Parry Island: Their Social and Religious Life.*

Miller, Elmer. (1980) *Harmony and Dissonance in Argentine Toba Society.*

Murdock, George P. (1980) *Theories of Illness: A World Survey.*

Reynolds, Barrie. (1957) *Magic, Divination and Witchcraft among the Barotese of Northern Rhodesia.*

Whiting, Beatrice B. (1950) *Paiute Sorcery.*

Whiting, John W. M. (1967) "Sorcery, Sin and the Superego: A Cross-Cultural Study of Some Mechanisms of Social Control." In *Cross-Cultural Approaches*, edited by Clellan S. Ford, 147–168.

SOUL

In all cultures people believe that they and other humans have a spiritual or mystical essence that is distinct from their physical being. In Western cultures and religions this essence is commonly referred to as the soul, or more precisely, the individual soul. While in some cultures the soul is defined as an individual's "personality," experts generally agree that the concept of "the soul" refers to a deeper and broader essence. While the soul can be discussed as a concept in and of itself, in all religious systems beliefs about the soul are enmeshed in a broader system of belief and practice. Other features of belief and practice closely tied to beliefs about the soul are ancestor worship, death and afterlife, and supernatural beings. While a belief in the individual soul is universal, there is much variation across cultures in beliefs about the nature, number, forms, shapes, behavior, and meaning of the soul. For example, the Aymara of Peru believe that the soul is like one's shadow and is located throughout a person's body where it looks and acts like the physical body. In fact, the two are so alike, that one Aymara man noted: "Unless you know that a man is dead, it is sometimes difficult to say whether you have seen him or whether it was his soul you saw." The Aymara are vague about where one's soul comes from, although they believe that a child's soul is weak and vulnerable to injury and that the soul develops as does the physical body and then declines in old age. When a person dies, his or her soul leaves the body and lives on. The Aymara believe that the soul is immanent—part of the physical body and usually inseparable from it until death. In about 50 percent of cultures the soul is conceptualized as immanent. In the other 50 percent, people believe that the soul and body are distinct and that parts of the body can be used to access the souls of other people and to derive power from them. The use of hair, nails, or body fluids in magic, the taking of heads or scalps, and ritual cannibalism are all attempts to obtain the power or attributes of the soul of another for oneself.

For the Toradja of Indonesia, beliefs about the soul are complex and involve four related concepts—*sumanga'*, *penaa*, *bombo*, and *deata*. Sumanga' is the soul or life-force that is present in all living things. It is capable of leaving the body and might be stolen by a malicious spirit.

It may also be enhanced by taking the sumanga' of an enemy. Penaa is the Toradja term for the vital essence of each living person. It means breath, heart, or spirit and the association with breath is not confined just to the Toradja but is a belief found in many cultures. Thus, for the Toradja, the penaa is one's individual soul and also, because it can grow and change, represents an individual's connections to others in the community. When a Toradja dies or is near death, his or her penaa disappears and is replaced by the bombo, the soul of the deceased. The bombo closely resembles the individual in physical appearance and remains in the community until the funeral ritual—which may take up to seven days—is completed. If the funeral is conducted correctly, the bombo goes to the Land of the Souls (Puya), taking with it all of the material wealth offered and sacrificed at the funeral. If the funeral is not conducted correctly, the bombo lingers about as a possible source of trouble until it is appeased through prayer and offerings. Not all bombo go to Puya; among those who do not, in addition to those whose funerals are performed incorrectly, are special souls such as those of women who die while pregnant, of lepers, of people who commit suicide, and of people who die unjustly. All of these souls continue to lurk about the village and are feared as a cause of misfortune and illness. The bombo who reside in Puya—which is located in the southwest and closely resembles the world of the living—communicate with relatives still alive by appearing in dreams or through religious specialists who contact them on behalf of relatives. Deata, the fourth conception of the soul, are bombo who transcend Puya and move to the world of the gods and the life-force in the northwest where they become ancestor spirits who receive offerings and protect their descendants living on earth.

The Tarahumara of northern Mexico also equate the soul with breath, and their name for the soul—*iwigala*—means "to breathe." They believe that the soul is found in the heart (a common belief in many Western cultures as well) and that air to support the soul moves directly from the windpipe to the heart. The soul is linked to night and death and is often in a state opposite that of the living body. Thus, when a person is cold, his soul is hot and so on. When sleeping, the soul may wander outside the body and keep watch over the individual. At death, one's soul lives on in Heaven.

These three examples indicate some of the major common features of soul belief found in many cultures: (1) all individuals have a soul; (2) the soul might leave the body while the individual is still alive; (3) the soul leaves the body and goes elsewhere after death; (4) the soul is associated with the life-force.

In addition to believing that humans have souls, in many cultures people also believe that animals, or at least some animals, also have souls. For example, traditional peoples in Siberia believe that dogs—long important in hunting and herding activities—have souls. The Tarahumara believe that the soul allows one to speak or sing and thus, all animals have souls. Trees do not, but some plants that are reported to sing are believed to have souls. As with humans, Tarahumara animal souls go to heaven after death. In general, animals that are most important to humans are the ones thought to have souls. A belief in animal souls is often manifested in beliefs in animal reincarnation and funerals for animals, both of which reflect an interest in the soul after death.

Soul Plurality

A survey of sixty cultures indicates that in 34 percent of cultures people believe that individuals have more than one soul. In 15 percent they believe that individuals have two souls, in 10 percent three souls, in 2 percent four souls, and in 7 percent five souls. The Toradja mentioned above, for example, believe an individual has four souls, with each appearing at different times in the life cycle and after death. The Jivaro of Ec-

uador believe that a man has three souls. He is born with the *nekas* soul, which is quite weak and fades in importance after puberty when a boy obtains his *aruntum* soul from an ancestor through an initiation rite. He also possesses a *muisak* soul that resides in the head and protects the aruntum when a man is killed and the killer tries to add the aruntum to his own. In Dahomey, men have four souls and women and children have three. All people have a guardian soul they are born with, an individual soul that survives after physical death, and a soul that is a small piece of the creator spirit present in all Dahomeans. Only men have a fourth soul, a group soul associated with the survival of the family. Among the traditional cultures of the world, multiple souls are found mainly in cultures with relatively small, settled communities that rely on food grown through horticulture. In addition, in some of these cultures, people trace their descent both through their fathers' and mothers' families, although different sets of obligations and behaviors are associated with each line. Thus, a belief in multiple souls may reflect this divided allegiance to two kinship groups. Cultures that believe in only one soul tend to be ones that subsist by hunting-gathering or the herding of animals and that are nomadic. In these cultures, having to keep two or more souls together or all in the body, or keep track of their locations would be burdensome and would hinder travel.

The Soul after Death

In 90 percent of cultures people believe that the soul leaves the body and survives after physical death. While there is considerable variation across cultures in belief about what happens to the soul and where it goes, there is also considerable similarity across cultures in the factors that determine where a soul goes and the nature of its existence. One of the factors that determines the fate of one's soul is how the person died. As we saw for the Toradja mentioned above, the souls of certain persons such as lepers and those who commit suicide linger on earth while the souls of others go to Puya. Similarly, the Chamorro of Guam believe that the souls of those who met violent deaths go to a demon who cooks them continually in a cauldron. Those who die a natural death go to an underworld of paradise. A second determinant of the fate of one's soul in some cultures is the behavior of the individual. For example, the Chenchu of South Asia believe that those who have lived proper lives go to the land of the souls while those who are evil are denied admission and instead must exist on earth as ghosts. Similarly, the Malekula of Oceania believe that the souls of good and bad people live in separate places in the underworld. A third factor that determines the fate of one's soul in some cultures is the nature of the world of the living. That is, the structure of relations among souls in the afterworld mirrors the structure of people in the society. For example, Lakher society in South Asia is organized into three classes—royalty, nobles, and commoners—and the underworld is similarly composed of three regions mirroring the three classes on earth. An opposite pattern is found among the Siuai of Oceania who have a loose form of social organization with no rigid social classes. The Siuai underworld reflects this equality, as their are no rankings or segregation of souls.

Social scientists have long been interested in why in nearly all cultures people believe in a soul that survives after the death of the body. Attempts to answer this question are hampered by the ubiquitousness of the belief, which makes it impossible to compare cultures with the belief with those that do not believe in the survival of the soul. As an alternative, social scientists have produced a long list of factors, all of which are found in at least some cultures, that might lead people to believe that souls survive death. These factors are neatly summarized by the psychologist-anthropologist team of Alice and Irvin Child:

1. Dreaming of a deceased person may be seen as actual contact with the person.
2. Believing that one's behavior is caused by supernatural forces, including a soul of an ancestor, is a useful excuse for one's own bad behavior or position in life.
3. Environmental cues associated with a recently deceased person such as their clothes may create a sense that the person is still present.
4. A wish to complete unfinished activities with a deceased person creates the wish that he or she is still alive.
5. All people have thoughts about people who are close to them who have died and these thoughts may be interpreted as actual contact with the deceased.
6. It is not uncommon for people to see or hear or smell someone who has recently died, suggesting that they are still present.
7. Séances produce indirect contact with the dead or their spirits.
8. A belief in the survival of the soul is a component of funeral rites in many societies.
9. Other religious beliefs and practices such as ancestor worship, prayers for the dead, and reincarnation reinforce a belief in the survival of the soul.
10. People who have near-death experiences often report approaching an afterworld.
11. A fear of death and a wish to be immortal are powerful psychological forces in many cultures.
12. Child rearing practices in some cultures include using references to the power deceased ancestors have on the living to control behavior in children. (Child and Child 1993).

Soul Travel and Loss

In many cultures people believe that the soul is capable of leaving and then returning to the body while the individual is still physically alive. Such travel may be voluntary or involuntary and good or bad for the individual. For the Tarahumara it is voluntary and good, as the soul leaves the body at night when the person sleeps to watch over him, protect his herds, and warn of coyotes. While outside the body, the soul may also act just like a human—singing, dancing, and getting drunk. As in other cultures where the souls leaves voluntarily, it is important that the soul returns, or the person will die. The Aymara of Peru are particularly concerned about children accidently losing their souls. Since children's souls are weak they are not firmly attached and may be knocked loose when a child falls or is frightened. The soul remains where it fell and must be brought back into the body, usually by the child's mother who waves and yells at it. If it is not brought back, the child is susceptible to possession by evil spirits and might fall ill and die. This Aymara belief suggests another fairly common belief about soul loss—that it can cause sickness and death. In about 20 percent of cultures people believe that losing their soul temporarily causes illness. In another 10 percent of cultures, people believe that sorcerers can cause a person to become ill or to die by causing his soul to leave his body. Believing that soul loss causes illness seems to be related to the association of soul loss with death, as in most cultures the soul leaves the body when a person dies. Restoring the soul usually requires the expertise of a healer. Among the Tenino of Oregon, for example, some healers are able to identify the absence of a person's soul as the cause of depression that follows the death of a close relative or friend. The soul of the survivor has departed in order to follow the soul of the deceased to the afterworld. To bring the soul back, the healer dispatches a ghost to the afterworld to retrieve the soul, which is then returned to the body and the person's mood lifts.

See also ANCESTOR WORSHIP.

Adams, Kathleen M. (1993) "The Discourse of Souls in Tana Toraja (Indonesia): Indigenous Notions and Christian Conceptions." *Ethnology* 32: 55–68.

Child, Alice B., and Irvin L. Child. (1993) *Religion and Magic in the Life of Traditional Peoples*.

Cohen, Yehudi A. (1968) "Macroethnology: Large-Scale Comparative Studies." In *Introduction to Cultural Anthropology*, edited by James A. Clifton, 402–448.

Lumholtz, Carl. (1902) *Unknown Mexico: A Record of Five Years' Exploration of the Western Sierra Madre; in the Tierra Caliente of Tepic and Jalisco; among the Tarascos of Michoacan*.

Malefijt, Annemarie de Waal. (1968) *Religion and Culture: An Introduction to the Anthropology of Religion*.

Murdock, George P. (1980) *Theories of Illness: A World Survey*.

Somersan, Semra. (1981) *Death Symbolism: A Cross-Cultural Study*.

Swanson, Guy E. (1968) *The Birth of the Gods: The Origin of Primitive Beliefs*.

Tschopik, Harry Jr. (1951) *The Aymara of the Chucuito, Peru: 1. Magic*. Anthropological Papers of the American Museum of Natural History 44: 133–308.

SUPERNATURAL BEINGS

A belief in the presence of supernatural beings is a cultural universal, although there is enormous variation across cultures in the types of beings recognized, the number of beings, their appearance, their effect on human life, and how humans can best contact them. The number of supernatural beings recognized ranges from the over one million gods of Hinduism (although an individual Hindu believes in only a few) to the handful of nature spirits recognized by the Amahuaca of Peru. Despite the considerable variation, there are some clear, basic similarities across many cultures in beliefs about supernatural beings.

First, in all cultures the basic defining feature of supernatural beings is that they possess powers greater than those of humans and that those powers can be used to influence human existence. The power humans have to influence supernatural beings is far more limited and in all cultures people spend considerable time and effort communicating with the supernatural beings. Second, people in most cultures believe that their gods and spirits understand the land of the living and use this knowledge in their actions, which influence the living. Third, gods especially are often described in anthropomorphic terms; that is, they are believed to look like human beings. And, fourth, gods are often believed to have mental abilities similar to those of human beings. From the sociological viewpoint, these last three characteristics suggest that the supernatural beings people create and believe in are often copies of the people themselves. Another interpretation—which is the viewpoint of most believers around the world—reverses the causal direction and suggests that the supernatural beings resemble their human followers because the beings created humans in their image.

One salient dimension concerning beliefs about supernatural beings is their sex. A survey of 93 cultures indicates that 15 percent have only male supernaturals, in 36 percent male supernaturals are more numerous and/or powerful, in 19 percent males are either more powerful or more numerous, and/or in 30 percent of cultures male and female supernaturals are equal in numbers or power or females are more powerful or more numerous. In no society are female supernatural beings both more numerous and more powerful than male ones and no soci-

ety has only female supernatural beings. While it might seem obvious that this male bias in beliefs about the sex of supernaturals reflects male dominance in general, this seems not to be the case, as the sex of supernaturals is unrelated to other indicators of male dominance. Rather, cultures with many female supernaturals and cultures with female supernaturals with much power tend to be ones where the socialization of children (usually a female activity) is considered important by both men and women. While this seems self-evident in Western cultures, there are many cultures in the world where individuals trace their kin ties only through one parent and in these cultures the other parent may have less interest in the socialization of their children. This latter type of society tends to have exclusively or mostly male supernaturals, reflecting the fact that the kinship line of importance is more often the father's line. In cultures where kin ties are traced through both parents, both parents tend to be interested in and involved in raising their children and this is reflected in the world of the gods where both male and female deities are involved in human affairs.

Another major dimension of the issue of the nature of supernaturals is whether in a given society they are seen as generally benevolent or generally harmful. For example, the Dani of New Guinea devote considerable ritual activity to pleasing the ghosts of deceased ancestors who lurk about the villages looking to cause disease, bad luck, and death. The goal of Dani rituals is to drive them into the forest where they can do little damage. Similarly, the Sara of southern Chad believe in a creator god no longer active in human affairs as well as bush spirits and spirits of the dead, both of which are active and potentially harmful. Much of their annual cycle of ceremonies is devoted to pleasing these two categories of spirits in order to maintain or restore order to the natural and social worlds of the Sara. Typical of societies where supernaturals are seen as mainly benevolent are the Tahitians, who believe in a hierarchy of supernaturals composed of a high god, superior gods, and ancestor spirits. All are believed to be either potentially malevolent or benevolent, although benevolence is the usual result so long as they are contacted through appropriate ceremonies—the more important the supernatural the more elaborate the ceremony. In other societies, the nature of supernaturals may be more complex and humans may play a major role determining their relations with supernaturals. For example, the Mardudjara aboriginals of Australia believe in both benevolent and malevolent spirits but it is humans, under the watch of the spirits, who determine their own fate. Spirits associated with the creation of the Mardudjara and their environment are seen as mainly benevolent and wish humans well but those in distant places are hostile and the Mardudjara prefer to avoid them by staying near home. Whether a culture's customary beliefs about supernaturals is that they are benevolent versus malevolent is closely tied to child-rearing practices. In cultures where children are accepted, indulged, and nurtured, supernaturals are usually seen as benevolent. In cultures where children are rejected, severely punished, or ignored, supernaturals are usually seen as malevolent and also as capricious. For example, in the Bahamas, the parents who most frequently beat their children are the ones who are most afraid of supernatural spirits. Thus, people around the world seem to believe that their gods and spirits will treat them as they treat their children.

There are five primary categories of supernatural beings—gods, spirits, culture heroes, ancestor spirits, and ghosts, and a number of other more limited types such as vampires, devils, and fairies. One key distinction among these types is whether they are of supernatural or human origin. Gods and spirits are almost always of supernatural origin, culture heroes may be supernatural or human, and the others are of human origins with ancestor spirits, ghosts, and vampires all believed to be manifestations of the human soul, which survives after physical death.

Gods

Gods are the most powerful of supernatural beings. Every god in every religious system with gods (not all cultures have a belief in gods) has a name, personal characteristics, and a distinctive appearance. Within and across cultures a distinction can be made between high or supreme gods and superior gods. A high god has supernatural power, is the creator of the world and/or the ultimate power in the world, has a distinct name and persona, and is immortal or has a life span much longer than that of humans. A culture may have a high god and no other gods as in Judaism, Christianity, and Islam, or there may be a pantheon of gods with a high god and superior gods. For the Lozi of Zimbabwe, their high god and only god is Nymabe. Nymabe is the creator of all the forests, rivers, plains, animals, fishes, and first man and first woman. He also taught man the skills of carpentry and blacksmithing. Nymabe lived on earth with his first wife Vasilele and other wives like an African monarch. The aggressive behavior of Kamunu, the first man, who killed other animals, forced Nymabe to flee to safety in Litooma, above the earth where he continues to reside. Lozi kings are believed to be descended from Nymabe and one of his wives. Nymabe is an otiose high god as he maintains but does not interfere in the world as reflected in the Lozi saying, "Nymabe does not speak to anything; if he should at any time speak to anything, the world has come to an end." Thus, the Lozi can be said to honor Nymabe rather than pray for his help. Appeals for help are made only once a year in September when every household makes an offering of seeds to Nymabe and their wishes are communicated by the village headman:

O Nymabe, you are the creator of all.

Today we, your creatures, prostrate ourselves before you in supplication.

We have no strength.

You who have created us have all power.

We bring you our seed and all our implements that you may bless them and bless us also so that we may make good use of them by the power which comes from you, our creator.

Additionally, individuals may pray for help when they are ill or for assistance when hunting, although Nymabe is seen as not usually intervening directly in the affairs of the Lozi.

A belief in a high god is not a cultural universal and is found in only 50 percent of societies. In about 30 percent of these cultures the god is believed to be mainly inactive in human affairs. In the other 70 percent, the high god is thought to be active. A belief in a high god is typical of societies where individuals are responsible for securing their own food—pastoral and hunting societies—and also in societies where there are a number of independent social groups. In both situations it is the presence of individuals who are ultimately responsible for their own fates that meshes with the belief in high gods, who also are ultimately responsible for their domains.

Superior gods are found in only about 40 percent of cultures, sometimes in a pantheon consisting of a high god and a number of superior gods, and sometimes in a pantheon without a high god. Superior gods are like high gods in that they have names and distinct identities but differ in not being responsible for creation and having power over one particular domain rather than the world in general. The Saami of Scandinavia, for example, have eight superior gods:

Tiermes—god of thunder
Paive—god of the sun
Mano—god of the moon
Biegolmai—god of wind
Leibolmai—god of hunting
Sarakka, Uksakka, and Juksakka—
goddesses of childbirth

As this list suggests, superior gods are often associated with particular features of the environment or the human experience that are of special importance to the group. As the Saami lived traditionally through a combination of hunting and reindeer herding, their superior gods reflect a concern with those environmental factors that influence these activities. Unlike high gods who may be seen as relatively uninvolved in human affairs, superior gods are usually believed to influence the human situation directly. Tiermes, the god of thunder, for example, is seen as both benevolent and malevolent. He is malevolent, for like thunder itself, he scares animals, causes fires, and causes rock slides. He is benevolent because by bringing rain he drives out the trolls and spirits that cause sickness. Thus, like the rain, he cleanses the air.

Superior gods tend to be found most commonly in traditional societies with social classes and occupational specialization; that is, in societies where different people exclusively perform different tasks such as metal-working, pottery-making, tool-making, and so on. Thus, it seems that the division of labor in society is mirrored by the division of labor among the gods.

Culture Heroes

A culture hero is a mythical figure who is creator of the world and the people themselves. Culture heroes existed in the distant past and usually play no role in the current affairs of the humans they created. The tales of their exploits are passed from generation to generation through myths. Nanibush, the culture hero of the Ojibwa of North America, is a typical culture hero. He created the earth, lived among the creatures he created, and survived many dangerous and exciting adventures. His creation of the 30,000 islands of Georgian Bay is recounted by a Parry Island Ojibwa as follows:

> Nanibush was hunting the giant beaver, wabnik. He drove it from Lake Superior to Georgian Bay, where the beaver, thoroughly exhausted, crawled halfway out of the water and turned to stone. Nanibush, seeking its hiding place, smote the land with his club, and shattered it into the maze of islands that exist today. You can still see the beaver, three miles north of Parry Sound, its body on shore, its tail drooping down under the water. (Jenness 1935: 38)

After completing his work, Nanibush disappeared and the Ojibwa do not know for sure where he is. Some believe that he rules the land of the dead, others think he just lives there, and still others think he turned into a large rock on the shore of Lake Superior.

In some cultures, the culture hero acts as an agent of the high god who created the world. For example, the Cuna of Panama believe that God sent Ibeorkun, their culture hero, to earth 800 years ago to teach the Cuna how to behave, what to name objects, and how to use them. Ibeorkun was followed by disciples who continued his work and then ten lesser gods who informed people about the supernatural world. While this myth reflects traditional Cuna beliefs it also incorporates aspects of Christian belief learned from missionaries. This is not an uncommon feature of myths about culture heroes in many cultures, as the people merge their own beliefs with beliefs about the Christian God, biblical creation, and Jesus Christ taught to them by missionaries.

Spirits

Spirits are lesser supernaturals than high gods or superior gods and are often created by gods to carry out their work on earth. However, in their domains spirits do have tremendous power that is far greater than the power of humans. Spirits in any given society are usually referred to collectively and do not have personal names or a distinct persona, although they may be associated with certain peoples, places, or objects. The Amahuaca of Peru, for example, have a category of supernaturals called *yoshi* (spirit) who are active in human affairs. The yoshi inhabit specific animals and plants; the animals being those such as jaguars, pumas, and eels, which the Amahuaca fear or dislike and the plants being ones that they rarely eat. While the yoshi are believed to dress and look like the Amahuaca, they have no names, do not eat or sleep, and generally wander about the forest. Some are good, some bad, and others both. While the Amahuaca are curious about them, they do not pray to them or make offerings, although they do see yoshi in dreams and in séances conducted to communicate with them. While yoshi can cause evil through sorcery, they can also be used for beneficial purposes such as curing illness.

A category of spirits of special significance in some cultures is ancestor spirits, which are thought to be present in 75 percent of cultures and which are thought to influence the lives of the living in 42 percent of cultures. The Bemba of Africa, for example, have a pantheon of supernatural beings that includes a high god; superior gods; nature spirits who reside in animals, trees, plants, hills, ponds, and so on; and ancestor spirits, who are believed to have much influence on the affairs of their living descendants. Each house has a shrine for the family's ancestors, who are prayed to and given offerings of food at life-cycle events such as birth, marriage, illness, and death. The ancestors of the village headman are involved in the affairs of the entire village and prayers and offerings are made at their shrine outside the headman's hut.

Another special category of spirits is personal guardian spirits, who are responsible for the well-being of specific individuals. An individual usually acquires a guardian spirit as part of a vision quest when he makes contact with the spirit.

Ghosts

Ghosts are manifestations of deceased persons that can be seen or heard or sensed or whose effects can be perceived by the living. Ghosts are a cultural universal and in 94 percent of cultures the ghost that is perceived is a recently deceased individual to whom the perceiver was close. And in 84 percent of cultures ghosts are feared. However, there is considerable variation across societies in how many and how often ghosts are perceived. While in some Western societies people believe that ghosts do not exist and view as odd people who claim to perceive them, in most other societies people generally expect to perceive the ghost of a relative or close relative who has recently died. Belief in ghosts and the view that such a belief is natural is common around the world for a number of reasons. First, various environmental cues such as a deceased person's clothing cause survivors to think of the deceased and perhaps think they are still present. Second, dreams about the deceased can also create a sense the person is still present. Third, thoughts about the deceased may lead some people to believe that they have actually been in contact with the deceased. And, fourth, people may wish for the presence of ghosts as their presence allows survivors to complete unfinished business with the deceased. A fear of ghosts may especially reflect the need to finish uncompleted business, as the relationship between the deceased and survivor may have been hostile, or the survivor fears that the deceased wants the survivor to join him or her (perhaps reflecting the survivor's wish to do so), or by fearing the ghost, the survivor can place some emotional distance between himself and the deceased.

The Trukese of Oceania are a typical society in that among them ghosts are generally feared. One woman reported the following experience with a ghost:

When I was about twelve I went to bathe one afternoon, and on the way back a ghost came out of the bush and bit me; I saw him as he left: he was a grown man but small

like a very small man who lives on Romonum now, I think he was the spirit of a brother of my father. That night I was sick, with pains and chills, but the next morning I was better. I did not take any medicine. I do not know why he came. (Gladwin and Sarason 1953: 66)

In many cultures, the fear of ghosts is passed from generation to generation in folktales, and the Trukese are no different:

When they used to tell folktales about ghosts I used to be frightened thinking about them, and would think they were going to eat me. I used to pull my knees up in front of me and put my arms around them because I was scared. When my mother was out somewhere around the island at night just my father and I slept in the house. But we did not sleep very close together and a ghost could come in and bite one of us easily; I was very worried. It was not good that way. (Gladwin and Sarason 1953: 68)

For the Ganda of Uganda, beliefs in ghosts went well beyond the individual experience and were an important component of their indigenous religion. In general ghosts were seen as benevolent and as providers of good fortune to members of the kinship they had belonged to. Shrines were built for ghosts and at the door beer was provided to quench their thirst and firewood and clothes to protect them from the cold. So long as people attended to ghosts in these ways that acknowledged thanks for the ghosts' help, ghosts would cause no harm. However, if these responsibilities were neglected, or the grave was neglected, or heirs to the deceased not chosen in a timely fashion, ghosts could cause harm, by possessing a person and causing him or her to fall ill. Typical of ghost sickness was general malaise or mild insanity in which the ill person had fits. These illnesses required the intervention of a healer who burnt herbs to drive the ghost out of the victim's body and restore health. Health could also be restored by visiting an oracle to identify the ghost and then making offerings to it.

Devils

The concept of the devil is associated with death, evil, and sin. Devils may be of supernatural origin, as in Christianity where Satan is a fallen angel, or of human origin, as in societies where they may be spirits of the dead. While devils are often inherently and purely evil, they are not always so, as with the Islamic *jinn* who are feared but do not always cause harm. In some cultures the devil is a solitary figure, with a name and a distinct appearance. In others there may be a number of evil supernatural beings. The Khasi of India, for example, do not believe in one devil, but rather a pantheon of demons whom they label *ksuid*, who divide the devil's work among themselves, a sampling of which is listed below:

u siem thylliew	god of smallpox
ka duba	demoness of fever
ka rinh	demoness of malaria
ka khlam	demoness of cholera
ka byrdaw	demoness of cramps
ka tyrut	demoness of violent death
u kyrtep	devil of blindness
u jungbih-u lasam	demoness of mouth of tooth disease
u 'suid-um	devil of sterility and miscarriage
u tynjang	devil who tickles people to death
u thlen	devil of wealth and comfort who can only be worshipped by human sacrifice
ka jumai	demoness of earthquakes
u 'suid-kynta-maram	devil of headaches

For the Khasi, such evil forces are associated with the idea that humans are sinful and much religious activity is devoted to pacifying these evil spirits so as to avoid illness or other misfortune.

One noteworthy feature of the devil is his appearance. In many cultures, he looks like members of other ethnic groups whom the people fear or consider inferior. For example, the Tarahumara of northern Mexico believe that they are children of God while the Mexicans are the children of the devil. They also believe that the devil has a wife, also a devil, who bore him children who were the first Mexicans. Not surprisingly, the Tarahumara personify the devil as a man with a thick beard, like the Mexicans. For the Amhara of Ethiopia, the devil is dark-skinned and has Black African features, and thus resembles the most despised people in Ethiopian society.

Vampires

A vampire is the soulless corpse of an evil person that is possessed by the devil, a witch, or some other evil force that fills it with blood sucked from the living so that the deceased might "live." Living in this sense means moving about at night, flying, changing its form, and sucking blood from and engaging in sex with the living. Vampire beliefs date back several hundred years among the peasants of eastern Europe and the continuing popularity of the Dracula legend attests to the basic interest of the subject matter. Vampire stories remain popular because they touch on some major issues addressed by religious beliefs and practices in all cultures—good versus evil, death and afterlife, and the lifegiving yet potentially polluting nature of blood. Because vampires are evil and can damage the living, those who believe in vampires go to great lengths to protect themselves from them. For example, in Serbia in the nineteenth century priests would drive a stake through the heart of a corpse of a suspected vampire. In the twentieth century, measures in the Balkans are less extreme and include lighting a candle on graves, walking a stallion through a graveyard to identify vampires (stallions will not cross a vampire's grave), burning a cross of sulphur and gunpowder on the grave, and sticking knives into the grave to prevent the corpse from rising. While vampire belief is most pronounced in Europe, it occurs in other cultures in Africa and North and South America as well. The following Iroquois legend from New York State indicates the fear that vampires invoke around the world:

Once upon a time, a man and his wife went out to hunt. The hunting ground was a two day's journey away, and on their way home, heavily laden with meat, they came to the cabin, where the owner, a famous medicine man, was dead. Because it was already dark, the husband decided that they should spend the night there, in spite of the fact that the dead man's body lay on a shelf in a bark coffin. The husband gathered wood and lit a fire and then lay down to rest while his wife cooked meat and cornmeal cakes. After a while he fell asleep. The wife went about her work. Suddenly the woman heard a noise behind her, near where her husband lay; it was like the sound of someone chewing meat. She thought about the corpse on the shelf and remembered that the dead man was a witch, so she put more wood on the fire and made it blaze up, and then she looked again. She saw a stream of blood trickling out from the bunk. At once she knew that her husband had been killed by the dead man. But she pretended that she did not notice. She said, as if speaking to her husband, "I must make a torch and bring some water." She made a torch of hickory bark, long enough to last until she could run home. Then she took the pail and went out; but as soon as she was outside the door, she dropped the pail and ran through the woods as fast as she could. She had gotten halfway home before the vampire realized that she had gone. He ran after her, whooping. She heard him behind her; the whooping came nearer and nearer. She was so scared she almost fell, but she ran on until her torch was almost out and at last reached the lodge in her village where people were dancing. She burst into the lodge and fainted.

When she revived, she told the story of what had happened to her and her husband. In the morning a party of men went to the cabin, where they found the bones of the husband, from which all the flesh had been eaten. The face and hands of the skeleton in the bark box were found to be bloody. Thereupon the chief said it was not right to leave dead people that way. They took the bones of the vampire and buried them in a hole that they dug in the ground, and they brought the bones of the husband back to the village and buried them there also. And thereafter the dead were no longer placed on scaffolds or on shelves in bark lodges, but were buried in the ground. (Wallace 1972: 99–100)

Other Supernatural Beings

The mythology of many cultures is rich with tales of the troublesome activities of little people, gnomes, fairies, goblins, monsters, trolls, and other mythical beings. While a part of mythology, in many cultures people believe that such creatures exist and claim to have seen them as proof of their existence. For example, the Ashanti of West Africa are convinced that a people called *mmoatia* (little folk or fairies) live in the forests. They are about one foot tall; are black, red, or white; and their feet are backwards. The black ones are harmless, but the red and white ones are filled with mischief, often stealing wine and uneaten food. To skepticism expressed by outsiders, the Ashanti retort: "Ah, but perhaps you have not got the right mind for seeing the little folk."

The Ashanti experience with the little people is typical of most cultures—little people are usually disruptive and difficult, but they cause no major harm. In some cultures, however, the little people are seen as generally helpful. The Saami, for example believe that their little people, called *saiva*, are an underground people who had once been Saami but now live apart and are always happy and satisfied. Saami communicate with saiva and recruit them as assistants to provide support in daily activities.

Another category of supernaturals are tricksters—beings who play tricks on humans. Tricksters may be a specialized form of supernatural being such as the coyote in Native American mythology or a god or spirit that sometimes plays tricks on humans.

See also ANCESTOR WORSHIP; SOUL; VISION QUEST.

Carneiro, Robert L. (1964) "The Amahuaca and the Spirit World." *Ethnology* 3: 6–11.

Carroll, Michael P. (1979) "The Sex of Our Gods." *Ethos* 7: 37–50.

Collinder, Bjorn. (1949) *The Lapps.*

Davis, William D. (1974) *Societal Complexity and the Nature of Primitive Man's Conception of the Supernatural.*

Ferndon, Edwin N. (1981) *Early Tahiti as the Explorers Saw It.*

Gladwin, Thomas, and Seymour Sarason. (1953) *Truk: Man in Paradise.*

Heider, Karl G. (1990) *Grand Valley Dani: Peaceful Warriors.* 2d ed.

Jenness, Diamond. (1935) *The Ojibwa Indians of Parry Island, Their Social and Religious Life.*

Karsten, Rafael. (1955) *The Religion of the Samek: Ancient Beliefs and Cults of the Scandinavian and Finnish Lapps.*

Levine, Donald N. (1965) *Wax and Gold: Tradition and Innovation in Ethiopian Culture.*

Levinson, David, and Martin J. Malone. (1980) *Toward Explaining Human Culture.*

Lodge, Olive. (1941) *Peasant Life in Jugoslavia.*

Lumholtz, Carl. (1902) *Unknown Mexico: A Record of Five Years' Exploration of the Western Sierra Madre; in the Tierra Caliente of Tepic and Jalisco; and among the Tarascos of Michoacan.*

Malefijt, Annemarie de Waal. (1968) *Religion and Culture: An Introduction to the Anthropology of Religion.*

Marshall, Donald S. (1950) *Cuna Folk: A Conceptual Scheme Involving the Dynamic Factors of Culture, as Applied to the Cuna Indians of Darien.* Unpublished manuscript, Harvard University.

Otterbein, Charlotte S., and Keith F. Otterbein. (1973) "Believers and Beaters: A Case Study of Supernatural Beliefs and Child Rearing in the Bahama Islands." *American Anthropologist* 75: 1670–1681.

Rattray, R. S. (1927) *Religion and Art in Ashanti.*

Reyna, Stephen P. (1995) "Sara." In *Encyclopedia of World Cultures. Volume 9. Africa and the Middle East,* edited by John Middleton and Amal Rassam, 304–307.

Rohner, Ronald P. (1975) *They Love Me, They Love Me Not.*

Roscoe, John. (1911) *The Baganda: An Account of Their Native Customs and Beliefs.*

Rosenblatt, Paul C., R. Patricia Walsh, and Douglas A. Jackson. (1976) *Grief and Mourning in Cross-Cultural Perspective.*

Simpson, John H. (1984) *High Gods and the Means of Subsistence. Sociological Analysis* 45: 213–222.

Stegmiller, P. F. (1921) "The Religious Life of the Khasi." *Anthropos* 16: 407–441. Translated from the German for the Human Relations Area Files.

Swanson, Guy E. (1968) *The Birth of the Gods: The Origin of Primitive Beliefs.*

Tonkinson, Robert. (1978) *The Mardudjara Aborigines: Living the Dream in Australia's Desert.*

Turner, Victor W. (1952) *The Lozi Peoples of North-Western Rhodesia.*

Wallace, Anthony F. C. (1972) *The Death and Rebirth of the Seneca.*

Whiteley, Wilfred. (1950) "Bemba and Related People of Northern Rhodesia." *Ethnographic Survey of Africa: East Central Africa.* Part II, 1–32, 70–76.

Whyte, Martin K. (1978) "Cross-Cultural Codes Dealing with the Relative Status of Women." *Ethnology* 17: 211–237.

SUPERNATURAL EXPLANATIONS FOR ILLNESS

Explanations for illness and death across cultures cite either natural causes or supernatural causes. While natural causes such as infection, accident, or stress are usually cited in modern societies that rely primarily on Western medicine for health care, most non-Western cultures in the past and to some extent today attribute illness and death to supernatural causes. And in nearly all cultures (137 out of 139 cultures in one survey) at least some types of illness are attributed to the actions of supernatural forces. This belief is found in all regions of the world and is especially strong in cultures in East Asia and the Mediterranean region. Another survey indicates that in 53 percent of traditional non-Western cultures, all or most illness is attributed to supernatural forces, including witchcraft and sorcery. However, beliefs in witchcraft and sorcery as major causes of illness mainly occur in different cultures—if people in a culture believe strongly in one of these, they will probably not believe strongly in the other. This suggests that these beliefs are alternative forms of the same basic belief in the potentially harmful effect of the supernatural world. Of course, while a specific culture may be characterized as having a strong belief in the harmful potential of spirits, this does not mean that all people in the culture share the belief or that they believe that they will be harmed. For example, the Central Thai believe strongly in the potential harm that might be caused by ghosts, but the majority of people in rural villages say that they personally have not been harmed by ghosts.

Supernatural explanations of illness fall into three general categories: (1) mystical causation, (2) animistic causation, and (3) magical causation. Many of the specific causes that fall into these categories as well as the supernatural treatment of illness are discussed in the appropriate entries elsewhere in this volume. The purpose of this article is to provide a broad understanding of the importance placed in many cultures on the role of the supernatural in illness.

Mystical Explanations

In this category of explanation, illness is attributed to some impersonal force acting in response to the victim's behavior and includes fate, ominous sensations, contagion, and mystical retribution. In mystical explanations no supernatural being directly causes the illness. Fate, ominous sensations (dreams, sights, sounds that cause illness), and contagion are quite rare across cultures as explanations. In only a minority of cultures are they cited at all and then always only rarely. Examples include the use of judicial ordeals among the Ganda of Uganda in which fate can cause death, certain visions experienced by Pawnee men that cause emotional problems, and contact with ghosts that can cause illness, poverty, and other miseries for rural Taiwanese. Mystical retribution, where disease results when someone violates a serious taboo or behaves in an immoral way, is more common and is a major or important explanation for illness in 21 percent of cultures. For example, in Central Thailand, Muslims are thought to be especially susceptible to diseases cause by the water ghost because they wash in ponds or canals after defecation and urination as required by Islam. This angers the water ghost because the water is no longer clean. Buddhists are not subject to such treatment as they wipe but do not wash. For the Sinhalese of Sri Lanka, illness or even supernatural punishment might result from the transgression of sexual mores, particularly if a man has intercourse with a woman who is a relative.

And the Mbuti of Central Africa attribute some illnesses or even death to violations of taboos involving the totemic animal of the individual's group. For example, if the totem is a chimpanzee, the individual may not kill it, eat it, eat from a container that held its flesh, or even eat berries, the chimp's favorite food. To avoid violating the taboos and becoming ill, the Mbuti will avoid chimps and hide or flee from them in the forest.

Animistic Explanations

In animistic explanations, illnesses are caused by a supernatural being such as a spirit, soul, or ghost and are of two types: soul loss and spirit aggression. Soul loss, although a worry in many societies where people believe that the soul leaves the body during sleep, is not cited as a major cause of illness in any society, is unimportant as a cause of illness in a minority of societies, and not cited at all as a cause in most societies. Spirit aggression, on the other hand, is the major supernatural explanation for illness and death across cultures. It is the primary causal factor in 42 percent of cultures and an important cause in another 21 percent of cultures. In many cultures, spirits who cause disease are minor ones; sometimes they are spirits whose main activity is causing disease, in other cultures ancestors unhappy with their descendants, and in other cultures ghosts, again unhappy with those left behind. In only a small minority of cultures do major spirits or gods concern themselves with the health of individuals.

Magical Explanations

This type of illness explanation attributes disease and often death to the actions of humans who use magical means to cause others to fall ill or die. These include the evil eye, sorcery, and witchcraft, all three of which are fairly common across cultures as explanations for illness.

See also DREAMS; EVIL EYE; MAGIC; POSSESSION AND TRANCE; PURITY AND POLLUTION; RELIGIOUS SPECIALISTS; SHAMANISM; SORCERY; SOUL; SUPERNATURAL BEINGS; WITCHCRAFT.

Baity, Philip C. (1975) *Religion in a Chinese Town.*

Justinger, Judith M. (1978) *Reaction to Change: A Holocultural Test of Some Theories of Religious Movements.*

Murdock, George P. (1980) *Theories of Illness: A World Survey.*

Putnam, Patrick. (1948) "The Pygmies of the Ituri Forest." In *A Reader in General Anthropology,* edited by Carlton S. Coon, 322–342.

Roscoe, John. (1911) *The Baganda: An Account of Their Native Customs and Beliefs.*

Textor, Robert B. (1973) *Roster of the Gods: An Ethnography of the Supernatural in a Thai Village.*

Weltfish, Gene. (1965) *The Lost Universe: With a Closing Chapter on the Universe Regained.*

Yalman, Nur. (1971) *Under the Bo Tree: Studies in Caste, Kinship, and Marriage in the Interior of Ceylon.*

SYNCRETIC RELIGIONS

Whenever two or more cultures come into contact there is a mixing of some elements from each of the cultures. Syncretism is one specific type of cultural blending that in its most extreme form results in the development of a new culture or ethnic group characterized by numerous cultural traits and institutions that are an amalgam of traits drawn from different cultures. A less extreme form of syncretism involves the development of new forms of cultural institutions through a blending of traits but not a transformation of the entire culture. Religious syncretism is a common phenomenon around the world, due in large part to culture contact and the influence of missionaries in the past and present, whose efforts to covert peoples have often resulted in new religions combining elements from the traditional and the introduced religion. All major religions in the world today are syncretic ones, to the extent that all when they began and as they developed they incorporated elements from other religions. Thus, Judaism was influenced by Babylonian and other Middle Eastern religions of the time, Christianity and Islam by Judaism, Buddhism by Hinduism, and so forth.

Syncretic religions resulting from culture contact are especially common in Latin America and include African Brazilian Candomblé, Cuban Santería, and Haitian Vodou, all of which formed through a combination of theology and practices from African religions brought by slaves and the Roman Catholicism of the European colonizers. Vodou, for example, is based on African elements primarily from the Fon of Benin, the Yoruba of Nigeria, and the Kongo of Zaire and Angola and the form of Roman Catholicism imposed by the French colonists. From African religions come various spirits, although they are often redefined in terms of their roles to fit the Haitian situation. These include the Yoruba ironsmithing spirit, Ogou, called Ogan in rural Haiti and seen as the spirit of military power; the image of Africa itself as the homeland and the home of the spirits; and African rites for serving the spirits. Added to this African base and merged with it are elements taken from Roman Catholicism including specific rites such as baptism, mass, and confession; Catholic prayers;

the names of saints; and the role of "bush priest," whose status is based on his ability to conduct Catholic rites in the original Latin. In Haitian Vodou and other syncretic religions, the elements do not simply exist side-by-side, but are often merged in various ways. For example, the African God Bondye, the "Good God," is linked with the Christian God while the snake deity, Danbala, is linked to St. Patrick, who is depicted in pictures with snakes around his neck. Earlier in the twentieth century, social scientists viewed syncretic elements of a culture such as the Vodou religion as an adaptive response to the colonial situation that enabled oppressed peoples to live in both their own and the world of the colonists. More recently, syncretism has become a mechanism of resistance and revolt, through which African-ancestry communities in Brazil, Suriname, Haiti, and elsewhere developed their own sense of a unique ethnic consciousness and used that consciousness to seek recognition and political power. In Brazil, syncretic religions are an important element in the black consciousness movement, while in Haiti, Vodou played a role in the overthrow of the Duvalier government in 1986, as it had in the slave revolt of 1789–1804 that ended French rule.

Syncretism is a poorly understood phenomenon and little is known about how cultural elements become integrated or why some aspects of culture, such as religion, are more open to syncretization than are other aspects, such as the kinship system, which is more likely simply to change, with the traditional replaced by the new. One factor that does seem to affect religious syncretism is the extent to which new elements fit with the old. For example, the recent worldwide phenomenon of many Gypsy peoples converting from Catholicism to Pentecostal Protestantism (both of which are merged with Gypsy beliefs and practices) is due to the magical, expressive nature of Pentecostalism, which fits the Gypsy ethos.

Apter, Andrew. (1991) "Herskovits's Heritage: Rethinking Syncretism in the African Diaspora." *Diaspora* 1: 235–260.

Bastide, Roger. (1960) *The African Religions of Brazil: Toward a Sociology of Interpretation of Civilizations*. Translated by H. Sebba.

Courlander, H., and Rémy Bastien, eds. (1966) *Religion and Politics in Haiti*.

Herskovits, Melville J. (1966) *The New World Negro: Selected Papers in Afroamerican Studies*. Bloomington: Indiana University Press.

Murphy, Joseph. (1988) *Santería: An African Religion in America*.

and economic implications as they kept the chief and his family separate from the rest of the population. The use of taboos to maintain political authority is not confined to Polynesian chiefdoms, as suggested by the taboo in monarchial Britain on nonroyalty looking at the king.

The belief that a violation of taboos will anger supernatural beings while adhering to them will please them or at least keep them neutral is apparent in the taboos associated with economic activities in many cultures. The Ojibwa of North America, for example, had many taboos involving hunting:

> Do not throw beaver or bear bones to the dogs, but place them in the water or hang them to trees; for the beaver and the bear will use these bones again when they are reincarnated. If you violate this taboo the boss beaver and the boss bear will be offended.
>
> Do not skin and dress an animal right away, lest its shadow learn of you and prevent you from killing other animals of the same species. Wait a half hour before you skin your quarry.
>
> Never torture an animal. If you do you will torture your own soul and surely meet with misfortune. If you do your child will fall sick, or suffer.
>
> Never boil two kinds of fish in the same pot simultaneously.
>
> Never scale trout. If you do the weather will be stormy and you will be unable to fish. (Jenness 1935: 80)

TABOO

A taboo is an action that is prohibited and the object to which the prohibition applies. The word *taboo* is an English rendering of the Polynesian term *tapu*, which in a number of Polynesian island cultures has two related meanings. First, it means "sacred" and is used in reference to the gods, chiefs (who are descended from gods), and the temples and objects associated with all three. Second, it means "prohibited," in reference to individuals or objects that are to be avoided. Explicit in the Polynesian conceptualization of taboo is that one who violates a taboo will be subject to supernatural sanction. In the modern usage, the notion of supernatural sanction has been dropped and taboo is now more generally used to refer to any action that is strongly prohibited. In Polynesia taboos can be either permanent as with the chiefs or temples, which must be avoided by commoners at all times, or they may be temporary, such as with food taboos placed on the family of someone who has recently died. In Polynesian societies permanent taboos of the sacred type traditionally had important political

For the Kapauku of New Guinea, taboos are relevant to agriculture in two ways. First, general taboos that apply to many activities are also relevant to agriculture. For example, a new mother is forbidden from leaving her house for five days and this includes going into the fields to plant sweet potatoes. Similarly, as part of the menstrual taboo, a girl is prohibited from entering gardens during the first two days of her first two menstrual periods. Second, there are specific taboos prescribed by shamans in order to treat an illness or remove a curse that limit or prohibit involvement in agriculture. For example, in 1955 the people of an entire village were prohibited from all farming for seven days in order to cure a man from an illness caused by an evil spirit. Violation of the taboo would have led to another attack by evil spirits.

In addition to customary taboos that apply to all people or to certain categories of people, in most cultures there are also personal taboos, which are recognized by the culture as legitimate, but differ from person to person in their details. For example, among the Mbuti of central Africa, many individuals have personal taboos that require them to not eat certain animals or other foods. These taboos usually result from some accident involving the animal or a food allergy.

Considerable attention has been devoted by social scientists to explaining taboo in general as well as to the specific categories of taboo discussed below. One explanation focuses on the role taboos play in creating cognitive boundaries so that people or objects that do not fit neatly in a society's model of the universe can be excluded. Another explanation focuses on the social role of taboos in defining the role of individuals in a society and creating social boundaries.

Food Taboos

In all cultures there are customary rules that prohibit the eating of certain foods. Food taboos come in a variety of forms, including (1) general taboos in which a certain food is taboo at all times to all people, such as the eating of pork by Jews or Muslims; (2) occasional taboos in which certain foods are taboo only at certain times, such as the traditional Roman Catholic taboo on the eating of fish on Friday; (3) ritual taboos in which certain foods are taboo during rituals such as birth or death ceremonies; and (4) person-specific taboos in which certain foods are taboo only to specific categories of people such as pregnant women, shamans, hunters, children, or warriors.

The Pawnee of the American Plains had a number of different food taboos. Wolf, mountain lion, coyote, otter, and wildcat meat were taboo to all, although buffalo and deer were not. All, except chiefs and religious specialists, could eat fish. Children were not allowed to eat the most tender buffalo meat, with a violation of the taboo resulting in failure in future raids on enemy villages. The stomach of cows was taboo for girls and boys and violating this taboo would cause the boy to be injured in war and the girl to injure her leg in adulthood. For the Ifugao of the Philippines, the most severe food taboos concerned betel, wine, or water supplied by enemy kinship groups. The taboo was enforced by the belief that a violation would lead spirits to cause illnesses such as malaria and tuberculosis that were resistant to cure by the usual curing rites. This Ifugao taboo, of course, prevented peace to be reached by warring kinship groups and was instead actually a component of the ongoing conflict. Each group would employ sorcerers to direct the concentrated aromas of their food to the other group, with the hope that their smelling it by accident would be sufficient to cause them to fall ill. The only way an afflicted Ifugao could recover was to appeal to and satisfy powerful spirits, which might also involve making peace.

Pregnancy Taboos

As with food taboos, pregnancy taboos are found in all cultures and usually involve food taboos and the curtailment of sexual activity at some point in the pregnancy. Pregnancy taboos in general are meant to protect the mother's and unborn child's health and are of two types. First are those designed to protect the mother's and unborn child's health because they remove from the diet items or restrict activities that might be harmful. Second are those that are not beneficial in that they prohibit harmful activities but that will result in harm if they are not followed. These include the continuation of the usual food taboos and other taboos such as speaking the name of a dead ancestor. Pregnancy taboos, while focused on the mother, may also involve other members of the family, often the father. For example, the Santal of India believe that malevolent spirits and witches will harm a pregnant woman. To protect herself, she rarely leaves her house in the evening, never crosses a stream, does not cry at the death of a relative, and sits only certain ways in the courtyard. Her husband protects her by avoiding death—he never kills an animal, stays away from funeral ceremonies, and avoids dead bodies.

Incest Taboo

The incest taboo is a prohibition on sexual relations between certain categories of relatives. In all cultures the taboo applies to members of the nuclear family (parents and children and siblings) and also to at least some other categories of relatives beyond the nuclear family, although there is much cross-cultural variation in the specific categories of relatives. Since the incest taboo prohibits sexual relations, the individuals who are prohibited from engaging in sex are also prohibited from marrying one another. Thus, the incest taboo is tied to rules that govern who may marry whom. In modern nations, the incest taboo applies to members of the nucleur family, grandparents, and various categories of other relatives such as cousins, aunts, and uncles. Violation of the incest taboo in modern nations is no longer punished by supernatural sanction but is handled by judicial or mental health agencies. In many other societies where ties of kinship, often traced just through one parent's line, are important in organizing community life, the in-

cest taboo often applies to all members of one's kin group such as to all members of their lineage or clan. While the incest taboo is found in all societies, there is much variation not only in which relatives are taboo but also in how seriously the taboo is regarded and how severely violations are punished. The Kachin of Myanmar (Burma), for example, have a complex kinship system and marriage and therefore sexual relations are prohibited between a man and all women in his lineage. However, the distribution of potential partners is such that the rule is frequently broken and men often marry women whom Westerners would call cousins, although they are usually from a different village. For the Mbuti of central Africa the incest taboo applies to members of the nuclear family as well as cousins. When the taboo regarding cousins is violated, people might look the other way unless the guilty man is caught and then punishment is severe:

> He has been driven to the forest . . . and he will have to live there alone. Nobody will accept him into their group after what he has done. And he will die, because one cannot live alone in the forest. The forest will kill him. And if it does not kill him he will die of leprosy. (Turnbull 1965: 112)

The Kapuaku of New Guinea prohibit sexual relations and marriage between a man and women in his kin group under the penalty of death and take the taboo quite seriously as suggested by the following case:

Case 31.

Place: Jiib (Pona Region)
Date: ca. 1947
Parties:
    a) Defendant: Bo Wog of Jiib
    b) Executioner: Bo Deg of Jiib, half brother of the defendant
    c) Authority: Bo Gek of Jiib
Facts: The culprit was known as a notorious thief who stole many garden products

and food from other people. He raped many women, including the wife of his half brother. Finally, he seduced his second parallel paternal cousin.

Outcome: All the people were upset by this outrage and the half brother of the defendant volunteered, after the decision of the authority, to execute the criminal. He killed him with a bamboo-tipped arrow shot from ambush. (Pospisil 1963: 164)

Because of their relation to marriage rules and to the wider kinship system, social and behavioral scientists have devoted much effort to explaining why the taboo is found in all cultures. Some experts argue that the taboo serves to prevent conflict within the family, others that forcing people to marry outside the kin groups creates alliances among kin groups, and still others that it results from people who grow up together usually having no sexual interest in each other. Other experts take a biological perspective and suggest that the taboo serves to control the harmful effects of inbreeding that would result from reproduction by close biological relatives. The criticism of this argument that in many cultures people did not relate sexual intercourse to the birth of a child nine months later is countered by some who argue that the harmful effects of inbreeding would, through the process of natural selection, caused societies without the taboo to die off long ago in human history, while those with the taboo would have survived.

Menstrual Taboo

In most cultures people other than the menstruating woman pay attention to this monthly event and in most cultures the woman is considered to be impure and potentially dangerous during this period so restrictions are placed on her that limit contact with other people, animals, plants, or objects that she might pollute. However, cultures vary widely in the degree to which a woman's activities are restricted. Cultures may

be ranked on a six-point scale of intensity of the menstrual taboo, with those cultures ranked at each point having all of the taboos at that point and also at all points above it on the scale:

1. informal concern for menstruation
2. menstruants prohibited from engaging in sexual intercourse
3. menstruants subject to personal restrictions such as on the eating of certain foods and loud laughing
4. menstruants not allowed to touch male objects such as tools or weapons
5. menstruants not allowed to cook for men
6. menstruants confined to menstrual huts

An example of a relatively low level of concern about menstruation and therefore a limited taboo are the Tahitians of Polynesia. Women go about their usual routine while menstruating, although some—especially older women—believe that if a menstruating woman touches a plant or fish it will spoil. Younger women reject this view:

> I've always gone [while menstruating] to fertilize the vanilla blossoms, to plant food crops; I've gone fishing—nothing bad ever happened. The vanilla flourishes all the time. There are plenty of flowers around the house. I go and pick them and I don't tell people I am menstruating. I just go and pick them. Did the flowers die? It all lives. (Levy 1973: 62–63)

Among the Andaman Islanders of South Asia, the taboo is more intense as women are required to avoid certain foods such as pork, turtle, honey, yams, and certain fish. If she were to eat any of these, she would become ill. As in many cultures, special attention is paid to the first menstruation, and during her first period and the accompanying ceremony, men do not touch the girl for fear their arm will swell. Bemba women of Zimbabwe are subject to even more restrictions. Fires are of special ritual importance to the Bemba and must be kept pure so that they can be used to purify the home. Menstruating women are considered impure and therefore may not touch the family fire and must keep one of their own. If it goes out, they may relight it only with material taken from the fire of a postmenopausal woman or from a premenstrual girl. The menstruating woman may not have intercourse with a man nor may she wash in a stream where others wash for fear of causing others to fall ill. If she violates any of these taboos, she is forced to sit over a fireplace until her flesh blisters. At the end of her period, the family fire is extinguished and a new one lit, in a ceremony that is equivalent to the one performed when a village has been polluted by death. Severe menstrual taboos were found among many Native American groups, as the customs of the Tlingit of the Northwest Coast and the Pawnee of the Plains indicate. The Tlingit believed that menstrual blood and childbirth discharges were exceedingly polluting and harmful to men, animals, and the spirits. Thus, during their menstrual cycle women were confined to the small, red cedar birth house, had to stay out of sight of men, could not touch men's possessions, and had to stay away from salmon streams. All of these restrictions were designed to prevent the "bloody woman" from causing others to become ill. For the Pawnee, the menstrual taboo was directly tied to their religion, as they believed menstrual blood, with its human aroma, would pollute the sacred bundles and their contents, which had a nonhuman sweet-grass aroma. To keep them away from the sacred bundles, girls who were daughters of the keepers of the sacred bundles were isolated in a menstrual hut called the "place-sitting-with-blood" where they were attended to by their grandmother but were prohibited from eating meat, bathing, or combing their hair. Other menstruating women were not so isolated but were prohibited from touching the sacred

bundles and from attending ceremonies where they were used. The presence of the menstrual taboo in many traditional Native American nations is not an accident but rather seems related to the fact that menstrual taboos are more common in societies that rely on hunting than in other types of societies. And, since many Native American societies relied on hunting, menstrual taboos were more common in North America. Why hunting societies often had a menstrual taboo is not clear, although it may be related to the belief found in many cultures that menstrual blood will harm or scare off animals.

Across cultures, it seems that menstrual taboos are an aspect of male/female relations and relate to ideas and other customs concerning power, social distance, and male and female roles. Experts disagree, however, in how these factors are reflected in menstrual taboos: some claim that the taboo reflects male control of female sexuality, others believe that the basic cause is male castration anxiety, and still others argue that the taboo is a custom that reinforces male/female differences. Missing from the cross-cultural literature are full discussions of female attitudes about the taboo, although there is some evidence that women do not necessarily find isolation during their menstrual period to be unduly burdensome.

Name Taboos

Across cultures, name taboos take three forms: taboo on using one's own name; taboo on using the name of certain categories of relatives; taboo on using the names of the dead. Name taboos are common across cultures, although only in a minority of cultures are they reinforced by the threat of supernatural punishment. A taboo on using one's own name is found in 28 percent of cultures and in most of these cultures people think it is rude or too personal to use one's name in public. This belief is not confined to non-Western cultures, as evidenced by British academics, many of whom prefer to use only the initials for their first and second names on their publications, the reason being that it is too personal to reveal your name to strangers.

Taboos on using the names of relatives apply to parents (30 percent of cultures), spouses (26 percent), parents-in-law (28 percent), grandparents (16 percent), siblings-in-law (16 percent), parents' siblings (13 percent), siblings (10 percent), and children (7 percent). This taboo seems to be a component of a general pattern of ritualized relations among relatives that is common in many societies. It serves to maintain distance between different categories of relatives and makes clear their status relative to each other. For example, the restriction on the use of one's parents' names by children in the United States indicates that parents are superior and children subordinate—they are not social equals.

A taboo on the names of the dead is practiced in 30 percent of cultures, most of them small, hunting/gathering cultures in which there is also a taboo on using one's own name. This taboo is found in this type of culture because, from a social and material point of view, the dead are not as important as in other cultures. This is because they pass little in the way of wealth or social status on to their descendants. In other cultures where social and material goods are passed on, remembering the dead is important and failure to do might result in punishment meted out by their spirits.

See also MANA; PURITY AND POLLUTION; RITUAL.

Alford, Richard D. (1988) *Naming and Identity: A Cross-Cultural Study of Personal Naming Practices.*

Barton, Roy F. (1946) *The Religion of the Ifugao.*

Biswas, P. C. (1956) *Santals of the Santal Parganas.*

de Laguna, Frederica. (1972) *Under Mount Saint Elias: The History and Culture of the Yakutat Tlingit.*

Dorsey, George A. (1940) "Notes on Skidi Pawnee Society." *Field Museum of Natural History, Anthropological Series* 27: 65–119.

Ember, Carol R., and David Levinson. (1992) "The Substantive Contributions of Worldwide Cross-Cultural Studies Using Secondary Data." *Behavior Science Research* 25: 79–140.

Firth, Raymond. (1939) *Primitive Polynesian Economy.*

Jenness, Diamond. (1935) *The Ojibwa Indians of Parry Island, Their Social and Religious Life.*

Leach, E. R. (1972) *Political Systems of Highland Burma.*

Leavitt, Gregory C. (1995) "Incest Taboo." In *Encyclopedia of Marriage and the Family, Vol. 2*, edited by David Levinson, 374–378.

Levinson, David, and Martin J. Malone. (1980) *Toward Explaining Human Culture.*

Levy, Robert I. (1973) *Tahitians: Mind and Experience in the Society Islands.*

Pospisil, Leopold J. (1958) *Kapauku Papuans and Their Law.*

———. (1963) *Kapauku Papuan Economy.*

Radcliffe-Brown, A. R. (1922) *The Andaman Islanders: A Study in Social Anthropology.*

Richards, Audrey. (1956) *Chisungu: A Girls' Initiation Ceremony among the Bemba of Northern Rhodesia.*

Turnbull, Colin M. (1965) *The Mbuti Pygmies: An Ethnographic Survey.*

———. (1961) *The Forest People: A Study of the Pygmies of the Congo.*

Young, Frank W., and Albert Bacadayan. (1967) "Menstrual Taboos and Social Rigidity." In *Cross-Cultural Approaches*, edited by Clellan S. Ford, 95–110.

TAOISM

Meaning "the Way," Taoism is one of the two religious philosophies, along with Confucianism, that has shaped Chinese life for the last two thousand years. Taoism originated in ancient China during the period of Warring States (481–221 B.C.E.) as a philosophy. It is very difficult to describe Taoist concepts in Western terms because Taoism is about defining the undefinable. Tao is the cosmic force behind all phenomena. It later evolved into a religion with many different manifestations and dominated China for several centuries before being supplanted by Buddhism. Taoism still has many adherents throughout the world and its philosophy remains an important influence in Asia and has a growing following in many other parts of the world.

Historic Development

Taoism dates back to the period of Warring States in China and received influences from many different philosophies developing then. Lao Tzu is considered the founder of Taoism, based on his teachings described in the Tao Te Ching. It is unclear whether Lao Tzu was a legendary or historic figure. The classic Chinese book Chuang Tzu, which is named after its author, states that Lao Tzu was a Taoist master who was an elder contemporary of Confucius in the third century B.C.E. Another account in the *Shih-chi* (Historical Records) from the Chinese Classic period states that Lao Tzu was an archivist in the royal court and met Confucius before heading west, never to be heard from again. Modern scholars question whether Lao Tzu even existed.

Nonetheless, the Tao Te Ching and later writings by Chuang Tzu provided the foundation for a philosophical Taoism that came to dominate imperial courts throughout much of China until the second century when a religious form of Taoism evolved in the province of Szechuan. Chiang Ling claimed to receive a revelation from Lao Tzu, who instructed him to implement his "orthodox and sole doctrine of the authority of the covenant." Chiang Ling later ascended to Heaven and earned the title Heavenly Master. A succession of followers, also called Heavenly Masters, founded an independent organization to instruct the faithful on the work of Lao Tzu, with an emphasis on teaching the right actions and good works. In C.E. 215, Chiang Ling's grandson Chang Lu gave allegiance to the Wei dynasty, thus giving Taoism imperial recognition as an organized religion.

Heavenly Masters often acquired influential roles in Chinese courts as intermediaries between the ruler and the people. By 300, most of the powerful families in northern China had become adherents to Taoism and before long religious Taoism was being imposed on southeastern China. As Taoism spread, the Heavenly Masters practiced increasingly diverse and elaborate ceremonies and rituals, including hygienic and respiratory techniques, exorcisms, and other activities. The founders of the Tang (618–907) and Ming (1368–1644) dynasties often followed Taoist practices. The founder of the Tang dynasty, Li Yuan, said he was a descendent of Lao Tzu and was accepted by Taoists as the fulfillment of messianic prophecy. Taoism became the ideology of the state. Despite its widespread growth, however, religious Taoism never established a central authority. Taoism became a scattering of different sects, all of which looked back to Lao Tzu as their founder, but many of which placed different emphases on the scriptures and observed independent ritualistic ceremonies.

The spread of Buddhism in China heavily influenced Taoism, which in turn also influenced Buddhist practices (some Taoists believe that Lao Tzu became Buddha when he ventured west from China). The continuing interaction between the two belief systems created a situation in which many Chinese consider themselves to be both Buddhists and Taoists.

老子

Taoism's founder, perhaps a legendary figure, perhaps a historic figure, Lao Tzu, a contemporary of Confucius, is frequently depicted riding an ox and carrying a scroll.

Taoist philosophy remains an important influence in the daily life of much of Asia. Religious Taoism is not nearly as widespread as it once was other than in Taiwan, where the religion has enjoyed a renaissance in recent years.

Texts

There is a vast quantity of sacred Taoist literature dating throughout its history. The founding document is Tao Te Ching, which traditionalists say was written by Lao Tzu. The anthology, which is believed to have been written between the sixth and fourth centuries B.C.E. is a collection of paradoxical statements on the nature of Tao (the Way). The text lays out the five fundamental principles of Taoism: Tao, relativity, nonaction, return,

and government. Chuang Tzu, named after its author, is considered to be the other fundamental Taoist scripture. Written in the third or fourth century B.C.E., the text describes Taoist philosophy and includes accounts of "spirit journeys," descriptions of Taoist Masters and disciples, and techniques on breathing, meditation, sexual activity, and diets.

Two other significant texts are the T'ai-p'ing Ching (Classic of the Great Peace) and the Pao P'u Tzu (Master Embracing Simplicity). Both were written in the third and fourth centuries and describe ways for Taoists to seek immortality through special diets, sexual activities, and alchemical substances.

Beliefs and Practices

Tao is a single, imperceptible, formless state that underlies both being and nonbeing. It is a purposeless, amoral, and impersonal cosmic entity that serves as the underpinning for everything that exists. "Look it cannot be seen—it is beyond form," states the Tao Te Ching. "Listen, it cannot be heard—it is beyond sound. Grasp, it cannot be held—it is intangible."

The concept of nonaction as representing the natural course of things is a fundamental belief in Taoism, though this does not mean that Taoists adhere to passive activities. Rather it refers to the constant interaction between the *yang* and the *yin*, two antithetical and complementary aspects of the Tao that create the natural order. The yang represents good, masculine, warmth, and positive principles. The yin represents cold, feminine, evil, and negative principles. However, the concept of relativity, or *chiao*, withholds any judgment of good and bad, large and small, or beauty and ugliness as absolutes. These are not polar opposites, but rather values placed by people depending on the individual circumstances of the person. What is cold for one person in Florida may be quite warm for an Alaskan resident, for example. All dualities, Chuang Tzu said, are not really opposites but identical aspects of the same reality.

The law of the Tao states that all phenomena go through a process of reversal in which they return to their original state. Since the Tao becomes everything, everything returns to the Tao. This return takes place through a constant transformation of each individual. Life is seen as an infinite process of change that makes human life immortal.

Tao religious practices are aimed at allowing people to discover the Tao through a wide variety of rituals and ceremonies. The goal is to strip a person of the cluttering outside influences that obstruct understanding of the cosmic Tao forces and allow him or her to become at one with the Tao. Taoists discourage passions and emotions that deflect the spiritual power of the Tao, and they encourage the mastery of the physical senses so that they can be used to focus on the Tao. The avenues for understanding are many. Perhaps the most important of the Taoist contemplative practices is the *shou-i* (or "meditating on the One") in visualization exercises of the heavenly bodies and planets. Other techniques involve breathing exercises, gymnastics, prescribed sexual practices, and alchemy (the Taoist search for different chemical compounds resulted in the discovery of gunpowder).

Religious Taoism has historically involved a highly organized system of ceremonies, temples, and priesthoods dating back to the second century that attracted all classes of Chinese society. The Heavenly Masters were a married, hereditary priesthood who oversaw the rituals. Some Taoist sects developed monasteries consisting of religious communities designed to facilitate everyday observance of Taoist meditation, liturgy, hygiene, and other matters.

The most important Taoist ceremony is the *chiao*, in which the community renews its communication with the gods. A chiao of three, five, or seven days is still celebrated in Taiwan. There are other chiao rites for the ordination of priests, the birthdays of gods, and the warding off of disasters. All chiao are celebrated on two levels: a feast in the village and a liturgy inside the closed temple. Incense-burning plays a significant role in the celebration of rituals. An incense burner is the central object in temples and is an essential part of all Taoist rites.

Welch, Holmes, and Anna Seidel, eds. (1979) *Facets of Taoism*. New Haven: Yale University Press.

TOTEMISM

Totemism is the customary belief that one's social group has a special relationship with some element of nature such as an animal, bird, plant, or physical feature. A totem is the specific feature of nature that is the object of the special relationship. Usually the totem is an animal or bird and less often a plant or feature of the landscape that is very common, or of considerable importance to the people, or one that possesses certain qualities considered desirable by the people. The word itself is from the Chippewa Indian word *ototeman*, the stem of which (*ote*) referred to a specialized form of relation among relatives. Totemism has drawn the attention of various social theorists from Emile Durkhiem, the founder of sociology, to Sigmund Freud, the founder of psychoanalysis, to the French anthropologist Claude Lévi-Strauss, all of whom have stressed the key role played by totemism in the evolution, structure, and functioning of human societies. While totemism does exist in different cultures around the world, there is no one type of totemism and across cultures totemism takes a wide variety of forms. Totemism in somewhat different forms is most common in Australian aboriginal societies and among Native American cultures in North and South America, but is also found elsewhere around the world, including Africa and South Asia.

The major beliefs and practices associated with totemism in these cultures (although the distribution of these beliefs and practices varies widely across cultures) are the association of a specific group with a specific animal, bird, plant, or natural feature; a belief that the group is descended from its totem; the group naming itself after its totem; a belief that a supernatural spirit appears in the form of the totem; a rule that people show respect for their totem and do not kill or harm it; various taboos associated with the totem such as not eating it; the carving and display of symbols of association with the totem; and the requirement that people marry outside their totem group—that is, one must marry someone who comes from a group associated with a different totem. Across cultures, the only three features shared by all cultures with totemic beliefs are (1) an association with a specific feature of nature; (2) the totem is the object of association for a specific social group such as a clan (a kinship group composed of people descended from a common ancestor) or a fraternal organization; and (3) totemism has a strong emotional component for members of the group. The second cross-cultural feature of totemism—association with a specific social group—is often played out across cultures in the assigning of the name of the totem to the group. For example, the Santal of northern India have nine totemic clans (and among these, twenty-two totemic subclans):

Besra	Hawk
Hasdak	Wild Goose
Hembram	Betel Palm
Marndi	Grass
Murmu	Nilgai

Saren	Pleiades
Pauria	Pigeon
Chore	Lizard
Bedea	Sheep

The emotional component tends to be played out in ritual behavior that symbolizes the importance of the totem to the group and the individual. For example, the Ganda of Uganda prohibit the eating of the totem animal and plant and believe that the child of someone who violates the prohibition will develop a rash. Similarly the Kapauku of New Guinea prohibit people from eating and burning totemic plants and to avoid becoming deaf by violating the prohibition, Kapauku men hire men from the neighboring Ijaaj group to clear their garden plots.

Totemism is especially common among the aboriginal peoples of Australia and takes a variety of forms. Individual totemism involves one person and his or her ties to a feature of nature. In sex totemism the male and female members of a culture each have different totems, which tends to reinforce a rigid division between men and women. In moiety totemism the entire culture is divided into two groups, with each group having its own totem. In section totemism, each of the primary kin groups in the culture has its own totem. In clan totemism, which is also common among native peoples of the New World, all members of each clan share the same totem—hence names such as Bear Clan, Wolf Clan, and Raven Clan. In local totemism, people who reside in the same territory and share a spiritual attachment to it share the same totem. Finally, some cultures are characterized by multiple totemism, in which a number of the above types coexist.

The most important types in traditional aboriginal cultures were those such as section and clan totemism in which identification with the same totem united smaller groups into larger ones for ritual and other purposes. Traditional aboriginal societies were composed of small, nomadic bands, a number of which through ties of kinship and marriage formed larger groups known as clans. Each clan had a unique totem—an animal or plant—took its name from the totem, and could not harm the totemic plant or animal. The totem represented the relationship among the supernatural, nature, and human beings. In addition, a particular totem was a clan's emblem and the totemic design was carved on sacred stone or wood slabs and some members of the clan scarified their bodies with the design in order to enhance their own ties to the supernatural and the group.

In North America, many native cultures also had totems, which were thought of as guardians or protectors of the person or group adopting the totem. In addition, in some cultures such as the Iroquois in New York State, clans were identified by totemic names and persons were required to marry persons from outside their own clan. In some cultures persons were born into the totemic group while in others affiliation was by individual choice. For example, among the Omaha, anyone who had seen a bear during his personal vision quest became a member of the Bear Society. Some groups in the Northwest, such as the Haida and Tlingit, displayed their totemic emblems on totem poles, which when placed in front of their houses identified the residents as members of a particular totemic group.

Another form of totemism is cult totemism, which is more individualistic and involves an individual's personal choice to associate himself or herself with a particular totem. Cult totemism reflects an individual's desire to bring some aspect of nature into his or her life and in the contemporary world is reflected in the use of the names of animals or birds in the names of fraternal organizations such as the Loyal Order of Moose or the Elks Lodge and in the names of sports teams such as the Chicago Bears, Seattle Seahawks, or Michigan Wolverines.

Biswas, P. C. (1956) *Santals of the Santal Parganas.*

Child, Alice B., and Irvin L. Child. (1993) *Religion and Magic in the Life of Traditional Peoples.*

Hodge, Frederick W. (1959) *Handbook of American Indians North of Mexico.*

Lessa, William A., and Evon Z. Vogt, eds. (1965) *Reader in Comparative Religion: An Anthropological Approach,* 2d ed.

Mair, Lucy P. (1935) "Totemism among the Baganga." *Man* 35: 66–67.

Malefijt, Annemarie de Waal. (1968) *Religion and Culture: An Introduction to the Anthropology of Religion.*

Pospisil, Leopold J. (1963) *Kapauku Papuan Economy.*

Vision quests of all types are an important means of interacting with the supernatural world and obtaining supernatural power among Native American peoples of North America (and to a lesser extent South America as well), although there is much variation in the actual components of the quest and its purposes both across and within cultures. For example, cultures on the Plains and in the Northwest used deliberate quests to obtain power, while in California cultures only some individuals were visited by spirits, usually in dreams, and only they obtained spirit guardians. The vision quest was also an important component of training to become a healer in many Native American and Siberian cultures. Highly romanticized and idealized images of Native American vision quests have in the last decades become prominent in the New Age movement, although their use in this context seems more geared toward self-discovery and control over one's life than in obtaining supernatural power. Elsewhere in the world, other methods of gaining supernatural power—such as through obtaining and learning to use sacred objects, ceremonies, taking a human life, or as a gift received from the supernatural—are more common than vision quests.

VISION QUEST A vision quest is the deliberate seeking of supernatural power through experiences that enable an individual to see or hear a supernatural being, usually a spirit. A key feature of vision quests is that once the person acquires supernatural power, he or she may use that power without having to call again upon the assistance of the spirits. Sometimes also classified as vision quests are experiences where a person sees or hears a spirit, without deliberately seeking to do so. In these situations, however, the person does not usually obtain supernatural power but rather a spirit guardian whom he or she can call upon in times of need. For example, the Aymara of Peru do not engage in vision quests, but individuals who become religious practitioners, which requires the ability to communicate with the spirits, obtain their status through a vision. The vision usually takes place in a remote region when the person is knocked unconscious by lightning and upon regaining consciousness recalls his vision and tells others about it.

Key elements of Native American vision quests are indicated by the quests of the Ojibwa of the Great Lakes region, the Klamath of Oregon, and the Tlingit of the Alaskan coast. Among the Ojibwa, the vision quest began when a boy reached the appropriate age—when his soul had become fully "awake." His father built him a small hut some distance from the family wigwam where the boy went to pray and sleep each night, attempting to receive his vision during a dream. The father would also offer advice about which spirit his son should try to contact; if the father had enjoyed a successful life, he, of course, wanted his son to have a vision experience with the same spirit who had guided him. During the day the boy continued his usual

251

routine around the camp, although he fasted or only drank liquids. Some boys had visions quickly, others took days or even months, and some never had one. Those who failed to have a vision because they were too young or for other reasons would become ill and required healing before attempting another vision. Failure to have a vision was a serious matter as it meant that the soul and body would not be able to work in harmony. A boy who failed to obtain a vision through fasting and dreaming in the hut might sleep for several nights on the grave of a famous warrior or healer in order to contact the soul of the deceased, which would aid him from the afterlife.

For the Klamath, the vision quest is an activity open to all and most people engage in many quests throughout their lives. The first one is undertaken at puberty, although it may not succeed. Throughout one's life quests are often taken during difficult times, such as following the death of a parent, spouse, or child. They may also be taken to achieve or renew one's status as a healer or to gain spiritual assistance in hunting, marriage, gambling, and other undertakings. Quests take a variety of forms and may involve sweating, fasting, hiding in the woods, running until exhausted, praying, diving in water, and singing. Diving in particular pools of water is common, as certain spirits are known to inhabit certain pools. The quest might involve a vision but must always involve a song received during a dream that the seeker sings upon awakening. Subsequent quests are not to contact the same, but, rather, different spirits.

The Tlingit rely on the vision quest to train and initiate those who become healers:

> Nobody is born to be an Indian doctor. They got to do certain things. Any man wants to be a good Indian doctor has to go in the woods. He has another man to watch over him and take care of him—his sidekick. Sometimes he [the latter] would become a doctor himself, if he wanted to. Any tribe,

when an Indian doctor dies, his nearest relative, brother or nephew, has to become an Indian doctor himself, whether he likes it or not. (de Laguna 1972: 674)

The Tlingit recognize that someone is well suited to become a healer by the songs they sing that show a link to specific spirits whose powers are used by the healers. Once identified as a potential healer, the novice is placed under the supervision of men who had served as assistants to the previous healer. Since the role of healer is hereditary, they are often not in line to inherit the role but are responsible for training the new healer, which includes vision quests. Quests are undertaken not just as part of the training but subsequently to renew one's power and to meet and derive additional power from other spirits. Before the quest, the novice or healer and his assistants must refrain from sexual relations and during the quest they must fast or limit intake of food and liquids. A typical quest and contact with the spirits is described as follows:

> His spirit starts coming to him. These shamans go out in the woods and don't eat. Sometimes they get small as a baby when they get back. They cut a tongue [of an animal]. These animals drop dead when they get there—they don't kill them. They cut the tongue and put it away where nothing can bother it. And the spirit of the animal is his yek [spirit]. They split the side of the tongue—just split it on the side, and wrap it up good. If they don't do it right, the man will get crazy, insane. But he got to live right. If he don't, he just get a lot of trouble. (de Laguna 1972: 676)

As these three samples show, the purpose of a vision quest is to establish contact with a spirit so as to acquire supernatural power or supernatural protection. While the details vary, quests generally involve isolation from the community, guidance by elders, and negative consequences if one fails to have a vision. In most cultures, it is men who go on vision quests. When women participate, it is often in a more limited manner—to gain protection rather than power, and by obtaining visions through dreams.

See also SHAMANISM.

Child, Alice B., and Irvin L. Child. (1993) *Religion and Magic in the Life of Traditional Peoples*.

de Laguna, Frederica. (1972) *Under Mount Saint Elias: The History and Culture of the Yakutat Tlingit*.

Jenness, Diamond. (1935) *The Ojibwa Indians of Parry Island: Their Social and Religious Life*.

Spier, Leslie. (1930) *Klamath Ethnography*.

Tschopik, Harry, Jr. (1951) *The Aymara of Chucuito, Peru: 1. Magic*. Anthropological Papers of the American Museum of Natural History 44: 133–308.

A witch is inherently evil and has direct access to the supernatural world and through this supernatural access can cause harm. In some cultures, such as the Azande in Africa, people believe that a witch acts consciously in causing misfortune, although persons accused of witchcraft rarely confess and are surprised upon being accused of being a witch. In other cultures, such as the Tlingit in North America, a witch is believed to act without conscious control of her actions and is not aware of being a witch.

Witchcraft differs from sorcery, although the two are often confused. Sorcery, unlike witchcraft, requires the use of a ritual specialist (called a sorcerer, shaman, medicine man, or witch doctor) who through his or her knowledge of formulae and rituals can direct supernatural power. Sorcerers, unlike witches, cannot simply cause supernatural forces to affect the lives of the living by wishing them to. While it is possible to discuss sorcery and witchcraft as separate phenomena, in reality the two are often closely linked in two ways. First, the types of misfortunes caused by both—illness, death, crop failures, and so on—are often the same and thus, from the perspective of the victim, it makes little difference whether the cause was sorcery or witchcraft. Second, the steps taken to prevent or cure the effects of sorcery or witchcraft often require the use of a sorcerer who is able to prevent or reverse the work of a witch or another sorcerer.

The attribution of at least some misfortune to witchcraft is found in 58 percent of societies. Cultures like the Garo in India, where no one "... gives a moment's thought to being himself endangered by witchcraft" are in the minority around the world. In cultures with a belief in witchcraft, witchcraft belief always involves witchcraft attribution as people believe it to be a cause of at least some illnesses, accidents, deaths, and other misfortunes. In some cultures witchcraft might not just cause specific misfortunes

WITCHCRAFT

Witchcraft is about jealousy, envy, anger, and getting even. In many cultures it is a way that people cause misfortune to happen to others. The Azande of Africa say that if "his condition is bad" witchcraft is present. Azande witchcraft beliefs are typical of many cultures in the range of misfortune that is attributed to witches:

> A man's ground-nuts [peanuts] are blighted. What does he say? He says, "It is witchcraft. Witchcraft has spoilt my ground-nuts." A man's wife falls ill. What does he say? He says, "Witchcraft has injured my wife." A man is told by the poison oracle that his journey is inauspicious. What does he say? He says, "Witchcraft has spoilt my journey." A man has a nightmare. What does he say? He says, "I have been bewitched in a dream." (Evans-Pritchard 1937: 100)

A witch (a witch is a female, a male witch is called a warlock) is someone who can cause harm to an individual, a family, or even an entire community by simply wishing the harm to take place.

to befall someone but may lead to a more general state of harm. The Tlingit, for example, say "You're not yourself when that witch spirit comes on you. You don't even know what you're doing." (de Laguna 1972: 733) Witchcraft is not distributed evenly among the cultures of the world; it occurs far more commonly in societies bordering the Mediterranean Sea, in sub-Saharan Africa, and in communities in the New World formed by descendants of immigrants from the Mediterranean region. It has been suggested that witchcraft beliefs began in Mesopotamia as beliefs in the evil eye and protective formulae were present among the Babylonians at least as early as 1750 B.C.E. Witchcraft beliefs were also fairly common in traditional Native American cultures, although unusual elsewhere in the world and virtually absent in East Asia.

Cross-Cultural Patterns

Across cultures, witchcraft beliefs share a number of common features. First, there is always the delineation of a category of persons as witches and a list of personal characteristics that identify these individuals as witches. Across cultures, witches are of two types—everyday and nightmare. Everyday witches are people who live within the community in which they cause misfortune, although they are often not full members of the community, as they may be individuals descended from people from another community, are of mixed ancestry, or are foreigners. For example, among the Tzeltal of Guatemala, people who have recently settled in a village are more likely to be accused of witchcraft than are longtime residents. Across cultures individuals are accused of being witches by others in the community because of their antisocial behavior (they live alone, eat alone, are unsociable), which often leads others in the community to dislike them. The Tzeltal, for example, often say that someone who is widely disliked is a witch, while someone who is popular is said to be *suente*, the possessor of good luck, which, like witchcraft, has supernatural origins. In some cultures a person's eyes mark that individual as a witch because they stare at others, in other cultures because they never look another in the eye, and in many cultures because their eyes are red. Everyday witches cause misfortune because they are envious of the good fortune of others in the community.

Nightmare witches are inherently evil and violate all rules of social behavior. They prowl or fly about at night doing their damage, unlike normal people who do their work during the day and sleep at night. They turn themselves into animals forms, feast on the flesh of the dead, move rapidly, and engage in wild orgies. They often work their evil by inserting foreign objects into the bodies of their victims. And, unlike everyday witches, they are not people who live in the community but come instead from somewhere else—from the sky, the supernatural world, or the forest. For example, the Toradja of Indonesia believe that nightmare witches live in their own villages outside the communities where normal people live.

In some cultures people believe in only one type of witch—nightmare or everyday—while in other cultures people believe in both types or even a variety of witch types. The Toradja believe in three types: *tau mepongko*, which operate day and night; *tau mebutu*, which operate at night only; and *to lambunu*, who come from outside the community and appear in human form asking for assistance and when not properly received eat the liver of the individual denying them their wish or perhaps even the livers of all inhabitants of the village. In a few cultures witches are believed to be hereditary. The Tlingit believe that witches recruit children to help them gain access to the personal possessions of people in the household and that this witchcraft role is passed on from one generation to the next.

While it generally assumed that most witches are women, across cultures it seems that men and women are about equally likely to be accused of being witches or of being the source of supernatural misfortune, although women are more likely to be considered the most threatening type of witch.

Second, in all cultures with witchcraft, there is a list of misfortunes attributed to witches. In a sample of 186 societies, witchcraft was the predominant cause of illness in 4 percent, an important secondary cause in 10 percent, and a minor cause in 14.5 percent. In addition to illness, witches also cause all other sorts of misfortune including crop failures, death of livestock, a bad marriage, a difficult pregnancy, and accidents. In all cultures with witchcraft belief, some misfortunes experienced by individuals are attributed to witchcraft and in some cultures widespread misfortune, such as a drought or an epidemic, is also attributed to witches.

Third, it is generally believed that witches are motivated by envy and fear. In this regard, witchcraft is much like other forms of supernatural aggression, such as the use of sorcery for evil purposes or the evil eye, in that people often believe that those most likely to be bewitched are those who have personal traits that are envied by others, such as wealth or beauty.

Fourth, it is believed that witches do their work in secret and often at night. The Wolof of Senegal believe that *doma* (witches) may attack in a number of ways: (a) in animal form so as to frighten the victim so that he or she cannot speak and they can then enter the victim's body through the throat; (b) by poisoning the victim's food or drink; or (c) by touching the victim—"They are always your friend; some day one will make you laugh and slap you on the back. The spot where he slapped you swells and you die." (Ames 1959: 267)

Fifth, in all cultures witches are not fully human in that their evil power is innate and is supernatural in origin and in that they can alter their physical appearance. Across cultures a common belief is that witches can appear as animals, reptiles, birds, or insects.

Sixth, it is believed that witches reverse the normal rules of behavior and behave in ways that are not socially acceptable, such as by causing harm or operating at night.

Seventh, witchcraft is always disapproved and rarely discussed with outsiders because of the seriousness of accusing an individual of being a witch, the fear of being accused oneself, and the misfortune that results from witchcraft.

Eighth, in all cultures there are means to protect oneself from witches and to reverse the misfortune they have caused. In many cultures people use protective devices to prevent witch attacks from ever occurring. The Toradja use charms worn on clothing or attached to cradles or placed in cavities in their teeth. The Wolof wear amulets and repeat prayers from the Quran in the belief that witches fear God. Iroquois False Face Societies hold pubic rituals to remove disease, storms, witches, and bad luck from the village. In addition, the Iroquois believe that the best way to protect oneself is to behave in an inconspicuous manner so as to avoid making anyone jealous. The Tzeltal seek to prevent witch attacks by confining their relationships mainly to compadres who are not likely to feel envious.

Short of prevention, in some cultures people watch for signs that help them detect the presence of a witch. The Tlingit know a witch is present by the sound of its footsteps, which sound like cracking ice, while the Toradja believe a witch is present when the tengko bird calls at night instead of day, when a dog repeatedly shows its teeth, or a cat meows at odd times.

Despite efforts to prevent witches from attacking or to detect and avoid them, witches are often successful in causing misfortune. When this happens, the only alternative is to take action to undo the misfortune, which in most cultures and most situations requires the skill and knowledge of a ritual specialist who is often called a shaman, medicine man, witch doctor, sorcerer, or curer. Sometimes the specialist is a general practitioner who deals with all supernatural matters, not just witchcraft, in other cases he or she might be a witchcraft specialist. For example, the Santal in India have three types of practitioners: *Ojha*, who have the power to reverse all types of evil; *Sakha* (sorcerers), who can identify witches; and the *Jan Guru*, who are specially trained to find witches.

These ritual specialists work by either performing rituals that reverse the misfortune or by identifying the witch. Ritual reversal often takes the form of curing the illness caused by the witch, which often involves removing the foreign object placed in the victim's body by the witch. For example, Iroquois specialists would use poultices applied to the body, massage, and sucking cures to remove objects such as balls of fur or stones from the victim's body. In many cultures successful treatment is often followed by rituals designed to protect the victim from future attacks. Tzeltal curers, for example, place crosses on the bedposts and doorway to blind the witch if she tries to return. Specialists also employ ritual methods, including consulting oracles, ordeals, and prayer, in order to call upon supernatural assistance in identifying witches. For example, Tlingit specialists would kill a mouse slowly and observe the members of the community, as the one who exhibited the same suffering as the mouse was the witch. The Turkana of East Africa have three ways of identifying witches. First, witches are thought to have unusual eyes, although in what way they are unusual is not easily described. Second, if one puts one's hand over one's mouth and pulls it away quickly, the name of the witch will be spoken. Third, a diviner can be consulted to discover the name of the witch. Once the witch is identified, the victim can ascertain why he was

bewitched or seek compensation from or revenge on the accused witch.

As a last resort in some cultures, witches are killed. The Iroquois, for example, would kill only witches who caused great damage or were beyond rehabilitation. When a witch is killed, the concern is that he or she be completely destroyed—the rationale for burning witches or for the Tzeltal practice of hacking the body into dozens of pieces.

Many of the essential features of witchcraft as it exists in contemporary societies are displayed by small-town Mexican-Americans in rural southern Texas. Bewitchment is the most serious of diseases and a matter the people are reluctant to discuss with outsiders. A belief in witchcraft is strongest among lower-class and lower-middle-class adults and generally dismissed as unimportant or ridiculed by those in the upper class and children. Believers fear both male and female witches (*brujo*), with female witches more common. Witches can fly and often take the form of an animal, usually a cat or an owl. The signs that one has been bewitched include a chronic illness, mental illness, insomnia, and misfortune that soon follows good fortune. Although many are suspected, a witch is rarely identified and accusations are made only after a person dies or leaves town. A person who is a witch can act directly while a nonwitch will hire a witch to place a hex. Witches act out of envy (this is why misfortune after good fortune is attributed to witchcraft), sexual jealousy, and to revenge a real or perceived offense. The hex can be removed by identifying the witch and getting her to remove it, or more often by retaining a specialist to reverse the hex, or by destroying an object thought to cause the hex, such as a dead toad or bat.

Causes

Social scientists assume that witchcraft is not "real" but is a creation of the human imagination. This view contrasts with that of people who believe in witchcraft, who instead experience it as quite real and view it as a daily part of their lives. Explanations that seek to explain the causes of witchcraft across cultures focus on the functions of witchcraft beliefs and its role in society.

Anthropologist Clyde Kluckhohn studied witchcraft among the Navajo extensively and suggests the following function of witchcraft:

> . . . witchcraft is a potential avenue to supernatural power. Power seems to be an important central theme in Navaho culture of which gaining wealth, disposing of enemies, and even, to some extent, obtaining possession of women are merely particular examples. (1944: 85)

Kluckhohn's description applies equally well to many other cultures, as does his conclusion that:

> Since most hostile impulses must to greater or lesser extent be suppressed, there is a need in every society for hate satisfaction. But unless there are some forms of hating which are socially acceptable and justified, everyone will remain in an intolerable conflict situation, and neuroticism will be endemic in the population. (Ibid.: 86)

Thus, witchcraft serves three purposes: it helps maintain social order by providing an outlet for aggression, it marks individuals who are different and therefore are not full members of the group, and it alleviates individual stress that might result from unexpressed anger.

Social explanations for witchcraft emphasize the presence of "unlegitimized social relationships" among people in societies where witchcraft attribution occurs. These are relationships in which people interact closely, work toward common goals, but do not necessarily enter into these relationships willingly,

and where disputes cannot be resolved in commonly agreed-upon ways. Unlegitimized relationships tend to occur in communities when any of the following conditions obtain: marriage partners typically come from other communities, there are conflicts between the generations, people are differentiated on the basis of wealth or social status, one group in the community is the conqueror of the other group, individuals owe allegiance to more than one competing group, and there are no duly recognized individuals or councils with the authority to settle disputes. All of these conditions may produce feelings of jealousy, envy, rivalry, and mistrust, which lead to anger and feelings of aggression that are manifested in wishes to cause others harm and the expectation that others will cause oneself harm. As the people live close to one another in small communities and must interact peacefully on a daily basis, the expression of anger must be indirect and hidden, as in witchcraft.

In some cultures witchcraft works to control and channel this anger and aggression through witchcraft accusation. When something goes wrong in the community, a person is accused of being a witch and killed, thus relieving tension in the community by transferring community anger to a scapegoat. This was exactly the situation in the Salem, Massachusetts, witchcraft hysteria of 1692, when hundreds were accused and twenty were executed as witches. Community harmony was disrupted by deep disputes about civil versus church authority, morality, and wars with the local Indians leading to a breakdown of traditional legal procedures and the resulting scapegoating of local citizens. While the accused individuals suffered, the trials provided a needed outlet for stress in the community.

See also EVIL EYE; SORCERY; SUPERNATURAL EXPLANATIONS FOR ILLNESS.

Ames, David W. (1959) "Belief in 'Witches' among the Rural Wolof of the Gambia." *Africa* 24: 263–273.

Burling, Robbins. (1963) *Rengsanggari: Family and Kinship in a Garo Village.*

de Laguna, Frederica. (1972) *Under Mount Saint Elias: The History and Culture of the Yakutat Tlingit.*

Downs, Richard E. (1956) *The Religion of the Bare'e-Speaking Toradja of Central Celebes.*

Evans-Pritchard, E. E. (1950) *Witchcraft, Oracles, and Magic among the Azande.* 2d ed.

Gray, J. Patrick. (1979) "The Universality of the Female Witch." *International Journal of Women's Studies* 2: 541–550.

Gulliver, Philip H. (1951) *A Preliminary Survey of the Turkana: A Report Compiled for the Government of Kenya.*

Hunt, Muriel E. V. (1958) *The Dynamics of the Domestic Group in Tzeltal Villages: A Contrastive Comparison.*

Kluckhohn, Clyde. (1944) *Navaho Witchcraft. Papers of the Peabody Museum of American Archaeology and Ethnology* 22 (2).

Mair, Lucy. (1969) *Witchcraft.*

Marwick, Max, ed. (1970) *Witchcraft and Sorcery.*

Masden, William, and Andre Guerrero. (1973) *Mexican-Americans of South Texas.*

Mukherjea, Charulal. (1962) *The Santals.*

Murdock, George P. (1980) *Theories of Illness: A World Survey.*

Naroll, Raoul, Gary L. Michik, and Frada Naroll. (1976) *Worldwide Theory Testing.*

Nash, June. (1970) *In the Eyes of the Ancestors: Belief and Behavior in a Maya Community.*

———. (1967) "Death as a Way of Life: The Increasing Resort to Homicide in a Maya Indian Community." *American Anthropologist* 69: 455–470.

Swanson, Guy E. (1968) *The Birth of the Gods: The Origin of Primitive Beliefs.*

Wallace, Anthony F. C. (1972) *The Death and Rebirth of the Seneca.*

Whiting, Beatrice B. (1950) *Paiute Sorcery.*

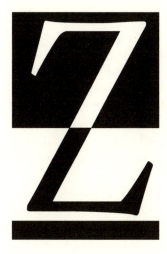

was marked by several miracles. Instead of crying at birth, he was laughing. When a cattle stampede nearly trampled him as a boy, a bull stood over him to protect Zoroaster from death. Similarly, a stallion protected him from runaway horses.

When, as a priest, the thirty-year-old Zoroaster was attending a spring festival preparing for a *haoma* ritual, he saw an angel who led him to the ancient Iranian god Ahura Mazada and the five Immortals. This was the first of several revelations in which Zoroaster was instructed by Ahura Mazada to preach the true religion. In the face of intense hostility from other priests because of his condemnation of their orgy-like rituals and self-serving practices, Zoroaster preached for only one decade and could only claim one convert, his cousin Maidhyoimah. His big opportunity, however, came at the age of forty-two when King Vishtaspah was willing to listen to Zoroaster after he cured one of his royal horses of paralysis. Vishtaspah and his royal court became believers and helped spread the religion throughout Persia and as far as China.

Zoroastrianism declined when Alexander the Great conquered Persia in 330 B.C.E. and burned Persepolis, the royal capital, and destroyed the definitive copy of Zoroastrian scripture, Avesta. Alexander's arrival and the subsequent contacts with Greek and Middle Eastern cultures, however, led to an intermingling of cultures with long-lasting implications. The Magi who visited the Christian Virgin Mary for the birth of Jesus Christ, for example, are believed to have been members of the Maga brotherhood, a group of influential Zoroastrian priests.

Zoroastrianism recovered during the Parthion period (247 B.C.E.–C.E. 227) and became the dominant religion of that era. Vologasses I (51–80) reconstructed the Avesta by gathering manuscripts and recording oral tradition in a new, definitive text. Zoroastrianism conflicted with several other religions during the Sassanid period (227–651), but nonetheless

ZOROASTRIANISM Founded in ancient Persia, Zoroastrianism heavily influenced the development of Judaism, Christianity, and Islam. Concepts such as heaven and hell, the resurrection of the body, the arrival of the Messiah, judgment at death, and the Armageddon battle at the end of this era are believed to originate from Zoroastrianism. Despite its heavy influence in these major religions, there are only about 200,000 Zoroastrians today, largely in Iran and also India, where they are called Parsis. The Parsi community has had a disproportionate influence in India because of the high levels of education attained by Parsis and their roles as business and political leaders.

Historical Development

Zoroaster, a trained priest in ancient Persia during the seventh and sixth centuries B.C.E., is traditionally considered the founder of Zoroastrianism, although many scholars question the time period during which he lived and some doubt that he is a real historical figure. Born in what is now Azerbaijan, Zoroaster's childhood served as an important influence until the Arab Muslims conquered the Persian Empire in 651. Islamic rulers clamped down on Zoroastrianism, forcing many people to convert. A small community of Zoroastrians has remained in what is now Iran to this day. In the eighth and ninth centuries a group of Zoroastrians fled to India. Known as the Parsis, they settled in the Bombay area and have became a very important influence in India despite numbering fewer than 100,000. Parsis place a very high emphasis on education and tend to be professionals or business people.

Religious Beliefs

Zoroaster's visions revealed a new religion that placed Ahura Mazada (meaning "Wise Lord") as the supreme god, a departure from the polytheistic religions of the time, which envisioned networks of multiple gods and devils. For Zoroastrians, Ahura Mazada is an eternal source of goodness and the creator of all being.

Zoroaster viewed humanity as a constant struggle between good and evil, represented by the two offspring of Ahura Mazada. The beneficent spirit Spenta Mainyu and the hostile spirit Angra Mainyu explain the origins of good and evil. They represent the prototypes of the moral judgments between good and evil that individuals must make during their lives. Zoroastrians assist in the battle of good over evil through the pursuit of "good thoughts, good words and good deeds." At the end of a person's life, he or she is judged according to the choices they made. In the morning after the third night after the person's death, the soul leaves the body and is taken by the angel Sorush to the judgment tribunal (*aka*). The soul must then cross the Chinvat bridge. Those whose lives have been righteous cross the bridge without incident to heaven, accompanied by a beautiful young woman or handsome man. But for those who have led sinful lives, the bridge narrows to the width of a razor's edge and the person falls into

hell. Thus, each person is free to choose his or her own destiny in Zoroastrianism. The pursuit of good thoughts, words, and deeds is accomplished by individuals through God's gifts to mankind: body, soul, and mind, the most important of which is mind. There is no course for atonement in Zoroastrianism. Eternal salvation is determined by decisions made here and now. The pursuit of goodness is considered a reward in itself.

Zoroastrians view history as four distinct three-thousand-year periods. During the first trimillennium, the primary forces of good were dormant. But at the era's conclusion, Ahriman—the principal source of all evil—saw the light of good and ascended from his dark domain. He prepared to unleash his army of wizards and agents of sin into the good world but Ahura Mazada struck a deal in which Ahura Mazada would rule for the second trimillennium and Ahriman for the third. The fourth and final era would consist of a struggle between the two for mastery. But Ahura Mazada tricked Ahriman during his three-thousand-year period by creating animals and humans to act as his agents, and by sending Zoroaster to muster their forces on behalf of good. Ahriman retaliated by digging a great hole to serve as hell and creating people with evil thoughts and wicked desires. Men from the two sides will clash in a final, immensely destructive conflict until so many soldiers will be killed that a "thousand women will seek to kiss one man." In the final great battle of Armageddon, Ahura Mazada will ultimately triumph. Ahriman and his followers will descend into the pit of hell to be annihilated in flames, everything will be destroyed, and a new universe will be created in which Ahura Mazada rules supreme.

Texts

The sacred scriptures of Zoroastrianism are known as the Avesta. It consists of four writings: (1) the Yasna, a collection of prayers that contains a group of hymns called the Gathas,

Zoroaster, founder of Zoroastrianism, according to D.F. Karaka from an 1884 history of the Persian religion, which dates from the seventh or sixth century B.C.E. Presently there are some 200,000 adherents, most of whom live in Iran and India, where they are known as Parsis.

written by Zoroaster; (2) the Visparat, written as an invocation to the celestial lords; (3) the Khorde Avesta, a book of daily prayers; and (4) the Videvdat, a series of writings concerned mainly with ritual purification.

Observances

All Zoroastrian children participate in an initiation ceremony when they are between seven and ten years of age called *naojote*, in which they pledge their devotion to the religion and become responsible for honoring Zoroastrian duties. The ceremony, which is overseen by a Zoroastrian priest, includes a recital of the articles of faith, which include the pledge to "praise good thoughts, good words and good deeds." This pursuit embodies a purity of thoughts, words, and deeds that is assisted through a series of purification rituals. The *padyab* is a form of absolution performed daily. *Nahn* consists of a bath observed on special occasions such as holy days, naojote, or marriage. Priests must go through a complicated ritual known as *bareshnum* that lasts several days. Those who have come into contact with a corpse perform a *riman* ritual to cleanse themselves.

Fire is extremely important in Zoroastrianism. It represents purity, light, warmth, and power. It is the central symbol in Zoroastrian temples and it is present in all Zoroastrian homes. The fire in people's homes must be constantly lit. One of the most egregious sins is to put out the fire.

As part of the purification rites, Zoroastrians historically placed a person's body after death on the top of a *dakhma*, or Tower of Silence. Zoroastrians consider a corpse to be very polluted and want to hasten its decomposition. Stripped of its clothing, the body would be exposed to the sun and vultures. This practice is no longer used and instead the body is placed on a metal stretcher and placed in a cement box so that dirt does not fall on the body.

Sects

The historical developmental experience of Zoroastrianism has lead to three different groupings of Zoroastrians in Iran, India, and a smaller group in Tadjikstan with differing customs. The biggest difference between religious sects, however, does not concern theology, but rather the dates for celebrating seasonal festivals. The three groups are the Shenshahi, Qadimi, and Fasli.

Boyce, Mary. (1971) "Zoroastrianism." In *Historia Religionum: Handbook for the History of Religions*, edited by C. Jouco Bleeker and George Widengren, vol. 2, 211–236.

Gnoli, Gherardo. (1986) "Zoroastrianism." In *The Encyclopedia of Religion*, edited by Mircea Eliade, vol. 15, 579–591.

Kulke, Eckehard. (1976) *The Parsees in India: A Minority as Agent of Social Change.*

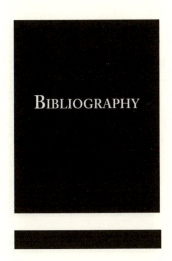

BIBLIOGRAPHY

Adams, Kathleen M. (1993) "The Discourse of Souls in Tana Toraja (Indonesia): Indigenous Notions and Christian Conceptions." *Ethnology* 32: 55–68.

Ahern, Emily M. (1973) *The Cult of the Dead in a Chinese Village.*

———. (1976) "The Power and Pollution of Chinese Women." In *Studies in Chinese Society,* edited by Arthur P. Wolf, 269–290.

Ahmad, Imatiaz, ed. (1981) *Ritual and Religion among Muslims in India.*

Alford, Richard D. (1988) *Naming and Identity: A Cross-Cultural Study of Personal Naming Practices.*

Allison, Robert W. (1992) "Mount Athos." In *Encyclopedia of World Cultures. Vol. 4: Europe.* Edited by Linda Bennett, 174–177.

Ames, David W. (1959) "Belief in 'Witches' among the Rural Wolof of the Gambia." *Africa* 24: 263–273.

Ames, Michael M. (1964) "Magical-Animism and Buddhism: A Structural Analysis of the Sinhalese Religious System." *Journal of Asian Studies* 23: 21–52.

Appleton, George, et al. (1985) *The Oxford Book of Prayer.*

Apter, Andrew. (1991) "Herskovits's Heritage: Rethinking Syncretism in the African Diaspora." *Diaspora* 1: 235–260.

Arens, W. (1979) *The Man-Eating Myth: Anthropology and Anthropophagy.*

Arguelles, Jose. (1992) *Mandala.*

Atkinson, Jane M. (1992) "Shamanisms Today." *Annual Review of Anthropology* 21: 307–330.

Avery, Jeanne. (1982) *The Rising Sign: Your Astrological Mask.*

Baity, Philip C. (1975) *Religion in a Chinese Town.*

Balzer, Marjorie M., ed. (1990) *Shamanism: Soviet Studies of Traditional Religion in Siberia and Central Asia.*

Barrett, David B. (1994) "Annual Statistical Table on Global Mission: 1994." *International Bulletin of Missionary Research* 18: 24–25.

Barrett, David B., ed. (1982) *World Christian Encyclopedia: A Comparative Study of Churches and Religions in the Modern World, A.D. 1900–2000.*

Barrett, Leonard. (1977) *The Rastafarians: The Dreadlocks of Jamaica.*

Barry, Herbert III, and Alice Schlegal, eds. (1980) *Cross-Cultural Samples and Codes.*

Barton, Roy F. (1946) *The Religion of the Ifugao.*

Basso, Keith H. (1970) *The Cibecue Apache.*

Bastide, Roger. (1960) *The African Religions of Brazil: Toward a Sociology of Interpretation of Civilizations.* Translated by H. Sebba.

Benz, Ernst. (1963) *The Eastern Orthodox Church: Its Thought and Life.*

Bhardwaj, Surinder M. (1973) *Hindu Places of Pilgrimage in India.*

Bilu, Yorum. (1985) "The Woman Who Wanted To Be Her Father: A Case Analysis of Dybbuk Possession in a Hasidic Community." *The Journal of Psychoanalytic Anthropology* 8: 11–27.

Birth, Kevin K. (1994) "Bakrnal: Coup, Carnival, and Calypso in Trinidad." *Ethnology* 33: 165–177.

Biswas, P. C. (1956) *Santals of the Santal Parganas.*

Bodine, John. (1979) "Taos Pueblo." In *Handbook of North American Indians*, edited by Alfonso Ortiz, vol. 9, 255–267.

Bogoras, Waldemar. (1904–1909) *The Chukchee.*

Bohannan, Paul, and Laura Bohannan. (1957) "Tiv Markets." *Transactions of the New York Academy of Sciences*, Series II, 19: 613–621.

———. (1969) *A Source Notebook on Tiv Religion in Five Volumes.*

Bourguignon, Erika. (1973) *Possession.*

Bourguignon, Erika, ed. (1973) *Religion, Altered States of Consciousness, and Social Change.*

Bowden, Henry W. (1981) *American Indians and Christian Missions: Studies in Cultural Conflict.*

Bradfield, Richard M. (1973) *A Natural History of Associations.*

Braha, James T. (1986) *Ancient Hindu Astrology for the Modern Western Astrologer.*

Brennan, Richard P. (1992) *Dictionary of Scientific Literacy.*

Broude, Gwen J. (1994) *Marriage, Family and Relationships: A Cross-Cultural Encyclopedia.*

———. (1995) *Growing Up: A Cross-Cultural Encyclopedia.*

Brown, Paula, and Donald Tuzin, eds. (1983) *The Ethnography of Cannibalism.*

Buechler, Hans C., and Judith M. Buechler. (1971) *The Bolivian Aymara.*

Bunnag, Jane. (1973) *Buddhist Monk, Buddhist Layman: A Study of Urban Monastic Organization in Central Thailand.*

Burling, Robbins. (1963) *Rengsanggari: Family and Kinship in a Garo Village.*

Burridge, Kenelm. (1991) *In the Way: A Study of Christian Missionary Endeavours.*

Cameron, Barbara. (1981) *Mahabote: The Little Key.*

———. (1984) *Turning the Tables: A Mitigation Manual.*

Carneiro, Robert L. (1964) "The Amahuaca and the Spirit World." *Ethnology* 3: 6–11.

Carrington, Patricia. (1977) *Freedom in Meditation.*

Carroll, Michael P. (1975) "Revitalization Movements and Social Structure: Some Quantitative Tests." *American Sociological Review* 40: 389–401.

———. (1979) "The Sex of Our Gods." *Ethos* 7: 37–50.

Cather, Willa, and Georgine Milmine. (1993) *The Life of Mary Baker Eddy and the History of Christian Science.*

Chagnon, Napoleon A. (1968) *Yanomamö: The Fierce People.*

Chan, W. T. (1963) *A Sourcebook on Chinese Philosophy.*

Child, Alice B., and Irvin L. Child. (1993) *Religion and Magic in the Life of Traditional Peoples.*

Christensen, James B. (1954) *Double Descent among the Fanti.*

Cipriani, Lidio. (1966) *The Andaman Islanders.* Translated by D. Taylor Cox.

Clark, Charles A. (1932) *Religions of Old Korea.*

Cobb, John B., Jr. (1960) *Varieties of Protestantism.*

Cohen, Yehudi A. (1964) *The Transition from Childhood to Adolescence: Cross-Cultural Studies of Initiation Ceremonies, Legal Systems, and Incest Taboos.*

———. (1968) "Macroethnology: Large-Scale Comparative Studies." In *Introduction to Cultural Anthropology*, edited by James A. Clifton, 402-448.

Cohn, Norman. (1957) *The Pursuit of the Millenium.*

Cohn-Sherbok, Dan. (1992) *The Blackwell Dictionary of Judaica.*

Colby, Kenneth M. (1963) "Sex Differences in Dreams of Primitive Tribes." *American Anthropologist* 65: 1116–1122.

Collinder, Bjorn. (1949) *The Lapps.*

Constantelos, Demetrios J. (1990) *Understanding the Greek Orthodox Church: Its Faith, History and Practice.*

Courlander, H., and Rémy Bastien, eds. (1966) *Religion and Politics in Haiti.*

Cox, Harvey. (1995) *Fire from Heaven: The Rise of Pentecostal Spirituality and the Reshaping of Religion in the Twenty-first Century.*

Crapo, Rickley H. (1990) *Cultural Anthropology: Understanding Ourselves and Others.*

Cross, F. L., ed. (1993) *The Oxford Dictionary of the Christian Church.*

Culshaw, W. J. (1949) *Tribal Heritage: A Study of the Santals.*

DaMatta, Roberto. (1991) *Carnival, Rogues, and Heroes.*

Danforth, Loring M. (1989) *Fire Walking and Religious Healing.*

Davis, William D. (1974) *Societal Complexity and the Nature of Primitive Man's Conception of the Supernatural.*

de Coppet, Daniel, ed. (1992) *Understanding Rituals.*

de Groot, Jan Jacob Maria. (1912) *Religion in China: Universism. A Key to the Study of Taoism and Confucianism.*

de Laguna, Frederica. (1972) *Under Mount Saint Elias: The History and Culture of the Yakutat Tlingit.*

de Silva, Alcionilio Bruzzi Alves. (1962) *The Indigenous Civilization of the Uaupes.*

DeGlopper, Donald R. (1974) *City on the Sands: Social Structure in a Nineteenth-Century Chinese City.*

Densmore, Frances. (1929) *Chippewa Customs.*

Diamond, Norma J. (1969) *K'un Shen: A Taiwan Village.*

Dieterlen, Germaine. (1951) *An Essay on the Religion of the Bambara.* Translated by Katia Wolf.

Dirks, Robert. (1988) "Annual Rituals of Conflict." *American Anthropologist* 90: 856–870.

Dorsey, George A. (1940) "Notes on Skidi Pawnee Society." *Field Museum of Natural History, Anthropological Series* 27: 65–119.

Douglas, Mary T. (1966) *Purity and Danger: An Analysis of the Concepts of Pollution and Taboo.*

Downs, Richard E. (1956) *The Religion of the Bare'e-Speaking Toradja of Central Celebes.*

Dundas, Paul. (1992) *The Jains.*

Dundes, Alan, ed. (1981) *The Evil Eye; A Folklore Casebook.*

Eliade, Mircea. (1964) *Shamanism: Archaic Techniques of Ecstasy.* Translated by Willard R. Trask.

———. (1969) *Immortality and Freedom.*

———. (1977) *From Primitives to Zen.*

Eliade, Mircea, ed. (1987) *The Encyclopedia of Religion.*

Elliot, C. (1969) *Japanese Buddhism.*

Ember, Carol R., and David Levinson. (1992) "The Substantive Contributions of World-wide Cross-Cultural Studies Using Secondary Data." *Behavior Science Research* 25: 79–140.

Encyclopedia of Islam. 2d ed. (1954–).

Encyclopedie de la Divination. (1965).

Erling, Jorstad, ed. (1973) *The Holy Spirit in Today's Church: A Handbook of the New Pentecostalism.*

Esposito, John L. (1995) *The Oxford Encyclopedia of the Modern Islamic World.*

Esslemont, J. E. (1980) *Baha'u'llah and the New Era.* First published in 1923.

Evans-Pritchard, E. E. (1950) *Witchcraft, Oracles, and Magic among the Azande.* 2d ed.

Falassi, Alessandro, ed. (1987) *Time Out of Time.*

Fenton, William N. (1962) "This Island, the World is on the Turtle's Back." *Journal of American Folklore* 75: 283–300.

Ferndon, Edwin N. (1981) *Early Tahiti as the Explorers Saw It.*

Filipovic, Milenko S. (1954) "Folk Religion among the Orthodox Population in Eastern Yugoslavia." *Harvard Slavic Studies* 2: 359–374.

Firth, Raymond. (1939) "The Analysis of Mana: An Empirical Approach." *The Journal of the Polynesian Society* 48: 483–510.

———. (1939) *Primitive Polynesian Economy.*

Ford, Clellan S., and Frank A. Beach (1951) *Patterns of Sexual Behavior.*

Forrest, Steven. (1984) *The Inner Sky, The Dynamic New Astrology for Everyone.*

Foster, Michael K. (1974) *From the Earth to Beyond the Sky: An Ethnographic Approach to Four Longhouse Iroquois Speech Events.*

Frayser, Suzanne G. (1985) *Varieties of Sexual Experience.*

Frazer, James G. (1880) *The Golden Bough: A Study in Magic and Religion.*

Freedman, Maurice. (1958) *Lineage Organization in Southeastern China.*

Friedrich, Paul, and Norma Diamond, eds. (1994) *Encyclopedia of World Cultures. Vol. 6. Russian and Eurasia/China.*

Garg, Ganga Ram. (1992) *Encyclopedia of the Hindu World.*

Gennep, Arnold Van. (1960 [1909]) *The Rites of Passage.*

Gillies, Eva. (1995) "Zande." In *Encyclopedia of World Cultures. Vol. 9. Africa and the Middle East,* edited by John Middleton and Amal Rassam, 397–400.

Gladwin, Thomas, and Seymour Sarason. (1953) *Truk: Man in Paradise.*

Glasse, Cyril. (1989) *The Concise Encyclopedia of Islam.*

Glazier, Michael, and Monika K. Hellwig. (1994) *The Modern Catholic Encyclopedia.*

Glock, Charles Y., and Robert N. Bellah. (1976). *The New Religious Consciousness.*

Gluckman, Max. (1954) *Rituals of Rebellion in South-East Africa.*

Gomes, Edwin H. (1911) *Seventeen Years among the Sea Dyaks of Borneo: A Record of Intimate Association with the Natives of the Bornean Jungles.*

Gough, Elizabeth K. (1969) "Caste in a Tanjor Village." In *Aspects of Caste in India, Ceylon, and North-west Pakistan,* edited by Edmund R. Leach, 11–60, 147–148.

Gray, J. Patrick. (1979) "The Universality of the Female Witch." *International Journal of Women's Studies* 2: 541–550.

Griaule, Marcel. (1938) *Dogon Games.*

Gross, Daniel R. (1971) "Ritual and Conformity: A Religious Pilgrimage to Northeastern Brazil." *Ethnology* 10: 129–148.

Grottanelli, Vinigi L. (1969) "Gods and Morality in Nzema Polytheism." *Ethnology* 8: 370–405.

Gulliver, Philip H. (1951) *A Preliminary Survey of the Turkana: A Report Compiled for the Government of Kenya.*

Hallowell, A, Irving. (1942) *The Role of Conjuring in Salteaux Society.*

Halpern, Joel. (1958) *A Serbian Village.*

Handy, E. S. Craighill. (1923) *The Native Culture of the Marquesas.* Bernice P. Bishop Museum, Bulletin No. 9.

Harner, Michael. (1977) "The Ecological Basis for Aztec Sacrifice." *American Ethnologist* 4: 117–135.

———. (1982) *The Way of the Shaman: A Guide to Power and Healing.*

Harrell, C. Stevan. (1979) "The Concept of Soul in Chinese Folk Religion." *Journal of Asian Studies* 3: 519–528.

Harrell, Clyde Stevan. (1983) *Belief and Unbelief in a Taiwan Village.*

Harris, Marvin. (1977) *Cannibals and Kings: The Origins of Cultures.*

———. (1985) *The Sacred Cow and the Abominable Pig.*

Hart, David M. (1976) *The Aith Waryaghar of the Moroccan Rif.*

Heider, Karl G. (1990) *Grand Valley Dani: Peaceful Warriors.* 2d ed.

Herskovits, Melville J. (1966) *The New World Negro: Selected Papers in Afroamerican Studies.* Bloomington: Indiana University Press.

Hickey, Gerald C. (1964) *Village in Vietnam.*

Hieb, Louis A. (1979) "Hopi World View." In *Handbook of North American Indians. Vol. 9. Southwest,* edited by Alfonso Ortiz, 577–580.

Hodge, Frederick W. (1959) *Handbook of American Indians North of Mexico.*

Howell, William. (1908–1910) *The Sea Dyak.*

Hsu, Francis L. K. (1948) *Under the Ancestors' Shadow.*

Hultkranz, Åke. (1992) *Shamanic Healing and Ritual Drama: Health and Medicine in Native North American Religious Traditions.*

Humphreys, Christmas. (1984) *A Popular Dictionary of Buddhism.*

Hunt, Muriel E. V. (1958) *The Dynamics of the Domestic Group in Tzeltal Villages: A Contrastive Comparison.*

Ingersoll, Jasper C. (1969) *The Priest and the Path: An Analysis of the Priest Role in a Central Thai Village.*

Jaini, Padmanabh S. (1979) *The Jaina Path of Purification.*

Janelli, Dawnhee Yim, and Roger L. Janelli. (1982) *Ancestor Worship in Korean Society.*

Jenness, Diamond. (1922) *The Life of the Copper Eskimos.*

———. (1935) *The Ojibwa Indians of Parry Island, Their Social and Religious Life.*

Jochelson, Waldemar. (1933) "The Yakut." *Anthropological Papers of the American Museum of Natural History* 33(2): 33–335.

Jones, Marc Edmund. (1972) *Astrology: How and Why It Works.*

Jordan, Mary Kate. Personal communication.

Justinger, Judith M. (1978) *Reaction to Change: A Holocultural Test of Some Theories of Religious Movements.*

Kalland, Arne. (1996) "Geomancy and Town Planning in a Japanese Community." *Ethnology* 35: 17–32.

Kamal, Ahmad. (1961) *The Sacred Journey.*

Kane, Steven M. (1979) *Snake Handlers of Southern Appalachia.*

Karsten, Rafael. (1955) *The Religion of the Samek: Ancient Beliefs and Cults of the Scandinavian and Finnish Lapps.*

Kaufman, Howard. (1960) *Bangkhuad: A Community Study in Thailand.*

Kemp, Phyllis. (1935) *Healing and Ritual: Studies in the Technique and Tradition of the Southern Slavs.*

Kendall, Laurel. (1985) *Shamans, Housewives, and Other Restless Spirits: Women in Korean Ritual Life.*

Khanna, Ashok, and Pramesh Ratnakar. (1988) *Banaras: The Sacred City.*

Kluckhohn, Clyde. (1944) *Navaho Witchcraft. Papers of the Peabody Museum of American Archaeology and Ethnology* 22 (2).

Knez, Eugene I. (1970) *Sam Jong Dong: A South Korean Village.*

Kollek, Teddy, and Moshe Pearlman. (1970) *Pilgrims to the Holy Land.*

Kopytoff, Igor. (1971) "Ancestors as Elders in Africa." *Africa* 41: 129–142.

Kraemer, Augustin. (1932) *Truk.*

Krauss, Friedrich S. (1888) *Yakut Shamanism.*

Lagae, C. R. (1926) *The Azande or Niam-Niam.*

Lambrecht, Francis. (1954) "Ancestor's Knowledge among the Ifugaos and Its Importance in the Religious and Social Life of the Tribe." *Journal of East Asiatic Studies* 3: 359–365.

Lantenari, Vittorio. (1963) *The Religions of the Oppressed: A Study of Modern Messianic Cults.*

Lattimore, Owen. (1941) *Mongol Journeys.*

Leach, E. R. (1972) *Political Systems of Highland Burma.*

Leavitt, Gregory C. (1995) "Incest Taboo." In *Encyclopedia of Marriage and the Family, Vol. 2*, edited by David Levinson, 374–378.

Leighton, Dorothea C., and John Adair. (1966) *People of the Middle Place.*

Léonard, Émile C. (1965–1968) *A History of Protestantism.*

Lessa, William A., and Evon Z. Vogt, eds. (1965) *Reader in Comparative Religion: An Anthropological Approach.* 2d ed.

Lesser, Alexander. (1933) *The Pawnee Ghost Dance Hand Game.*

Levine, Donald N. (1965) *Wax and Gold: Tradition and Innovation in Ethiopian Culture.*

Levinson, David. (1989) *Family Violence in Cross-Cultural Perspective.*

Levinson, David, and Marilyn Ihinger-Tallman. (1995) "Marriage Ceremonies." In *Encyclopedia of Marriage and the Family*, edited by David Levinson, 466–468.

Levinson, David, and Martin J. Malone. (1980) *Toward Explaining Human Culture.*

Levy, Robert I. (1973) *Tahitians: Mind and Experience in the Society Islands.*

Lewis, Oscar. (1965) *Village Life in Northern India.*

Lindenbaum, Shirley. (1972) "Sorcerers, Ghosts, and Polluting Women: An Analysis of Religious Belief and Population Growth." *Ethnology* 11: 241–253.

Lodge, Olive. (1941) *Peasant Life in Jugoslavia.*

Lofthus, Myrna. (1980) *A Spiritual Approach to Astrology.*

Ludlow, Daniel H., ed. (1992) *Encyclopedia of Mormonism.*

Lumholtz, Carl. (1902) *Unknown Mexico: A Record of Five Years' Exploration of the Western Sierra Madre; in the Tierra Caliente of Tepic and Jalisco; and among the Tarascos of Michoacan.*

McBrien, Richard P. (1995) *The HarperCollins Encyclopedia of Catholicism.*

McCreary, John L. (1974) *The Symbolisms of Popular Taoist Magic.*

McDaniel, June. (1989) *The Madness of the Saints: Ecstatic Religion in Bengal.*

MacDougall, Robert D. (1971) *Domestic Architecture among the Kandyan Sinhalese.*

McLeod, W. H. (1990) *The Sikhs.*

Mair, Lucy P. (1935) "Totemism among the Baganga." *Man* 35: 66–67.

———. (1969) *Witchcraft.*

Malefijt, Annemarie de Waal. (1968) *Religion and Culture: An Introduction to the Anthropology of Religion.*

Malinowski, Bronislaw. (1935) *Coral Gardens and Their Magic.*

Maloney, Clarence, ed. (1976) *The Evil Eye.*

March, Arthur C. (1986) *A Glossary of Buddhist Terms.*

Marett, Robert R. (1909) *The Threshold of Religion.*

Marshall, Donald S. (1950) *Cuna Folk: A Conceptual Scheme Involving the Dynamic Factors of Culture, as Applied to the Cuna Indians of Darien.* Unpublished manuscript, Harvard University.

Marty, Martin E. (1973) *Protestantism.*

Marwick, Max, ed. (1970) *Witchcraft and Sorcery.*

Masden, William, and Andre Guerrero. (1973) *Mexican-Americans of South Texas.*

Masters, William M. (1953) *Rowanduz: A Kurdish Administrative and Mercantile Center.*

Matthews, John. (1992) *The World Atlas of Divination.*

Melton, J. Gordon, Jerome Clark, and Aidan A. Kelly. (1990) *New Age Encyclopedia.* 1st ed.

Messing, Simon D. (1957) *The Highland Plateau Amhara of Ethiopia.*

Miller, Carol. (1975) "American Rom and the Ideology of Defilement." In *Gypsies, Tinkers, and Other Travelers,* edited by Franham Redhfisch, 41–54.

Miller, Elmer. (1980) *Harmony and Dissonance in Argentine Toba Society.*

Mills, Watson E. (1985) *Speaking in Tongues: A Guide to Research on Glossolalia.*

Minc, L., and K. Smith. (1989) "The Spirit of Survival: Cultural Responses to Resource Variability in Alaska." In *Bad Year Economics: Cultural Responses to Risk and Uncertainty,* edited by Paul Halstead and John O'Shea, 8–39.

Mischel, Walter, and Frances Mischel. (1958) "Psychological Aspects of Spirit Possession." *American Anthropologist* 60: 249–260.

Montellano, Bernard R. Ortiz de. (1978) "Aztec Cannibalism: An Ecological Necessity?" *Science* 200: 611–617.

Mooney, James. (1965 [1896]) *The Ghost-Dance Religion and the Sioux Outbreak of 1890.* Edited and abridged by Anthony F. C. Wallace.

Moore, Marcia, and Mark Douglas. (1948) *Astrology: The Divine Science.*

Moore, Omar K. (1957) "Divination—A New Perspective." *American Anthropologist* 59: 69–74.

Moore, Sally F., and Barbara G. Myerhoff, eds. (1977) *Secular Ritual.*

Mukherjea, Charulal. (1962) *The Santals.*

Murdock, George P. (1934) *Our Primitive Contemporaries.*

———. (1980) *Theories of Illness: A World Survey.*

Murie, James. (1914) *Pawnee Indian Societies.*

Murphy, Joseph. (1988) *Santería: An African Religion in America.*

Myerhoff, Barbara. (1974) *Peyote Hunt: The Sacred Journey of the Huichol Indians.*

Naroll, Raoul, Gary L. Michik, and Frada Naroll. (1976) *Worldwide Theory Testing.*

Nash, June. (1967) "Death as a Way of Life: The Increasing Resort to Homicide in a Maya Indian Community." *American Anthropologist* 69: 455–470.

———. (1970) *In the Eyes of the Ancestors: Belief and Behavior in a Maya Community.*

Neill, Stephen. (1986) *A History of Christian Missions.* Revised for the Second Edition by Owen Chadwick.

The New Age Catalogue: Access to Information and Sources. (1991).

Ngubane, Harriet. (1977) *Body and Mind in Zulu Medicine.*

Nigosian, S. A. (1994) *World Faiths.*

Nivison, D. S., and A. F. Wright, eds. (1959) *Confucianism in Action.*

Nordenskiöld, Erland. (1938) *An Historical and Ethnological Survey of the Cuna Indians.*

O'Connell, Joseph, et al., eds. (1988) *Sikh History and Religion in the Twentieth Century.*

Otterbein, Charlotte S., and Keith F. Otterbein. (1973) "Believers and Beaters: A Case Study of Supernatural Beliefs and Child Rearing in the Bahama Islands." *American Anthropologist* 75: 1670–1681.

Pagès, G. (1933) *A Hamitic Kingdom in the Center of Africa: In Ruanda on the Shores of Lake Kiva (Belgian Congo).*

Park, George K. (1963) "Divination and Its Social Contexts." *Journal of the Royal Anthropological Institute of Great Britain and Ireland* 93: 195–209.

Parman, Susan M. (1972) *Sociocultural Change in a Scottish Crofting Township.*

Paulme, Denise. (1940) *Social Organization of the Dogon (French Sudan).*

Peel, Robert. (1989) *Health and Medicine in the Christian Science Tradition: Principle, Practice, and Challenge.*

Pennick, Nigel. (1979) *The Ancient Science of Geomancy.*

Phillips, James M., and Robert T. Coote, eds. (1993) *Toward the 21st Century in Christian Mission.*

Picken, Stuart D. B. (1994) *Essentials of Shinto: An Analytical Guide to Principal Teachings.*

Pierson, Donald. (1967) *Negroes in Brazil: A Study of Race Contact at Bahia.*

"Pilgrimage." (1987) *Encyclopedia of Religion*, edited by Mircea Eliade. Vol. 11, 327–354.

Playfair, A. (1909) *The Garos.*

Pospisil, Leopold J. (1958) *Kapauku Papuans and Their Law.*

———. (1963) *Kapauku Papuan Economy.*

Price, Barbara J. (1978) "Demystification, Enriddlement, and Aztec Cannibalism: A Materialist Rejoinder to Harner." *American Ethnologist* 5: 98–115.

Putnam, Patrick. (1948) "The Pygmies of the Ituri Forest." In *A Reader in General Anthropology*, edited by Carlton S. Coon, 322–342.

Radcliffe-Brown, A. R. (1922) *The Andaman Islanders: A Study in Social Anthropology.*

Rathburn, Robert R. (1976) *Processes of Russian-Tlingit Acculturation in Southeastern Alaska.*

Rattray, R. S. (1927) *Religion and Art in Ashanti.*

Reyna, Stephen P. (1995) "Sara." In *Encyclopedia of World Cultures. Vol. 9. Africa and the Middle East*, edited by John Middleton and Amal Rassam, 304–307.

Reynolds, Barrie. (1957) *Magic, Divination and Witchcraft among the Barotese of Northern Rhodesia.*

Richards, Audrey I. (1939) *Land, Labour, and Diet in Northern Rhodesia: An Economic Study of the Bemba Tribe.*

―――. (1956) *Chisungu: A Girls' Initiation Ceremony among the Bemba of Northern Rhodesia.*

Richardson, Don. (1988) "Do Missionaries Destroy Cultures?" In *Tribal Peoples and Development Issues: A Global Overview,* edited by John H. Bodley, 116–121.

Roberts, John M. (1967) "Oaths, Autonomic Ordeals, and Power." In *Cross-Cultural Approaches,* edited by Clellan S. Ford, 169–195.

Rogers, Erik N. (1976) *Fasting: The Phenomenon of Self-Denial.*

Rohner, Ronald P. (1975) *They Love Me, They Love Me Not.*

Roscoe, John. (1911) *The Baganda: An Account of Their Native Customs and Beliefs.*

Rosenblatt, Paul C., R. Patricia Walsh, and Douglas A. Jackson. (1976) *Grief and Mourning in Cross-Cultural Perspective.*

Rossbach, Sarah. (1984) *Feng Shui.*

Rowe, David N. and Willmoore Kendall, eds. (1954) *China: An Area Manual.*

Sahlins, Marshall. (1979) "Cannibalism: An Exchange." *New York Review of Books* 26: 45–47.

Salamone, Frank A. (1974) *Gods and Goods in Africa.*

Sanday, Peggy R. (1986) *Divine Hunger: Cannibalism as a Cultural System.*

Schaden, Egon. (1962) *Fundamental Aspects of Guarani Culture.*

Selby, John. (1992) *Kundalini Awakening: A Gentle Guide to Chakra Activation and Spiritual Growth.*

Serpenti, I. M. (1965) *Cultivators in the Swamps.*

Shankman, Paul. (1969) "Le Rôti et le Bouilli: Lévi-Strauss' Theory of Cannibalism." *American Anthropologist* 71: 54–69.

Shapiro, Judith. (1987) "From Tupa to the Land without Evil: The Christianization of Tupi-Guarani Cosmology." *American Ethnologist* 14: 126–139.

Sheils, Dean. (1975) "Toward a Unified Theory of Ancestor Worship: A Cross-Cultural Study." *Social Forces* 54: 427–440.

―――. (1980) "A Comparative Study of Human Sacrifice." *Behavior Science Research* 15: 245–262.

―――. (1980) "The Great Ancestors are Watching: A Cross-Cultural Study of Superior Ancestral Religion." *Sociological Analysis* 41: 247–257.

Shipps, Jan. (1984) *Mormonism: The Story of a New Religious Tradition.*

Siewert, John A., and John A. Kenyon, eds. (1993) *Mission Handbook: USA/Canada Christian Ministries Overseas.*

Silberbauer, George B. (1981) *Hunter and Habitat in the Central Kalahari Desert.*

Simpson, George E. (1971) "The Belief System of Haitian Vodun." In *Peoples and Cultures of the Caribbean,* edited by Michael M. Horowitz, 491–521.

Simpson, John H. (1984) *High Gods and the Means of Subsistence. Sociological Analysis* 45: 213–222.

Skinner, Elliot P. (1989) *The Mossi of Burkina Faso: Chiefs, Politicians, and Soldiers.*

Skrefsrud, Lars O. (1942) *Traditions and Institutions of the Santals: Hororen Mare Hapramko Reak' Katha.*

Somersan, Semra. (1981) *Death Symbolism: A Cross-Cultural Study.*

Soustelle, Jacques. (1962) *Daily Life of the Aztecs.* Translated by Patrick O'Brian.

Spier, Leslie. (1930) *Klamath Ethnography.*

Spiro, Melford. (1970) *Buddhism and Society: A Great Tradition and Its Burmese Vicissitudes.*

Steadman, Lyle B., and Charles F. Merbs. (1982) "Kuru and Cannibalism." *American Anthropologist* 84: 611–627.

Steadman, Lyle B., Craig T. Palmer, and Christopher F. Tilley. (1996) "The Universality of Ancestor Worship." *Ethnology* 35: 63–76.

Stegmiller, P. F. (1921) "The Religious Life of the Khasi." *Anthropos* 16: 407–441. Translated from the German for the Human Relations Area Files.

Strathern, Andrew. (1989) "Melpa Dream Interpretation and the Concept of Hidden Truth." *Ethnology* 28: 301–315.

Stutley, Margaret, and James Stutley. (1977) *Harper's Dictionary of Hinduism: Its Mythology, Folklore, Philosophy, Literature, and History.*

Suttles, Wayne. (1957) "The Plateau Prophet Dance among the Coast Salish." *Southwestern Journal of Anthropology* 13: 352–396.

Swanson, Guy E. (1968) *The Birth of the Gods: The Origin of Primitive Beliefs.*

Talmage, James E. (1976) *A Study of the Articles of Faith: Being a Consideration of the Principal Doctrines of the Church of Jesus Christ of Latter-Day Saints.* 51st ed.

Tatje, Terrence, and Francis L. K. Hsu. (1969) "Variations in Ancestor Worship Beliefs and Their Relation to Kinship." *Southwestern Journal of Anthropology* 25: 153–172.

Teksbury, William J. (1967) "The Ordeal as a Vehicle for Divine Intervention in Medieval Europe." In *Law and Warfare: Studies in the Anthropology of Conflict,* edited by Paul Bohannan, 267–270.

Tester, Jim. (1987) *A History of Western Astrology.*

Textor, Robert B. (1973) *Roster of the Gods: An Ethnography of the Supernatural in a Thai Village.*

Thompson, L. G. (1979) *Chinese Religion.* 3d ed.

Thompson, Laura. (1940) *Southern Lau, Fiji: An Ethnography.*

Thrupp, Sylvia L., ed. (1970) *Millennial Dreams in Action: Studies in Revolutionary Religious Movements.*

Titiev, Mischa. (1971) *Old Oraibi: Study of the Hopi Indians of the Third Mesa.*

Tonkinson, Robert. (1978) *The Mardudjara Aborigines: Living the Dream in Australia's Desert.*

Tripathi, B. D. (1978) *Sadhus of India.*

Tschopik, Harry Jr. (1951) *The Aymara of the Chucuito, Peru: 1. Magic.* Anthropological Papers of the American Museum of Natural History 44: 133–308.

Turnbull, Colin M. (1961) *The Forest People: A Study of the Pygmies of the Congo.*

———. (1965) *The Mbuti Pygmies: An Ethnographic Survey.*

Turner, Victor W. (1952) *The Lozi Peoples of North-Western Rhodesia.*

Turner, Victor W., and Edith Turner. (1978) *Image and Pilgrimage in Christian Culture.*

Turner, Victor W., ed. (1982) *Celebration: Studies in Festivity and Ritual.*

Tylor, Edward B. (1958) *Primitive Culture.* Originally published in 1871.

Van Esterik, John L. (1978) *Cultural Interpretation of Canonical Paradox: Lay Meditation in a Central Thai Village.*

Wallace, Anthony F. C. (1956) "Revitalization Movements." *American Anthropologist* 58: 264–281.

———. (1966) *Religion: An Anthropological View.*

———. (1972) *The Death and Rebirth of the Seneca.*

Walters, D. (1991) *The Fengshui Handbook.*

Wang, Hsing-ju. (1948) *The Miao People of Hainan Island.*

Waters, Frank. (1963) *Book of the Hopi.*

Watts, Alan. (1957) *The Way of Zen.*

Weekes, Richard V., ed. (1984) *Muslim Peoples: A World Ethnographic Survey.*

Welch, Holmes, and Anna Seidel, eds. (1979) *Facets of Taoism.* New Haven: Yale University Press.

Weltfish, Gene. (1965) *The Lost Universe: With a Closing Chapter on the Universe Regained.*

Werblowsky, R. J. Zwi, and Geoffrey Wigoder, eds. (1986) *The Encyclopedia of the Jewish Religion.* Rev. ed.

Whiteley, Wilfred. (1950) "Bemba and Related People of Northern Rhodesia." *Ethnographic Survey of Africa: East Central Africa.* Part II, 1–32, 70–76.

Whiting, Beatrice B. (1950) *Paiute Sorcery.*

Whiting, John W. M. (1967) "Sorcery, Sin and the Superego: A Cross-Cultural Study of Some Mechanisms of Social Control." In *Cross-Cultural Approaches*, edited by Clellan S. Ford, 147–168.

Whyte, Martin K. (1978) "Cross-Cultural Codes Dealing with the Relative Status of Women." *Ethnology* 17: 211–237.

Williams, Francis E. (1923) *The Vailala Madness and the Destruction of Native Ceremonies in the Gulf Division.*

Winkelman, Michael. (1986) "Magico-Religious Practitioner Types and Socioeconomic Conditions." *Behavior Science Research* 20: 17–46.

———. (1990) "Shaman and Other 'Magico-Religious' Healers: A Cross-Cultural Study of Their Origins, Nature, and Social Transformations." *Ethos* 18: 308–352.

Wolf, Arthur P. (1974) *Religion and Ritual in Chinese Society.*

Worsley, Peter. (1957) *The Trumpet Shall Sound.*

Wright, Robin M., and Jonathan D. Hill. (1986) "History, Ritual, and Myth: Nineteenth Century Millenarian Movements in the Northwest Amazon." *Ethnohistory* 33: 31–54.

Yalman, Nur. (1971) *Under the Bo Tree: Studies in Caste, Kinship, and Marriage in the Interior of Ceylon.*

Yogananda, P. (1946) *Autobiography of a Yogi, Self-Realization.*

Young, Frank W., and Albert Bacadayan. (1967) "Menstrual Taboos and Social Rigidity." In *Cross-Cultural Approaches*, edited by Clellan S. Ford, 95–110.

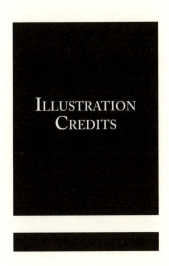

ILLUSTRATION CREDITS

16 UPI/Corbis-Bettmann

27 Corbis-Bettmann

35 Corbis-Bettmann

39 Corbis-Bettmann

44 Corbis-Bettmann

47 Paul Barker. Reuters/Corbis-Bettmann

54 Corbis-Bettmann

61 Corbis-Bettmann

71 Chandu Mhatre. Reuters/
Corbis-Bettmann

84 Corbis-Bettmann

93 Corbis-Bettmann

100 Corbis-Bettmann

105 Corbis-Bettmann

114 UPI/Corbis-Bettmann

130 UPI/Corbis-Bettmann

139 Library of Congress LC-USZ62-17351

155 UPI/Corbis-Bettmann

173 Corbis-Bettmann

183 Corbis-Bettmann

191 UPI/Corbis-Bettmann

197 UPI/Corbis-Bettmann

203 Gendreau Collection.
Corbis-Bettmann

214 Corbis-Bettmann

246 Corbis-Bettmann

263 From Karaka, D. F. (1884) *History of the Parsis*, Vol. II, 146. Corbis-Bettmann.

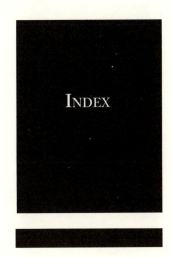

INDEX

Abbas Effendi, 24
Abraham, 94, 102
Abu Bakr, 92
Ainu, 7
Aleut, 134
Ali, 92
Allah, 93
Alms giving, 94
Alorese, 5
Amahuaca, 227, 230
Amaterasu, 213
American Firewalking Movement, 169
American Indians. *See specific groups*
Amhara, 36, 45, 74, 163–165, 183, 185
Amida Buddhism, 213
Amulets, 182, 183
Anabaptists, 172
Anastenaria, 169
Ancestor spirits, 230
Ancestor worship, 3–6, 119
Andamen Islanders, 34, 182, 242
Angad, Guru, 218
Anglican Church, 172, 173, 174, 175
Animals
    reincarnation as, 181
    sacrifice of, 201, 202–203

souls of, 224
spirits, 7–8
totemism, 247
Animatism, 7
Animism, 7–8, 236
Anointing the sick, 200
Apache, 45
Aquinas, Thomas, 199
Aranda, 113
Aranyakas, 83
Armageddon, 262
Asceticism, 9–13, 188
Ashanti, 233
Assemblies of God, 151
Astrology, 14–22
    applications of, 21–22
    growth-centered, 21–22
    houses of the zodiac, 19, 20
    Indian, 20–21
    planets and, 15, 18–19, 20
    signs of the zodiac, 16–18, 20
Atman, 85
Augustine of Hippo, 60, 199
Australian Aborigines, 45, 56, 228, 248
Avesta, 262
Avignon papacy, 196
Aymara, 115, 125, 222, 226, 251
Azande, 181, 255
Aztecs, 37, 205

Ba Chin, 73
Baganda, 182–183
Baha'i, 23
Baha'u'llah, 23–24
Balinese, 125, 203
Bambara, 204
Baptism, 64, 115–116, 200
    Holy Spirit and, 136, 149
Baptistic Pentecostalism, 151
Bar Mitzvah, 107
Bemba, 126, 204, 230, 242–243
Benedictines, 195
Bennett, Dennis, 152
Benson's Method, 132
Berber rituals, 110–113, 118
Bhavanaya meditation, 129

Bible, 38
    Judaism and, 104–106
    Protestantism and, 172, 174–175
    translation, 134–135, 172
    vernacular translation, 61, 134–135, 172
Birth chart (horoscope), 15
Birth rituals, 109–110, 113–114
Bishops, 63, 199
Black magic, 126
Bodhisattvas, 31
Book of Mormon, 141, 142
Brahma, 88
Brahman, 9
Brahman-Atman, 85
Brahmanas, 83
Brahmans, 177
Brahmo Samaj, 82
Breath spirit, 8
Breathing meditation, 131–132
Buddhism, 9, 25–31
    asceticism, 11
    beliefs, 29–30
    emanational mystical monotheism, 138
    festivals, 31, 72–73
    Hinduism and, 81
    history, 25–29
    meditation and, 129
    practices, 31
    priests, 187–188
    sects, 30–31
    Shintoism and, 28, 213, 215
    Taoism and, 245
    texts, 30
    Zen, 31, 132, 213
Burial, 4, 112

Calendar, Muslim, 91
Calvin, John, 172
Calvinism, 172, 173, 174
Candomblé, 161, 165–167, 237
Cannibalism, 33–37, 205
Cao Dai, 72, 73
Cardinals, 199
Cargo cults, 190, 192
Carib, 33
Carnival, 69, 73–74

Carrington, Patricia, 131, 132
Caste, 81, 86, 177–178
Catholic Church. See Roman Catholicism
Celibacy, 9, 10. See also Sexual restrictions
Central Thailand. See Thai cultures
Ceremonies. See Festivals; Rituals
Cerularios, Michael, 60
Charismatic missions, 136
Charismatic Pentecostalism, 149
Charity, 94
Chenchu, 225
Childhood, 114–116
Chiliastic cults, 190
China
    ancestor worship, 4
    Buddhism, 28
    Confucianism, 43–45
    cosmology, 48–49
    geomancy (feng shui), 77–79
    Taoism, 245–247
Chippewa, 64, 117, 120
Chrismation, 64
Christ. See Jesus Christ
Christian Science, 41–43, 150
Christianity, 38–41
    Hinduism and, 82
    missions, 133–137
    Shinto and, 215
    theistic dualism, 138
    See also Eastern Orthodox Christianity;
        Pentecostalism; Protestantism; Roman
        Catholicism
Christmas, 175, 200
Chuang Tzu, 246
Chukchee, 36, 185
Church of Australia, 174
Church of Christ, Scientist. See Christian Science
Church of Jesus Christ of Latter-Day Saints 136,
    141. See also Mormonism
Circumcision, 97, 106, 116–117
Clan totemism, 248
Clinically Standardized Meditation (CSM), 131
Code of Manu, 83
Communion, 64. See also Eucharist
Confession, 64, 200
Confirmation, 200
Conflict rituals, 74–75

Confucianism, 43–45
  Shintoism and, 213, 216
Confucius, 43–44
Congolese-Kinbangu cult, 190
Conservative Jews, 106
Constantine, 40, 59, 195
Contextualization 135
Copper Eskimo, 45
Cosmogeny, 45
Cosmology, 45–50
  Chinese, 48–49
  Hopi, 50
  Iroquois, 48
  San, 50
  Western vs. non-Western, 47–48
Counter Reformation, 196
Crisis cults, 190
Crusades, 41
Cult of the dead, 3
Cult totemism, 249
Cuna, 56, 125, 168, 230

Dahomeans, 224
Dani, 227
Dead Sea Scrolls, 103
Death, 119–120
  Berber rites, 112
  rituals, 219
  soul and, 224–225
  Zoroastrian rites, 264
  Zuni rites, 110
Demons, 232
Devils, 232
Dharma, 29
Diaspora, 103
Divali, 88
Divination, 53–55
  astrology, 14–22
  mediums and, 186
Dogon, 113, 148
Dome of the Rock, 95
Dreams, 55–58, 251. *See also* Vision quests
Dybbuk possession, 162
Dynamism, 7

East Syrian Orthodox Church, 60
Easter, 64, 175, 200

Eastern Orthodox Christianity, 38, 59–64
Ecclesiastes, 106
Economic magic, 126
Ecstatic divination, 53
Eddy, Mary Baker, 41–42, 150
Emanational mystical monotheism, 138
End of the world, 151
Epics, 83
Epiphany, 64, 200
Episcopal Church, 174
Eskimo, 8, 45, 134
Essenes, 103
Eucharist, 64, 199–200
Evangelical missions, 135
Evangelical movement, 174
Evil eye, 64–67, 110
Evolutionary theories of religion, 7
Exorcism, 162

Faith, 198
Fasli, 264
Fasting, 9–10
  Islam and, 94–95
Feng shui, 77–79
Festivals, 69–75
  Baha'i, 25
  Buddhist, 31
  Catholic, 200
  communitas, 69, 70
  Hindu, 70–72, 88–89
  inversion, 73–75
  Islamic, 97
  Jewish, 107
  Protestant, 175
  Serbian cycle, 70
  Shinto, 217
  Sikh, 219
  Taoist, 247
  Vietnamese, 72–73
Fetishes, 182–183
Fijians, 128
Finished Work Pentecostalism, 151
Fire-walking, 168, 169
Fon, 237
Food restrictions, 11–12, 209, 240, 242
Fore, 37
Forrest, Stephen, 22

Funeral rites, 4, 119
    cannibalism and, 35

Ganda, 186, 231, 235, 248
Gandhi, Indira, 82
Gandhi, Mahatma, 82, 84, 218
Garo, 3, 202, 255
Geomancy, 4, 77–79
Ghost Dance, 161, 190, 192
Ghosts, 227, 231–232, 235
    spirit possession, 162
    See also Spirits
Glossolalia, 150
Goajiro, 125
God
    Islam and, 93
    Judaism and, 102
    monotheism and polytheism, 138–140
    Sikhism and, 218
Godparents, 115, 116
Gods and goddesses, 226–229
    Hindu beliefs, 83, 85, 88
    polytheism, 138, 140
    Shinto, 213
Golden Temple, 218
Good Samaritan parable, 38
Gospels, 38
Greek Orthodox Christianity, 62
Growth-centered astrology, 21–22
Guarani, 10
Guardian soul, 224
Guardian spirits, 230
Guided meditation, 133
Guru Angad, 218
Guru Granth Sahib, 219
Guru Nanak, 217–218
Gurus, 189
Gusii, 5
Gypsy cultures, 47, 237
    marime system of purity and pollution, 177,
    178

Hadith, 96
Haida, 249
Hair-cutting ritual, 115
Halloween, 73
Hallucinogenic trances, 158, 161

Hanafi, 96
Hanbali, 96
Handsome Lake religion, 190
Hanukkah, 107
Hare Krishna movement, 82
Hasidicism, 104
Hausa, 134
Healers, 184, 185–187, 252
Healing, 127, 202, 206–207. *See also* Illness;
    Possession
Henry VIII, 173
Heresy, 40
Hermits, 11, 12
Herzl, Theodore, 104
Hesychasm, 61
Hinduism, 9, 81–89
    asceticism, 11, 12
    astrology, 15
    beliefs, 83–87
    caste system, 81, 86, 177–178
    emanational mystical monotheism, 138
    festival cycle (Rampur), 70–72
    history, 81–82
    meditation and, 129
    pollution concepts, 47
    practices, 88–89
    reincarnation beliefs, 182
    sects, 87–88
    Sikhism and, 217
    texts, 83
Hokkien, 181
Holi, 89
Holiness churches, 150–152
Holism, 145
Holly Rollers, 152
Holocaust, 104
Holy Spirit
    Eastern Orthodox Christianity and,
        60, 62, 63
    Pentecostalism and, 136, 149
    Trinity, 198
Holy war, 95
Hopi, 50, 70, 119, 158–159, 170–171
Horoscopes, 15, 21
Houses of the zodiac, 19, 20
Huguenots, 173
Huichol, 158

Human sacrifice, 201
Hus, J., 171, 196
Hutchins, Julia W., 151
Hymns, 64

Iban, 57
Icons, 64
Ifugao, 5, 240
Illness, 163, 235–236, 257–258. *See also* Evil eye;
  Healing; Possession; Witchcraft
Imams, 23
Immaculate conception, 38
Incense burning, 247
Incest taboos, 241
Indian astrology, 20–21
Indigenization, 134–135
Initiation rites, 110, 115, 116–118
  Sikh ceremony, 219
  women, 117
  Zoroastrian children, 264
Intuitive divination, 53
Iroquois, 49, 57, 69–70, 233, 249, 257, 258
Islam, 91–97
  Baha'i and, 23
  beliefs, 93–95
  fasting, 10
  Five Pillars of, 94–95
  Hinduism and, 82
  history, 91–93
  missionaries, 133, 134
  observances and festivals, 97
  pollution concepts, 47
  sects, 96–97
  Sikhism and, 217
  texts, 95–96
Israel, 102, 104

Jainism, 99–102
Japan
  Buddhism in, 28, 31
  Shinto, 28, 212–217
Javanese, 45, 47
Jehovah's Witnesses, 136
Jerusalem, 103
  Archbishopric of, 174
  Islam and, 95
  pilgrimages to, 154

Jesuits, 196
Jesus Christ, 38–40
  Christian doctrinal differences, 149
  in Christian Science, 42–43
  Eastern Orthodox Christianity and, 62–63
  Essenes and, 103
  Islam and, 94
  Mormonism and, 141, 142
  Pentecostalism and, 152
  Rastafari and, 191
  Roman Catholic beliefs, 198
Jesus Only Pentecostalism, 151
Jesus Prayer, 61
Jewish nationalism, 104
Jews. *See* Judaism
Jihad, 95
Jivaro, 116, 224
Job, 105
John XXIII, 198
John Frum movement, 190
John the Baptist, 38
Judaism, 102–107
  fasting, 10
  history, 102–104
  observances and festivals, 106–107
  pollution concepts, 47
  sects, 106
  texts and beliefs, 104–106
Justinger, Judith, 193

Kachin, 241
Kachina society, 110
Kali, 85
Kandyan, 65–66
Kapauku, 34, 125, 239, 241, 248
Kaplan, Mordecai, 106
Karma, 86, 101, 182
Kethuvim, 104
Khasi, 232
Kimam, 10
Kitab-i-Aqda and Kitab-i-Iqan, 24
Klamath, 251, 252
Koans, 132
Kongo, 237
Koran. *See* Quran
Korean shamanism, 206
Kundalini, 129

Kurds, 156, 168
Kuru, 37
Kwakiutl, 118

Lamaism, 28
Lao Tzu, 245, 246
Lau, 128
Lent, 10, 200
Leo IX, 60
Leo XIII, 198
Life-cycle rites, 109–120
    birth, 109–110, 13–114
    childhood, 114–116
    death, 119–120
    initiation. *See* Initiation rites
    marriage, 118–119. *See also* Marriage
Little folk, 233
Lotus position, 131
Lourdes, 154, 155, 157
Love magic, 125
Lozi, 222, 228
Lukang, 74
Lunar mansions, 20–21
Luther, Martin, 171, 172, 196
Lutheranism, 172, 174

McPherson, Aimee Semple, 151
Maccabaeus, Judas, 103
Madhyamika, 31
Magic, 123–127
    black, 126
    curative, 127
    economic, 126
    evil eye, 64–67
    love, 125
    protective and preventive, 126–127
    religious objects, 182–183
    sorcery, 220–222
    war, 125
    witchcraft, 220, 221, 255–259
Magico-religious practitioners, 184–188, 206–212
Mahabharata, 83
Mahadeva, 88
Mahavira, 99
Mahayana Buddhism, 30
Malaki, 96
Malekula, 225

Maloney Clarence, 65
Mana, 127–128
Mandala, 132
Mantras, 85, 131
Maori, 179
Mardudjara, 228
Marett, Robert R., 7
Marime, 177, 178
Marquesas Islanders, 204
Marriage, 118–119
    Berber, 111–112
    Catholic sacrament, 200
    incest taboos, 241
    Islamic practices, 97
    Judaism and, 107
    sacrament, 64
    Sikh ceremony, 219
    Zuni, 110
Mass hysteria, 192
Mbuti, 236, 240, 241
Mecca, 91, 94, 95, 154
Medina, 91, 95
Meditation, 11, 128–133
Medium, 186
Melanesian mana beliefs, 127–128
Melanesian revitalization movements, 190
Melpa, 56
Menstruation, 117, 176, 178, 240, 242–243
Messiah, 38
Messianic cults, 190
Methodism, 174
Mexican-American witchcraft beliefs, 258
Midrash, 106
Millenarian movements, 189–190
Millenial cults, 190
Missions, 133–137
Mitra, 83
Monarchic monotheism, 138
Monasticism, 1
    Buddhist, 28
    Catholic, 195, 199
    Eastern Orthodox Christianity and, 63
Monotheism, 138–140
Moon, 15
Mormonism, 133, 136, 141–143
    fasting, 10
Moses, 102, 104
Mossi, 138

Mount Athos, 12, 63
Muhammad, 91–92, 23
Muslims. *See* Islam

Name taboos, 243–244
Naming, 111, 113
Nanak, Guru, 217–218
Nationalism
    Eastern Orthodox Christianity and, 63
    Jewish, 104
    Protestantism and, 173
Native American Church, 161, 190
Nativistic movements, 190
Neo-Confucianism, 44
Nestorian Orthodox Church, 60, 168
Neviim, 104
New Age movement, 136, 145–146, 206
    American Firewalking Movement, 169
    vision quests, 251
New Pentecostalism, 152
New Testament, 38, 149–150, 172,
    174–175, 199
Nicea, Council of, 40, 60
Nicene Creed, 40
Nightmare witches, 256
Nirankari, 219
Nirvana, 30–31, 129
Nzema, 140

Objects, religious, 182–183
Offering and sacrifice, 201–205
Ojibwa, 11, 36, 220, 229–230, 239, 251
Old Testament, 38, 104, 199
Omaha, 249
Oneness Pentecostalism, 151
Orasac festivals, 70
Ordeals, 147–148
Oriental Orthodox Church, 60
Original sin, 198
Orokolo, 192
Orthodox Judaism, 106
Ottoman Turks, 92

Paiute, 192
Parham, Charles Fox, 150, 151
Parsis, 261–262
Passover, 10, 107
Paul, 40, 150, 172

Pawnee, 125–126, 161, 235, 240, 243
Penance, 64, 200
Pentecostal Assemblies of the World,
    151–152
Pentecostalism, 149–153, 237
    missions, 133, 134, 136
    snake-handling, 168, 169
Peyote, 158, 161, 190
Piests, 174
Pilgrimage for Spruce, 158–159
Pilgrimages, 95, 153–159, 218
    indigenous cultures and, 157–159
    shrines and centers, 156–157
    types of, 154–156
Pius VI, 197
Pius IX, 197
Pius X, 199
Planets, 15, 18–19, 20
Pollution, 47, 117, 176–179. *See also* Menstruation
Polygyny, 142, 143
Polynesian mana beliefs, 127–128
Polytheism, 138, 140
Popes and the papacy, 40, 60, 195–199
Possession, 159–167
    Cadomblé, 165–167
    divination, 53
    role and function, 167–168
    Vodou spirits, 162
    zar spirits, 163–165, 186
Poverty, ascetic, 9, 10–11
Prayer, 94, 170–171
Prayer-sticks, 170
Preanimism, 7
Pregnancy, 113, 240–241
    Zuni rites, 109
Priests, 187–188
    asceticism, 11–12
Prophet cults, 190
Prophets, 188–189
Protective magic, 126
Protestant ethic, 174
Protestant Reformation, 41, 171, 196
Protestantism, 38, 41, 171–175
    beliefs and practices, 175
    history, 171–174
    missions, 136
    texts, 174–175
    See also Pentecostalism

Puberty rites, 117
Pueblo, 115
Pukupuka, 119
Puranas, 83
Pure Land Buddhism, 31
Purification rituals, 176
    Hindu, 88
    Sikh, 218
    Zoroastrian, 264
Puritans, 174
Purvas, 99–100

Qadimi, 264
Quakers, 175
Quran, 91, 93, 95–96, 257

Ramadan, 10, 94–95, 97
Ramakrishna movement, 82
Ramayana, 83
Rampur festivals, 70–72
Rastafari movement, 190, 191–192
Rebirth, 29
Reconstruction Judaism, 106
Reform Judaism, 106
Reformation, 41, 171, 196
Reincarnation, 85–86, 101, 181
Relative cultural deprivation, 193
Religious objects, 182–183
Religious specialists, 184–189
    asceticism, 11–12
Reorganized Church of Jesus Christ of Latter Day
        Saints, 141, 142
Resurrection, 198
Revitalization movements, 189–193
Ritual reversal, 258
Rituals, 194
    conflict, 74–75
    festivals and, 69
    life cycle, 109–120. See also Life-cycle rites
    magic and, 125
    purification, 176
    sacrifice and offerings, 201–205
    See also specific practices
Roberts, Oral, 152
Roman Catholicism, 9, 38, 40–41, 194–200
    beliefs, 198–199
    fasting, 10

history, 195–198
life-cycle rites, 115–116
missions, 135–136
Protestant Reformation and, 171, 196
sacraments, 199–200
symbolic cannibalism, 36
syncretic religions, 237
texts, 199
Rome, pilgrimages to, 154
Rosh Hashanah, 107
Roy, Ram Mohun, 82
Rundi, 148
Russian Orthodox Christianity, 61, 62, 134

Saami, 140, 229, 233
Sabbath, 107
Sacraments
    Eastern Orthodox Christianity and, 64
    Protestant, 172
    Roman Catholic, 199–200
Sacrifice, 201–205
    animal, 201, 202–203
    in Hinduism, 85
    human, 37, 204–205
Sahajdharas, 219
Samadhi, 129
Samsara, 85–86
San, 50, 138
Santal, 115, 241, 248, 258
Santería, 161
Sara, 227
Satan, 138
Savonarola, Girolamo, 171
Science and Health with Key to the Scriptures, 42
Seance, 210–212
Seclusion, 9, 11
Second Work Pentecostalism, 151
Sectarian Shinto, 216
Serbian festivals, 70
Serbian magic beliefs, 124
Serbian Orthodoxy, 70, 124
Sex totemism, 248
Sexual restrictions, 9, 10, 113
    asceticism, 13
    incest taboos, 241–242
Seymour, William Joseph, 151
Shafi'i, 96

Shamanism, 206–212
    healers, 184–186
Shariah, 96
Shenshahi, 264
Shiite Muslims, 92, 96
    Baha'i and, 23
Shinto, 28, 212–217
Shiva, 88
Shoghi Effendi, 24
Shrine Shinto, 215, 216
Shrines, 154, 156–157
Siberian shamanism, 206–212
Siddhartha Gautama, 25–27, 81
Signs of the zodiac, 16–18, 20
Sikhism, 82, 138, 217–220
Sin
    original, 198
    penance, 64, 200
Singh, Guru Gobind, 218
Singha Sabha, 219
Singhs, 219–220
Sinhalese, 11, 65–66, 129, 235
Siuai, 225
Smith, Joseph, Jr., 141–142
Smriti, 83
Snake handling, 168–169
Sorcery, 188, 220–222, 235, 255
Soul, 222–226
    of animals, 224
    animism and, 7–8
    Baha'i and, 24
    Buddhist beliefs, 29
    dreams and, 57–58
    Hindu beliefs, 85
    infant, protecting, 113
    reincarnation, 181–182
    trance and, 160
    Zoroastrianism and, 262
Soul loss, 226, 236
Soul travel, 158, 160, 210, 225–226
Speaking in tongues, 150, 151, 152
Spirit baptism, 136, 149
Spirit double, 8
Spirits, 228, 230–232
    ancestor, 3, 230
    animism and, 7–8
    cannibal, 36

causes of illness, 236
    guardian, 230
    possession by, 159–167
    sacrifice to, 204
    seance, 210–212
    shamanistic, 185
    vision quests and, 251
    Vodou (Haiti), 162
    zar (Amhara), 163–165, 186
Sruti, 83
Subanum, 202
Sufism, 9, 97, 132
Suku, 5
Sun, 15
Sunna, 96
Sunni Muslims, 92, 96
Superior ancestor worship, 6
Supernatural beings, 226–228
    culture heroes, 229–230
    devils, 232
    gods, 226–229
    little people, 233
    spirits and ghosts, 230–232
    vampires, 232–233
    See also God; Gods and goddesses
Syncretism, 236–237

Taboo, 239–244
Tahi, 113, 115
Tahitians, 228
Tai Ch'i, 132
Taiwanese cultures, 115, 235
    ancestor worship, 4, 5
    pollution beliefs, 179
    reincarnation beliefs, 181
    soul travel beliefs, 160
Talismans, 182
Talmud, 104, 106
Tamil, 9
Tao, 48
Tao Te Ching, 245, 246
Taoism, 132, 245–247
Taos, 158
Tarahumara, 223–224, 232
Teachers, 189
Teda, 116
Ten Commandments, 102–103

Tendai, 31
Tenino, 226
Thai cultures, 11
    Buddhist priests, 187–188
    ghosts and, 235
    magic beliefs, 126, 129
    possession beliefs, 162
    reincarnation beliefs, 181
Thanksgiving, 69
Theistic dualism, 138
Theravada Buddhism, 30
Tibetan Buddhism, 28
Tien Thien, 73
T'ien-T'ai, 31
Tikopia, 128
Tiv, 13
Tlingit, 9, 10, 13, 36, 45, 48, 134, 183, 243, 249,
    251, 252, 255, 256, 258
    shamanism, 207, 208, 209, 211
Toba, 221
Toradja, 223, 224, 256, 257
Torah, 102, 104
Totemism, 247–249
Trance, 158, 159–161, 165
    role and function, 167–168
Transcendental meditation (TM), 131
Transubstantiation, 36
Tricksters, 234
Trinity, 62, 198
Tripitaka, 28, 30
Trobriand Islanders, 123
Trukese, 12, 231
Tucano, 36, 74
Tupi-Guarani Free Land movement, 190
Turkana, 258
Tylor, Edward B., 7
Tzeltal, 113, 256, 258

Udasis, 219
Unification Church, 136
United Pentecostal Church, 152
Untouchables, 86, 177
Upanishads, 83

Vailala madness, 192
Vampires, 232–233
Vanuatu, 190
Varuna, 83

Vedas, 83
Vietnamese festivals, 72–73
Vipassana, 129
Virgin Mary, 38, 62
Vishnu, 83, 88, 138
Vision quests, 117, 158, 230, 251–253
Vodou, 161, 162, 237

Wallace, Anthony, 189
War magic, 125
Wayto, 92
Weber, Max, 174
Wesley, John, 174
Wesleyan Pentecostalism, 151
Wisdom divination, 53
Witchcraft, 188, 220, 221, 235, 255–259
    cannibalism and, 36
    Zuni rites and, 110
Wolof, 137, 257
World Council of Churches, 41, 174
Worldview, 45
Wycliffe, John, 171, 196

Yakut, 201
    shamanism, 206–212
Yang, 48, 246
Yanomamö, 161
Yin, 48, 246
Yir Yront, 56
Yoga, 87, 88
Yogi, Maharishi Mahesh, 131
Yom Kippur, 10, 107
Yoruba, 237
Young, Brigham, 142

Zande, 137
Zar doctors, 185–186
Zar spirits, 163–165, 186
Zealots, 104
Zen Buddhism, 31, 132, 213
Zionism, 104
Zodiac, 15
    houses of, 19, 20
    signs of, 16–18, 20
Zoroastrianism, 138, 261–264
Zulu, 179
Zuni, 109–110, 115, 117, 118
Zwingi, Huldrych, 172